4X4 ROUTES

THROUGH SOUTHERN AFRICA

MapStudio

First edition published in 2011 by MapStudio™ South Africa

ISBN 978-1-77026-290-4

Project Author Philip Sackville-Scott
Production Manager John Loubser
Editor Thea Grobbelaar
Designer Nicole Bannister
Cartographic Manager Genené Hart
CD-Rom & Digital Map Compilation Anthony Davids
Proofreader Roelien Theron
Reproduction Resolution Colours (Pty) Ltd, Cape Town
Marketing Manager Adrian Kaplan (adriank@mapstudio.co.za)
Feedback research@mapstudio.co.za
Photo credits © 2011 All images supplied by contributing authors,
excluding the following pages: pp44–53 – Johan Swanepoel; pp98, 99, 101 top – Dawie
Verwey; p176 – Walter Knirr/Images of Africa; pp184, 186, 187 – Riaan Haasbroek;
p184 inset – Michael Steyn; p183 – Willem Olivier
Printed and bound by Times Offset (M) Sdn. Bhd.
Terrain background for maps kindly supplied by the Peace Parks Foundation

"VISION – Peace Parks Foundation envisages the establishment of a network of protected areas that links ecosystems across international borders. Given the proximity of the region's protected areas to each other, the possibility exists to create wildlife dispersal routes between them or in certain instances link them. MISSION – Peace Parks Foundation facilitates the establishment of transfrontier conservation areas (peace parks)* and develops human resources, thereby supporting sustainable economic development, the conservation of biodiversity and regional peace and stability. Our GIS Programme now in its 10th year has offered mapped visual support to the various countries and agencies' planning, decision making and management structures across the full network of these southern African protected areas. Please visit www.peaceparks.org for more detailed information"

MapStudio™
80 McKenzie Street, Cape Town
PO Box 1144, Cape Town, 8000
Tel: 0860 10 50 50
www.mapstudio.co.za

Maps © 2011 MapStudio™
© MapStudio™ 2011

MapStudio™ and the MapStudio™ device are trademarked to New Holland Publishing (South Africa) (Pty) Ltd.

THE NAME YOU CAN TRUST
SINCE 1958

Contents

4X4 ROUTES

THROUGH SOUTHERN AFRICA

Introduction

What better feeling of excitement and anticipation can there be for lovers of the outdoors than getting behind the wheel of a 4X4, turning the key and edging out of the driveway to start an outdoor journey of discovery, a great off-road adventure?

You and your family have no doubt spent many hours researching likely destinations, preparing yourselves and the vehicle, and selecting the style in which you would prefer to spend this time together experiencing the diverse wonders and sense of freedom that an off-road holiday offers.

There are as many options for an off-roading holiday as there are 4X4 models. You could:

▶ go it alone
▶ hook up with a few close family friends
▶ make new friends and join a club outing
▶ sign up with a commercial off-road operator

Your choice of accommodation could be:

▶ staying in chalets and lodges
▶ camping
▶ a combination of chalets and camping
▶ fully catered
▶ partially catered
▶ self-catering.

Your decision as to the style in which you choose to undertake such a trip will most likely depend on a combination of certain determining factors, such as:

▶ your personal level of off-road driving training and experience
▶ your family's overlanding expertise
▶ your family's likes and dislikes
▶ the level of preparedness of your vehicle
▶ the kit you have accumulated
▶ the time you have available to plan and book your trip
▶ the availability of all family members (annual leave, school and university holidays, house-sitter, dog-sitter, etc.)
▶ and last, but not least, the budget.

But herein lies the beauty of embarking on a multi-day, expedition-style off-road tour of the type written about in this book. There is literally something for everyone. Some people are adequately prepared to undertake a week-long trip into the Tankwa Karoo or Richtersveld National Park on their own, while they wouldn't dream of driving into Kaokoland or Angola unless under the stewardship of a trained and competent off-road guide. Some simply do not have the time or know-how to do the route planning, make the reservations, calculate logistics and safely lead a group, while others regard all this as fun and an integral part of the trip.

Depending on your knowledge of navigation, your bush orientation, your ability to set up backup plans for unforeseen eventualities (be they mechanical, medical or otherwise), you may choose to do your trip with an experienced friend. If you do not know anyone that fits the bill, you would probably join an organised convoy, where you quite literally tag along or 'follow the leader', without (hopefully) a further care in the world! After all, you are on holiday, so if someone else can assume the mantle of responsibility, why not?

This book is a compilation of popular Southern African off-road adventure tours with the emphasis on guided, self-drive, expedition-style (multi-day), self-catering camping trips – a bit of a mouthful, but a comprehensive description nevertheless. Its intention is to stimulate interest in off-road touring among those who haven't tried it yet as well as to suggest new destinations to those who do have some experience. All those 4X4s that ply the highways need to get into the bush at least once in their lifetimes!

We acknowledge that there are many extremely experienced and highly skilled off-road drivers who have been doing some of these routes for years. There are also experts in specific fields of interest – such as geology, flora, fauna, rock art, photography, geography and history – who may not find great depth in our descriptions of the experiences on these tours. We have not attempted to impart in-depth detail, but rather to provide an overview across many aspects. The aim is to provide interesting information about the places that we visit in order to make the tours more exciting, captivating and pleasurable to all occupants of the vehicle, not only the driver.

Most of the routes described are not difficult from a driving point of view, although some do contain specific obstacles that are more challenging, where a certain level of expertise is required. (Fear not, your 4X4 guide will see you safely through.) The focus is therefore not on showcasing routes that challenge the drivers, but tours that interest and stimulate all participants, while introducing the whole family to new destinations, new sights and sounds, and a fantastic and healthy lifestyle based on respect for and preservation of our natural heritage.

Camping in the Kalahari

A convoy of 4X4 vehicles driving along the Zambezi River

A selection of top off-road guides and operators have contributed chapters about routes that they regularly travel with groups of off-road tourists. They range from club guides to part-time commercial guides and full-blown off-road tour operators. What they all have in common is a love of the outdoors, an appreciation of nature and a willingness to promote the off-road lifestyle and share it with the public. These professionals know their routes like the backs of their hands and are able to impart information on the places of interest along the way, while ensuring your safety and enjoyment of the great outdoors. (*See* page 222 for more information on them and their companies or clubs.)

We have selected 20 tours in Southern Africa, eight of which are within South African borders and the rest to neighbouring states, with the Serengeti migration tour being an extended expedition up to Tanzania. This is by no means a comprehensive coverage of Southern Africa's off-road destinations, nor do we wish to imply that they are the most popular. Suffice it to say that they are all routes that we, the guides, love and enjoy and they are a good sample of what you can expect the next time you venture off the tar.

Jurgens Schoeman of Live The Journey Tours shares his immense knowledge of the Angola, Khaudum/Caprivi and Namib Desert routes, while André van Vuuren of Explore Africa Adventures shares his Serengeti Migration and Liuwa Plains experience. Simon Steadman of Mafunyane Adventures describes the Kgalagadi and Central Kalahari Game Reserve trips, and Johann du Toit of African Expeditions takes us on a tour of Lesotho. Andrew Brown of the Offroad Adventure Club writes about longer trips to Botswana and Zimbabwe. Johan Snyman, who is an expert on the Kaokoland area of Namibia, has submitted a chapter, as has Hugo Potgieter of Mozambique 4X4 Safaris on his favoured area of Southern Mozambique.

Of the trips within the borders of South Africa, Dave van Graan of Masazane Expeditions writes on the Soutpansberg, Greg van der Reis of the 4X4 Offroad Adventure Club covers the Richtersveld, and Philip Sackville-Scott of Sackville Safaris presents adventures to the Tankwa Karoo and Cederberg, the West Coast, Namaqualand and the Transkei Wild Coast, and also follows the Molopo River and the Old Ox-wagon Route.

Some routes are only operated by concession holders, while other areas pose too many dangers for you to attempt venturing there on your own. The benefits of being led by a trained and experienced off-road guide are many – not only from a safety point of view, but particularly in that you will be taken to, and shown, sights that you could easily have driven straight past, not knowing that they were even there. As most of these destinations are hundreds if not thousands of kilometres from home, who knows when you will get the opportunity to return?

This book is aimed at all off-road enthusiasts, irrespective of your experience and the type of vehicle you own, or wish to own some day, as long as it is a 4X4. We hope that you enjoy reading it and that it leads to your contacting one of the 4X4 guides to book your family on an off-road adventure of a lifetime!

OVERVIEW MAP OF 4X4 ROUTES

Equator

GABON

CONGO

KENYA

Kisangani

Mbandaka

DEMOCRATIC
REPUBLIC OF
THE CONGO

Kinshasa

RWANDA

BURUNDI

Lake
Victoria

Mwanza

Arusha

Moshi

Dodoma

TANZANIA

Zanzibar

Dar es Salaam

(10)

Lake
Tanganyika

Mbeya

Lake
Malawi

MALAWI

Lilongwe

Blantyre

Pemba

Nampula

Quelimane

Mbuji-
Mayi

Lubumbashi

Kolwezi

Kitwe

Ndola

(10)

ZAMBIA

Lusaka

(14)

Harare

ZIMBABWE

Luau

Malanje

ANGOLA

Mavinga

(13)

Livingstone

(10)

*Okavango
Delta*

(4)

Huambo

Lobito

Luanda

*Etosha
Pan*

(4)

Grootfontein

Ondangwa

(12)

Namibe

(12)

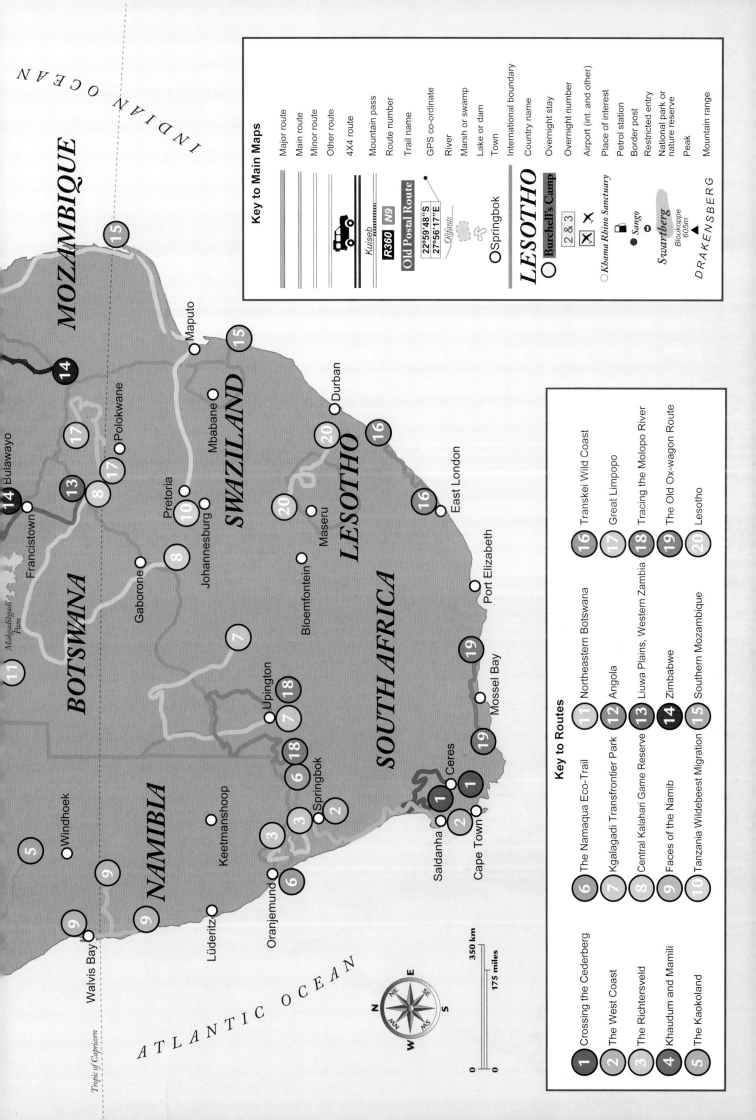

Key to Main Maps

Major route
Main route
Minor route
Other route
4X4 route
Mountain pass
Route number
Trail name
GPS co-ordinate
River
Marsh or swamp
Lake or dam
Town
International boundary
Country name
Overnight stay
Overnight number
Airport (int. and other)
Place of interest
Petrol station
Border post
Restricted entry
National park or nature reserve
Peak
Mountain range

Kuiseb

R360 N9

Old Postal Route

22°59'48"S
27°56'17"E

Olifants

◦Springbok

LESOTHO

● Burchell's Camp

2 & 3

◦ *Khama Rhino Sanctuary*

● *Sango*

Swartberg

Bloukoppe 605m

DRAKENSBERG

Key to Routes

1 Crossing the Cederberg
2 The West Coast
3 The Richtersveld
4 Khaudum and Mamili
5 The Kaokoland

6 The Namaqua Eco-Trail
7 Kgalagadi Transfrontier Park
8 Central Kalahari Game Reserve
9 Faces of the Namib
10 Tanzania Wildebeest Migration

11 The Namaqua Eco-Trail
12 Angola
13 Liuwa Plains, Western Zambia
14 Zimbabwe
15 Southern Mozambique

11 Northeastern Botswana
16 Transkei Wild Coast
17 Great Limpopo
18 Tracing the Molopo River
19 The Old Ox-wagon Route
20 Lesotho

INDIAN OCEAN

MOZAMBIQUE

BOTSWANA

NAMIBIA

SOUTH AFRICA

SWAZILAND

LESOTHO

ATLANTIC OCEAN

Tropic of Capricorn

Makgadikgadi Pans

Maputo
Bulawayo
Polokwane
Pretoria
Johannesburg
Mbabane
Maseru
Durban
East London
Port Elizabeth
Mossel Bay
Bloemfontein
Gaborone
Francistown
Windhoek
Keetmanshoop
Lüderitz
Oranjemund
Springbok
Upington
Saldanha
Cape Town
Ceres
Walvis Bay

350 km
175 miles

N NE E SE S SW W NW

1 Crossing the Cederberg – Tankwa to Sandveld

by Philip Sackville-Scott

TOP 10 ATTRACTIONS OF THIS TRIP

❶ Varied off-road driving conditions – sand and rock, mountainous ❷ Wide open spaces ❸ Photographic opportunities ❹ Prolific fynbos ❺ Spring flowers if travelling here at the right time of year ❻ Floral diversity ❼ Rock art ❽ Clear night skies for stargazing ❾ Cultural heritage ❿ Proximity to Cape Town

TRIP OUTLINE

We will be exploring an area generally known as the Greater Cederberg Biodiversity Corridor (GCBC), with Kagga Kamma as its southern and Graafwater as its northern boundary. To the east it is bound by the gravel R355, the longest uninterrupted road between two towns in South Africa, while the western boundary is the cold Atlantic coast.

Being within a few days' drive of Cape Town, this is an area not usually associated with multi-day overlanding trips, as one would think of a Namibian or Richtersveld experience, but the uninitiated will be surprised at how many similarities there are with these two better-known off-roading destinations.

The Cederberg has been a favourite of hikers, climbers, birders, botanists and general off-road holiday-makers for many years and this trip highlights what makes it so special.

The geology is important, as it creates the varied conditions for the diversity of flora to flourish. From the flat coastal plain the Cederberg range rises up to over 2000m at Sneeukop, elevating the cold and moisture-laden sea air which discharges onto the Cederberg as rain or mist. These mountains act as an impenetrable watershed, so that the area to the east, the Tankwa Karoo, obtains minimal rainfall – just 50–70mm per annum.

This trip starts at Kagga Kamma, north of Ceres, and progresses northwards up the western edge of the Tankwa, before crossing up into the Cederberg and turning southwards again through Wuppertal to Matjiesrivier and then in a northwesterly direction to Graafwater. From here we meander westwards to Lambert's Bay, before zigzagging eastwards again towards Citrusdal and the N7 artery back to Cape Town.

SEE DETAILED MAP ON PAGE 12 ▶▶

APPEAL RATING

5/5

The change in climate and flora – from the barren wastelands of the Tankwa Karoo (Succulent Karoo) to the fynbos-rich Cederberg and the coastal Sandveld – is one of the most dramatic you can experience in South Africa within such a short distance and time span.

- Biodiversity – you travel through three biomes
- Part of a World Heritage Site
- The Tankwa Karoo is fascinating in its barrenness
- Dramatic sandstone rock formations of the Cederberg
- San rock art, rooibos tea plantations and a sandstone mine
- The diversity of the landscape holds the whole family's attention throughout
- The quaint mission station of Wuppertal and its satellite villages
- Deep, vast canyons eroded by the Doring, Tra-Tra and Tankwa rivers

THE BEST TIME TO TRAVEL HERE

There is something for everyone all year round.

- The region experiences winter rainfall, making it the best time to see running rivers and waterfalls
- Depending on rainfall, the spring flowers are a great draw card in August and September
- Summers can be hot, but due to the altitude of much of this route the heat isn't unbearable – and it's likely to be dry

FAMILY-FRIENDLY RATING

4/5

- A great diversity of attractions awaits travellers on this route, with plenty that is of interest to all ages
- Children can be taught about the abundant flora, and the rock art and geology are fascinating too
- The camp sites are generally comfortable, if sparse in certain instances
- The elderly could suffer from the extremes of temperature
- This is predominantly a camping trip, although alternative accommodation is available at most (not all) of the sites

SELF-SUFFICIENCY RATING

3/5

At all times you will be within one or two hours' drive of help, so although comprehensive planning and the selection of equipment are essential for your comfort, they aren't critical to your survival.

- Fuel is available along the route, so no long-range capacity is necessary
- A comprehensive selection of food is available in Ceres, Clanwilliam and Citrusdal, but replenishment in-between is not guaranteed
- Water is clean and drinkable throughout the Tankwa and Cederberg, though brackish in the Sandveld
- Except for the camps at Kagga Kamma and the Doring River, all other camps have hot showers and flushing toilets

MAP 1 CROSSING THE CEDERBERG – Tankwa to Sandveld

12

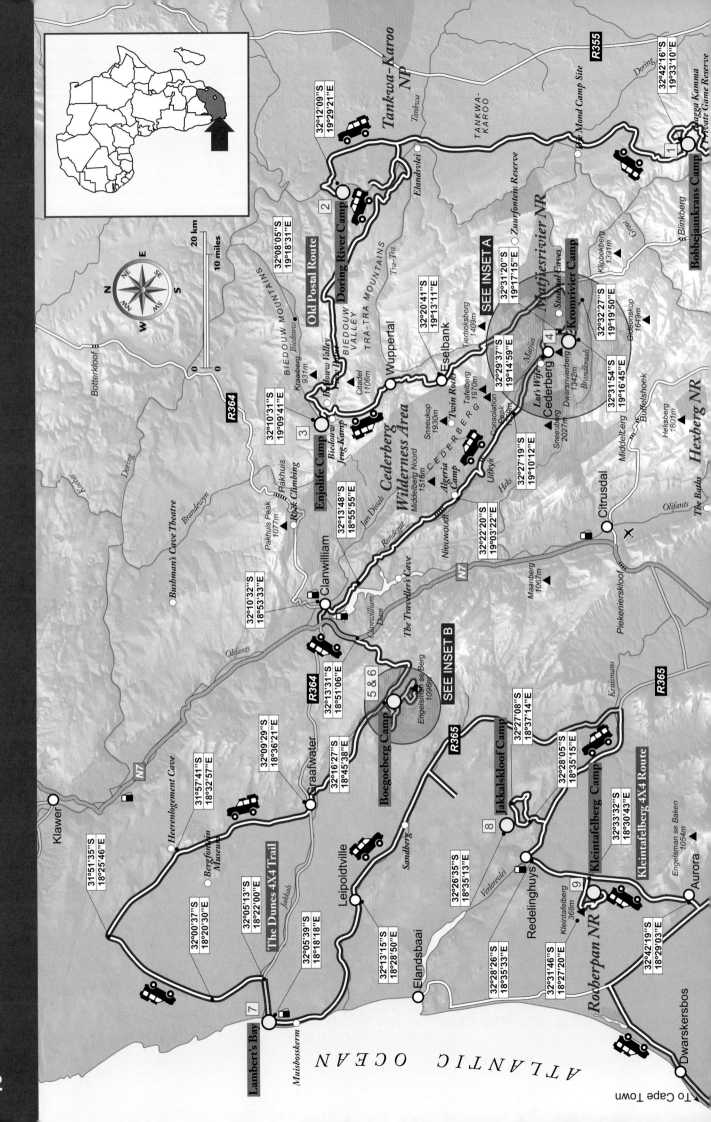

Tankwa-Karoo NP

32°12'09"S 19°29'21"E

32°08'05"S 19°18'31"E

Old Postal Route

Doring River Camp

2

32°42'16"S 19°33'10"E

R355

Die Mond Camp Site

Bobbejaankrans Camp

1

Sagga Kamma Private Game Reserve

Doring

Blinkberg

BIEDOUW MOUNTAINS

Elandsvlei

Klipbokberg 1391m

Zuurfontein Reserve

32°20'41"S 19°13'11"E

SEE INSET A

Matjiesrivier NR

Tra-Tra

TRA-TRA MOUNTAINS

BIEDOUW VALLEY

Wuppertal

Eselbank

Tierhoeksberg 1409m

32°31'20"S 19°17'15"E

32°29'37"S 19°14'59"E

Stadsaal Caves

Matjies

Kromrivier Camp

32°32'27"S 19°19'50"E

Gideonskop 1649m

Hexberg NR

Heksberg 1801m

Biedouw Valley

Krom River

Citadel 1106m

Kraaiberg 931m

Biedouw

Tafelberg 1970m

Twin Rocks

Sneeukop 1930m

4

Cederberg

Sneeuberg 2027m

Dwarsrivierberg 1342m

Brandtwak

R364

32°10'31"S 19°09'41"E

3

Enjolife Camp

Jeps Kamp

Biedouw

32°13'48"S 18°55'55"E

Rock Climbing

Pakhuis

Pakhuis Peak 1077m

Jan Dissels

Cederberg Wilderness Area

Middelberg Noord 1516m

Algeria Camp

Consolation Peak

Uitkyk

Lot's Wife 1596m

Heks

32°27'19"S 19°10'12"E

Middelberg 1361m

Buffelshoek

Bushman's Cave Theatre

32°10'32"S 18°53'33"E

Clanwilliam

The Traveller's Cave

Nieuwoudt

32°22'20"S 19°03'22"E

Citrusdal

Olifants

The Baths

Botterkloof

R364

Rondegat

N7

Maanberg 1067m

Kliphuis

Brandewyn

Doring

Klodee

32°13'31"S 18°51'06"E

5 & 6

SEE INSET B

Engelsman se Berg 1096m

Piekenierskloof

Olifants

Clanwilliam Dam

Boegoeberg Camp

R365

R365

32°27'08"S 18°37'14"E

Jakkalskloof Camp

Kruismans

R365

32°05'13"S 18°22'00"E

The Dunes 4X4 Trail

32°09'29"S 18°36'21"E

Graafwater

32°16'27"S 18°45'38"E

8

32°26'35"S 18°35'13"E

Veloorvlei

Redelinghuys

Kleintafelberg 368m

32°28'05"S 18°35'15"E

Kleintafelberg Camp

9

Kleintafelberg 4X4 Route

Rocherpan NR

Engelsman se Baken 1054m

Aurora

Klawer

31°51'35"S 18°25'46"E

Heerenlogement Cave

31°57'41"S 18°32'57"E

Bergfontein Museum

Jakkals

N7

Leipoldtville

Sandberg

32°28'26"S 18°35'33"E

32°31'46"S 18°27'20"E

32°42'19"S 18°29'03"E

Dwarskersbos

Muisbosskerm

32°00'37"S 18°20'30"E

32°05'39"S 18°8'18"E

Lambert's Bay

7

32°13'15"S 18°28'50"E

Elandsbaai

ATLANTIC OCEAN

To Cape Town

N

NE

E

SE

S

SW

W

NW

20 km

10 miles

0

0

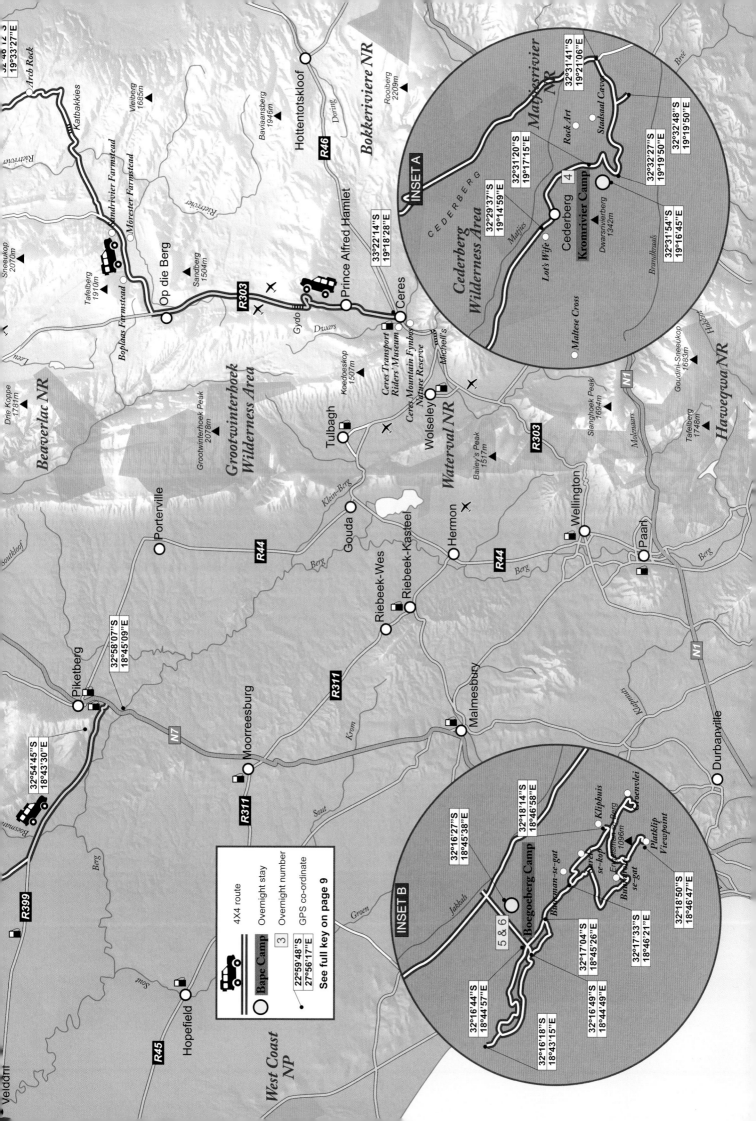

Day 1	Ceres to Kagga Kamma	120km	4 hr
Day 2	Drive to camp on Doring River	90km	5 hr
Day 3	Old Postal Route to Biedouw Valley	75km	4 hr
Day 4	Biedouw via Wuppertal to Kromrivier	90km	5 hr
Day 5	Kromrivier to Boegoeberg	100km	4 hr
Day 6	Drive Boegoeberg Trail	50km	5 hr
Day 7	Boegoeberg 4X4 to Lambert's Bay	120km	6 hr
Day 8	Lambert's Bay to drive Jakkalskloof Trail	120km	5 hr
Day 9	Jakkalskloof to Kleintafelberg 4X4	50km	6 hr
Day 10	Kleintafelberg 4X4 to Piketberg	70km	2 hr

VEHICLE REQUIREMENTS

- Four-wheel-drive with low-range transfer case
- Recovery points front and back
- Good ground clearance
- Proper off-road tyres with high profile for rocky ground
- Rear diff-lock or traction control an advantage

TRAILER-FRIENDLY RATING

3|5

- This trip is suited to smaller, lighter camping trailers, but is difficult for heavy off-road caravans
- There are some very tight twists and turns and steep ascents and descents over loose rocky ground
- The limited manoeuvrability of a large trailer could cause delays
- We stay at different camp sites every night except for the two nights at which we camp at Boegoeberg

GENERAL WARNINGS FOR THIS ROUTE

There are no major safety concerns on this trip, except that the Tankwa is renowned for being harsh on tyres. As always in wilderness areas, you need to be bush-wise and take basic precautionary measures.

- Use sun-protection creams, hats and long-sleeved shirts
- Protect eyes against glare
- Hydrate regularly
- The weather in the mountains can change rapidly, so wet-weather clothing and warm clothing and bedding are essential as backup, even during summer months
- Malaria-free throughout
- No large predators on this route – Cape leopard, caracal and jackal are about, but rarely seen
- Local population is sparse, so criminal activity is low and unwanted attention is rare

DAY 1

The tour group assembles in the wonderful Warm Bokkeveld town of Ceres (named after the Roman Goddess of Fruitfulness), centre of the most important deciduous fruit-growing area of the Western Cape. It's a medium-sized town, with various stores where you can obtain provisions, including groceries, vehicle spares, and camera and camping equipment. This is also the last opportunity to refuel for a good few days.

Spend a few hours in the Ceres Transport Riders' Museum, learning about the agricultural importance of the area, its pre-colonial history and the many mountain passes that characterise the approach to this idyllic town. On the outskirts of town, the Ceres Mountain Fynbos Nature Reserve covers 30ha of pristine flora, and on your walk you can view caves with San rock art.

Our meeting time is at midday at a local fuel station where introductions are made, administration is finalised and the group is informed about the rest of the day's driving.

The convoy heads northwards out of town on the tarred R303, via Prince Alfred Hamlet and the Gydo Pass to the Koue Bokkeveld town of Op Die Berg, where the plateau height is 1015m. Looking back towards Cape Town, on a clear day you can see Table Mountain, Devil's Peak and Signal Hill.

DID YOU KNOW?

Prince Alfred Hamlet was named in honour of a visit to the Cape by Prince Alfred, the Duke of Edinburgh, during the late 1800s. The visit coincided with the laying out of the initial 80 plots to form the new town.

Some 200m beyond Op Die Berg we turn right, heading northeast through the Valley of the Van der Merwes (named for the many families of that name who have farmed here for generations) towards the Ceres Karoo. At 17.3km from this turn-off, the tar road ends and the gravel continues north to Matjiesrivier in the Cederberg.

We turn right here onto gravel and head for the Katbakkies Pass and into the Swartruggens Conservancy. Along the way we pass established farmsteads, such as Môrester and Sandrivier, that have rich and colourful histories. Boplaas, for example, was established in 1743 and is currently farmed by the 11th generation of Van der Merwes.

Camping at Kagga Kamma, day 1

Steep descent on day 2 down to Joubert's Kloof, Kagga Kamma

Out among the rock formations we make our camp. The air is crystal clear and the stars seem close enough to touch. At full moon you don't even need a torch to walk around at night, so bright is the moonlight. As the fire burns down, we drift off to our tents and the first of many peaceful nights' rest.

DAY 2

The day dawns to prolific birdsong and brilliantly changing skies – the deep blue of night makes way for a lighter blue, then a deep orange that turns to yellow as we get our first sight of the golden sun breaching the horizon.

After a lazy breakfast and packing up camp, we head out onto the trail, our destination (Kliphuiskloof on the farm Elandsvlei) some 60km due north. The rough, rocky Grade 2–3 trail leads us westwards to the boundary fence around some very tight twists and turns, where one has to be particularly vigilant against sidewall cuts to the tyres. There are a few testing sections, typically the steep descents, where a good ground clearance is needed and where it is good practice to guide the vehicles through one by one. These situations provide many great photo opportunities and also allow the group to bond by assisting each other.

Once safely down at Joubert's Kloof, the view up the deep, narrow kloof is stunning. A prominent feature here is a giant old fig tree growing out of the side of the rock cliff face.

The Katbakkies Pass, named after the rock formations that look like cats' faces, takes us up onto the Swartruggens plateau after a short, sharp climb of around 300m. The soil here is a deep red and the Karoo bushes low. This is where the holiday feeling begins.

After 20km we reach the turn-off (left) for the Kagga Kamma Private Game Reserve, which we follow due north for a further 15km until we reach the entrance gates. Monumental sandstone rock formations line the road and the lighting effects here at sunset are quite spectacular.

Once through the entrance gates, we veer west towards reception and then south onto deep sand twin tracks to do some game-viewing and explore the rock formations in search of San rock art. (On a previous trip here we saw a vast herd of eland grazing with some Burchell's zebra, and further to the north we came across gemsbok, springbok and white-tailed gnu. The rock art paintings we found in the southernmost section of the reserve were both clear and well preserved, painted in great detail to record the animals that roamed the area during the time of the San.)

With the sun now starting to set on a long first day, we turn north and drive via twisting and turning twin tracks to the northern end of the reserve and out onto the 4X4 trail section in search of our first night's camp site at Bobbejaankrans. This is a typical wilderness camp with absolutely no facilities.

Dried mud patterns

Hoodia plant

SPECIFIC KIT REQUIRED FOR THIS TRIP

- ▶ Full camping gear, bedding, tents, table and chairs
- ▶ Full kitchen and braai utensils
- ▶ Water reserves for two days (2 litres per person per day minimum)
- ▶ A fridge in the vehicle is a necessity
- ▶ GPS and trig survey maps if you are going without an off-road guide
- ▶ Licensed and working 29MHz radio
- ▶ Comprehensive tyre-repair kit, including bead-breakers (one per group) and gaiters
- ▶ Consider taking a second spare tyre

ESSENTIAL REQUIREMENTS FOR THIS TRIP

- ▶ Puncture-repair kit, tyre-pressure gauge and compressor
- ▶ Kinetic strap or rope and tow strap or rope
- ▶ Spade
- ▶ High-lift jack or inflatable airbag – one in the group is sufficient
- ▶ Basic tools and basic spares for your vehicle
- ▶ Lighting, 12V or gas
- ▶ First-aid kit catering at least for sores and cuts, hay fever, sore eyes, headaches, nausea, bites and stings

SEE FULL PACKING LIST ON PAGE 218 ▶▶

BIODIVERSITY HOTSPOTS

Three of the 34 biodiversity hotspots in the world are in the Western Cape.

The Cape Floral Region contains an estimated 9500 species, of which 70% are endemic. Only 9% of this region is formally protected.

TRA-TRA RIVER

A tributary of the Olifants, it flows first into the Doring River. The word 'Tra-Tra' is thought to mean 'bushy' or 'overgrown'.

TANKWA

Of Khoisan origin, the name is thought to mean 'Place of Thirst'. Sometimes spelt 'Tanqua', its plains stretch from the Cederberg in the west to the Roggeveld Mountains in the east and from the Koedoesberge in the south to the Bokkeveld and Hantamsberg to the north near Calvinia.

Wrecks on Joubert's Farm, day 2

Continuing north on the rock-strewn trail we reach the last of the serious descents after 2km. Drive this pass very slowly in first gear low range and you will easily reach the bottom in safety. The remains of Joubert's Farm lie at the base of this descent and this is also another of the designated camp sites. Here on the plains it is quite sandy underfoot and the spring flowers display a purple carpet after good winter rains. Beware of the aardvark holes.

It is about a three-hour drive to get from the previous camp at Bobbejaankrans to the northernmost end of the property, where the hidden Kagga Kamma Kloof leads you out onto the plains of the Tankwa Karoo, a moon-like landscape strewn with stones and rocks. Following the telephone lines is easier than trying to make out the tracks until you reach the graded gravel road leading to a little-known holiday farm and camp site called Die Mond. This oasis lies just east of where the Groot and Matjies rivers have combined to form the Doring River, and a weir ensures wonderful swimming all year round. We stop for a light lunch and a swim, a most welcome respite from the dry summer heat.

The infamous R355 between Calvinia and Ceres lies just 14km to the east at this point, as we drive northwards on a parallel farm dirt road. The landscape is dry and barren as we

KAGGA KAMMA – PLENTIFUL WATERS

The owners bought three adjacent farms in 1986, and in 1988 turned the 15,000ha property into a private reserve, introducing animals that had historically occupied the area, such as Burchell's zebra, eland, gemsbok, kudu, white-tailed gnu, wildebeest, bontebok and springbok. Smaller duiker, klipspringer and steenbok occur here, as well as some grey rheebok and Cape grysbok.

The bird life is rich too, with ostrich, secretary bird and kori bustard among the larger species on the plains, while Verreaux's eagles soar above. Typical sounds in the Kagga Kamma veld include those of the southern black korhaan and Namaqua sandgrouse.

The San heritage is rich here too, with much rock art to be seen in the sandstone formations.

Full species lists, in the form of printed pamphlets, are available from their reception for your further enlightenment.

drive through a succession of farm gates, a stark contrast to the verdant growth lining the banks of the rivers in the area.

The change in the flora is abrupt when we exit the Kagga Kamma Kloof. South of here the Karoo bush and succulent growth is quite strong, if low in height. At the kloof exit, the north-facing hillside is covered in aloes – a magnificent sight when in full bloom. In the north succulents seem to flourish, although along the river courses acacia thorn trees are abundant.

At this stage of its journey the Doring River flows north towards the Olifants River. Just at Elandsvlei the Tankwa River feeds in from the east, and 3km later the Tra-Tra River joins in from the west. It then meanders north through deep, beautiful canyons. If you thought this area was flat, you are mistaken!

The farm Elandsvlei was once a bustling settlement, with a school and a post office. It was the hub of a vast farming area and the only habitation of any substance between Calvinia and Karoopoort in the south.

From Elandsvlei we drive a few kilometres north to a neighbouring farm where we turn west down into the canyon, crossing the river via a long concrete drift (which should first be walked) to find our camp site for the night on the banks of the Doring River. The freshly flowing water allows us to cool off and wash the day's dust from our hair as we settle in and relax after a great day's off-road driving.

DAY 3

Our spot at the river is stunning and we are reluctant to leave. Those with plenty of time at their disposal can easily spend a second night here just chilling. It is a great pity, though, that the river has become infested with the highly poisonous invasive oleander shrub.

Initially we retrace our route back towards Elandsvlei, before crossing the Doring and starting out on the Old Postal Route. Legend has it that a local farm lass walked from here across the mountains to Wuppertal to deliver the mail, a two-day walk in either direction. She'd rest a day at either end before starting

Posing on a pan in the Tankwa

back again. Those were hard times before e-mail!

This is a beautiful off-road track, initially leading northwest from Elandsvlei over the typical rock-strewn landscape of the Tankwa before it gains altitude and heads into the eastern slopes of the Cederberg range. Around 20km into the day's travel, the road has climbed considerably and the change in vegetation is remarkable. Periodically we spy the Cederberg's Tafelberg (1970m) away to the west.

The higher the altitude, the more fertile the soil and the wetter the conditions – condensation rates are higher here than down on the plains. This leads to full-on fynbos, prolific protea, restio and erica diversity, with wabome ('wagon trees') over 5m in height. This is a veritable Garden of Eden to gladden the heart of anyone with a feel for botany, and fynbos in particular. Agtdaegeneesbos ('eight days to heal bush') with its recognisable blue flowers brightens the landscape. The San believed that a tea brewed with the leaves of this bush would cure any ailment within eight days. (Don't most ailments heal within eight days anyway?)

The track gains more height before levelling out at around 1000m at Agterfonteinskloof. Here one finds commercially cultivated rooibos plantations on a large scale and the mood changes from a feeling of being in the middle of nowhere to now actually sensing people around you. Along the way you get a wonderful eastern view of the Citadel (1106m), looking just like a conical Lesotho hat.

The track eventually turns north and you reach the edge of the very high Kraaiberg and Osberg escarpment, dropping almost 600m down into the Biedouw Valley and our preferred overnight camp at Enjolife under shady acacia trees beside the east-flowing Biedouw River (another tributary of the Doring River).

Many visitors to this area only get to enjoy the Biedouw during the mad rush to view spring flowers. This is indeed a sight to behold, but the valley offers much beauty and tranquillity all year round.

Interesting bush ablutions in the Biedouw Valley

DAY 4

On day four we explore down to the eastern extreme of the Biedouw Valley, with the Biedouw Mountains to the north and the Tra-Tra Mountains along the south, to the drift crossing known as Uitspanskraal, where the Doring River runs deep and is impassable for many months of the year. We then head back, returning westwards again and leaving the more remote and rugged eastern Cederberg behind us as we head for the Moravian mission station of Wuppertal.

A sign on a gate, reading 'Biedouw Jeug Kamp', marks a worthy diversion to a group of waterfalls and potholes in a very beautiful setting. Atop the pass is a turning to the right and, time permitting, you can visit Heuningvlei, one of the 14 outstations of the mission.

The descent down a well-maintained broad gravel road into Wuppertal is very steep and drivers should take care not to overheat their brakes. A slow descent in first gear high range, using engine compression braking, is recommended.

This picturesque village is famous for its leather factory (where a good variety of shoes is manufactured), a glove factory, and a range of cosmetics made with rooibos tea. It is really worthwhile to wander around the village for an hour or so, drinking in the history and photographing its many oddities. Basic commodities can be bought at the shop, as well as lovely fresh baked bread on weekdays.

Support the community by enjoying a light lunch at the tearoom with the *leiwater* (trough-fed irrigation) flowing gently in the background. Then visit the Leipoldt House.

Continuing southwards out of Wuppertal we cross the Tra-Tra River at a low concrete bridge before commencing a steep climb up a pass marked '4X4 vehicles'. Most of the worst eroded sections have had concrete strips laid to reduce wear and tear, so it isn't such a difficult drive, although the roadway does get pretty narrow at certain points.

Once on the plateau, the road levels out considerably and we have a pleasant drive, passing the rooibos plantations of Wuppertal as we head for the small village of Eselbank. Along the way you will see on your right-hand side some of the most remarkable rock formations in the Cederberg – children can be kept occupied for hours as they look for recognisable shapes.

Just before Eselbank we stop at the waterfalls, where the Tra-Tra River has cut its way in dramatic fashion through the sandstone, for a swim and some lunch before continuing southwards to Matjiesrivier Nature Reserve, home to the Cape Leopard Project. Here we turn right (west) to visit the landmark Stadsaal Caves and view their world-famous rock art.

From here we head westwards to Kromrivier, our camp site, where basic cottages and chalets can be rented or you can camp when it isn't too cold.

DAY 5

This is a transit day. Leaving the hospitality of the Nieuwoudts at Kromrivier, we travel northwest through the parts of the Cederberg that are familiar to hikers, mountain bikers and campers. In the vicinity are such well-known landmarks as Dwarsrivier, Lot's Wife, the Maltese Cross and Sneeuberg. The road continues over the Jan Dissels River up the Uitkyk Pass, with Tafelberg, Consolation Peak and Middelberg viewable to the east of this scenic valley as we make our way to CapeNature's Algeria camp site for a midmorning tea break.

Just 400m past Algeria the road splits, with the left option leading you over the Nieuwoudt Pass and via a low bridge to the N7. We take the northern option, going via the Rondegat River to the Olifants River and along the lower eastern reaches of the Clanwilliam Dam to the town of Clanwilliam itself, where we stop to refuel and stock up on provisions for the remaining four days that lie ahead.

After lunch we join the N7 and head south for 7km before turning right onto gravel for 11km, where we again turn right and head for the farm Lambertshoek, which we reach after a further 7km.

Lambertshoek is owned by Sybrie de Beer and is home to Boegoeberg 4X4. Situated in the Engelsman se Berg, it overlooks Graafwater, Lambert's Bay, Elandsbaai and

The Cederberg south of Wuppertal, day 5

Clanwilliam. The 30 camp sites are all shady, and a wonderful sandstone lapa is the focal point for all meals, either self-catering or served by Sybrie and his team.

The afternoon is spent at leisure, relaxing beside the huge swimming pool, getting tents set up for our two nights here and generally enjoying some time out of the vehicles for a change.

DAY 6

After a late breakfast and a relaxed start, we take a guided tour of the farm and visit the sandstone quarry where this stone is still chiselled and cut by hand. This is one of the major sources of sandstone tiles stocked by many retailers in the Cape.

At the right time of year, generally the height of summer, you can watch the harvesting of rooibos on the lands. Sybrie gives a wonderful explanation of the entire process, from the gathering of the tiny seeds, to the cultivation of the plants in a nursery, to the planting out in the

Rooibos seedlings at Boegoeberg

lands. The harvested rooibos is cut and stored and then finely chopped before being laid out on sloping concrete floors to drain. The heaps need to be turned periodically as the heat build-up is quite substantial.

And then of course there's buchu, another product of the farm. In fact the many mountain tracks that now constitute the 4X4 trails were previously used to harvest the buchu. Before the tracks were built, the buchu was transported down the mountain by donkey or by hand.

Later we head for the hills. From the start of the trail, the climb up Engelsman se Berg begins taking us past places with interesting names – like Buurman-se-gat, Sarel-se-kop, Kliphuis, Die Poort, Groenvlei and Stillerus – until we reach the Platklip viewpoint, where a panoramic view awaits. From here it's down to Buurvrou-se-gat and a magic lookout point towards Elandsbaai. Then we continue to a waterfall/swimming hole/picnic spot. There are numerous places to stop along the way to take in the surroundings or simply to enjoy a cup of tea (see www.encounter.co.za/boegoeberg-4x4-trail.html).

The 30km 4X4 trail offers a variety of challenges, from steep ascents and descents to technical driving sections where large rock formations need to be negotiated. On the last section to Platklip, the trail crosses a stream a few times. The difficulty of this section varies according to the season, and driving skills and the ability to maintain traction will be frequently tested. But fear not – vehicle damage is highly unlikely.

DAY 7

It is with reluctance that we pack up and say farewell to Boegoeberg, such a relaxing and energising mountain retreat. However, leave we must and today we travel the longest distance of all the days on this trip as we leave Lambertshoek behind us and travel northwest to Graafwater and then detour due north for 30km to visit the Heerenlogement Cave.

This cave (the name translates as 'Gentleman's Lodgings') had a fresh supply of water and as such was favoured by early explorers, including Olaf Bergh and Simon van der Stel (the latter sheltered there in 1685 on his journey to Namaqualand in search of copper). Many have carved their initials on the cave walls as a permanent record of their stay here. A neighbouring farmer on Klipfontein has a fascinating private museum relating to the early settler history of this dry sandy area in the Sandveld.

OLAF BERGH

The Swede, Olaf Bergh, was one of the first explorers to journey to Namaqualand. The purpose of his journeys was to negotiate with the 'Sousequase and Gourisse Hottentots', to trade and to familiarise himself with the West Coast. Isaac Schrijver and the botanist Thunberg were also sent to explore the area (see www.vanriebeecksociety.co.za/catalogue.htm).

Bergh was one of the wealthiest men at the Cape in his time and a considerable landowner. His properties included the farm De Kuilen (today Kuilsriver), a house on the Heerengracht, another behind it, a house near the Groote Kerk, a house in Table Valley, the farm Constantia and two bungalows in Piketberg. Quite how much of this wealth was the loot from plundering shipwrecks is anyone's guess. Surely an official of the VOC didn't earn enough to acquire all those properties?

The Sandveld stretches from Hopefield in the south to Lutzville in the north and from the Cederberg in the east to the Atlantic Ocean in the west. As the name suggests it is very sandy – a vestige of when this entire area was below sea level. The region is famous as a potato-growing area and produces wonderful fynbos-fragranced honey. It has limited cattle and wheat production to the south bordering the Berg River.

We now head for Lambert's Bay on the coast, where the colonies of gannets, penguins and cormorants on the island in the bay are a sight to behold. It is predominantly a fishing village and famed for its crayfish factory. Good authentic West Coast cuisine can be sampled at the Muisbosskerm,

Typical rough track approaching the Sandveld

Bosduifklip and Plaaskombuis restaurants.

A little-known fact is that the only known naval engagement between Boer and British forces occurred here, when Smuts raided the Cape and found a small Royal Navy gunboat anchored in the bay. They fired upon it from the safety of the dunes and the Navy returned a few shots.

In the evening we set up camp, then take a break from our camp-fire cooking routine and dine at one of the wonderful restaurants in Lambert's Bay.

> **DID YOU KNOW?**
> It is illegal to pick or collect flora or fauna without the written consent of CapeNature. The illegal trade in fauna and flora continues to present a major threat to biodiversity conservation in the Western Cape.
>   Report suspicious individuals and behaviour to Paul Gildenhuys of The Biodiversity Crime Unit (BCU) on 082 551 8312.

DAY 8

We leave Lambert's Bay, driving south along the coast before swinging inland to Leipoldtville, not well known for much apart from having been founded as a Dutch Reformed congregation by CJ Leipoldt, father of C Louis and son of Johann Gottlieb, one of the founders of Wuppertal.

Continuing through this major potato-growing region, we arrive shortly at Sandberg, one of the largest farms in the Sandveld. Tours of their hothouses and processing plants can be arranged. A lone hill stands prominent on the farm, and the family has created a nature reserve with the most amazing cave accommodation built into the natural rock formations. There are also some permanent tents, complete with open-air showers. Known as Donkieskraal, this has been categorised as a private nature reserve, and it has various big antelope species. Game-viewing vehicles take guests on game drives, and if the staff have the time they will lead you to the rock art sites and other places of interest on the farm.

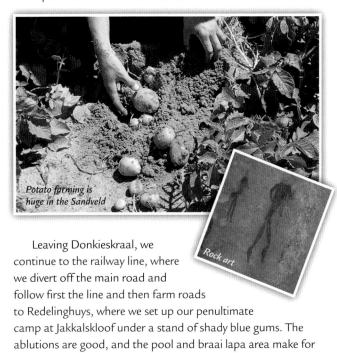

Potato farming is huge in the Sandveld

Rock art

Leaving Donkieskraal, we continue to the railway line, where we divert off the main road and follow first the line and then farm roads to Redelinghuys, where we set up our penultimate camp at Jakkalskloof under a stand of shady blue gums. The ablutions are good, and the pool and braai lapa area make for

wonderful socialising later on. The farmhouse is rather special, being the old stables and wagon shed that were adapted 50 years ago to replicate a castle, complete with castellations and turrets. Well worth a visit, Jakkalskloof has been in the Kotze family since 1841 and the current custodian, Izak Kotze, has plans to renovate the *hartbeeshuisie*, the original farmhouse.

In the afternoon, we drive Izak's short sand route for a bit of light relief. The route isn't difficult but can be tricky in summer when the sand is hotter and therefore very soft.

The pool provides welcome relief after the good fun of the trail. Our now seasoned off-road travellers cool off, light a camp fire and get some water on for a *moerkoffie*. Later, the chatter of good friends lasts well into the night.

Roadside lunch stop – Jakkalskloof

DAY 9

And so we head to our last camp site at the Kleintafelberg 4X4 Route, another professionally run operation where considerable investment has been made by the owner, Steven Burger. To get there, though, we first need to drive northwest for 3–4km across the Jakkalskloof farm to the Redelinghuys road, through deep sand, before turning south and driving the 5km into town.

There isn't much to see in this small Sandveld village, but you can refuel, if you can find the attendant! The small café has general supplies and there is even a rudimentary municipal camp site in town as well as a fairly decent guesthouse.

It is 10km down the road southwards through typical Sandveld countryside, with rooibos plantations mixed in with flat expanses of fallow pastures, and then a further 5km before you arrive at the entrance to Kleintafelberg, with its majestic sandstone formation towering overhead. The sandy entrance is very deep and soft in places and a 4X4 with deflated tyres is necessary just to get to reception.

The camp is set in a shady, sandy area, with really great ablutions, a swimming pool, braai lapa and an entertainment area where large groups can be accommodated. Apart from the camp sites, there are four fully furnished and well-appointed chalets for those who by now are tired of camping.

Our arrival here is generally midmorning, so we have plenty of time to explore the two 4X4 routes – the sand route through old rooibos lands, and the rock route, which snakes its way to the top of the mountain where a well-positioned picnic spot

The mountain track on Jakkalskloof's trail

provides the opportunity for a welcome rest at the halfway mark. You are afforded tremendous views over the surrounding farmlands and the various agricultural activities from here, with patches of rapidly reducing renosterveld also visible in-between the cultivated lands.

Although we are only about two hours' drive from Cape Town, it still feels as though you are miles away from civilization, so unpopulated is the landscape.

It is with some trepidation that we gather for the last evening around the communal camp fire. Ten days ago most of us were strangers, now we're friends for life, bonded by the trials of the road, the joint efforts of repairing punctures and recovering our stuck convoy buddies. We have experienced the dry wastelands of the Tankwa, the imposing wind-eroded sandstone creations that are the Cederberg, and the exposed sea bed that has become known as the Sandveld.

We traipse off to bed with thoughts of the last week's experiences floating around our heads.

DAY 10

As if by way of a thank you, the dawn's golden rays light the Kleintafelberg and the whole area takes on a magical feel – even the birds chirp merrily as if understanding our melancholy mood.

The tour can end in two ways: either by turning towards the sea and paying a visit to the Rocherpan Nature Reserve (especially if there are keen birders in the group) and then continuing to Laaiplek, Velddrif and over the Berg River southwards past Langebaan on the R27 and so back to Cape Town. Otherwise, we go first south to Aurora and then southeast on the R399 to its junction with the N7 just south of Piketberg. Either way, there is plenty to see and experience – you just have to look around you as you drive.

MURDER AT HOUDENBEK
At Houdenbek (near Ceres) in 1825 there was a slave uprising stemming from the French revolutionary ideas of the 1790s, when the slaves at the Cape sought their emancipation. The Houdenbek slaves were treated well and entrusted by their owner, Willem van der Merwe, to carry guns. The slaves Abel and Galant led a rebellion and shot Van der Merwe, a visitor to the farm and the tutor in cold blood. A commando was raised and the gang was hunted down. Back in Worcester they were immediately sentenced to death, shot and beheaded. As a deterrent, their heads were displayed on stakes at the hill Koppieshoogte.

2 The West Coast – !Kwha ttu to Hondeklipbaai and beyond

by Philip Sackville-Scott

TOP 10 ATTRACTIONS OF THIS TRIP

❶ Great sand off-road driving ❷ Proximity to the seashore ❸ Photographic opportunities ❹ Fresh salt-laden air ❺ Spring flowers if travelling here at the right time of year ❻ Clear night skies for stargazing ❼ Sighting of whales and dolphins ❽ Crayfish and other wonderful seafood ❾ A San cultural experience ❿ Visiting coastal national parks

TRIP OUTLINE

We travel along the West Coast of South Africa, from just north of Cape Town, through the Sandveld region and up into the restricted diamond-mining coastline section of the Northern Cape at the southern edge of the Kalahari basin.

The route hugs the coast all the way to Hondeklipbaai. Here adventurers have the option to continue north into the restricted diamond concession area from Koiingnaas via the Shipwreck Trail to Kleinsee and on to Springbok, or to veer northeast inland into the Namaqua National Park and on to Nababeep via the Buffelsrivier Eco-Trail. We prefer the latter, allowing guests to visit the Shipwreck Trail on their own (as an add-on to this vacation), should they so wish.

SEE DETAILED MAP ON PAGE 24 ▶▶

APPEAL RATING

★ 5/5

The stark barren coastline of the West Coast borders the cold Atlantic Ocean.

- Every night we camp as close to the beach as permitted
- Catch fish and pick mussels off the rocks
- Swim, surf and dive for crayfish
- Drive the western edge of South Africa
- Experience typical West Coast humour, characters, food and hospitality
- Visit places with odd names, like Tietiesbaai, Koekenaap, Gert du Toit se Baai, Malkopbaai, Hondeklipbaai and Jurg se Kaya to name but a few

THE BEST TIME TO TRAVEL HERE

There is something for everyone all year round.

- The midwinter months are cold and rainy, making this the least pleasant period to visit the West Coast
- Depending on rainfall, the spring flowers are a great draw card in August and September in the northern sections of the route
- Summers are hot, with many hours of sunlight, but the sea breezes do have a wonderfully cooling effect – this is the best time here

FAMILY-FRIENDLY RATING

5/5

- People of all ages can always find something to do at the seaside
- Children, especially, love to splash in the surf and explore rock pools
- Camping on soft beach sand is comfortable for all
- This is exclusively a camping trip but alternative accommodation is available at some of the stops

SELF-SUFFICIENCY RATING

3/5

At all times you will be within one or two hours' drive of help, but detailed planning and the selection of provisions and equipment are essential for your comfort.

- Fuel is available along the route, so no long-range capacity is necessary
- A comprehensive selection of foodstuffs is available as far as Lambert's Bay, after which you need to carry sufficient food for the remainder of the trip, ending in Springbok (the basics are available at Hondeklipbaai)
- Fresh water is scarce from Lambert's Bay onwards
- After Lambert's Bay, none of the camps have hot showers or flushing toilets

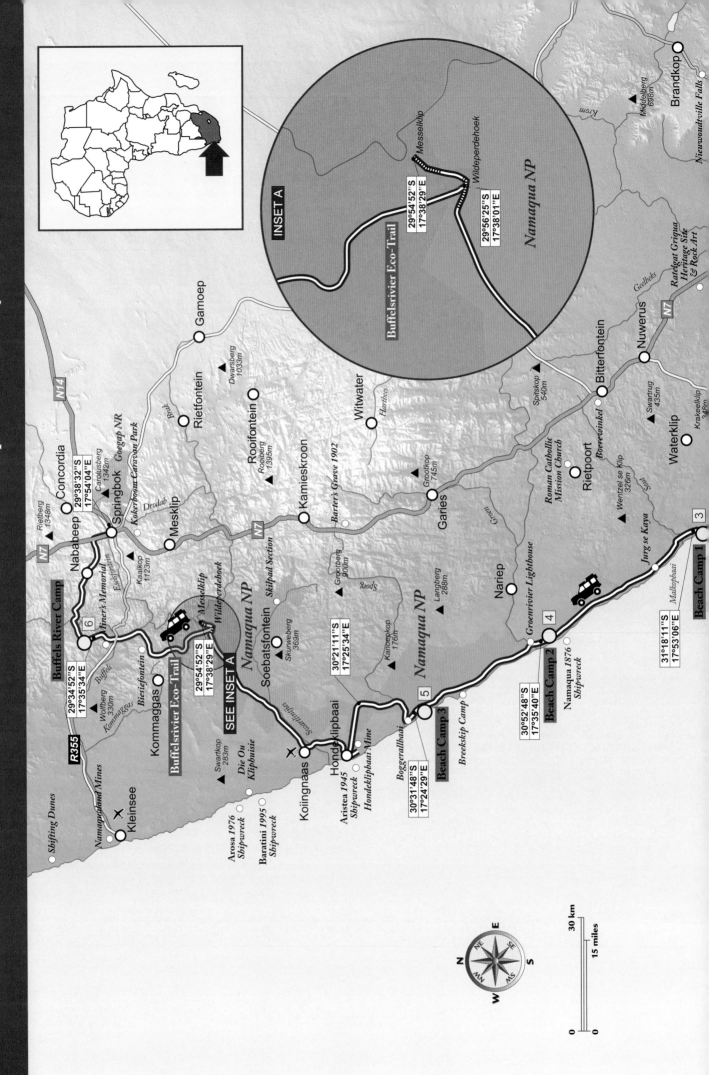

MAP 2 THE WEST COAST – !Kwha ttu to Hondeklipbaai and beyond

INSET A

Buffelsrivier Eco-Trail

Namaqua NP

Messelklip

Wildeperdehoek

29°54'52"S
17°38'29"E

29°56'25"S
17°38'01"E

Brandkop

Middelberg
698m

Krom

Nieuwoudtville Falls

Ratelgat Griqua
Heritage Site
& Rock Art

Geelbeks

N7

Nuwerus

Bitterfontein

Boeretoinkel

Spitskop
540m

Swartrug
435m

Waterklip

Krakeelklip
34m

Roman Catholic
Mission Church

Rietpoort

Wentzel se Klip
326m

Jurg se Kuya

Scott

Gamoep

Dwarsberg
1033m

Rietfontein

Brak

Rooifontein

Rooiberg
1395m

Witwater

Hartbees

Kamieskroon

Barter's Grave 1902

Grootkop
745m

Garies

Groen

Langberg
288m

Nariep

Grootberg
900m

Spoeg

Namaqua NP

Kanoepkop
176m

Groenrivier Lighthouse

Malkopbaai

Maltkopbaai

31°8'11"S
17°53'06"E

Beach Camp 1

Namaqua 1876
Shipwreck

30°52'48"S
17°35'40"E

Beach Camp 2

4

Breekskip Camp

Beach Camp 3

5

Boggerallbaai

30°21'11"S
17°25'34"E

Soebatsfontein

Skilpad Section

Skurweberg
369m

Namaqua NP

Messelklip

Wildeperdehoek

SEE INSET A

29°54'52"S
17°38'29"E

Buffelsrivier Eco-Trail

Kommaggas

Biesiefontein

Swartkop
283m

Die Ou
Klipbuisie

Swartlijntjies

Koiingnaas

Hondeklipbaai

Aristea 1945
Shipwreck

Hondeklipbaai Mine

30°31'48"S
17°24'29"E

Baratini 1995
Shipwreck

Arosa 1976
Shipwreck

Shifting Dunes

Namaqualand Mines

Kleinsee

R355

Wolfberg
330m

Buffels

Kommaggas

6

Buffels River Camp

Miner's Memorial

Eselsfontein

Kaalkop
1123m

29°34'52"S
17°35'34"E

N7

Nababeep

Rietberg
1348m

N14

Concordia

29°38'32"S
17°54'04"E

Springbok

Carolusberg
1342m

Gogap NR

Kokerboom Caravan Park

Drodab

Mesklip

30 km

15 miles

0

0

N
NE
E
SE
S
SW
W
NW

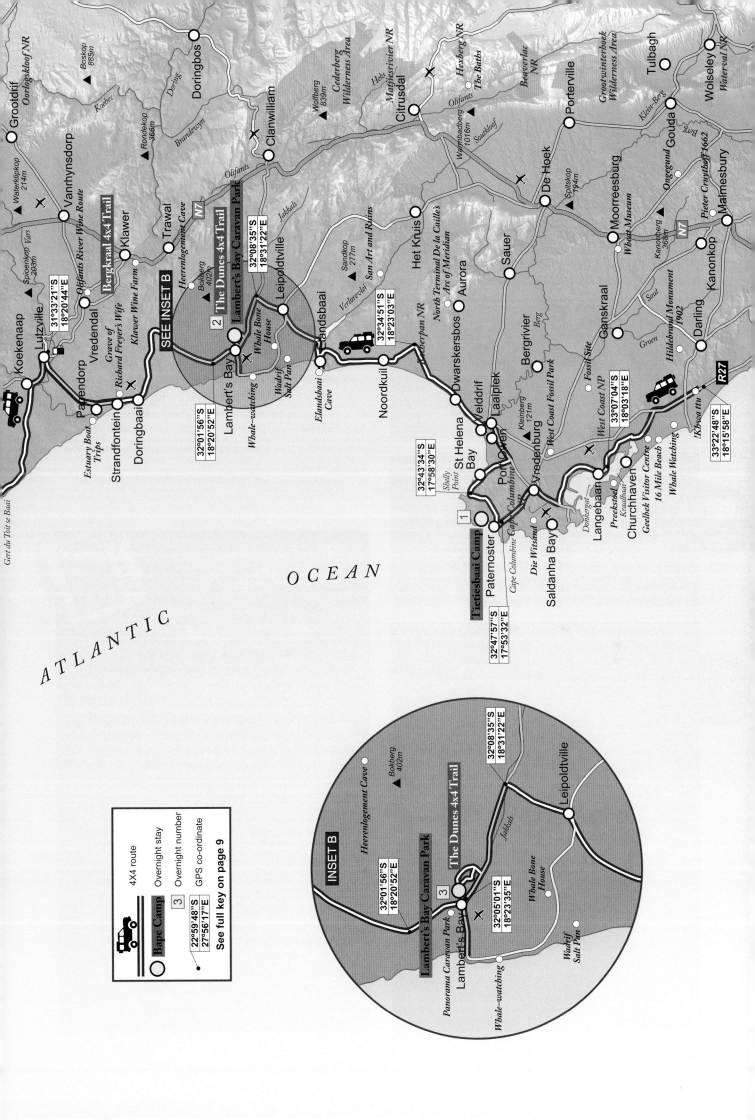

Grootdrif

Oorlogskloof NR

Boskop 885m

Waterkliphop 214m

Koekenaap

Vanrhynsdorp

Spioenkop 203m

Gert du Toit se Baai

Lutzville

31°33'21''S 18°20'44''E

Olifants River Wine Route

Vredendal

Papendorp

Grave of Richard Freyer's Wife

Klawer Wine Farm

Bergkraal 4x4 Trail

Klawer

Trawal

Clanwilliam

Strandfontein

Estuary Boat Trips

Doringbaai

Doring

Rondekop 366m

Doringbos

Brandewyn

Olifants

N7

Heerenlogement Cave

Bokberg 402m

SEE INSET B

The Dunes 4x4 Trail 2

32°08'35''S 18°31'22''E

Leipoldtville

32°01'56''S 18°20'52''E

Lambert's Bay Caravan Park

Lambert's Bay

Whale-watching

Whale Bone House

Wadrif Salt Pan

Elandsbaai

Elandsbaai Cave

Jakkals

Verlorevlei

Sandkop 277m

San Art and Ruins

Het Kruis

Wolfberg 839m

Cederberg Wilderness Area

Heks

Matjiesrivier NR

Olifants

Citrusdal

Warmbadberg 1016m

Soutkloof

The Baths

Hexberg NR

Beaverlac NR

Porterville

Grootwinterhoek Wilderness Area

Klein-Berg

Ongegund

Gouda

Tulbagh

Waterval NR

Wolseley

Pieter Cruythoff 1662

Malmesbury

N7

Kanonkop

Darling

R27

Hildebrand Monument 1902

Kanonberg 368m

Sout

Groen

Moorreesburg

Wheat Museum

De Hoek

Spitskop 794m

Sauer

Aurora

North Terminal De la Caille's

Arc of Meridian

Bergrivier

Berg

Rocherpan NR

Dwarskersbos

Laaiplek

Velddrif

St Helena Bay

Shelly Point

32°43'34''S 17°58'30''E

Noordkuil

Port Owen

Vredenburg

Kleinberg 121m

West Coast Fossil Park

Fossil Site

West Coast NP

33°07'04''S 18°03'18''E

'Kbwag ttu

33°22'48''S 18°1'58''E

Paternoster

Tietiesbaai Camp 1

32°47'57''S 17°53'32''E

Cape Columbine

Cape Columbine NR

Die Witsand

Saldanha Bay

Donkergat

Langebaan

Preekstoel

Kraalbaai

Churchhaven

Geelbek Visitor Centre

16 Mile Beach

Whale Watching

32°34'51''S 18°23'03''E

A T L A N T I C O C E A N

Base Camp

4X4 route

Overnight stay

3 Overnight number

GPS co-ordinate

22°59'48''S 27°56'17''E

See full key on page 9

INSET B

Heerenlogement Cave

Bokberg 402m

32°08'35''S 18°31'22''E

Leipoldtville

The Dunes 4x4 Trail

Lambert's Bay Caravan Park

Panorama Caravan Park

Lambert's Bay

32°01'56''S 18°20'52''E

3

32°05'01''S 18°23'35''E

Jakkals

Whale Bone House

Whale-watching

Wadrif Salt Pan

DAILY DRIVING DISTANCE AND TIME

Day 1	Cape Town to Paternoster	170km	6 hr
Day 2	Paternoster to Lambert's Bay	170km	6 hr
Day 3	Lambert's Bay to beach camp 1	150km	5 hr
Day 4	Beach camp 1 to beach camp 2	90km	5 hr
Day 5	Beach camp 2 to beach camp 3	100km	4 hr
Day 6	Beach camp 3 to Buffelsrivier Eco-Trail	50km	5 hr
Day 7	Buffelsrivier Eco-Trail to Springbok	50km	2 hr

VEHICLE REQUIREMENTS

- Four-wheel-drive with low-range transfer case
- Recovery points front and back
- Good ground clearance
- Proper off-road tyres with high profiles that can safely be deflated to 1 bar
- Rear diff-lock or traction control an advantage

TRAILER-FRIENDLY RATING

3/5

- This trip is suited to smaller, lighter camping trailers, but is difficult for heavy off-road caravans
- There are some very tight twists and turns and steep ascents and descents over loose rocky ground
- The limited manoeuvrability of a large trailer could cause delays
- We stay at different camp sites every night

GENERAL WARNINGS FOR THIS ROUTE

There are no extraordinary safety concerns on this trip. As always in remote wilderness areas, you need to be bush-wise and take basic precautions.

- Use sun-protection creams, hats and long-sleeved shirts
- Protect eyes against glare
- Guard against unexpected wave action when clambering over the rocks
- Adhere to accepted water safety precautions, especially where young children and non-swimmers are concerned
- Make sure that you have the necessary permits to fish or gather other marine resources
- Don't over-inflate tyres – they cause damage to the track (in thick sand sections you'll get stuck, particularly on very hot days, when the sand is at its least dense)
- Fresh water is scarce, but you need to hydrate regularly
- The weather along this coast can change rapidly when thick fog banks roll in off the sea; wet-weather clothing and warm clothing and bedding are essential as backup, even in summer
- Malaria-free throughout
- No large predators on this route – caracal and jackal are about, but rarely seen
- Local population is sparse, so criminal activity is low and unwanted attention is rare

Driving the sand tracks

DAY 1

The story of the West Coast is the story of the San and other pre-settler peoples that inhabited this area over many centuries, so it is fitting that we commence this journey at !Khwa ttu on the R27, just before Yzerfontein. The group gathers in the restaurant for registration and a cup of tea, before being taken on a two-hour tour led by San guides who introduce us to their culture and share the ancient oral history of their traditional lifestyle, including tracking and hunting skills, village life and celebration dances.

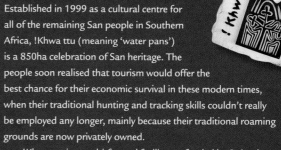

!KHWA TTU

Established in 1999 as a cultural centre for all of the remaining San people in Southern Africa, !Khwa ttu (meaning 'water pans') is a 850ha celebration of San heritage. The people soon realised that tourism would offer the best chance for their economic survival in these modern times, when their traditional hunting and tracking skills couldn't really be employed any longer, mainly because their traditional roaming grounds are now privately owned.

!Khwa ttu is a multi-faceted facility, co-funded by Swiss donors, who enabled the run-down sheep and wheat farm Grootwater to be purchased, stripped of its Port Jackson, and rehabilitated to the point where antelope species could be introduced. Buildings had to be rebuilt and renovated and other infrastructure installed.

Now the focus is on education, training San candidates selected from communities throughout Southern Africa to become fully functional participants in the tourism industry, be they guides, waiters, cooks or housekeeping, front-of-office or kitchen staff.

Their mission includes educating their children and providing the adults with training in literacy, entrepreneurship, health issues, community development, craft production, marketing and gender awareness.

There are two scheduled tours per day, when visitors are introduced to the San culture past and present and traditional methods are demonstrated with dignity and pride.

Attractions include a restaurant, accommodation, guided tours, a craft shop and conferencing facilities. These all contribute to a self-sustaining entity. Visit their website at www.khwattu.org for further information, directions and prices.

WEST COAST NATIONAL PARK – LANGEBAAN LAGOON

The Langebaan Lagoon is the focal point of this coastal reserve, with Postberg creating seasonal interest to the west. Sea birds such as gannet, cormorant and pelican flock to the rocky shores, and flamingoes and migrant waders (from Siberia) invade the salt marshes. The calm waters provide a haven for aquatic enthusiasts, from skiers and sailors to kayakers and kite surfers. Mountain bikers and hikers, too, find themselves in an idyllic playground setting. Whale-watching and the annual wildflower displays attract many tourists during spring.

Top attractions include an unforgettable stay on a houseboat at Kraalbaai, game-viewing from your own vehicle (where you can see eland, grysbok, red hartebeest and caracal) and most definitely a visit to a replica of Eve's footprints in the Geelbek Visitor Centre. These footprints, discovered in 1995 by David Roberts, date back 117,000 years to the time of the emergence of *Homo sapiens* and are the oldest known footprints of an anatomically modern human.

Botany lovers are not disappointed either as fynbos and succulent species proliferate around the lagoon edges. Find unusual plants such as the *Gethyllis* (kukumakranka, the original Khoi name), a bulbous plant whose infusion in brandy or *witblits* was an early Cape remedy for colic and indigestion.

Accommodation options range from camping to dormitory-style huts, chalets and quaint cottages.

Educational walks and guided tours can be arranged.

After a divine lunch in the restaurant we head north along the R27 for the turn-off into the West Coast National Park some 15km away. Arriving at a fork we turn right and drive north along the eastern edge of the Langebaan Lagoon, popping in at the Geelbek Visitor Centre on the way. If you have extra time, take the left turn to Churchhaven, Preekstoel and Kraalbaai to check out the houseboats. Further on is the Postberg section of the park and the old whaling station (now a Special Forces base) at Donkergat on the point.

In Langebaan town, we stop for an ice cream and a stroll on the beach before continuing past Club Mykonos and the ore

PATERNOSTER

Named after a Dutch merchant vessel wrecked at the spot some 300 years ago, this sleepy fishing village is a must-see along the West Coast. The coastline here is rocky but with many wide sandy coves. Fresh seafood is usually available, the people are eccentric and the beaches are welcoming.

The local hotel was built by the community in 1863 from limestone from the area. Initially it was a multi-purpose building containing a clothes store, snooker tables and a jail. The dining room hosted dances as well as church services and corn was stored in an open area. It was only converted into a hotel in 1940. The local bar has particular appeal!

Cape Columbine, with its nature reserve and lighthouse (the last manned lighthouse on the South African coast), is 3km away.

When the *Lisboa* ran aground on Soldiers Reef in 1910, it was the first time that radio was used in South Africa to summon assistance for a ship in distress.

VREDENBURG

Following the names of this settlement over the years tells the story of this business hub of the West Coast. Originally known as Twisfontein, it then became Prosesfontein and ultimately Vredenburg.

A feud sprang up between two farmers over a freshwater spring on the border of Heuningklip and Witteklip in the 18th century, at which time it was named Twisfontein or 'Fountain of Dispute'. After the commencement of court proceedings to sort out the dispute, it was temporarily renamed Prosesfontein or 'Lawsuit Fountain'. Only after the building of a Dutch Reformed Church alongside the spring did the process run its course. The dispute was settled and the growing town was renamed Vredenburg, meaning 'peaceful settlement'.

Today it is home to numerous fishing and other commercial businesses and is central to the local agricultural enterprises in the area.

SALDANHA ORE PIER

Opened in 1976 to load iron ore from the Sishen mines 861km away to the northeast, this structure spikes out into the natural harbour of Saldanha Bay, dividing it almost perfectly in half. Ore trains of 4km in length comprise 10 locomotives and 342 wagons, each with a 100-ton payload, making these the longest production trains in the world. Mammoth wagon-lifters pick up the laden ore wagons and tip the contents into the bulk carriers berthed alongside the jetty, creating quite a racket during the loading process. Ore-inspiring!

Interestingly, the spiritual leader of the Griqua, Andrew Abraham Stockenstrom le Fleur I, latterly known as the Kneg ('Die Kneg van God' – The Servant of God) prophesied before his death in 1941 that this railway line would be built. He accurately located the crossing over the Sout River and in great detail foretold the route that it would follow.

pier to Saldanha, Vredenburg and our overnight camp site at Tietiesbaai just north of Cape Columbine, near the wonderful fishing village of Paternoster.

During the summer months of extended daylight hours, you can spend many hours exploring around the Columbine Reserve, visit the lighthouse and enjoy a few drinks at the Paternoster Hotel.

Sunset over the West Coast

SPECIFIC KIT REQUIRED FOR THIS TRIP

- ▶ Full camping gear, bedding, tents, table and chairs
- ▶ Full kitchen and braai utensils
- ▶ A means to provide shade – an awning, gazebo or plain old beach umbrella
- ▶ Water reserves for three days (2 litres per person per day minimum)
- ▶ A fridge in the vehicle is a necessity
- ▶ GPS and trig survey maps if you are going without an off-road guide
- ▶ Licensed and working 29MHz radio
- ▶ Comprehensive tyre-repair kit, including bead-breakers (one per group) and gaiters

ESSENTIAL REQUIREMENTS FOR THIS TRIP

- ▶ Contact elanza.vanlente@sanparks.org for updated info on reservations and permits
- ▶ Puncture-repair kit, tyre-pressure gauge and compressor
- ▶ Kinetic strap or rope and tow strap or rope
- ▶ Spade
- ▶ High-lift jack or inflatable airbag – one in the group is sufficient
- ▶ Basic tools and basic spares for your vehicle
- ▶ Lighting, 12V or gas
- ▶ First-aid kit catering at least for sores and cuts, hay fever, sore eyes, headaches, nausea, bites, stings and sunburn

SEE FULL PACKING LIST ON PAGE 218 ▶▶

WEST COAST FOSSIL PARK

Phosphate mining in the Langebaan area between the 1950s and the early 1990s exposed one of the world's richest fossil beds. So far, over 200 species of fossilised remains have been excavated. These date back to the Pliocene era (five million years ago) when this area was well watered and forested, unlike its current appearance.

This National Heritage Site is well worth a visit as excavation continues under the guidance of Iziko Museums. There are daily guided tours and the adventurous may explore on their mountain bikes.

ELANDSBAAI

Originally a fishing village, these days it is better known for its international status as a great surfing spot. Great bird-watching may be enjoyed at the amazing Verlorenvlei ('Lost Marsh'), which is home to over 240 species.

The Sishen–Saldanha railway line meets the coast for the first time at Strandfontein to the north, before trundling through an 840m tunnel at Baboon Point on its way to Saldanha Bay.

A large rock overhang on the sea-facing side of Baboon Mountain hosts the Elandsbaai Cave, where 10,000-year-old San rock art can be seen close up. You can drive up a short dirt track almost to the cave mouth and climb a few steps into this cave. The sea views at sunset are stunning – the perfect spot for a sundowner.

Elandsbaai Cave, with its associated shell middens and archaeological and palaeontological sites nearby, provides evidence of the cultural history of San hunter-gatherers and Khoi herders and their ancestors. It is the only site on the entire African continent where rock paintings can be found so close to the coast.

Baboon Point provided strategic value during World War II when several radar installations were built here to exploit the commanding sea views. Later, under the apartheid system, they were used for exploitation of a more sinister kind, when they were converted to house migrant labourers serving the local fishing industry.

DAY 2

Today we need to start early to reach our destination at Lambert's Bay, over 170km to the north, and it is with reluctance that we leave this peaceful cove. We try to hug the coast as much as is legal and so we head for Shelley Point and St Helena Bay and around to the fishing villages of Velddrif and Laaiplek, passing the up-market Port Owen Marina along the way.

Some 10km further, situated in the middle of St Helena Bay, you come to the seaside resort town of Dwarskersbos ('Cross Candle Bush'), which made history when it was flooded by a tidal wave in 1969.

Rocherpan Nature Reserve, famous for the many bird species that visit the pan, makes a pleasant stop, time permitting. (You should bear in mind that time moves slower

Self-sufficiency is essential when camping on the beach

Typical cosy beach along the West Coast

here on the West Coast and as such is a precious commodity. This trip can easily take you twice as long if you stop to explore all the amazing offerings on show.)

Our lunch-time stop is in Elandsbaai, where we take you to the Elandsbaai Cave on Baboon Point, just around the bend from the crayfish factory. The energetic and those with a high tolerance for the cold can attempt a swim in the cold Atlantic surf. Others will prefer to browse the shops and bistros in town or visit the hotel, where the men's bar is not for the faint-hearted!

Leaving town, we travel east for about 10km along the northern banks of the bird-rich Verlorenvlei, before continuing north again en route to Leipoldtville and our second camping site at Lambert's Bay Caravan Park. These are the last hot showers and flushing toilets for a while, so enjoy it while it lasts!

In the late afternoon we take a short trip into the Lambert's Bay dunes to practise our sand-driving techniques and enjoy a sundowner overlooking the whitest of white dunes with the golden sun sinking beneath the horizon in the background.

Then it's back to camp for a convivial evening around the first of many camp fires in the days to come.

NAMAQUA SANDS MINING

The operation is located at three separate sites on the West Coast. The mine and concentration plants are at Brand se Baai, the separation plant at Koekenaap and the smelters at Saldanha. At Koekenaap, ilmenite, zircon and rutile are recovered and transported to the smelters by rail. The two smelters produce titanium slag and pig iron.

Titanium is the primary product of the mineral sands industry and it is mined in the form of ilmenite and rutile. Over 90% of the world's titanium dioxide production is used in the manufacture of pigment for paints, papers and plastics. It is also used for the production of titanium metal, welding rods and titanium-based chemicals.

Pig iron is produced as a co-product of titanium slag and is used in the foundry and steel industry.

Zircon is used in ceramics, chemicals, refractories, TV glass and a range of other applications.

DAY 3

The route north from Lambert's Bay follows the coastline to Doringbaai, Strandfontein and Papendorp at the mouth of the Olifants River. Salt is mined here, and this wetland and estuary system is a Ramsar site, being an important habitat for migratory birds along this coastline.

Lutzville is the last opportunity to refuel until we reach Hondeklipbaai, so it is compulsory to do so before we continue onto the beach route, from Gert du Toit se Baai onwards. This is where the trip starts to take on its magical feel. The preceding days have set the scene and acclimatised you to the sights and sounds of the West Coast lifestyle. Now this tranquil, unspoilt natural beauty takes over, welcoming you into her arms and wooing you into a lifelong love story of your own writing.

The driving is along twin tracks that vary from very thick sand conditions with a high centre mound, where low tyre pressures are essential, to hard compacted rock and crushed shell where the going is easier.

The route passes the vast mining operation of Namaqua Sands Mining and the salt works at the mouth of the Sout River just north of Brand se Baai.

For the next three nights we will camp near to the beach somewhere along this stretch of coast. Sometimes we arrive at our preferred camp sites to find other groups already settled, so we move off a few kilometres and find another sheltered cove

Sand tracks weave along the shoreline

or sandy beach at which to overnight. This is the old-fashioned considerate way. There is plenty of space here, so it isn't necessary to impose on others. Hopefully others will respect this simple principle too!

In the days before 4X4 driving was banned on our beaches, this was a very popular coastline for off-road enthusiasts and fishermen to explore. Although some natural rehabilitation has occurred through the reduction of vehicular traffic, the scars of a myriad tracks remain an eyesore. In time, the authorities will no doubt have the resources to start a beautification and restoration programme here.

It is gratifying to know that, among other species, the African black oystercatcher ('swarttobie') has returned in numbers and breeding is prolific, with a high survival rate, now that their dune nests are relatively undisturbed.

DAY 4

There is no need to rise early today.
Rather take the time to unwind – enjoy the sea air, take an early morning stroll along the beach and explore the rock pools – before the sun gets too hot. (The only shade here is provided by the contraptions you bring along, be they fancy roof-mounted awnings, basic gazebos or good old beach umbrellas!)

On the trail again, we wend our way this way and that, following the tracks up the coast and calling in at interesting bays and coves as we feel like it.

Jurg se Kaya is a landmark spot where rudimentary accommodation is complemented by warmth and world-class hospitality. Feel free to amend the itinerary to include a night here with Jurg and Buurman who will regale you with stories from the time you arrive until the sun rises the next day!

There is generally a 'main track' from which many lesser tracks lead down to the beach to favourite fishing spots or rock pools. Given time, it would be a treat to explore each one, but time doesn't permit when you only have a week.

Stopping for a look at the view

Cosy fireplace just north of Groenrivier

At Island Point, remnants of the boilers of the *Namaqua* are still visible on the rocks as you pass by. She was a Union Company Iron Screw Coaster, built in Sunderland, England, in 1872 and wrecked in 1876 en route from Table Bay to Port Nolloth.

We camp in the vicinity.

DAY 5

Now setting into a regular beach-bum routine, we go about our chosen morning activity, pack up and continue north beside the coast. After the Groenrivier Lighthouse we turn slightly inland in order to cross through the Groenrivier itself, just after where the 'holiday squatter camp' used to be – this has now been cleared.

From here northwards we are under the jurisdiction of SANParks, who have obtained management of this coastal section up to Hondeklipbaai and are doing a fine job with rehabilitation and blocking off access to the many lesser tracks leading down to the beach. At the time of writing, many formal camp sites had already been constructed, all complete with long-drop toilets and wind-protection stone walls and fireplaces. Water is not supplied, so bring enough with you.

Their efforts are commendable, considering the vast distances needed to travel for routine maintenance and the harsh conditions prevalent in this area. The fruits of their labours are there for all to see: an aesthetically much-improved environment for us off-road tourists and, presumably, a more accommodating one for the natural inhabitants!

When the mood takes us, we stop for tea breaks and

lunch, arriving at our preferred camp site near the Bitter River mouth at Plat Bay. The usual late-afternoon routine calls for setting up camp, a walk on the beach, trying to have a warm shower (generally cause for much hilarity as the results are not guaranteed) and then the lighting of a camp fire, communal braaiing and convivial conversation until the sleeping bags call.

DAY 6

We make an early start and leave our beachcombing ways behind us as we move off for the final stretch of shoreline, taking us past the remains of a sheep kraal and fresh water spring en route to the aptly named Boggerallbaai.

The highlight for today is a visit to the Spoeg River mouth and the wonderful cave on the southern bank – from a distance the twin openings of the cave resemble a giant owl face carved from the granite outcrop by wind and water erosion. Radiocarbon dating of pottery and bone fragments found during excavations done in the cave in 1987, and again in 1994, yielded a date of 2400 years old for the sheep bone found at the lowest levels below the pottery layers. This provides evidence for the oldest known sheep domestication in South Africa, and shows that one of the places where sheep were first introduced to South Africa was along the West Coast.

The level of the estuary is maintained by groundwater seepage and water salinity is therefore low. Animals found in the area include Cape fur seal, steenbok, porcupine, duiker, bat-eared fox, water mongoose, meerkat and various rodents, while a wide variety of bird life is present. Flora is largely Strandveld and can be described as semi-succulent scrub.

The route into Hondeklipbaai from here winds its way over rough tracks, ending up at the main gravel road from Garies. Here we turn west into town. The evidence of vast mining operations is all around and you have to be constantly vigilant for the large scrapers and trucks hurtling around the place.

Initially the town doesn't appear to offer much, but on closer inspection a range of delights is revealed. There are various accommodation options, from camping to chalets and guesthouses, with some nice eateries thrown in.

Hondeklipbaai's harbour, from which copper ore brought by ox-wagon from Springbok was exported before the port was supplanted by Port Nolloth, now serves fishing and diamond-mining boats.

The 'dog'-shaped rock fell over some time ago, but the name still stands.

Leaving Hondeklipbaai, we turn north 5km out of town in the direction of Koiingnaas, before the road swings northeast along the Swartlintjies River to the inland section of the Namaqua National Park. The wide gravel road is flat and in good condition. During the heat of the day little life is visible, but be aware so as not to crush the world's smallest tortoise, the Namaqua speckled padloper. If you are lucky you may glimpse gemsbok, steenbok and smaller mammals.

Soon the road starts to climb the Wildeperdehoek Pass from where the view back over the coastal plain is quite breathtaking. At the top of this pass the road turns 90° left, and in the apex of the turn you take a left off the main gravel pass onto the Buffelsrivier Eco-Trail.

If you have time, continue along the Wildeperdehoek Pass for around 5km until you get to the Messelklip Pass and check out the old prison.

Back on the Buffelsrivier Eco-Trail, the road becomes a minor track and leads to some farms up in the mountains. It meanders this way and that, and without GPS or a good

Namaqua National Park viewed from the Wildeperdehoek Pass

Once down the mountain we find ourselves among farms, and the road widens as it runs down the valley alongside the Buffels River. Drive slowly through the settlement so as to reduce dust clouds, or the community may not be as welcoming the next time you pass by!

The dirt road leads us to a junction with the tarred R355 between Springbok in the east and Kleinsee in the west. We cross straight over and head up a seldom-used pipe track. Flat initially, it gradually climbs, getting steeper and steeper as we progress. There are some very sharp turns, with bad traction and deep undulations thrown in, which keep the driver's attention focused on the road, despite the spectacular scenery. At the top of the climb, after a few harrowing detours, the track turns sharp left and proceeds along a ridge, with panoramic views to west and east.

Along the way we find the bush camp and settle in for our last night together around the camp fire, reminiscing about what has been a momentous trip for all. We have experienced San culture, West Coast hospitality and quirkiness, isolated beaches, seal colonies, shipwrecks, wildlife in the national park, and we have been lulled to sleep by the rolling surf and enjoyed seafood, great company and brilliant off-road driving to boot.

For the last time on this trip we turn our eyes to the great black sky above and marvel at the universe's celestial display, before crawling into our sleeping bags, knowing that our lives have been enriched and our souls brightened just by having passed this way.

off-road guide it is easy to take a wrong turning. At a few points the going gets a bit challenging, mainly due to erosion gullies in the track, but this is why you have a 4X4 vehicle with high ground clearance, is it not? This mountain section of the trip is far different to the preceding five days on sand. Here you are exposed to steep inclines, declines and narrow rocky tracks.

It's very beautiful, especially if you're here in the soft light of late afternoon. At Biesiefontein, the ruins of a substantial farmhouse alongside the road bear testimony to the agricultural prosperity of the region in earlier years. Shortly after the ruins the track leads you past a huge striated granite outcrop, nicknamed the Zebra Rock due to the distinctive stripes on the rock face.

Soon the track starts its long and steep descent to the Buffels River, an undertaking which can take some time, especially when towing unbraked heavy trailers and off-road caravans. Take care not to overheat brakes as descending under engine compression alone doesn't reduce your speed sufficiently.

Some parts of this track are greatly eroded and you should get out of your vehicle to pick a safe line if you are in any doubt.

The farmhouse ruins at Biesiesfontein

Zebra Rock on the Buffelsrivier Eco-Trail

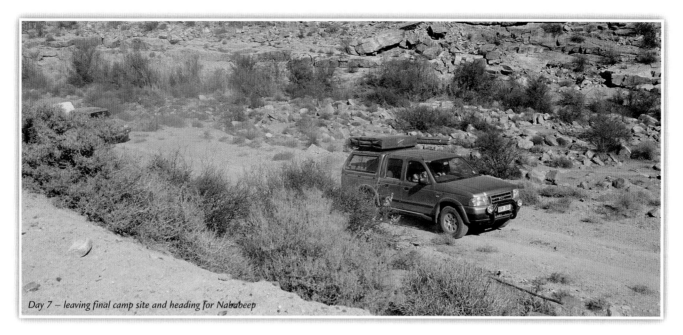
Day 7 – leaving final camp site and heading for Nababeep

DAY 7

With the dawning of the final day, the early risers stoke the camp fire, throw on a few twigs and brew that last kettle of *moerkoffie*. The 'hard-core okes' toast some bread on a stick and pick at the leftovers of last night's braai, while the more refined mix a bowl of muesli and yoghurt. Those who slept under the stars roll up their bedrolls, and the caravanners systematically implode their rigs.

We leave our bush camp and wend our way down the winding gravel road to the small town of Nababeep for a quick visit to the mining museum, before proceeding to Springbok, our journey's end, where we visit the Springbok Lodge for the obligatory burger and milkshake before hitting the tar road for home.

It doesn't matter who you are, what level of luxury you prefer, or whether you are experienced or a 'newbie' – the off-road touring lifestyle has a place for everyone.

All you have to do is pack your family into your vehicle and head out on another life-altering experience.

NABABEEP

Nababeep is the largest Namaqualand copper-mining town, yet few travellers bother to stop and discover its rich history and experience its quaint appeal.

The town derives its name from two Nama words, *naba* (meaning 'hump of an animal') and *bib* (meaning 'small spring'). Combined they denote *Nababib*, 'The Spring Behind the Hill'.

Nababeep developed in the 1850s when a copper mine was opened by the Cape Copper Company. Copper lost its value in 1919 and the mine was closed. It only reopened in 1937 after an American company did intensive prospecting in the 1920s.

The copper ore was taken by steam train some 175km northwest to Port Nolloth until the railway line from Cape Town was extended to Bitterfontein, approximately 190km south of Nababeep, which is considerably further away. Curiously, the Cape Town line still ends at Bitterfontein, so everything had to be trucked there before proceeding by rail.

At the mine museum visitors can learn about the development and history of the copper-mining industry in the region. *Clara*, the last steam locomotive used on the Port Nolloth line, is mounted on rails outside the museum.

For the nature enthusiast, the two-day Skaaprivier ('Sheep's River') Hiking Trail is an experience not to be missed.

KOEKENAAP

Situated on the banks of the Olifants River, this tranquil one-horse town owes its survival to sheep farming, the growing of tomatoes, gem squash, potatoes and grapes, and wine production in neighbouring Lutzville. The mineral separation plant for Namaqua Sands Mining is here too.

The origin of the town's name seems to derive from the misinterpretation of a remark made by a German missionary. While admiring the view of the beautifully verdant valley, he said to his colleague, 'Guck hinab' (or 'look down there'). To their Khoi guide this sounded like Koekenaap and the name has stuck. It is unlikely that a direct translation into current Afrikaans ('Cake and Ape') has any relevance!

3 The Richtersveld – a place of splendour

by Greg van der Reis

TOP 10 ATTRACTIONS OF THIS TRIP

❶ Lots of interesting towns to visit ❷ Mine tours can be arranged if you travel via Alexander Bay ❸ Talk to local people in the town and hear their stories ❹ Varied off-road driving conditions – sand, rock and possibly some mud ❺ Driving is easy to moderate ❻ Opportunity to hone your overlanding skills ❼ Photographic opportunities second to none ❽ Birders' paradise, especially on the river banks ❾ Visit a World Heritage Site and meet the people ❿ Visit the Alexander Bay Ramsar wetland

TRIP OUTLINE

This is an amazing place with a fascinating history. Despite the heat and the dryness, the landscape, seemingly lifeless, is home to an abundance of plants and animals. The Richtersveld, a mountain desert, has the largest variety of succulents of any place on earth. It is also home to the halfmens tree and quiver tree or kokerboom. It has a certain esoteric beauty, but why should such an apparently barren place be worthy of World Heritage status? The Richtersveld is unique and there's more than first meets the eye.

The Richtersveld National Park, set in a great loop of the Orange River, is rugged, desolate and in parts hauntingly beautiful. This is a place of deep canyons, jagged mountain ranges, landscapes of many colours, and extremely rare succulents. We will be exploring the South African side only.

It is widely accepted that the Richtersveld begins at the Steinkopf–Port Nolloth road and covers the area to the north, with the Orange River being the northern boundary. It was named after Dr Richter, the Inspector of the Rhenish Missionary Society of Berlin, which ran a mission station established at Steinkopf in 1836. Details of Dr Richter's travels are sketchy, but since he started visiting the area in 1830 it can be assumed that he travelled to the Orange River as well as to its mouth. A few years later, mission stations were established at Lekkersing and Kuboes, and both Richtersveld towns are mentioned regularly in early prospectors' journals.

SEE DETAILED MAP ON PAGE 36 ▶▶

APPEAL RATING

5/5

The Richtersveld is pure wilderness and for almost 200 years has been the heartland of the prospectors in the Northern Cape – the region has seen fortunes lost by many a dreamer. By travelling through the Richtersveld National Park one can feel the call of the wilderness. Although not that remote, it gives 4X4 enthusiasts the experience of staging a mini-expedition, having to be completely self-sufficient and having to plan for the 'what ifs'.

- ▶ Overlanding skills and vehicle preparedness are required
- ▶ The transition from river bank to arid interior is extreme but still immensely beautiful
- ▶ The Richtersveld is a photographer's dream, with amazing colours, abundant bird life and many interesting plants

THE BEST TIME TO TRAVEL HERE

- ▶ From March to October is the best time
- ▶ It's usually warm all year round, with midsummer temperatures reaching 40°C plus; evenings can vary from 30°C in summer to -4°C in winter, but the average temperature is pleasant
- ▶ It helps to acclimatise by not using your vehicle's air conditioner
- ▶ August and September are suggested for flowers; although you might experience rain, it is still the best time to visit the area

FAMILY-FRIENDLY RATING

4/5

- ▶ The area is hot and if you plan on driving all day the children will get restless
- ▶ Due to the fact that there are scorpions and snakes, young children need to be supervised at night (get a 12V UV light and see them glow blue at night)
- ▶ The whole family will love the river and the children will happily spend hours playing in the water, fishing and just being kids
- ▶ This is a holiday where one can camp or use the accommodation available, thus pleasing all members of the family

SELF-SUFFICIENCY RATING

5/5

- ▶ This is a wilderness experience so you have to take everything you may need with you (even if you choose a chalet, you will still need food, clothing, water, firewood, recovery equipment, etc.)
- ▶ Medical help can be between one and six hours away (this could possibly be provided by the mining companies, otherwise Springbok is up to eight hours away), so you need to take a comprehensive medical kit and know how to use it
- ▶ Fuel is generally available in Steinkopf, Port Nolloth and Alexander Bay and sometimes at Sendelingsdrif, but, to be safe and not spoil your holiday, allow for 500–600km of fuel at your worst four-wheel-drive off-road consumption (the amount of fuel needed varies according to your route and daily driving distances)
- ▶ Take four litres of drinking water per person per day – the inland camps do not have water; river water can be boiled or have purification tablets added (although 'orange', it is free from bilharzia and pollutants)
- ▶ No wood may be gathered in the Richtersveld, so bring your own (usually one bag of wood per vehicle per night); wood can be purchased from the park office at Sendelingsdrif
- ▶ A selection of food is available in Springbok and Port Nolloth
- ▶ All camps have cold showers and toilets, but do not rely on these facilities when booking the inland camp sites

MAP 3 THE RICHTERSVELD – a place of splendour

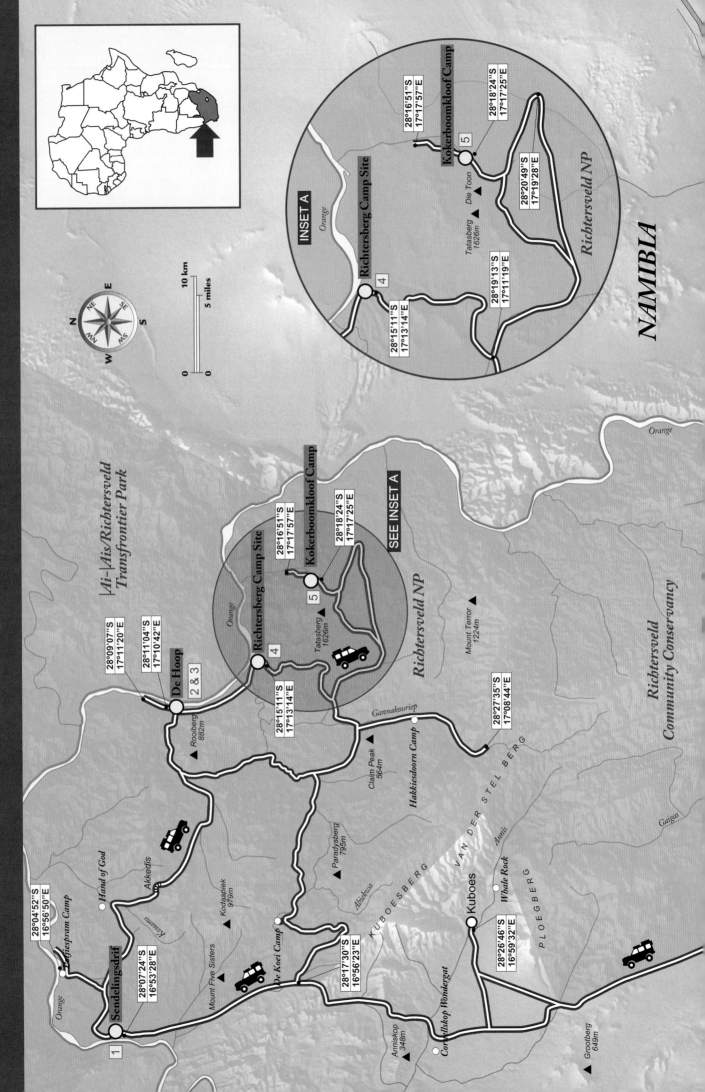

INSET A

Richtersberg Camp Site

28°15'11''S
17°13'14''E

Kokerboomkloof Camp

28°16'51''S
17°17'57''E

28°8'24''S
17°17'25''E

Kokerbloomkloof Camp

Tatasberg
1626m
Die Toon

28°20'49''S
17°9'28''E

28°9'13''S
17°11'19''E

Richtersveld NP

NAMIBIA

Orange

10 km

5 miles

|Ai-|Ais/Richtersveld
Transfrontier Park

28°09'07''S
17°1'120''E

28°11'04''S
17°0'42''E

De Hoop

2 & 3

Rooiberg
882m

Richtersberg Camp Site

28°5'11''S
17°13'14''E

Kokerboomkloof Camp

28°16'51''S
17°17'57''E

28°8'24''S
17°17'25''E

SEE INSET A

Tatasberg
1626m

Richtersveld NP

Mount Terror
1224m

Gannakouriep

Claim Peak
564m

Hakkiesdoorn Camp

28°27'35''S
17°9'8'44''E

VAN DER STEL BERG

28°04'52''S
16°56'50''E

Fonteinpram Camp

Orange

Hand of God

Akkedis

Kasums

Sendelingsdrif

28°07'24''S
16°53'28''E

1

Kodaspiek
979m

Mount Five Sisters

De Koei Camp

28°17'30''S
16°56'23''E

Paradysberg
795m

Abiekwa

KUBOESBERG

Anniis

PLOEGBERG

Kuboes

Whale Rock

28°26'46''S
16°59'32''E

Cornellskop Wondergat

Anniskop
348m

Grootberg
649m

Gaigas

Richtersveld
Community Conservancy

Orange

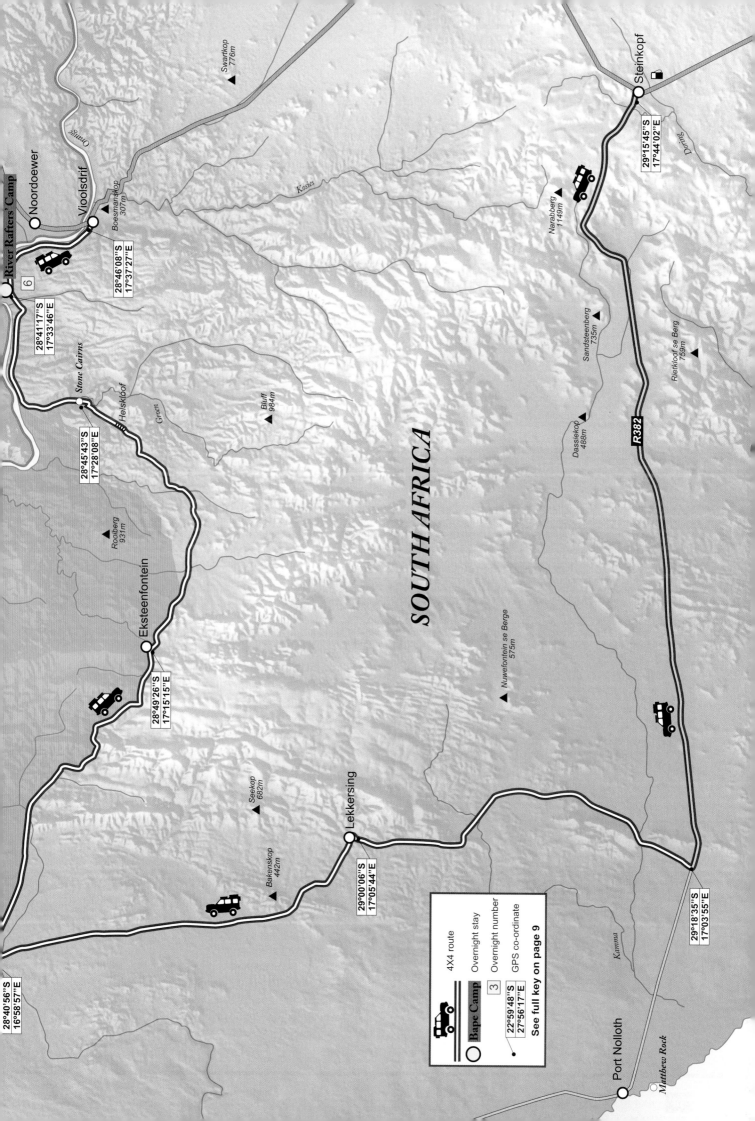

Noordoewer

River Rafters' Camp

28°40'56"S
16°58'57"E

6

Vioolsdrif

28°41'7"S
17°33'46"E

Orange

Boesmanskop
307m

28°46'08"S
17°37'27"E

▲ *Swartkop*
776m

Kosies

Steinkopf

29°15'45"S
17°44'02"E

Narabberg
1149m

Dorivis

Stone Cairns

28°45'43"S
17°28'08"E

Helskloof

Groen

▲ *Bluff*
984m

Sandsteenberg
735m ▲

Rietkloof se Berg
759m ▲

Rooiberg
931m

SOUTH AFRICA

Dassiekop
488m ▲

R382

Eksteenfontein

28°49'26"S
17°5'15"E

Nuwefontein se Berge
575m

Nuwefontein se Berge
575m ▲

Seekop
682m ▲

Lekkersing

Bakenskop
442m ▲

29°00'06"S
17°05'44"E

29°18'35"S
17°03'55"E

Kamma

28°40'56"S
16°58'57"E

4X4 route

Bape Camp Overnight stay

3 Overnight number

22°59'48'S
27°56'17"E GPS co-ordinate

See full key on page 9

Port Nolloth

Matthew Rock

DAILY DRIVING DISTANCE AND TIME

Getting to the park should be part of the adventure and various route options exist.

Steinkopf to Sendelingsdrif:

Via the R382 (Port Nolloth road)		220km	3 hr
Vioolsdrif and Helskloof		234km	5 hr
Port Nolloth and Alexander Bay		267km	3 hr

Once you have arrived at the Richtersveld National Park you can drive as much or as little as you please, with various routes being available. A suggested itinerary for this trip would be:

Day 1	Steinkopf via Kuboes to Sendelingsdrif	235km	6 hr
Day 2	Sendelingsdrif via Potjiespram to De Hoop	60km	4 hr
Day 3	Chill out at De Hoop	20km	2 hr
Day 4	De Hoop to Richtersberg	50km	4 hr
Day 5	Richtersberg to Kokerboomkloof	45km	4 hr
Day 6	Kokerboomkloof via Eksteens-fontein to a river rafters' camp	210km	6 hr
Day 7	Vioolsdrif to home		

VEHICLE REQUIREMENTS

Before your trip, get your vehicle serviced by an expert who will check all the essentials.

- Spare fan belts, radiator hoses, fuses, hose-pipe clamps, insulation tape and a good tool kit
- Two-wheel-drive vehicles with good ground clearance can cope, but no sedans
- Four-wheel-drive recommended, especially when towing a trailer
- Good ground clearance is essential
- Recovery points front and back
- Proper off-road tyres will be an advantage (we suggest you take at least two spare wheels as the road to the park can be corrugated – and make sure you remember to take the key to your spare wheel lock)
- Try a pressure of 1.6 bars for the rocky roads and 1.2 bars in the sand, and deflate further if necessary
- We suggest purchasing a tyre monitoring system for the trip, as this enables you to check the tyre pressure while driving, and repair or pump a tyre before it gets damaged beyond repair
- Rear diff-lock or traction control could be an advantage in the thick sand conditions

TRAILER-FRIENDLY RATING

5/5

This trip is definitely suited to those who like to tow their creature comforts with them.

- Towing is from camp site to camp site on Grade 2–3 tracks; remember to deflate the trailer tyres when deflating the vehicle tyres

There are various routes to the park entrance and once there, numerous options open up for you to follow. Which camp sites you choose is also a matter of personal preference. The other factors determining your preferred route include the capabilities of your vehicle, your level of self-sufficiency, the amount of time you have available to you and, naturally, your specific interests.

The gateway to the area is Steinkopf, 50km north of Springbok on the N7. Steinkopf has limited facilities but does have two fuel stations and a general dealer where one can buy necessities. The local people are very friendly and helpful. On Good Friday in 2007, when one of our team damaged a tyre, one of the local men helped us source a second-hand tyre and even went so far as to help us fit it.

Negotiating a rocky dry river bed

As mentioned above, from Steinkopf you have options when going into the park, namely:

- Proceed to Vioolsdrif and turn left onto the Modderdrif Road. This road follows the Orange River for about 24km before turning south at Modderdrif. There are various camp sites run by rafting operators, and all allow overnight camping by 4X4 drivers at a reasonable fee. This road will eventually take you to Eksteenfontein some 38km further on, and then to Sendelingsdrif, a total distance of 168km from Vioolsdrif. This road is interesting, with petroglyphs having been chipped onto large boulders alongside the road; it has been suggested that this rock art is more than 2000 years old. Further down this road is a turn-off to a lookout point and although the view is nice, it is not worth the 54km round trip. Then there are the stone cairns built by travellers entering Helskloof (which is narrow), with halfmens trees looking down on you from the hills. You are likely to see dassies and possibly a rhebok or steenbok.
- The longest route is via Port Nolloth, Alexander Bay and Brandkaros to Sendelingsdrif.
- As per the itinerary above, if you turn west at Steinkopf onto the R382, you can enter the park via the excellent gravel road that turns north 20km before Port Nolloth. This road takes one straight to Sendelingsdrif.

A suggested trip itinerary follows:

DAY 1

Having refuelled at Steinkopf, travel west along the R382 for 71km on tar, before turning to the north along the gravel road to Lekkersing and Kuboes. It is advisable to stop 100m or so from the intersection to allow everyone in the convoy to deflate their tyres (and trailer tyres too) to around 1.5 bar for a softer ride, as well as to engage four-wheel-drive. This gravel road is in fairly good condition for most of the way and good speeds can be maintained so as to reach the camp at Sendelingsdrif with time to spare in the afternoon. It is 40km from this junction to Lekkersing and a further 72km to Kuboes, an old mission community where the church was built in 1893. There is no fuel in the town, but there are a few general dealers and if you time your visit correctly you'll find steaming hot fresh bread.

The local people regard Kuboes as the heartland of Nama culture. This little town lies nestled between the mountains of Kuboesberg to the north, Van der Stel Berg to the east and Ploegberg to the south. The town was established by the Rhenish Missionary Society, and the nomads of the Richtersveld would commute for miles in order to attend church services and to enable their children to be educated.

The locals of Kuboes will gladly perform their traditional Nama dances and Namastap music and will take you on a magical ride with their famous storytelling.

A short detour to the southwest of Kuboes leads, along a very rough Grade 3 track, to Whale Rock, a sandstone formation bearing an uncanny resemblance to its namesake.

From Kuboes the road initially leads to the west for around 9.5km before continuing northwards. After a further 5km the turn-off to the Cornellskop Wondergat lies on your left.

The Wondergat is a sinkhole that, in Nama mythology, is the home of a large serpent called Heitsi-Eibib. The serpent is said to turn into a maiden and lure the young Nama men to their death in the river.

Another version explains that a man made a large hole in the ground and sat by it. He told those who passed by to throw a stone at his forehead. But when a person did this, the stone rebounded and killed the stone thrower, causing him to fall into the hole. At last, Heitsi-Eibib was told that many people were thus dying. So he went to the man sitting at the hole, who challenged Heitsi-Eibib to throw a stone at him. He declined to do that, but he drew the man's attention to someone on one side, and when the man turned around to look, Heitsi-Eibib hit him behind the ear. The man died and fell into his own hole, and the people then lived peacefully.

Continuing northwards for 17km, you will arrive at the entrance gate to the Richtersveld National Park, a 162,445ha mountainous desert at the most northwesterly part of South Africa. It has a harsh, dry climate with extremes of temperature and a rainfall as low as 50mm per annum.

Since its inception in 1993 the Richtersveld National Park has been run by both the local community and SANParks, and most mornings you will be woken by the sounds of goats moving past your camp site on their way to their grazing.

VIEW POINT

Whale-like rock formation near Kuboes

So why would you want to visit the Richtersveld? If you're a little adventurous, hate fences, love the feeling of open spaces, like being left to your own devices and want to explore old mines and their history, the Richtersveld is for you. The park is rough and, although there are ablutions, you can find yourself a corner and pretend that there is no one around for 1000km.

The question most frequently asked is: Do I need a 4X4 to visit the Richtersveld? The answer is no. Most vehicles with good ground clearance – such as a bakkie (pick-up) or kombi

WORLD HERITAGE SITE

It is slightly ironic that the reason the Richtersveld is a World Heritage Site is not because of its 'desolation' but because of its population.

The Nama people made this part of the world their home about two millennia ago and, because no one else has been willing or able to survive in this landscape, their lifestyle has not changed much in that time.

'The extensive communal grazed lands of the Richtersveld Cultural and Botanical Landscape are a testimony to land management processes which have ensured the protection of the succulent Karoo vegetation and thus demonstrates a harmonious interaction between people and nature.' (UNESCO: http://whc.unesco.org/en/list/1265)

– will suffice, but please note that sedans are not permitted in the park. There are some tracks, however, especially the track between De Hoop and Richtersberg, that do require the use of a 4X4 with good ground clearance – the sand here is like talcum powder and can exceed 400mm deep, and often soft-roaders end up with their bellies on the centre mound and all four wheels off the ground.

The roads in the park are reasonable but rutted and it takes you some time to get to your camp site. If you rush without being vigilant you might break something on your vehicle.

How long should you stay? I would suggest that you stay four to five nights and explore every corner of the park.

Having booked long in advance, you'll find yourself in Sendelingsdrif, signing in at the office. You feel something watching you and you see vervet monkeys and you are pleased that you closed the windows of your vehicle.

From the main gate, it is a further 20km to tonight's camp at Sendelingsdrif. Along the way you will pass the appropriately named Mount Five Sisters, with its five peaks. Sendelingsdrif has camp sites and also offers chalets with all the modern conveniences such as air conditioning, a fridge and stove. It also boasts a lovely deck looking out over the river and a pont with which you can cross into the Namibian side of the transfrontier park (passports required).

You frequently see vervet monkeys, so prepare for the chaos that these primates can cause if you leave the door to your chalet open while at the swimming pool!

Camp, day 2 – soft sand underfoot

DAY 2

In general, the camp sites situated on the banks of the Orange River are the most popular, and De Hoop and Richtersberg (your camps for the next two days) both boast ablution blocks with toilets, cold showers and sinks. Further inland, however, the attempt to create ablution facilities has been in vain and at Kokerboomkloof the tanks have not seen water for a long time.

The road from Sendelingsdrif initially leads inland to the east, before resuming its northerly direction, heading past the Potjiespram Mountain to Potjiespram Camp, the first riverside camp that you will find in the park. There are 18 sites and most people like to find a quiet, isolated spot on the river bank.

Typical camp site on the banks of the Orange River

Potjiespram (or Pootjiespram) comes from the name of the *pootjies* ('sheeps' hooves') which, after having been cleaned and before being cooked, reveal small humps that resemble *prammetjies* ('breasts'), a reference to surrounding mountains.

From here the trip to De Hoop will take you about five hours if you relax, explore and stop often for photographs. The road leads you first south, then east, then south and east again in giant zigzags, before delivering you to De Hoop, another idyllic camp on the banks of the Orange River.

Many of the park's famous features are to be found on this stretch between Potjiespram and De Hoop, including the Hand of God rock formation and the Akkedis Pass. Aim to arrive at De Hoop in the afternoon so that you can set up camp and watch the sunset over the water while the fire crackles. The tracks in the camp can be sandy but, as with all the other riverside sites, you can get by with deflated tyres.

DAY 3

Get up early, make coffee and enjoy the view of sunrise across the Orange River into Namibia. This is probably one of the most popular camps in the park, with 12 sites available. The camp is vast, covering many square kilometres along the sandy river bank, but there are a few trees offering sparse shade.

A farmer named Paul Avenant used to live here from 1926 until 1959, and the chimney from his house is all that remains of that era. Further down the valley are the remains of Ou Werf where another farmer, Albert Viljoen, lived. Albert's wife was the sister of Paul Avenant and they lived here until 1945.

The track up the river bank is not really very interesting, but can be challenging due to the thick powdery sand, and if you're going to get stuck anywhere, it's likely to be here! This rest day provides a wonderful opportunity for everyone to relax and do just as they please, be that swimming, fishing or exploring the surroundings.

ESSENTIAL INFORMATION FOR AN ENJOYABLE RICHTERSVELD EXPERIENCE

Dangers in the Richtersveld:
Don't dive into the Orange River as it can be shallower than expected and the bottom is strewn with rocks. Scorpions and snakes abound, so wear boots in the evening, even when sitting around the fire.

Clothing:
Wear UV-protective shirts – these are fantastic as you don't get sunburnt through them. Invest in a decent hat (not a cap) that will keep the sun off your neck and ears. As the area is usually hot during the day, shorts or a swimming costume is the perfect attire, but as the sun sets the nights can be chilly and so a light jacket or fleece is great in the evening. Pack according to the season; the only anomaly is winter where you can have temperatures of 35°C in the day whereas night temperatures can be -4°C.

Food:
Take your 12-volt freezer/fridge with you. If you do not have one, then rent or borrow one as this will make your trip so much more enjoyable. Plan your menu and pack the last day's food first (in the bottom) and the first day's food on the top. Freezing your vacuum-packed meat before loading it into the fridge works well and uses less battery power. A small gas stove with disposable cylinders is ideal for the morning coffee and tea unless you want to keep a fire going 24 hours a day. Most of the camping stores sell these stoves; take an extra gas cylinder or two.

Communications:
There is very limited cellphone reception in the park, but if you have roaming you can connect via the Namibian service provider. Most 4X4 enthusiasts use 29MHz radios during their travels and although the mountains limit the range, listen on Channel 1 and 14 for other users. VHF is a good option with better range, and you can try either of the ORRA (Off Road Radio Association) channels.

The Richtersveld isn't always dry

DAY 4

Leaving De Hoop, you have two options to get to Richtersberg. The trip southwards (upriver) will take about 90 minutes through thick sand. Cautious drivers should rather take the inland detour to Richtersberg, but you must allow much more time for this route. The track goes west for 7.3km before turning south for 23.8km and again northeast for a further 18.3km, passing Mount Richtersberg on your left.

The area between De Hoop and Richtersberg was frequented by Fred and Solly Ruppling, prospectors who had been searching for profitable quantities of minerals along the river for many years.

The Richtersberg camp site is also very popular, with 12 sites and great swimming holes that are deeper than 2m. Some 3km east of the camp site you'll find Tatasberg, which is now a luxury camp with fully equipped self-catering chalets. The camp manager lives close by and can assist if necessary.

Tatasberg was drilled extensively for copper in 1974 but no significant quantities were found. It was named after a Nama, Tatas, who had a *veepos* ('cattle post') camp at the foot of the mountain. After his death he was buried on the high bank overlooking the river and posthumously had the mountain (Tatasberg) and the local river named after him.

This is your last night of camping on the river banks inside the national park, so enjoy it while you can. Tomorrow night you'll be camping at the stunningly beautiful Kokerboomkloof Camp, before finishing the trip at a river rafters' camp closer to Vioolsdrif.

Old mine

DAY 5

From here you travel away from the river to Kokerboomkloof. The driving on this section is easy, with some great wide river beds to traverse. Initially you travel southwards via a wonderful viewpoint (a good opportunity to photograph the Tatasberg away to your east) to the Springbokvlakte, where the road then turns northeastwards once you have taken the left fork. It leads to a turn-off some 4km further, leading to another viewpoint, this time to the south of the Tatasberg. (This is a 2km diversion off the main road.)

Heading back to the main road, you then turn left again and after just over a kilometre there is yet another viewpoint, dead south of the Tatasberg, overlooking the Springbokvlakte away to your south. From here you have a 6km drive past the mountain known as Die Toon ('The Toe') to tonight's camp site, Kokerboomkloof.

This beautiful camp nestles under the shadow of Die Toon, a huge rock formation, and is easily accessible via a sandy road that is in good condition. The silence here is numbing and the plant life fascinating. The sandstone formations have names such as Baboon Skull Rock, Sphinx and Moon Rock. There is an abundance of kokerbome and this is probably the camp with the most photographic possibilities. The red and orange hues at dawn and dusk offer the best opportunities of making the rocks and kokerbome look extravagant.

Don't miss climbing Die Toon (you won't get to the actual top unless you are a rock climber), as the views over the plains make this well worth the effort.

The camp sites are set between huge boulders and the ablution blocks (when operational) will offer a reprieve from digging toilet holes.

Time permitting, you could stay an extra day here, if only for the additional photographic opportunities to be had, and to regain your strength for tomorrow's leg, the longest of the trip, being some 210km.

DAY 6

Today's route takes you 60km back to the park entrance gate away to the west. Initially you drive southwest back to the Springbokvlakte and then in a northwesterly direction, passing Claim Peak and the turn-off to Hakkiesdoorn Camp.

About 15km before the gate, you'll find a good viewpoint and the turn-off to De Koei, a nondescript camp site but, like many other places in the Richtersveld, once you start to look, you will find that the plants are diverse and interesting. Most visitors use De Koei as a stopover when leaving the park via the Helskloof Pass and, unless you are going to study the plant life, no more than one night is recommended.

Once out of the park, you'll travel south towards Lekkersing, taking the left turning to Eksteenfontein. This small town in the middle of the Richtersveld was originally called Stinkfontein (after the Stinkbossie found in the area) but soon changed its name to Eksteenfontein, in honour of Dominee Eksteen who worked with the community and in the area. The town, home to a number of the mineworkers, has a bottle store and small general dealer. One can purchase permits in Eksteenfontein to travel into the World

Interesting rock formations, day 6

Heritage Site, but these routes require 4X4 with low range and are very remote. These trails require a minimum of two vehicles, as some trails are Grade 4, and breaking down here on your own could add you to the statistics of people who get lost and die in the mountains every year.

From here on you travel in a general northeasterly direction, past a windmill and some halfmens trees, before descending the Helskloof Pass to the stone cairns which travellers have packed beside the roadway to mark their passing. The last stop is to see some petroglyphs, and then it's on to your final camp site at a river rafters' camp on the Orange River. (The roads in this section are generally in very bad condition and you can expect to drive bad corrugations until you reach Vioolsdrif.)

Soft green grass on which to pitch your tent and proper ablution facilities with hot and cold running water and flushing toilets allow you to end the trip clean and refreshed for the drive home the next day.

4 Khaudum and Mamili – explore the remote parks of the Caprivi Strip

by Jurgens Schoeman

TOP 10 ATTRACTIONS OF THIS TRIP

❶ Visit to the Hoba meteorite near Grootfontein ❷ San cultural interaction in Bushmanland – entrance to the Khaudum ❸ Varied off-road driving conditions – thick sand and deep-water channels ❹ Excellent photo opportunities ❺ The rare roan antelope in Khaudum ❻ Popa Falls ❼ Nyae Nyae pans ❽ The 'Dorslandboom' ❾ Remoteness – the Khaudum is one of the last true wilderness areas and not a lot of tourists visit the area, which will definitely give you a feeling of being alone in an authentic African wilderness ❿ Tiger fishing on the Okavango

TRIP OUTLINE

This journey promises to satisfy your hunger for wildlife, adventure and off-road endurance, all in one package! The areas that we will travel through have not really been discovered by the tourist masses. Ever-changing landscapes, vegetation and ecosystems keep the route interesting.

It starts in the north of Namibia at Grootfontein, from where we proceed to Tsumkwe, a town located in an area that was formerly known as Bushmanland. We then visit the Nyae Nyae plains and learn more about the San culture before entering the Khaudum National Park in northeastern Namibia, on the border with Botswana. We then spend a couple of days in the Khaudum park to really appreciate the wildlife and the contrasting vegetation types. Prepare yourself for a true African bush experience.

Once we leave Khaudum, we enter the Caprivi and travel on the Trans-Caprivi Highway, driving to Bagani where we visit the nearby Mahango (formerly Mahango Game Park, now incorporated into the Bwabwata National Park). This wonderful park is situated on the banks of the Okavango River where you will find a series of rapids, waterways and islands universally known as Popa Falls.

Back on the B8 the route will take you through the former Caprivi Game Park (now also incorporated into the Bwabwata National Park) to Kongola and then south towards the Mudumu and Mamili national parks. The journey will end at Katima Mulilo, the largest town in the Caprivi, which lies at the convergence of Angola, Namibia, Botswana, Zimbabwe and Zambia.

SEE DETAILED MAP ON PAGE 46 ▶▶

APPEAL RATING

5/5

Khaudum and Mamili are two of Namibia's lesser-known national parks. It is the remote and undeveloped nature of their settings and surroundings which makes for a truly memorable wilderness and bush experience.

▶ Heavy sand tracks for protracted distances in Khaudum ensure challenging driving conditions throughout

▶ Khaudum is the only park in Namibia that protects the Northern Kalahari Desert Biome environment

▶ Mamili National Park is the largest wetland area in Namibia with conservation status

▶ High water levels and flooded roads during certain times of the year can be very demanding on the vehicles and their occupants

▶ The wild experience of driving and camping in the unfenced Khaudum National Park's camps is a huge attraction for many

▶ Wonderful game-viewing and excellent bird-watching opportunities exist at every turn on this trip

▶ The wildlife can be a bit skittish as the animals are not used to the presence of humans nor vehicle activity

THE BEST TIME TO TRAVEL HERE

Weather conditions can be very hot during summer, with daily afternoon thunderstorms a regular phenomenon. The rainy season starts in October/November and can last up to April. The peak rainfall months are from late December up to March.

The average minimum temperature in winter (July) is 7°C and the average maximum during December and January is anywhere from 35 to 38°C. In summer the temperatures can go up to as high as 45°C.

During summer the bush and grass are also much denser, with some roads in Mamili flooded and impassable. The winter time has more moderate temperatures and it is drier, which is better for game-viewing. The Kwando River, originating in Angola, inundates the flood plains of Mamili. Be careful when crossing small rivers as the water levels can be higher than anticipated.

It is not advisable to visit the Khaudum park during the rainy season as there is a good chance that your vehicle will get stuck in one of the mud pans.

FAMILY-FRIENDLY RATING

3/5

▶ This trip can be very trying and difficult if you have small children forced to spend many long hours trapped in a hot vehicle

▶ The high temperatures experienced at certain times of the year can cause discomfort for all

▶ Bush camping with no facilities in Khaudum and Mamili can be difficult for those with smaller children and those not used to 'roughing it'

▶ Children cannot run and explore freely as camp sites are not fenced off from the wild, free-roaming game and especially the predator species

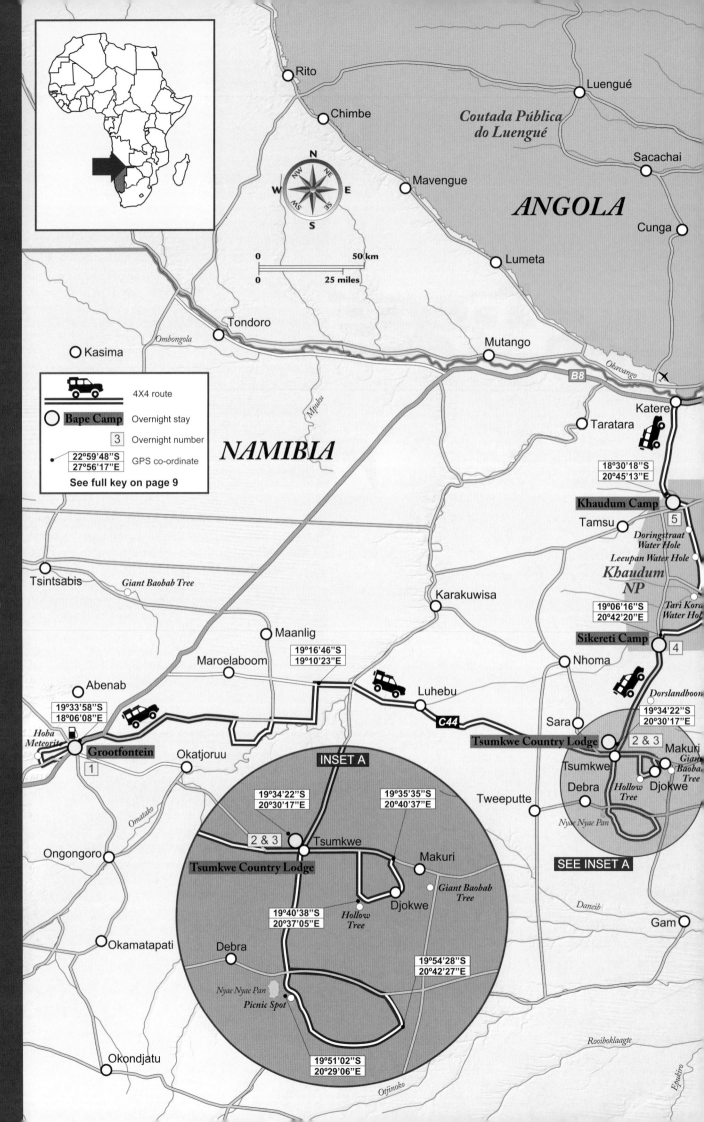

Key:

4X4 route

Bape Camp Overnight stay

3 Overnight number

22°59'48"S
27°56'17"E GPS co-ordinate

See full key on page 9

ANGOLA

Coutada Pública do Luengué

NAMIBIA

Rito

Chimbe

Luengué

Sacachai

Mavengue

Cunga

Lumeta

Tondoro

Ombongola

Mutango

Okavango

B8

Kasima

Katere

Taratara

18°30'18"S
20°45'13"E

Khaudum Camp

Tamsu

5

Doringstraat Water Hole

Leeupan Water Hole

Khaudum NP

Mpuku

Tsintsabis

Giant Baobab Tree

Karakuwisa

19°06'16"S
20°42'20"E

Tari Kora Water Hole

Maanlig

19°16'46"S
19°10'23"E

Sikereti Camp

4

Nhoma

Maroelaboom

Luhebu

C44

Dorslandboom

19°34'22"S
20°30'17"E

Abenab

19°33'58"S
18°06'08"E

Sara

Tsumkwe Country Lodge

2 & 3

Makuri

Hoba Meteorite

Grootfontein

Okatjoruu

Omatako

1

Tsumkwe

Giant Baobab Tree

Debra

Hollow Tree

Djokwe

INSET A

19°34'22"S
20°30'17"E

19°35'35"S
20°40'37"E

2 & 3

Tsumkwe

Tsumkwe Country Lodge

Tweeputte

Nyae Nyae Pan

SEE INSET A

Makuri

Giant Baobab Tree

19°40'38"S
20°37'05"E

Hollow Tree

Djokwe

Ongongoro

Daneib

Okamatapati

Debra

Nyae Nyae Pan

Picnic Spot

19°54'28"S
20°42'27"E

Gam

Okondjatu

19°51'02"S
20°29'06"E

Otjinoko

Rooiboklaagte

Epaliro

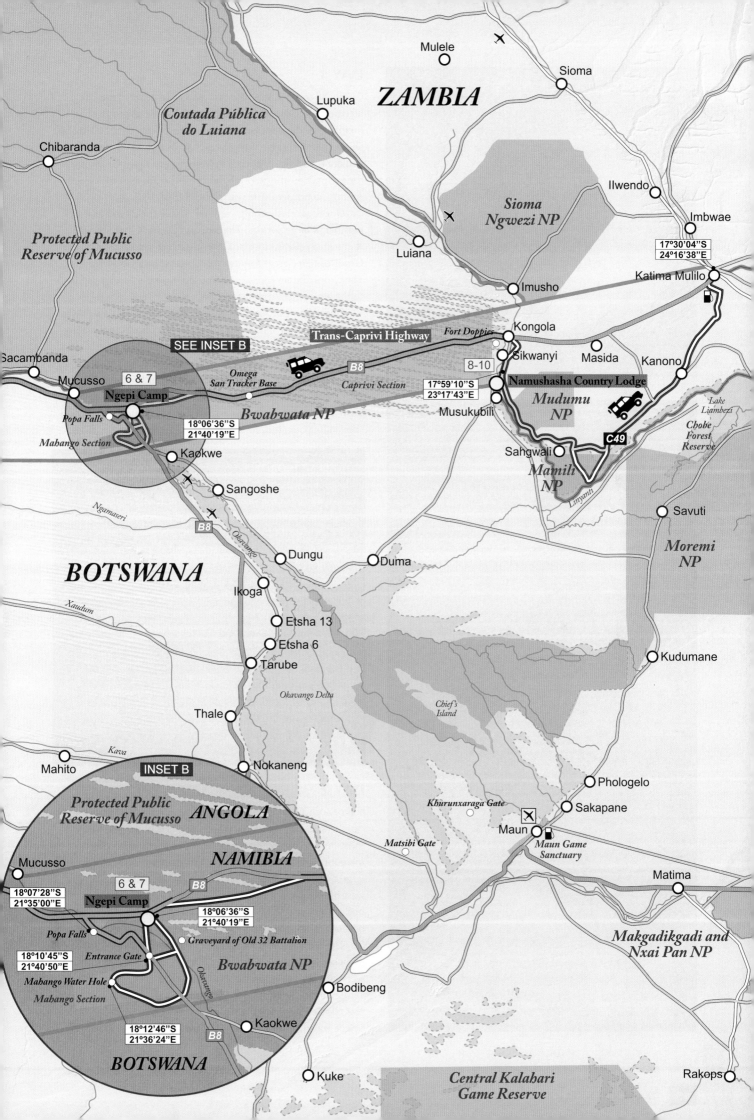

DAILY DRIVING DISTANCE AND TIME

Day 1	Meet at Grootfontein		
Day 2	Grootfontein to Tsumkwe	310km	7hr
Day 3	Nyae Nyae plains	80km	5hr
Day 4	Tsumkwe to Sikereti Camp	60km	6hr
Day 5	Sikereti to Khaudum Camp	170km	8hr
Day 6	Khaudum to Ngepi Camp	190km	8hr
Day 7	Mahango day drive	40km	4hr
Day 8	Ngepi to Namushasha Lodge	330km	8hr
Days 9 and 10	Mudumu and Mamili national parks	120km	6hr
Day 11	Kongola or Katima Mulilo	120km	4hr
Total distance from Grootfontein to Kongola		1420km	

SELF-SUFFICIENCY RATING

5/5

Thorough preparation is essential for a trip through the Khaudum and Mamili national parks as these parks do not offer any facilities at all.

- Be self-sufficient in the parks as far as fuel and drinking water are concerned
- The nearest fuel stations to Khaudum's Sikereti Camp are Grootfontein (360km from Sigeretti Camp) and Tsumkwe (60km from Sikereti Camp), but the latter only provides diesel and 93 leaded petrol
- The closest fuel stations to Khaudum Camp are Bagani/Divundu (about 150km from the camp) and Rundu (about 170km)
- Mamili's nearest fuel station is about 70km away at Kongola or about 120km away at Katima Mulilo
- Keep in mind that fuel consumption in sandy conditions is much higher than you are used to – petrol engines (this does vary from make to make) can travel between 2.5 and 4km per litre, and diesel-powered vehicles usually manage around 4–5km per litre
- Your daily personal liquid consumption will be more than usual too – make provision to carry 2 litres of drinking water per person per day in your vehicle (that is over and above the cool drinks and beer or water for the kitchen or shower)
- You must bring in all your wood for camp fires and braais, as the collecting of wood in the parks is not allowed
- The bush camps in the parks do not have any ablution facilities at all – no toilets, no showers, nothing
- Naturally, whatever you take in with you should leave with you – do not bury rubbish or leave plastic bags of garbage behind as there is no weekly garbage removal truck visiting here
- It is recommended that a minimum of two vehicles travel together for safety's sake and to recover each other
- Grootfontein, Rundu and Katima Mulilo all have well-appointed retail stores where you can stock up on supplies should you run short

DAY 1

Guests all travel in their own time so as to arrive in the late afternoon in Grootfontein in Namibia where all group members and guides will meet at a pre-arranged camp site. You should allow enough time to reach Grootfontein from wherever you are travelling; distances in Namibia are vast – Grootfontein, for example, is about 1250km from either the Noordoewer or Ariamsvlei border posts with South Africa.

Due to a relatively high annual rainfall the town has a number of large springs. The San and Damara that lived in the area referred to it as Gei-/ous, which translates as Grootfontein ('great fountain' or 'great spring') in Afrikaans. The Grootfontein Museum is housed in an old fort dating back to the era of German occupation.

During the border war between 1975 and 1990, there was a large army base at Grootfontein, which contributed in a big way towards the town's economy.

This first afternoon, we will meet up with the rest of the group, set up camp and enjoy a pre-tour briefing and familiarisation session around the camp fire. A genuine African bush adventure awaits you – it will recharge your batteries and rejuvenate your soul.

HOBA METEORITE

The Hoba meteorite lies not far from Grootfontein (to the west) and is the largest known meteorite on earth. It is estimated that it landed on earth about 80,000 years ago. It was discovered by accident when the owner of the farm was ploughing his fields. The plough ground to a halt when he heard a metallic sound as it scratched against a hard object. Jacobus Hermanus Brits was the scientist that first identified it as a meteorite, back in 1920. At that stage it weighed 66 tons, but the current mass is about 60 tons. This is due to erosion, scientific sampling and some vandalism. The lump of metal that you will see is composed of 84% iron and 16% nickel with small traces of cobalt.

In 1955 the Namibian (then South West African) government declared the Hoba meteorite a national monument. In 1987 the owner of the farm Hoba West, Mr Engelbrecht, donated the meteorite and the site to the State. A tourist centre was opened to protect the meteorite against vandalism, and tourists from all over the world visit the site annually.

DAY 2

Full of anticipation, we arise early and, after a wholesome catered breakfast, break up camp and first pay a visit to the most famous attraction in the Grootfontein area, the Hoba meteorite, before hitting the road to Tsumkwe. This, the world's largest meteorite, lies in a shallow depression about 20km west of the town of Grootfontein on the farm Hoba West. The meteorite was discovered in 1920. It has been uncovered, but because of its large mass it has never been moved from where it fell. The mass is estimated at over 60 tons and it consists mainly of nickel and iron. It is the most massive naturally occuring piece of iron known on the earth's surface.

Once finished at Hoba, we depart for Tsumkwe, but we are first allowed time to stock up on last-minute supplies and refuel before leaving Grootfontein. We follow the back roads and

Baobab, Tsumkwe

eventually join the C44 to the frontier town of Tsumkwe.

Tsumkwe is the main town in the area previously known as Bushmanland and is the ancestral land of the Ju/'hoan San people. Around Tsumkwe there are about 32 small communities which make up the Ju/'hoan San population of about 3000 living in the Nyae Nyae Conservancy. The Nyae Nyae Conservancy is a vast expanse of wooded savannah consisting of enormous boababs and seasonal pans. It was proclaimed as a conservancy in 1998 and is managed by the community themselves.

Upon arrival in Tsumkwe, we set up camp at the Tsumkwe Country Lodge.

During the afternoon we leave on a game drive to the Nyae Nyae Pan about 17km south of Tsumkwe to enjoy some bird-watching and game-viewing. The Nyae Nyae Pan is the largest and most scenic of the pans in the area. After good rains the saline surface of the pan is transformed into a water paradise for thousands of birds including large flocks of flamingoes. Although the area has been restocked with game, it is sometimes difficult to spot the animals due to the dense vegetation. The sound of approaching vehicles unfortunately also scares them off.

From the pan we backtrack on our route to Tsumkwe, as it is time to get settled around the camp fire. You are guaranteed to enjoy the wonderful view of the southern skies while the night sounds from the surrounding bush mix with the crackling sounds of the fire.

DAY 3

Today we continue our exploration of the Nyae Nyae Conservancy. We will follow a circular drive to include visits to two well-known baobabs in the area. Baobabs are also known as the 'upside down tree' and today you will definitely see why.

Proceeding in an easterly direction on the C44 for about 15km, we then turn right towards Djokwe. A sandy track will lead us to the Holboom. Holboom is Afrikaans for 'hollow tree'. It refers to the huge hollow in its stem. It is an amazing sight to witness and this tree is thought to be the world's largest baobab.

About 4km from Djokwe we will stop at the second giant baobab, Grootboom (Afrikaans for 'large tree'). You get the impression that a number of trunks have merged together into one conglomerate tree. The circumference of this monster is about 30m.

Our next stop is Makuri where we will visit a San settlement and take part in various traditional San activities offered by the community. You will have the opportunity to experience their customs and traditions by joining the women when they go in search of veld food or be amazed by the field knowledge of the male trackers.

Despite their current circumstances, the San are always welcoming and a visit will not be complete without traditional dancing and singing which are guaranteed to lift the spirits.

After this moving experience, we make our way back to our camp in Tsumkwe. On the return journey, stay vigilant and be on the lookout for elephants that frequent the area as well as kudus and other antelope species.

Elephant herds are a common sight when approaching Tsumkwe

DAY 4

As we head for the Khaudum National Park we leave civilisation behind us and enter an area that can best be described as an isolated wilderness. It is now time to deflate all tyres, as thick sand will have to be negotiated on our way to Sikereti Camp, our final destination for the day.

The southern boundary of the park is approximately 54km from Tsumkwe. From there it is only 7.5km to Sikereti. En route we will stop at the 'Dorslandboom', a landmark in the area. It was also a landmark for the Dorsland Trekkers, who camped under the tree en route to their destination in Angola. See if

DORSLAND TREK

The Dorsland Trek started when settlers were looking for a homeland of their own, where they would not be under foreign rule and would be free to practise their religion and culture without interference. In 1874 the first group, under the leadership of Gert Alberts, started the trek. They were followed shortly thereafter by a number of other groups. The trek route took them through the vast, arid and hostile Kalahari (today Botswana and Namibia). These extreme conditions gave the trek its name, Dorsland Trek ('Thirstland Trek').

They went on and entered Angola by crossing the Kunene River at Swartbooisdrift. Today you will find a monument there to commemorate the trek. After encountering some troubles with the Portuguese rulers in Angola, some settlers packed up and returned to what was then South West Africa to settle around the Otavi, Tsumeb and Grootfontein areas.

VEHICLE REQUIREMENTS

- A 4 x 4 vehicle with high- and low-range gear functions
- Vehicles with a high ground clearance are recommended
- Recovery points in the front and back
- You do not need specialist tyres to do the tour – most of the standard tyres with which 4X4s come equipped are perfectly suitable for the various types of terrain you will encounter on this trip
- Tyres known colloquially as old 'Marie Biscuit' tyres are too narrow and will not do well
- Modern so-called soft-roaders may struggle

TRAILER-FRIENDLY RATING

3/5

If you are inexperienced at off-road driving with a trailer, then this trip is definitely not recommended due to the deep soft sand tracks of Khaudum and also not for the many water crossings in Mamili. However, a good driver with adequate experience of towing off-road will be able to handle a trailer in the conditions of both Khaudum and Mamili.

TRAVEL DOCUMENTATION

- South African citizens will require a passport (but no visa) for Namibia; this requirement is applicable to children as well
- ZA sticker on the rear of your vehicle
- Vehicle registration papers
- Letter of authority to take the vehicle across borders, if the vehicle is not registered in your name
- Proof of vehicle insurance
- Travel insurance that will cover emergency evacuation for all vehicle occupants

GENERAL WARNINGS FOR THIS ROUTE

- The whole trip is through a malaria area; anti-malarial prophylactics are strongly advised
- The camp sites and bush camps are unfenced; be bush-wise and keep an eye on the children at all times
- The area is remote and isolated – there is no mobile phone coverage in Khaudum and only at a few places on the outskirts of Mamili
- The driving conditions vary a lot – be on the lookout for potholes and prepare yourself before the trip with the technical ability to drive in thick sand and deep-water channels
- It is important to have a radiator net to keep seeds from blocking the radiator fins
- It is recommended that at least two 4X4 vehicles travel together

you can still find the dates 1883, 1884 and 1891 carved into the tree trunk.

Shorter shrub and bush typify the vegetation in the south of Khaudum, with dominant species being purple-pod cluster leaf, kudu bush, bushwillow and blade thorn.

Buffalo wallowing

The Khaudum Game Park was proclaimed in 1989 to protect the Northern Kalahari Sandveld Biome. In 2007 it was given national park status and was renamed the Khaudum National Park, but it remains one of the less visited parks in Namibia, due to its isolation. Broad-leaved woodlands stabilise the undulating east-to-west trending dunes. The proliferation of trees tends to mask the dunes and make them hardly detectable. The sand in the area is noticeably white or grey in comparison with the red sand of the southern Kalahari. This is due to the high rainfall leeching minerals and nutrients from the sand.

Khaudum National Park is fence-free, except for the border with Botswana and about 55km of the western border of the park. This means the animals can roam freely and follow their natural migration routes within the vast area. Twelve artificial water holes sustain the wildlife during dry seasons and are ideal spots to spend some time watching the animals as they go about their daily routine, gingerly stepping down to drink, constantly vigilant for any signs or a whiff of impending danger from resident predators.

Having established our camp under the sporadic shade we again head out and drive west to the Tsoana water hole. The park has a large concentration of elephants and we are more than likely to come across some en route to this water hole. During the dry season over 3000 elephants were counted during a game count and aerial survey.

WHAT IS AN *OMURAMBA*?

The plural for *omuramba* is *omiramba*, a Herero word that refers to prehistoric river beds. About 16,000 years ago *omiramba* were rivers, but today they only have water after good rains. These dry river beds occur in the Kalahari Desert, but more specifically in the northeastern part of Namibia (Khaudum National Park) and northwestern part of Botswana. In Khaudum you will find the Chadum Omuramba, Cwiba Omuramba, etc. *Omiramba* provide irregular pools of water, and this makes the surrounding area more fertile and appealing for animals as well as for herdsmen. The San also tend to settle near *omiramba*.

With time and patience you will be able to see a variety of animals in the park, including elephant, giraffe, lion, leopard, spotted hyena, jackal, the scarce African wild dog (large packs of up to 30 wild dogs have been sighted in the park), kudu, steenbok, gemsbok, blue wildebeest, tsessebe, hartebeest, eland and reedbuck. Some 320 bird species have been recorded.

Remember that all the camps within Khaudum are unfenced and it is therefore not only advisable to, but life-threatening if you do not exercise extreme caution regarding how you walk around the camp. Wild animals can pass through the camp, and they do so especially at night, so you should use a strong light when visiting the ablution facilities. Always keep your tent zipped closed and pack all food away so that the tempting aromas do not tantalise the taste buds of the inquisitive and hungry wildlife.

Sikereti Camp, Khaudum

WARNING
DANGER!
BEWARE OF ELEPHANT, LION
& HYAENA IN CAMP AT NIGHT

DAY 5

Our journey continues northwards to Khaudum Camp, the most northerly camp of the park.

From Sikereti there are three possible routes to reach the camp. We follow the easternmost route closest to the border with Botswana, travelling from one water hole to the next in a bush version of a pub crawl, searching for game and seeking out the treasures of the area. The Tari Kora water hole will be our first stop from where we continue on our northerly heading for a further 25km to the Leeupan. About 16km north of Leeupan is the Doringstraat water hole. En route you will experience a definite change in the driving conditions, as the track becomes much sandier and a higher level of concentration is needed to negotiate the constantly twisting twin track with its undulations, bumps and soft patches.

Looking around you, it will also be noticeable how the vegetation changes as you progress northwards. The calcrete and clay make way for thick sand, and tall-standing woodland tree species replace the shrubs and bushes of the south. Some of the dominant species in this northern area are false mopane, wild syringa, Zambezi teak, Kalahari apple-leaf, Sandveld acacia, camel thorn, kiaat and African wattle.

Khaudum is home to the rare roan antelope. These animals like to spend their time browsing in the more northern parts of the park.

Khaudum Camp is located on a high dune, which allows for beautiful panoramic views of the surrounding area. Pitch your

tent under the shady trees and enjoy the sunset with a cold beer in your hand. The sounds of nature will fill the air after dusk and a pleasant evening around the camp fire will be a perfect ending for a day in the African bush. For those with a keen interest in astronomy, the stars here seem that much brighter and a whole lot closer too. It seems as though you would be able to touch them if you were able to stretch your hand out just a little bit further!

DAY 6

Today, once we have enjoyed another splendid, hearty bush breakfast, we pack up and leave our Khaudum camp behind us as we start the challenging 60km trip towards Katere through thick soft sand. It is difficult to build up sufficient speed and maintain your momentum along this sandy and dusty trail because the sections of deep corrugation require careful manoeuvring just to stay on the track.

Reaching Katere we join the B8 highway and continue driving in an easterly direction towards the Caprivi. This is a tropical area, with high temperatures and high summer rainfall, making it the wettest part of Namibia. The area is mostly made up of swamps, flood plains, wetland and woodland.

We head for Ngepi Camp (or any other of the well-maintained camp sites in this area) on the western side of the Okavango River. Here we will spend the next two days relaxing after the hard driving of the last couple of days and it will also allow time to enjoy the splendours of the Okavango River.

Having sorted ourselves out and settled into our new accommodation, we will depart late in the afternoon on a sunset cruise on the Okavango River and enjoy the wonders of a typical sunset over one of Southern Africa's largest waterways.

DAY 7

This morning we enjoy a drive to Mahango. The area is arguably one of Namibia's most beautiful and the Okavango River's metamorphosis from a stream to a swamp happens here. Mahango borders the Okavango River and the area is characterised by riverine forests, a broad flood plain and magnificent baobab trees. Plenty of game species are to be found here, so be on the lookout for elephant, red lechwe, buffalo, sable, roan antelope, Chobe

THE ROAN ANTELOPE THAT MADE HISTORY

In 1970 a group of 70 roan antelope was airlifted from the Khaudum to Etosha. A Hercules cargo plane made three flights to relocate the sedated animals from one reserve to the other. It was the first time in history this had been done over such a long distance.

These animals weigh about 250kg and measure around 1.5m at the shoulder. They have a reddish-brown colour with a lighter underbelly and a black face with white eyebrows and cheeks. Their horns are ringed and arch slightly backwards, and the males' horns can be as long as 1m.

The relocation of 70 of these animals was thus a truly remarkable project.

bushbuck, reedbuck, tsessebe, sitatunga and lots of hippos. You will often hear the 'voice of Africa' – the cry of African fish-eagles. Herds of elephant are regularly seen crossing the river to get to the islands in search of better food – an awesome sight to witness. It is interesting to see them marshalling themselves and organising the young calves, encouraging them to take the plunge and swim safely across to where the grass is greener.

Next, we visit the Popa Falls, which is really a series of rapids and not a waterfall in the true sense of the word, as the drop-off during the extent of the rapids is only about 4m in total. The rapids are not all visible at the same time as they extend for over 1km across the river. Small rocky outcrops create islands dividing the rapids into a variety of channels. If the water levels are low it is possible to jump across to some of the small islands. As there are plenty of hippos and crocodiles in the river, you have to be cautious and aware of with whom you are about to be sharing the river!

As you have the afternoon off and can spend these precious hours at leisure, doing as you please, you can hang around and soak up the natural beauty of the falls, or return to camp on your own steam to laze around camp, take a well-deserved nap

(aren't they all 'well deserved'?) or spend some time relaxing around the swimming pool.

For the keen fishermen in the group, you can join one of the many 'catch and release' fishing trips that are available on this stretch of the river. Threespot and green-headed tilapia are two of the more common species of game fish that occur in the Okavango River, but it is the tigerfish that has the reputation for putting up the best fight.

DAY 8

After two relaxing days here, we depart on the last section of the journey, eastwards through the Caprivi Strip. The former Caprivi Game Park (now part of Bwabwata National Park) is sandwiched between Angola to the north and Botswana to the south. The 5715km^2 park is 32km wide and it stretches for about 180km from the Okavango River in the west to the Kwando River in the east. The sight from the bridge over the Okavango River near Bagani is impressive and one that will stay with you for a long time. During the border war this bridge was always well guarded due to its location and strategic importance.

The park is a sanctuary for large and small game species alike, but visitors are not likely to see many of these animals as vehicular traffic is restricted to the main road between Kavango and Eastern Caprivi and exploring off the track is, naturally, prohibited.

About 15km from the Bagani Bridge in the Caprivi you will find the remains of the well-known military base, Buffalo, the headquarters of 32 Battalion. The legendary military strategist turned author, Colonel Jan Breytenbach, received orders from the former

THE HISTORY OF THE CAPRIVI

The Lozi kings ruled the Caprivi in the 19th century, when it was known as Itenge. The British took over the administration of the area as part of the protectorate they had of Bechuanaland (today Botswana). Britain also administered the island of Zanzibar, but in 1890 Germany laid claim to the island. A dispute arose that was settled at the Berlin Conference, which had the following outcome: Zanzibar was returned to Britain in exchange for the Caprivi Strip, which came under German rule. The strip was named after Chancellor von Caprivi who negotiated the deal. Germany thought that with the annexation of the Caprivi they would have access to the Zambezi River and eventually access to Tanganyika (today Tanzania). This never happened as the British stopped them before they reached the Victoria Falls.

The Caprivi became of strategic importance during the border war in the 1970s and 1980s. It was used as a jumping-off point and resupply route by South African troops in support of UNITA (the National Union for the Total Independence of Angola, who operated in southern Angola) and it was also an infiltration route for Swapo guerrillas.

government to form a guerrilla fighting unit that would operate within the borders of Angola and so 32 Battalion, commonly known as the 'Buffalo Soldiers' (named after the emblem on their berets), was born.

Some 70km further eastwards, we make a quick stop at Omega, location of the training bases for San trackers used by the former South African Defence Force (SADF). During the border war, this base was regarded as one of the most attractive on the Caprivi, with sleeping quarters laid out under a wonderful canopy of trees.

Further along the B8 we undertake a short detour to see the remains of another old SADF base at Fort Doppies. Fort Doppies was established in 1970 and derived its name from a vervet monkey who lived in the area and had the habit of rushing into the base to steal the spent copper cartridge cases (known as 'doppies' in Afrikaans) and then running away with his booty. It was at Fort Doppies where most of the Special Forces training took place during the border war.

From this place of forgotten history, we proceed to our next base camp at Kongola, from where we will explore the wonders of the Mudumu and Mamili national parks. Our preference is to settle into the accommodation at Namushasha Country Lodge, which is situated 24km south of Kongola.

DAYS 9 AND 10

By now well accustomed to bush travel in the Caprivi, we prepare to head south from Namushasha Country Lodge to the Mudumu and Mamili national parks.

Mudumu National Park is a vast 1010km² expanse of dense savannah and mopane woodland with the Kwando River as its western border. The park is home to small populations of sitatunga and red lechwe, while spotted-neck otter, hippo and crocodile inhabit the waterways.

To the south of Lianshulu the Kwando River branches off into a labyrinth of channels ultimately forming the Linyanti Swamp. This geographic feature is rich in bird life, but when in flood it makes access to the park difficult if not impossible. Some 70% of Namibia's bird life has been recorded in this Eastern Caprivi region.

We will be exploring the section of the Mudumu National Park that lies to the west of the C49 roadway, as well as the riverfront section, as animal activity in the area is normally high

and we should be able to record many successful sightings.

Rejoining the C49 we proceed even further south to the Mamili National Park. We reach the entrance to the park approximately 13km after turning off the C49. Mamili is Namibia's equivalent of Botswana's Okavango Delta – a watery paradise of river channels, islands and wetlands. The two largest islands are Nkasa and Lupala, both situated in the Linyanti River. During the dry season it is possible to reach the islands by road, but in the rainy season most of the area is completely covered by flood waters.

You will have to be very cautious when driving through these flooded channels. It is advisable to first determine how high the level of the water is at each crossing, so as to avoid any large concealed holes. The route that we will follow will be determined by the water levels in the park and our guides will make a judgement call, based on their experience of this area and their expertise at fording deep waters.

Water crossings are numerous in Mamili National Park

The route takes us back to the C49, from where we head north again to Katima Mulilo, the largest town in the Caprivi. Here, for the first time in many days, we will have the opportunity to replenish any dwindling supplies, stock up with lovely fresh beers and explore the town. (Don't miss the baobab tree with the toilet inside!) Tonight, it is with great sadness that the tour ends. For the last time the group of new friends gathers for dinner, reliving the experiences of the past week, swapping contact details and making plans to reunite and share photographs. (You know the drill!)

DAY 11

Katima Mulilo is the meeting place of many roads and the springboard to many exciting destinations. From here you can decide where your journey will take you next as you can head for Zambia, Zimbabwe, Botswana, Angola or follow the Golden Highway back to Windhoek.

5 The Kaokoland – an inhospitable wonderland

by Johan Snyman

TOP 10 ATTRACTIONS OF THIS TRIP

❶ Interesting cultures and people ❷ Varied and challenging driving conditions ❸ The chance to hone your overlanding skills ❹ Varied landscapes ranging from vast open spaces to mountainous areas ❺ Photographic opportunities ❻ Prolific bird life ❼ Interesting wildlife – especially the desert-adapted elephants ❽ Interesting geological formations ❾ Places of historical interest ❿ Clear skies with millions of stars at night

TRIP OUTLINE

The Kaokoland comprises an area of approximately 48,000km^2 and is to be found in the northwestern corner of Namibia. Its northern border is the Kunene River alongside Angola. Along the eastern border are Ovamboland and the Etosha National Park, south is Damaraland, and the Skeleton Coast National Park is along the western border.

The geological formations date back over 2 million years and consist of igneous and metamorphic rocks covered with a thin layer of sedimentary rock.

According to folklore, the area got its name when the Himba people entered the region with the rising sun behind them, the river on their right-hand side (*Okunene*) and the land on their left-hand side (*Okaoka*).

SEE DETAILED MAP ON PAGE 56 ▸▸

APPEAL RATING

5/5

Access to this fascinating part of Namibia was restricted during the Namibian War for Independence, but the number of visitors to the area has been increasing steadily for the past 20 years. This inhospitable wonderland bestows a life-altering experience upon the 4X4 adventurer with the right attitude.

- The remoteness of the area requires personal perseverance and adaptability, a vehicle that is prepared to 110% and a high level of overlanding skills
- Unsurpassed driving experiences ranging from good gravel roads to thick, loose sand in dry river beds to some very challenging boulder-strewn tracks
- You will pass through diverse landscapes, ranging from vast open plains to very mountainous areas
- Prolific bird life and mammals – you are likely to encounter elephant in some of the dry river beds.
- Some very interesting plants
- And last, but not least, the Himba people – a tribe that, for the most part, still lives in the Stone Age

THE BEST TIME TO TRAVEL HERE

May to October are the best months. This area falls in a summer-rainfall region where the precipitation is in the form of thunderstorms. This causes flash floods in the dry river beds and damage to roads and tracks. In summer, daytime temperatures reach the high 40 to low 50°C mark. From May onwards the temperatures become mild, but the area dries out rapidly and most trees shed their leaves.

FAMILY-FRIENDLY RATING

2/5

This will depend on the personalities of the people going on the trip!

- The chances are very good that children will become bored spending so many hours inside the confines of a vehicle; in many of the camp sites they will also not be able to run about, or do as they please, as crocodiles are a problem along the Kunene River, while elephant and lion could pose a major problem along the dry river beds
- The elderly could suffer from the extreme physical demands that travelling in this area will place on them

SELF-SUFFICIENCY RATING

5/5

- Careful planning needs to be done to ensure that sufficient equipment is taken along to maintain vehicle mobility and personal wellbeing, as this can be critical to your survival; on some sections of the route you will be days away from help, even if you have a satellite phone at your disposal
- Fuel is not readily available along the route, and between Ruacana and Fort Sesfontein you will have to carry enough fuel to enable you to travel approximately 1000km
- Vehicle repair facilities, medical facilities (hospitals) and shops for the replenishment of food supplies are only available at Kamanjab and Opuwo
- Water can be undrinkable at some camps
- Most of the camps have hot showers and flushing toilets; the standards vary, though, and at some camp sites there are no facilities

MAP 5 THE KAOKOLAND – an inhospitable wonderland

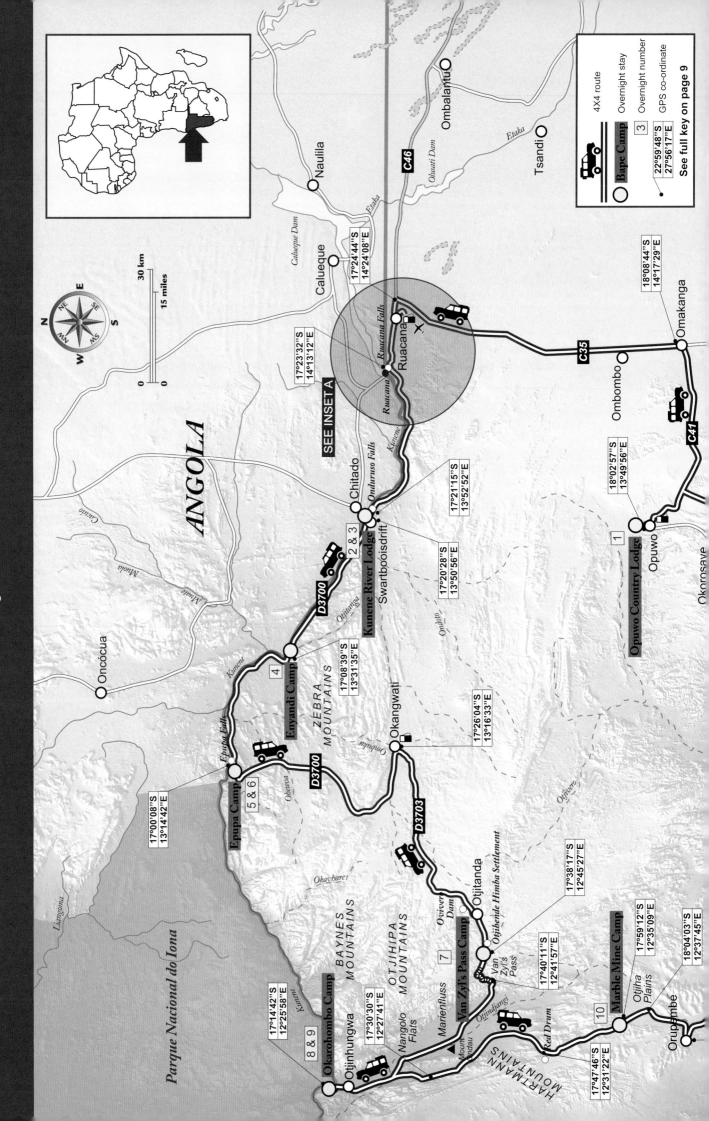

ANGOLA

Parque Nacional do Iona

4X4 route
Overnight stay
Overnight number 3
Bape Camp
GPS co-ordinate 22°59'48"S 27°56'17"E
See full key on page 9

30 km
15 miles

SEE INSET A

Naulila

Calueque Dam

Calueque
17°24'44"S 14°24'08"E

Ombalantu

Tsandi

Etaka

Olusati Dam

C46

Ruacana Falls
Ruacana
17°23'32"S 14°13'12"E

Onduruso Falls

Chitado

Kunene

Omakanga
18°08'44"S 14°17'29"E

C35

Ombombo

Opuwo
18°02'57"S 13°49'56"E

Opuwo Country Lodge 1

C41

Okorosave

17°21'15"S 13°52'52"E

Swartbooisdrift
17°20'28"S 13°50'56"E

Ondoto

Kunene River Lodge 2 & 3

D3700

Otjitanga

Enyandi Camp 4
17°08'39"S 13°31'35"E

ZEBRA MOUNTAINS

Okangwati
17°26'04"S 13°16'33"E

Ombuku

Otjivero

D3703

Oncócua

Mbiola

Cacato

Mbaio

Epupa Falls

Obetava

Epupa Camp 5 & 6
17°00'08"S 13°14'42"E

D3700

Kunene

Okavhare1

BAYNES MOUNTAINS

OTJIHIPA MOUNTAINS

Otjibende Himba Settlement
17°8'17"S 12°45'27"E

Otjitanda

Oruvervu Dam

Van Zyl's Pass
17°40'11"S 12°41'57"E

Van Zyl's Pass Camp 7

Marienfluss

Nangolo Flats

Otjindjangi

Liangoma

Otjinhungwa
17°30'30"S 12°27'41"E

Okarohombo Camp 8 & 9
17°14'42"S 12°25'58"E

Mount Ondau

Red Drum

HARTMANN MOUNTAINS

Otjiha Plains
17°59'12"S 12°35'09"E

Marble Mine Camp 10

Orupembe
18°04'03"S 12°37'45"E

17°47'46"S 12°31'22"E

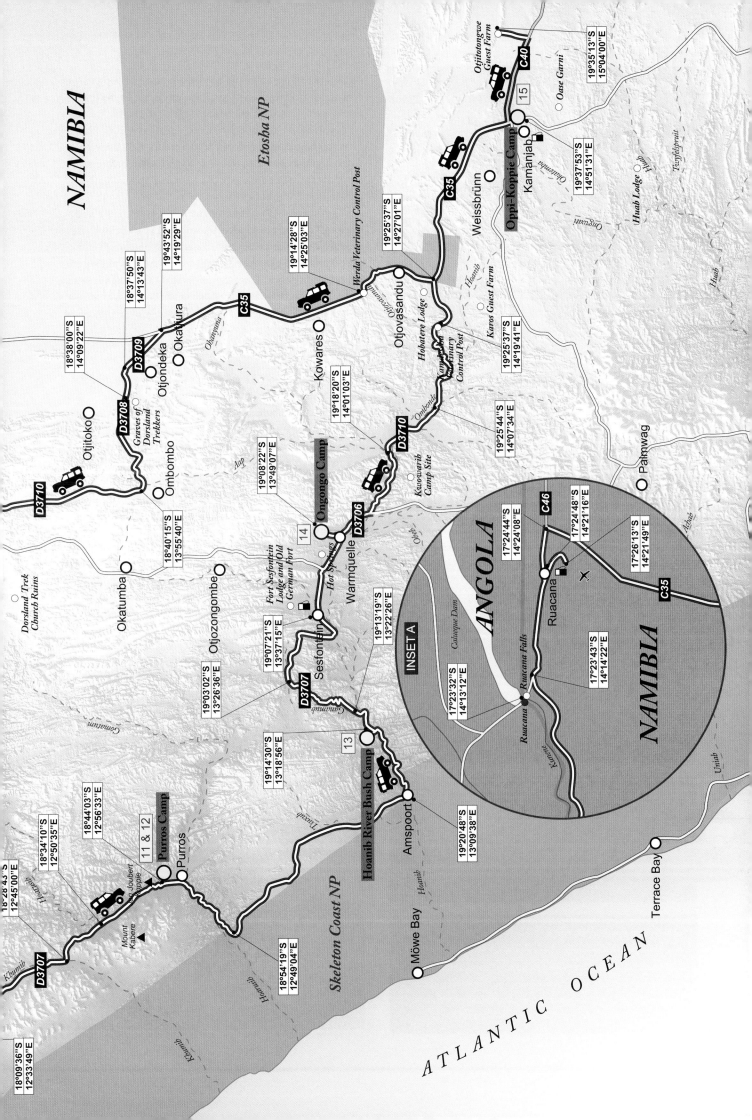

NAMIBIA

Etosha NP

19°43'52''S
14°19'29''E

18°37'50''S
14°13'43''E

18°38'00''S
14°09'22''E

D3709

D3708

Otjitoko ○

*Graves of
Dorsland
Trekkers*

Otjondeka
○ Okatura

C35

19°14'28''S
14°25'03''E

Werda Veterinary Control Post

19°25'37''S
14°27'01''E

Otjitotongwe
Guest Farm

19°35'13''S
15°04'00''E

C40

15

○ *Oase Garni*

Kamanjab

19°37'53''S
14°51'31''E

Huab Lodge ○

Huab

Tsvÿfelspruit

Ongarati

Huab

C35

Oppi-Koppie Camp

Weissbrünn

Hoanib

Karos Guest Farm

19°25'37''S
14°19'41''E

Otjovasandu ●

Hobatere Lodge ○

*Kaÿanÿabi
Veterinary
Control Post*

19°25'44''S
14°07'34''E

Ombonde

D3710

*Kaoÿvarib
Camp Site*

○ Palmwag

Ackab

Kowares ●

19°18'20''S
14°01'03''E

Okanÿana

18°40'15''S
13°55'40''E

○ Ombombo

D3710

Okatumba ○

*Dorsland
Trek Church Ruins*

Aap

Otjozongombe ○

19°08'22''S
13°49'07''E

Ongongo Camp

14

Hot Springs

D3706

Obeb

*Fort Sesfontein
Lodge and Old
German Fort*

Warmquelle ●

19°07'21''S
13°37'15''E

Sesfontein ●

19°03'02''S
13°26'36''E

D3707

Ganuamub

Gomatum

19°13'19''S
13°22'26''E

19°14'30''S
13°18'56''E

13

Hoanib River Bush Camp

19°20'48''S
13°09'38''E

Amspoort ●

Hoanib

Skeleton Coast NP

18°44'03''S
12°56'33''E

11 & 12

Purros Camp

18°34'10''S
12°50'35''E

Purros ●

*van Joubert
Koppie*

18°28'43''S
12°45'00''E

D3710

Hoarusib

▲ *Mount Kabere*

D3707

18°09'36''S
12°33'49''E

Khumib

Khumib

18°54'19''S
12°49'04''E

Taxaub

Hoanib

Möwe Bay ●

Terrace Bay ○

INSET A

ANGOLA

C46

17°24'44''S
14°24'08''E

17°24'48''S
14°21'16''E

Calueque Dam

Ruacana ●

✈

17°26'13''S
14°21'49''E

C35

17°23'32''S
14°13'12''E

Ruacana Falls

17°23'43''S
14°14'22''E

NAMIBIA

Kunene

Uniab

A T L A N T I C   O C E A N

DAILY DRIVING DISTANCE AND TIME

Start	Meet up with group near Kamanjab		
Day 1	Kamanjab to Opuwo	300km	8hr
Day 2	Opuwo to Kunene River Lodge	240km	8hr
Day 3	Rest day at Kunene River Lodge		
Day 4	Kunene River Lodge to Enyandi	50km	7hr
Day 5	Enyandi to Epupa	50km	6hr
Day 6	Rest day at Epupa	20km	1hr
Day 7	Epupa to Van Zyl's Pass camp site	145km	9hr
Day 8	Van Zyl's Pass to Otjinhungwa	75km	7hr
Day 9	Rest day at Otjinhungwa	10km	
Day 10	Otjinhungwa to the Marble Mine camp site	95km	7hr
Day 11	Marble Mine to Purros	110km	9hr
Day 12	Rest Day at Purros	40km	
Day 13	Purros to Hoanib River Bush Camp	130km	9hr
Day 14	Hoanib River Bush Camp to Warmquelle	105km	5hr
Day 15	Warmquelle to Kamanjab	160km	8hr
Day 16	Kamanjab to your own destination		

VEHICLE REQUIREMENTS

- Four-wheel-drive with low range
- Good approach and departure angles, as well as good ground clearance
- Recovery points front and back
- Proper off-road tyres with at least 50% tread remaining
- Two spare wheels
- Rear diff-lock or traction control can be to your advantage
- Remove spotlights and running boards, as they are likely to be damaged, and tow-hitch drop plates will restrict departure angles

TRAILER-FRIENDLY RATING

1/5

Although many people have completed this route while towing trailers and off-road caravans, this is not an advisable practice. It places an unnecessary amount of strain on your vehicle, manoeuvrability is diminished, and in some areas it is downright dangerous. It also results in a lot of track erosion.

PHOTOGRAPHING PEOPLE

Please note that while people, especially women dressed in traditional attire, make interesting photographic subjects, they have a right to privacy and human dignity. You therefore cannot photograph them without obtaining permission first, and in many instances some form of compensation will be demanded.

As visitors to the Kaokoland come from all over Southern Africa, the meeting place for participants is the Otjitotongwe Guest Farm, where we will be camping for the night. The turn-off to this farm is to your right-hand side off the C40, 121km after you have turned onto the C40 from the C38 between Outjo and the Etosha National Park, and 23km before you reach the town of Kamanjab. (Kamanjab is approximately 450km from Windhoek.)

The owners of the Otjitotongwe Guest Farm, Tollie and Roeleen Nel, operate a lodge, restaurant, bar and camp site at this facility. They provide a sanctuary for 'problem' cheetahs that would have been killed on surrounding farms as they are a threat to livestock. Three 'tame' cheetahs that were raised by hand (and can be petted) are living at the house, and there are a number of 'wild' ones in a securely fenced camp that can be visited at feeding time.

DAY 1

Please note that from here onwards we will be departing at 08:00 on travelling days and that vehicle odometers should be zeroed before leaving each camp, as all distances indicated on the route description are measured from the morning's departure point. We will not be running according to a fixed time schedule, but will stop for refreshment breaks at suitable locations.

We first travel to Kamanjab where we refuel the vehicles and can also stock up on some basic supplies. We then travel northwards on the tarred C35 until we reach the Werda Veterinary Control Post at 110km. Please note that no meat or dairy products may be brought out of the area that we are now entering. We continue north along the C35 until we turn off left onto the gravel D3709 after approximately 170km. Along this road we will begin to see the first small villages, and you need to be alert for children and livestock that wander onto the road in front of your vehicle.

We follow the D3709 until we reach the Otjondeka settlement at 186km, where we turn left again onto the D3708. This is a narrow sand and gravel track and is heavily overgrown in some places. You therefore have a good chance of damaging the paintwork of your vehicle. After 195km we arrive at Rusplaas, a place of historical significance where you will find some unmarked graves of the Dorsland Trekkers, ruins of structures that they had built, as well as a memorial erected in their honour.

Heading for Opuwo, day 1

At 225km we turn north onto the gravel D3710. This road crosses some wide open spaces and there are sections where the track is covered with a thick layer of powdery dust that makes driving conditions extremely hazardous because it hides the underlying potholes and ruts.

At 287km we turn west on the tarred C41, which we follow to Opuwo, the largest town in the area. It has a big OK Food Store, and this will be the last opportunity to stock up on food supplies. We also refuel the vehicles here. Although fuel should be available at Ruacana, we fill all the long-range tanks and fuel containers here as a precautionary measure. A number of different cultures are to be seen here, with local people wearing Western clothing while some Herero, Himba en Ovambo people are dressed in traditional attire.

From here we drive to the Opuwo Country Lodge on the outskirts of town where we will camp for the night. The ablution facilities are good and electricity is available at the individual sites. There is also cellphone reception. We may use the facilities at the lodge, which include a pool, restaurant, bar and curio shop. The lodge also has the largest thatched roof constructed to date in the southern hemisphere.

Beware, seemingly dry river beds can trip you up!

Ruacana Falls

DAY 2

We retrace our steps to Opuwo and drive east on the tarred C41 until we reach a settlement called Omakanga after 59km, where we then turn north onto the gravel C35. There is normally a manned police roadblock at this intersection, so make sure that you have your driver's license at hand and are wearing your safety belts. After 144km we will reach Ruacana where we refuel for the last time before reaching Fort Sesfontein, approximately 900km further.

From here we take a short detour through the Namibian border post to Angola (no formalities) to visit the viewpoint overlooking the Ruacana Falls. The energetic can climb down (and up again) the ±500 stairs leading to the inlet works of the hydroelectric power station and also view the falls from below.

At 180km we bid tarred roads farewell for a while as we start driving westwards along the D3700. This road was constructed in the 1950s by Victor Hartley, under the supervision of the late Ben van Zyl, in order to facilitate the establishment of veterinary control posts along the Kunene River to control the spread of foot-and-mouth disease. During the rainy season this road can sometimes be partly submerged, forcing you to drive some

extremely rocky detours and negotiate some very swampy areas.

At 221km we take another short detour towards the Kunene River to view the Onduruso Falls. Do not be misled by the name, as the falls are more a series of rapids located in a beautiful setting with large shade trees.

At 228km we reach the Kunene River Lodge camp site where we will be spending two nights. This is a very well-managed facility with camp sites situated beneath huge trees. The lodge has a restaurant, bar, pool and excellent ablution facilities, and the camp sites are supplied with electricity between 07:00 and 22:00.

DAY 3

This is a rest day in preparation for the two difficult days that lie ahead, and participants can pass the day in a variety of ways. The lodge offers rafting trips on the Kunene River, you can go on a fishing trip, and there are many interesting birds to be seen at the camp site.

DAY 4

After leaving the lodge, our first stop is Swartbooisdrift at 5km. This place is of historical interest as this is where the Dorsland Trekkers crossed the Kunene River into Angola in the early 1900s and also where they re-entered Namibia in 1928/9 after being repatriated by the Portuguese colonial authorities. A memorial has been erected in their honour and there are several graves to be seen dating from 1928/9. More recent graves belong to family members that were buried there subsequent to the trek.

From here onwards, driving conditions will become very demanding in places and we'll only cover 50km in a full day's driving. There are several tributaries of the Kunene that need to be crossed, and the level of the river determines the difficulty of these crossings. There are steep gradients with loose gravel and rock, as well as erosion gullies that need to be negotiated.

On your left-hand side you will see the aptly named Zebra Mountains – the patterns formed by the vegetation and rocks resemble the patterns of zebra skins. Numerous dwellings

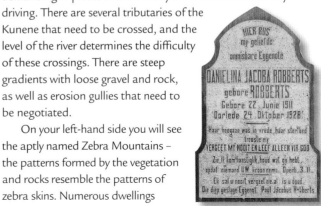

GENERAL WARNINGS FOR THIS ROUTE

Unless they are accompanied by a guide, inexperienced and unprepared travellers should stay out of this area as it is utterly inhospitable and you will be days away from any assistance should anything go wrong.

This is a long and strenuous trip. Do not underestimate the time that it will take to drive from one destination to the other or the amount of strain it will place on you and your fellow travellers – especially the ones in your vehicle.

As this area is remote and inhospitable, you must do everything in your power to stay mobile and keep out of harm's way. You need to take the following basic precautionary measures:

▶ Communications are limited, so it is sensible to take a satellite phone
▶ Do not expose your vehicle to unnecessary risks
▶ You need to protect your eyes and skin from the harsh sunlight
▶ You have to drink enough water to prevent dehydration
▶ Malaria is prevalent along the Kunene River
▶ Biting and stinging insects, venomous snakes, lion and elephant are to be found in the area
▶ Do not set up camp in the dry river beds

SPECIFIC KIT REQUIRED FOR THIS TRIP

▶ Camping gear – a rooftop tent will be a lot easier to use and also frees up much-needed space inside the vehicle
▶ Kitchen, cooking and braai utensils
▶ Water reserves for two days (5 litres per person per day minimum)
▶ A suitable fridge/freezer, unless you intend eating tinned food and drinking warm beverages
▶ A GPS with T4A maps installed as well as a proper paper map (topographical or T4A) if you are not accompanied by a guide
▶ Licensed 29MHz radio
▶ Field guides on mammals, birds and plants

ESSENTIAL REQUIREMENTS FOR THIS TRIP

▶ A comprehensively equipped first-aid kit
▶ Basic tools and spare parts for your vehicle
▶ An extra spare tyre, a puncture-repair kit, tyre-pressure gauge and compressor
▶ Recovery equipment, which includes a snatch rope, a tow rope, a spade and a high-lift jack
▶ The right attitude and a good sense of humour

SEE FULL PACKING LIST ON PAGE 218 ▶▶

and cultivated fields are to be seen along the river and we will encounter lots of children begging for sweets.

We camp at the Enyandi community camp site which, apart from being partially enclosed with a wooden fence, has no facilities whatsoever. You pitch your tent beneath mature makalani palms and the communal fire place is in the shade of a huge sycamore fig tree.

DAY 5

Today we continue our drive along the Kunene River, reaching Epupa Falls after 50km. Along the way we encounter numerous makalani palm trees, many of them dead or dying, with wooden stakes driven into the stems and devoid of any leaves at their crowns. This is the result of the local population tapping the sugary sap from the very top of the plant and then using it to produce a very potent wine.

We set up camp at the Epupa community camp site, situated right next to the falls and below makalani palm trees. The camp site has excellent ablution facilities. A new restaurant, with a deck overlooking the falls, has been constructed and basic foodstuffs can be bought here. There is cellphone reception at the camp site and you can use your phone as a modem to access the internet. The settlement of Epupa consists of scattered dwellings with a few small shops. The Namibian Defence Force and Police have a small base here.

Camp site under palms, day 5

DAY 6

Today we will be exploring the area around Epupa. We walk downstream along the river to get a closer view of the falls, but must take care as some of the viewpoints can be very slippery and dangerous. We may encounter crocodiles on some of the sandy beaches. There are numerous Himba dwellings in the immediate vicinity and although the Himba do not object to visitors coming to have a look at how they live, they will insist on compensation. It is in your best interest to reach an agreement on this before you start wandering about. They will also offer local arts and crafts for sale (and you will be swamped by children begging for sweets and people with a variety of ailments and sores, asking for medication). We will also drive to a nearby vantage point from where we have an excellent view of the falls.

DAY 7

Initially today we travel along the C43/D3700 towards Okangwati. This is a good gravel road in a wide road reserve,

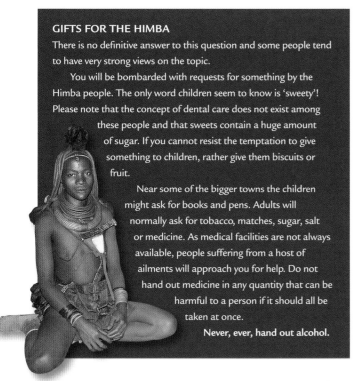

but the surface can become terribly corrugated at times and there are some sections with loose gravel. After 61km we take a short detour to a Himba Demonstration Village on the left-hand side of the road. This village used to be set up to receive visitors, but the young woman who acted as guide and spoke English has left and it is now almost impossible to communicate with the inhabitants.

After 70km we reach a village called Okangwati. This is a fairly large settlement with a few shops. Some of the local women bake delicious bread rolls right next to the road. There is a local entrepreneur who sells fuel and if he has stock, it is a good idea to support him. Buy your fuel in empty 5-litre water bottles so that you can ensure that the fuel is clean and that you get the quantity you paid for. This is your last opportunity to make a phone call, as you will only have cellphone reception again when we reach Fort Sesfontein.

From here onwards we will be travelling west on the D3703. Although this is a proclaimed road, it has not been maintained for more than a decade and the going will be demanding – especially if your vehicle does not have sufficient ground clearance, or if you're towing. At 78km we find a hot spring next to the road. This is a watering point for cattle and the herders accompanying the cattle usually bathe there. If there are people here when you arrive, park your vehicle(s) some distance away while one of the men in the party goes forward to tell them that you would like to come and look at the hot spring. This could save all parties involved considerable embarrassment!

At 90km you will find a cement dam wall on your left-hand side. This dam is actually filled with sand and a hole has to be dug into it to reach the water. This keeps the water clean and also prevents huge evaporation losses. At 100km we reach some cattle kraals next to the road where traders come to buy cattle. The sad part is that they often pay with beer, and you will see piles of empty beer bottles lying all over the place.

At 127km we take a short detour to the Ovivero Dam, built on the initiative of Ben van Zyl. It serves as a watering

place for cattle and you have to be careful not be caught up in a mini-stampede when the herds arrive.

At 134km we turn west onto a sandy track that goes past Otjihende and Otjitanda to our overnight stop at the Van Zyl's Pass community camp site. Along this track we encounter numerous Himba villages. Here you stop at your own peril, as you will normally be swamped by adult women, all asking for something at the same time without you being able to understand a single word they say.

There are three camp sites with basic facilities and you can spend the night around the camp fire convincing yourself, and the rest of the group, that you are not concerned about what lies ahead tomorrow …

DAY 8

Today we descend Van Zyl's Pass … what is all the fuss about?

Van Zyl's Pass is one of the toughest and most dangerous mountain passes in Southern Africa. It was built by the late Ben van Zyl in the 1960s, taking 20 labourers four months to remove trees and rocks to facilitate the passage of vehicles. It is approximately 10km long and in that distance you drop 640m in altitude, giving an average gradient of 1m drop for every 16m travelled. There are a few extremely dangerous descents and on three occasions you will be driving down a slope with a drop of 1m for every 1m travelled. Due to its narrow width and the steep gradients, the pass should only be driven from east to west. Once you have started travelling down the pass, there is no turning back.

There are many conflicting reports about how difficult or easy this pass is to negotiate. As time goes by and more and more people drive down the pass, the holes tend to get filled in and the bigger rocks get removed from the track, making the pass a lot easier to negotiate. But it only takes a rainstorm, an inconsiderate driver who insists on driving the wrong way up the pass, or the local Himba herdsmen driving their cattle herds up or down the pass a few times to reach grazing and water to alter the track completely. You will therefore only know for sure what conditions are like when you have reached the bottom of the pass, and either breathe a sigh of relief or seek a change of underwear.

We reach the start of the pass 1km after leaving our camp site and from here onwards the going will be slow. After 9km we take a short detour to the viewpoint overlooking the Marienfluss, a vast, grass-covered plain situated between the Otjihipa and Baynes mountain ranges on the right-hand side and the Hartmann mountain range on the left-hand side. From here to the bottom of the pass is 1km with a 380m drop

Van Zyl's Pass

in altitude, giving an average gradient of 1m drop for every 2.6m travelled. Some 400m after we leave the viewpoint we reach a tricky spot where we drop 86m in 94m and right at the end we encounter an area with loose gravel where we drop 86m in 127m. We have now reached the end of the pass and you are now also entitled to paint your name on a piece of flat rock and add it to the pile of those that have gone before you. If you dig around in the pile, you might be fortunate enough to find one with the late Jan Joubert's name on it.

From here we drive north through the Marienfluss to Otjinhungwa and camp at the Okarohombo community camp site for two days. The track consists of red sand and sections of it are badly corrugated, so serious erosion is taking place as travellers keep on making new tracks. Along the way you will see circular areas where no vegetation is growing. These are called 'fairy circles' since there is no scientific explanation as to how they are formed.

At 24km we reach the wreck of an old Land Rover. This vehicle burnt out when grass trapped around the exhaust pipe caught fire; you are advised to stop often to check that no grass is trapped beneath your vehicle. At 33km you will see a distinctively shaped mountain on your left-hand side. This is Mount Ondau, one of the most sacred places of the Himba people, and you should not trespass there.

At 53km you will see a vast open area, called the Nangolo Flats, on your right-hand side. After 71km we reach a small settlement called Otjinhungwa. There was a very nice camp site here, called Camp Syncro, but it was destroyed by fire in June 2010. We therefore have to carry on until we reach the Okarohombo community camp site at 74km.

The camp site is near the Kunene River and crocodiles pose a danger, while flies can be a nuisance. There are flushing toilets and solar-heated showers, and the camp sites are located beneath huge trees.

At tonight's camp site you can share your experience of the day with your fellow travellers.

DAY 9

This is a well-earned rest day to recuperate after two days of strenuous driving. There are some tracks that can be explored and there is a safe place to swim in the Kunene River.

DAY 10

We retrace our tracks for 21km before we turn right onto a track that leads south on the western side of Mount Ondau. There are some Himba settlements in this remote area and you will see that

An opencast marble mine

these people have caught up with Western technology, as there are a number of LDVs parked next to their huts.

At 60km we will pass the wreck of a vehicle that is said to have detonated a land mine during the war. Judging by the number of bullet holes in it, it seems to have served as a target as well.

At 71km we reach a landmark called Red Drum, a 44-gallon oil drum that has been painted red. There are three similar landmarks in the area called Blue, Orange and Green Drum. Here we turn left onto the track leading to Rooidrom Pass and a marble mine. The track is not very difficult to drive, but erosion damage does occur during the rainy season and there are steep sections with loose rock that have to be negotiated.

The community camp site was established adjacent to the marble mine. It has good facilities, with flushing toilets and hot showers. The mine itself is not in production on a continual basis, but pure white marble blocks are cut out of the mountain and there are a number of them lying in wait for transportation.

> **CAMPING IN KAOKOLAND**
> All the camp sites listed on this route, except the one in the Hoanib River, are formal camp sites. The commercial establishments are operated through an agreement with the local population, while the community camps were established with the aid of NGOs and are operated by local communities. In both instances the local people derive a benefit from visitors travelling through their area, and so-called 'wild camping' is frowned upon.

DAY 11

This can be a very long day, depending on how wet, or dry, the river beds are. About 4km after leaving camp we enter the Otjiha Plains, and after 11km we turn right onto a gravel track leading to Orupembe at 26km. This tiny settlement has a police station, a shop and a few houses.

From here we drive south along the D3707 until we turn right into the Khumib River bed at 30km. Soon after rains, this river bed can be impossible to drive in, while the sand becomes loose and deep when it dries out. Along here we may encounter giraffe, elephant and oryx. At 71km we leave the Khumib River, turning left onto a rocky track to cross the foothills of a mountain into the Hoarusib River. Here are some very impressive rock formations.

There are several permanent fountains in the Hoarusib River and we have to do a number of shallow-water crossings that normally don't present problems. At 92km we take a short detour to a viewpoint with good photographic prospects of the Hoarusib River and Mount Kabere.

The community camp site at Purros, with flushing toilets and hot showers, is situated beneath giant camel thorn and ana trees. Please note that elephant roam freely through this unfenced camp site.

DAY 12

This is a rest day, and we explore the area. Our first stop is Jan Joubert Koppie where we have a magnificent 360° view of the area. From there we drive to a small Himba kraal that is geared to receive visitors and then we can drive up and down the river looking for the elephant and lion that frequent the area.

DAY 13

Depending on the amount of water in the Hoarusib River, this can be a long day. If the river proves impossible to negotiate, we will take a detour south of this route.

About 7km after leaving the camp, we reach the point where the Hoarusib River starts flowing through a canyon. It is now a permanent stream of water and necessitates numerous shallow-water crossings. From December to May the river bed becomes a swamp that is normally impossible to navigate. Aquatic birds can be seen and you will usually encounter elephant and, sometimes, lion. There are also some interesting rock formations en route.

We turn south out of the river after 30km; 3km later we take a short detour to go and look at an interesting geological formation before we continue south across vast open plains. Sections of the track are terribly corrugated, and serious track erosion is taking place as travellers keep on making new ones. Look out for Namaqua chameleon, sandgrouse, oryx and ostrich. After 98km we enter the dry river bed of the Tsuxub River, which we follow until we reach the Hoanib River at Amspoort.

We drive in a northeasterly direction in the Hoanib River until we reach our overnight stop, a bush camp with no facilities. Along the way we should see elephant, giraffe, oryx and springbok. At night jackal tend to visit the camp and they will snatch food that is left unattended.

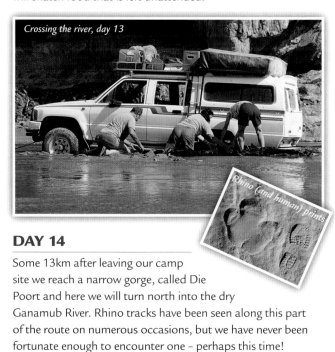

Crossing the river, day 13

Rhino (and human) prints

DAY 14

Some 13km after leaving our camp site we reach a narrow gorge, called Die Poort and here we will turn north into the dry Ganamub River. Rhino tracks have been seen along this part of the route on numerous occasions, but we have never been fortunate enough to encounter one – perhaps this time!

After 40km we reach the D3707 and turn east onto it towards Sesfontein. This road surface is usually in a terrible state. Sesfontein is a small, bustling village with several small shops, and we will stop here to refuel – if they have fuel in stock.

Sesfontein was a German military outpost from about 1886 and the fortified building housed the German Schutztruppe till it was abandoned in 1915. An entrepreneur turned it into a guesthouse in the 1980s. (Sesfontein has cellphone reception.)

From here we continue along the D3706 until we reach the turn-off to Ongongo Camp at 96km. The camp, situated in a gorge near Warmquelle, has flushing toilets and hot showers. The standard of the facilities varied a lot in the past, but this camp has been under new management since 2008 and this has

Scenery, day 13

brought some improvement. The camp site is best known for its natural pool, which is situated under an overhanging rock. A waterfall discharges cold water into the pool from above and warm water flows into it from below.

DAY 15

Returning to the D3706, we turn south towards Palmwag. At 16km we turn east onto the D3710. This road starts off innocently enough as a gravel road, but soon changes into a gravel track and then into a sandy river-bed track in the Hoanib River. Fountains in the river bed result in some shallow-water crossings. Interesting rock formations are to be seen along this part of the route. At around 30km we start to encounter the first patches of thick dust for which this route is renowned and we will have to increase the following distance between vehicles tenfold. The dust has the consistency of talcum powder and splashes like water in front of the wheels of your vehicle. At 39km we continue southeast in the dry river bed of the Ombonde River in alternating sections of dry river sand and patches of thick dust until we reach the veterinary control post at Kamdescha. Please note that we may not take any uncooked meat or dairy products through this gate. We then drive on a hard sandy track until we reach the tarred C35 at 107km.

We continue south until we reach Kamanjab, where we will be staying at the Oppi-Koppie camp site with its excellent facilities. The camp sites also have electricity and there is cellphone reception.

The first thing you need to do after setting up camp is to replace the air filter of your vehicle as it will in all likelihood be partly clogged with dust.

This will be our last night together and we spend it around our camp fire reminiscing about our experiences of the past few days.

DAY 16

Depart at your leisure and head off in the direction of home, or your next off-road destination.

ELEPHANT

These large mammals are not afraid of humans and can present a major problem. There are those who provoke these animals in order to be able to take 'action shots' of charging elephants – it is in your best interest to keep as far away from them as is possible. In camp sites, like Purros, the elephant are accustomed to people, and there have been numerous occasions where people were chased by them or where they destroyed camp sites to get at food.

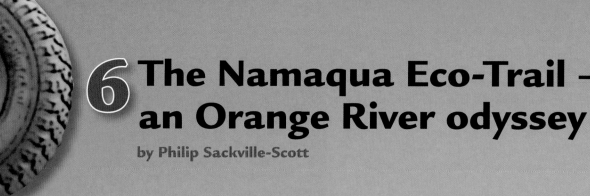

6 The Namaqua Eco-Trail – an Orange River odyssey

by Philip Sackville-Scott

TOP 10 ATTRACTIONS OF THIS TRIP

❶ Varied off-road driving conditions – sand and rock ❷ Unique Northern Cape scenery ❸ The cathedral in Pella ❹ Wide open spaces and sociable weaver nests ❺ Photographic opportunities around every turn ❻ Halfmens and quiver trees ❼ Clear air and blue skies of this World Heritage Site ❽ Area with the richest diversity of succulents in the world ❾ Camping beside the mighty Orange River for four nights ❿ Visit the largest date palm plantation in the southern hemisphere

TRIP OUTLINE

This is a journey of discovery along the mighty Orange River (also known as the Gariep River) in the northwestern sector of the Northern Cape province.

On this trip, we follow the southern bank of the river along the border between South Africa and Namibia, starting at Pofadder in the east and travelling downstream along the Namaqua Eco-Trail and past the border control post at Vioolsdrif before veering away from the river and into the Richtersveld Community Conservancy. We travel around the southern boundary of the Richtersveld National Park, before swinging north again as we head for our final destination, the mouth of the Orange River at Alexander Bay.

This is an area with a rich cultural heritage, great geological diversity and a particular wealth in minerals resulting from many years of diamond mining. There are several successful agricultural enterprises thanks to the constant availability of water.

SEE DETAILED MAP ON PAGE 66 ▶▶

APPEAL RATING

5/5

The strange place names of this area – Richtersveld, Kamgab, Abassas, Kuboes and Guadom to name but a few – are a compelling enough reason to want to visit and explore and find out more.

- Tracking the Orange River and free-camping on her banks
- The remoteness, quiet and peace all around
- Photographers' paradise
- Unusual plant species of the Richtersveld
- Geological and mineral diversity
- Visiting a 'mountain desert' – a rarity
- A World Heritage Site in your back yard

THE BEST TIME TO TRAVEL HERE

- The temperature in summer regularly exceeds 50°C
- Although the days are mild during midwinter, night-time temperatures can drop to freezing
- The spring and autumn months (August to October and March to May) are your best options
- Spring months see new growth blooming and the landscape transforms

FAMILY- FRIENDLY RATING

4/5

- There is plenty to interest people of all ages on this route
- Children enjoy the frequent stops along the river to swim and cool off
- The elderly could suffer from the extremes of temperature
- This is an out-and-out camping trip – no alternative accommodation is available along the route, except at the halfway mark

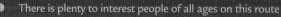

SELF-SUFFICIENCY RATING

4/5

Comprehensive planning of both route and logistics is critical to your safety and survival in this harsh environment. It is recommended to travel with a minimum of three vehicles.

- Although fuel is available along the route, either jerry cans or a long-range tank is recommended as a precaution
- Provisions are available in Pofadder, Steinkopf and at trail's end in Alexander Bay, with basic replenishments at Pella and Eksteenfontein
- The river water is drinkable
- No camps have showers or any kind of toilets

GENERAL WARNINGS FOR THIS ROUTE

!

There are no major safety concerns on this trip, but you need to be bush-wise and take basic precautionary measures.

- Sun-protection creams, hats and long-sleeved shirts
- Protect eyes against glare
- Hydrate regularly
- Scorpions are a constant threat
- Malaria-free throughout
- No large predators on this route, unless you divert into the national parks
- Local population is sparse, so criminal activity is low and unwanted attention is rare

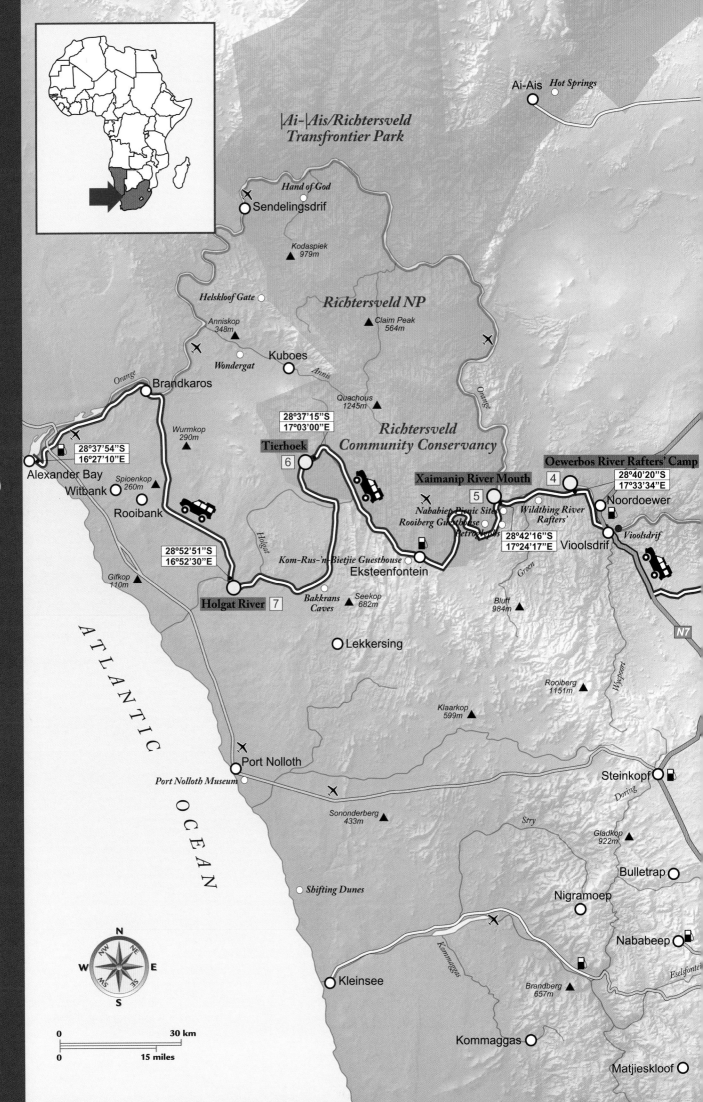

MAP 6 THE NAMAQUA ECO-TRAIL – an Orange River odyssey

Ai-Ais Hot Springs

|Ai-|Ais/Richtersveld
Transfrontier Park

Hand of God

Sendelingsdrif

Kodaspiek
979m

Richtersveld NP

Helskloof Gate

Anniskop
348m

Claim Peak
564m

Wondergat

Kuboes

Annis

Orange

Quachous
1245m

Orange

Brandkaros

28°37'15"S
17°03'00"E

Richtersveld
Community Conservancy

Wurmkop
290m

Tierhoek

6

Oewerbos River Rafters' Camp

Xaimanip River Mouth

28°40'20"S
17°33'34"E

28°37'54"S
16°27'10"E

4

5

Alexander Bay
Witbank

Spioenkop
260m

Nababiep Picnic Site
Rooiberg Guesthouse
Petroglyphs

Wildthing River
Rafters'

Noordoewer

Rooibank

Holgat

28°42'16"S
17°24'17"E

Vioolsdrif

Vioolsdrif

28°52'51"S
16°52'30"E

Kom-Rus-'n-Bietjie Guesthouse

Eksteenfontein

Green

Gifkop
110m

Holgat River 7

Bakkrans
Caves

Seekop
682m

Bluff
984m

Lekkersing

N7

Rooiberg
1151m

ATLANTIC

Klaarkop
599m

Port Nolloth

Port Nolloth Museum

Steinkopf

Doring

Sononderberg
433m

Stry

Gladkop
922m

OCEAN

Bulletrap

Shifting Dunes

Nigramoep

Nababeep

Eselsfontein

Kommaggas

Kleinsee

Brandberg
657m

N
NW NE
W E
SW SE
S

0   30 km
0   15 miles

Matjieskloof

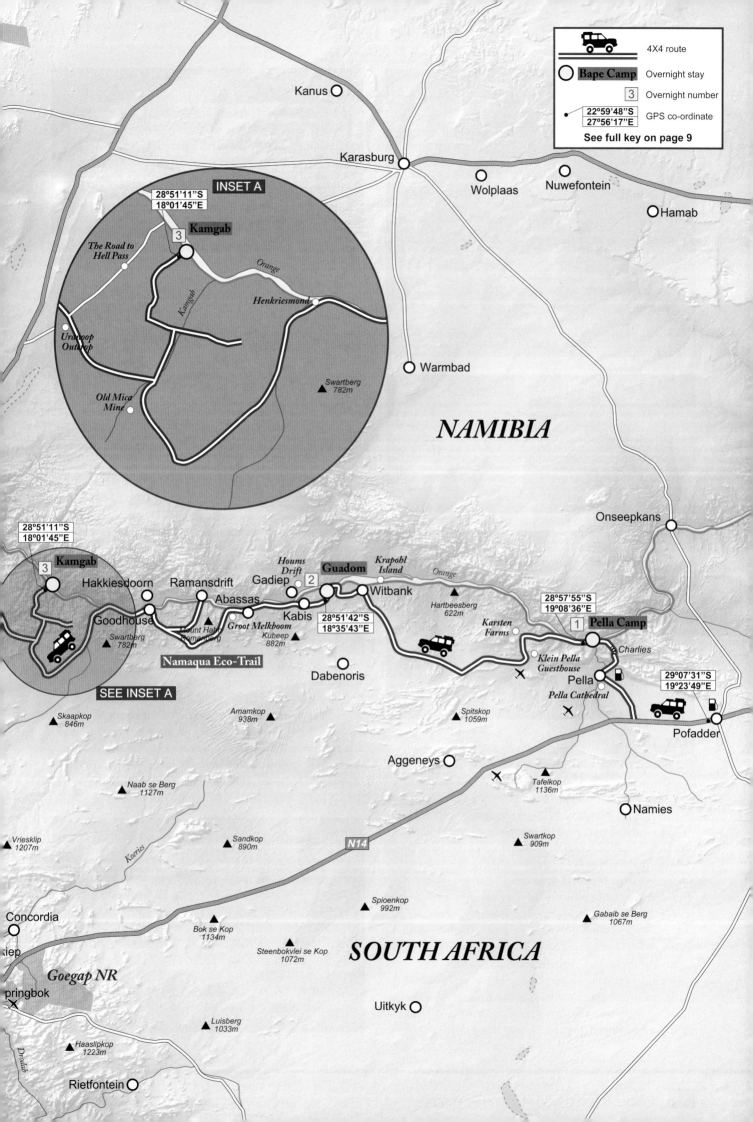

DAILY DRIVING DISTANCE AND TIME

	Cape Town to Pofadder	730km	
	Johannesburg to Pofadder	1020km	
Day 1	Meet and greet; Pofadder to Pella Camp	50km	2hr
Day 2	Pella Camp to Guadom	80km	5hr
Day 3	Guadom to Kamgab	160km	6hr
Day 4	Kamgab to Vioolsdrif	185km	5hr
Day 5	Vioolsdrif to Xaimanip Mouth	20km	3hr
Day 6	Xaimanip Mouth to Tierhoek	155km	6hr
Day 7	Tierhoek to Holgat River	65km	4hr
Day 8	Holgat River to Alexander Bay	95km	4hr

VEHICLE REQUIREMENTS

▶ Four-wheel-drive with low-range transfer case
▶ Recovery points front and back
▶ Good ground clearance
▶ Proper off-road tyres
▶ Adequate space to carry sufficient water, provisions and camping equipment for 4–6 days

TRAILER-FRIENDLY RATING

4/5

This trip is definitely suited to those who like to tow their creature comforts with them.
▶ Towing is from camp site to camp site on Grade 2–3 dirt roads and tracks
▶ There are some short but steep inclines and declines so braked axles are an advantage
▶ Each night is spent at a different camp site, so setting up and striking camp could get tedious
▶ The river-bank camp sites are on very thick soft sand

DAY 1

The meeting point is the small town of Pofadder, midway between Springbok and Upington on the N14 roadway. Pofadder offers minimal opportunities for provisions, but fuel and LPG gas are available and there is an agricultural co-op.

The meet and greet needs to take place at around lunch time to leave sufficient time to finally top up all fuel and water tanks for the week's exploring that lies ahead and to visit the afternoon's attractions and make camp on time.

The convoy forms up and heads west out of town along the N14 for 20km before leaving the tar and heading north along a sandy twin track. We stop to deflate our tyres (there's red sand under our feet) and admire the grassland all around us before continuing across country to the small town of Pella.

Prior to embarking on the trail proper, we need to report at the tourism office to show our permits. In order to reduce crowding on the trail, the authorities insist that it only be driven from east to west and that convoys are limited to 10 vehicles.

POFADDER

This very small town in the Northern Cape is apparently named after Klaas Pofadder, a Koranna captain of the area. Reverend Christian Schröder founded a mission station here in 1875, and farmers settled around the perennial spring from 1889 onwards. The locals farm primarily with sheep and goats.

As Timbuktu denotes a place in the middle of nowhere to many, so does Pofadder represent a faraway out-of-the-mainstream location to South Africans.

Camping on the river bank

We arrive in Pella between 14:00 and 15:00 and take a short tour of the mission and Pella Cathedral led by one of the resident sisters who will describe some of the history and the process of building the church. Being advocates of responsible tourism, we suggest that off-roaders bring old clothes, blankets, books and stationery for the mission to distribute. It is a small, poor community comprising mainly the descendants of Nama, San and Baster refugees from Namibia and Griqualand.

Leaving town, we opt for the Charles' Pass route down to our camp site on the Orange, passing through a most picturesque dry river course with the Great Pella Mountains dominating the skyline on either side.

Arriving at the river, we search for an open stretch of sandy beach to make camp for the night. Here the character of the river constantly changes as flooding alters the banks. You will not be disappointed as the bird life on the river is active at dusk and you can hear fish jumping once the breeze has died down.

A way upstream a pump station supplies water to the towns of Pella and Pofadder (and the large zinc mine at Aggeneys) via a small purification plant to remove sediment.

PELLA

Founded by London missionaries in 1814, this remote town was established as a settlement for Khoisan driven out of Namibia and named after the Macedonian town that had given refuge to Christians in biblical times. The town was abandoned in 1872, due to continued attacks by the cattle-rustling San, and was reopened by the Catholic Church in 1878.

Father Simon and Brother Wolf built the cathedral, with a picture in an encyclopedia as their only visual reference. Bricks were made on the river and the wood of old packing crates was used for pews and the altar. The church was consecrated in 1895, giving the community there more permanence.

The setting is idyllic, with high cliffs across the river on the Namibian side providing a backdrop for the sound of water flowing over some rapids 200m upstream. Our camp fire blazes and the cry of an African fish-eagle stirs the soul, setting the tone for the adventures that lie ahead.

A late-night swim washes away the braai fire smoke and cools things down in preparation for the best sleep of your life.

DAY 2

Having breakfasted and broken camp, we get off to a slow start, sympathetic of the long hours of driving we all put in the previous day. We backtrack some 300m up a wide, dry river bed in deep soft sand, before turning west onto a firmer rocky twin track that meanders along the southern bank of the Orange. The pace is leisurely and after around 10km in second gear high range we crest a rise – before our eyes lies the vast spread of green vineyards of Karsten Farms, where we stop for late-morning tea and to buy dates at the Klein Pella Guesthouse. Delicious!

KLEIN PELLA – DATE AND GRAPE FARM
Owned by Karstens Farming, this 87ha date plantation is the largest producer of Majool dates in the southern hemisphere, with 13,900 date palm trees. Many hectares are under vine as well. It is a quite unexpected sight to come across this vast flourishing agricultural enterprise amid the arid rugged landscape of Namaqualand. Here is the only guesthouse in close proximity to the river between Pella and Viooolsdrif.

From Klein Pella the route climbs away from the river on initially deep sand tracks, before we join a wide gravel road where we can increase speed safely as we head for Witbank down by the river once again. This section of the river is characterised by the main flow diverting into numerous channels creating a succession of islands and wetlands, depending on the river's height. The largest is Krapohl Island, named after Krapohl, one of the first people to survey the area.

To the east numerous tracks wind through the rugged countryside, but they're not always accessible due to erosion or overgrowing acacia trees. Given time, it is interesting to explore the area and observe the subsistence farmers' harsh lifestyle.

From Witbank, it is just a short drive to another wonderful camp site on the soft sand of the bank, somewhere between Guadom and Kabis, depending where you can get access. Care needs to be taken as the inexperienced can easily get bogged down in silty mud if the river has been high just before your visit. This drift is known as Houms Drift on the Namibian side.

As this is an unhurried trip, we try to arrive at our camp sites during mid-afternoon at the latest, allowing the group to relax, fish and swim. The adventurous chefs appreciate the extra time to be able to bake a pot-bread or a potjiekos stew.

DAY 3

Today we rise a bit earlier, as the distance to be travelled is one of the longest on this stretch of the river. Once again we hug the southern bank, passing a distinctive ruin (believed to be of a small church) and the old Abassas homestead, which is deteriorating fast. After about an hour's drive we get to the wide, sandy

confluence of a dry river bed and the Orange known as Groot Melkboom, named after the massive tree that dominates the site. In fact it is a Namaqua fig, and we take time out to walk around and enjoy a short tea break. The river frontage about 200m directly in front of the tree is very rocky, but if you drive a bit further around to the west there are some nice flat, sandy areas where camping is more comfortable, should you decide to overnight here.

Groot Melkboom

Leaving Groot Melkboom, the trail goes due south (at 90° to the Orange up a dry river bed) in order to circumvent Mount Hahn Romanberg. Initially narrow, it widens into a broad plain as it snakes around to the west and then due north again as you head back towards the river and your lunch spot at Ramansdrift.

After a refreshing swim, you backtrack to the south of Mount Hahn Romanberg, circling around to the west and then again north until you reach the river once more at Goodhouse. On the Namibian side the gravel D208 arrives from the north on the opposite bank, at a town called Hakkiesdoorn. There is a drift or fording point here at Goodhouse, as well as at Ramansdrift and Guadom. These three fords played a role in one of the first skirmishes of World War I when a British force, under Colonel Grant, secured them against possible threat from the German forces in German South West Africa, as Namibia was then known.

The current name Goodhouse is an anglicisation of the original Gudaus, thought to be a Nama word

ORANGE RIVER
This great river has its source at Mont aux Sources (3000m) near the Moteng Pass high in the Drakensberg mountains of northern Lesotho. Known as the Senqu River, it feeds the Katse Dam before traversing nearly the whole length of the country, accepting many tributaries along the way. It enters South Africa east of Zastron in the Free State and then fills the Gariep Dam, near Colesberg. It then heads northwest, filling the Van der Kloof Dam, and near Douglas it merges with the Vaal River before heading for Upington, cascading over the Augrabies Falls and heading out to the Atlantic coast at Alexander Bay. At 2200km, it is the longest river in South Africa.

In 1867 the first alluvial diamond was discovered near Hopetown on the Orange River. Diamonds are still mined along the final stretches of its flow, as well as on the beaches around its mouth.

SPECIFIC KIT REQUIRED FOR THIS TRIP

- Full camping gear, bedding, tents, table and chairs
- Full kitchen and braai utensils
- Drinking water for three days (5 litres per person per day minimum)
- A fridge in the vehicle would be a necessity
- GPS and trig survey maps if you are going without an off-road guide
- Licensed 29MHz radio
- A satellite phone in case of emergency evacuation

ESSENTIAL REQUIREMENTS FOR THIS TRIP

- Puncture-repair kit, tyre-pressure gauge and compressor
- Second spare wheel advisable
- Kinetic strap or rope and tow strap or rope
- Spade
- High-lift jack or inflatable airbag – one in the group is sufficient
- Basic tools and basic spares for your vehicle
- Lighting, 12V or gas
- First-aid kit catering at least for sores and cuts, hay fever, sore eyes, headaches, nausea, bites, stings and sunburn

SEE FULL PACKING LIST ON PAGE 218 ▶▶

describing the sound of sheep sloshing across the ford. There was once a pont crossing here too. Currently a pumping station near here supplies water to Steinkopf, Okiep, Springbok and Kleinsee.

Leaving Goodhouse on the way to Henkriesmond, you pass deserted agricultural fields where it is obvious that considerable infrastructural input has been squandered. Apparently it was a chilli farming scheme, funded by Americans, which failed. The pipes lie degrading in the harsh sun, but all couplings and valves are long gone. It's sad to witness such wastage.

At Henkriesmond the trail once again veers south, away from the river, along a fairly good, if extremely dusty, dirt road for about 20km of corrugations, whereafter you can thankfully turn off onto a twin track again in a northwesterly direction. About 10km along this track you arrive at a mica mine. It is fascinating to see how the thin leaves of mica are compounded to the quartz rock.

Approaching Kamgab, day 3

THE KOKERBOOM (QUIVER TREE – *ALOE DICHOTOMA*)

This aloe tree is indigenous to Southern Africa. It is named after the San practice of hollowing out its soft, tubular branches to use as quivers for their hunting arrows. The San called it *Choje*. The fleshy branches and leaves store moisture, and a white, powdery substance coating the branches reflects heat, making it fairly drought-resistant. It has the ability to kill off its own branches during extended dry periods to reduce moisture loss, regenerating them elsewhere when the stress period has passed.

However, the species is suffering higher than normal mortality rates due to climate change caused by global warming. It is estimated that 76% of the current population will be lost in the next 100 years. It is not the warming per se that affects species negatively, but the relatively rapid rate of this warming.

By the time you leave the mica mine it will be around 16:00, and the most picturesque section of the whole route lies ahead – the 20km trip down the Kamgab River to the camp site at its confluence with the Orange. This is a seriously beautiful track. Starting in wide open plains, dotted with quiver trees and euphorbias, it narrows as it winds among the bare rock faces of the surrounding mountains. The softer light of the late afternoon ensures wonderful photographic opportunities.

This is one of the few sections of the trail where you will need low range to crawl over the boulders and bare rock outcrops that litter the track. As the track twists and turns down the river bed, you need to concentrate to avoid the dreaded 'sidewall cuts' to your tyres. A few spots are very technical and it's advisable to get out of your car to inspect the trail and to ask an experienced person to guide you through.

Caution: Be constantly vigilant and aware of sharp, pointed rocks to the side of the track – these can slice through the sidewall of your tyres in a jiffy. Bizarrely these rocks often cut both the front and the rear tyres as you pass by, leaving you with a major problem if you can't plug them and if you don't have two spares.

Once you reach the river, you find yourself in paradise for the third successive night.

DAY 4

During this fourth day we complete the first half of the trail as we arrive at the N7. Having already done some 370km since leaving Pofadder, it is wise to recalculate your fuel supply and range for

THE BOSLUIS BASTERS

The Basters were a group of people descended from the Khoi and Cape Dutch farmers and were partly assimilated by either group, but generally kept to themselves and intermarried. These people were prohibited from worship in churches at the start of the 1900s, but the good Reverend Eksteen changed this. He set up a church in the 1940s, and the group eventually settled peaceably with the local Nama people in the Richtersveld towns of Lekkersing and Eksteenfontein. They became known as the Bosluis Basters because the majority came from a farm called Bo-Sluis ('Upper Sluice'). The history of the Bosluis Basters' difficult trek, their hardships, adventures and tales can be heard in Eksteenfontein, where they eventually overcame the oppression they suffered.

the remaining 360km of the trail to Alexander Bay. If you're not carrying extra fuel in jerry cans or don't have a long-range tank, you can either drive 50km south to refuel at Steinkopf, thus adding 100km to your overall journey, or nip across the border to Noordoewer, which will take some time and money. These are all points to ponder as you leave our wonderful Kamgab Mouth Camp and backtrack southwards up the Kamgab River.

Just over halfway back to the point where you turned off the trail yesterday is a turning to the left, marked 'View Point'. This 6km sidetrack meanders through a beautiful little valley, between rugged mountains and past a quiver tree that has been toppled by the weight of a sociable weaver nest, to a viewpoint with dramatic vistas to the east. A short walk up the hill provides an even better vantage point and is well worth the effort.

Backtracking through the Kamgab River bed, you soon rejoin the main trail and continue northwestwards. After about 12km you will see the conical Uranoop outcrop on your right-hand side. Not too far up the hill are a few halfmens trees (*Pachypodium namaquanum*) that are easy to walk to and inspect up close. Being well over 2m tall, they are estimated to be more than 500 years old, so look, but don't touch!

A few hundred metres further is a track turning off to the right. This is the infamous 'Road to Hell' and hard-core 4X4ers doing this trail may well want to spend additional time to divert down there. Be warned, however, that it isn't for the faint-hearted as there is a substantial chance that your vehicle will be damaged. Diff-locks front and back are almost essential, and so is plenty of experience with driving Grade 4–5 obstacles. (As this type of driving isn't the focus of this book, we'll leave it at that!)

From your stop at the halfmens trees, the trail leads first to the northwest before turning west through soft sand, zigzagging its way to the N7 in the vicinity of the Swartberg mine.

Here you either go south to Steinkopf for fuel, or continue north to Vioolsdrif on the tar, depending upon the outcome of your earlier deliberations around fuel consumption and range.

Just before the Vioolsdrif border post you turn left and west onto a wide and unbelievably corrugated gravel road and drive for about 15km to our overnight camp site at Oewerbos River Rafters' Camp. You will get here early in the afternoon, leaving you plenty of time to chill, do some washing, swim in the river or their pool, have a few drinks at the bar (or even a pizza) and enjoy a hot shower in their well-appointed ablutions.

Taking a break, day 4

This half day at leisure is welcomed by all, as the rigours of an extended overland trip can start to fray the nerves somewhat after a while. This evening you camp on lovely thick green lawn, just to add to the feeling of luxury. Naturally you can opt to break your overland journey and indulge in a short canoe trip on the river, or even just spend a few extra days here relaxing.

DAY 5

And so the second half of the trail commences in the late morning, with a short drive westwards along the river bank once more. We continue past Wildthing River Rafters', stopping to photograph petroglyphs by the roadside. These 2000-year-old engravings are dotted all over the Richtersveld and are thought to have been chipped into the black dolomite rock by the ancestors of the San.

VIOOLSDRIF

The name in Afrikaans means 'the ford (shallow river crossing) of the violin'. It is reportedly named after a Nama man, Jan Viool ('John Violin'), who is said to have played the fiddle in these parts in the 19th century. He used to guide ox-wagons across the ford and would play his fiddle on the river bank while waiting for wagons to arrive.

There are several motels, camp sites and river rafting companies operating in the vicinity.

Proceeding to the Nababiep picnic sites, we turn off the wide gravel road onto rough twin track once more. This leads down towards the river across a rock-strewn plain that soon turns to deep, thick soft sand.

This section requires great care, first gear, low range and guiding to get all vehicles over and around the large boulders along this 100m stretch. Considerable time can be spent here searching for the right track, packing rocks under the lower-slung vehicles and generally taking precautions to avoid damage to the vehicles.

But it is all good fun and helps to keep the off-road driving skills honed. At around lunch time we arrive at our last riverside camp site at the mouth of the Xaimanip River. This used to be a naturally terraced and grassed area, but flooding over the past few years has washed away some of the topsoil and changed the terrain. Still, you camp on soft sand once again and it is a very beautiful setting on a wide bend in the river, with Hamerkop (a rock outcrop) on the Namibian side.

THE HALFMENS ('HALF HUMAN' TREE – *PACHYPODIUM NAMAQUANUM*)

According to Khoi legend, fugitives from a warring tribe who looked back longingly at their homeland were changed into trees by a benevolent God, to alleviate their suffering in this desert land. From afar, clumps of them do resemble crowds of fleeing humans frozen in time. Their spiny trunks culminate in a ring of leaves, resembling a cloth cap. These deciduous succulents can grow to 3.5m in height. They are always found on the southern slopes of hills and their caps always point north, as though they are indeed looking over their shoulders. The species is classified Highly Endangered under the CITES convention.

DAY 6

The past two 'short days' are intended to recharge the batteries and you now find yourself refreshed and willing to explore the remainder of the trail into the Richtersveld and all the way to the mouth of the Orange. The official route of the eco-trail is over the Helskloof Pass some little way to the east, via the main gravel road from Vioolsdrif to Eksteenfontein. Our route is south from our camp site and up the dry Xaimanip River. It meanders this way and that for about 20km, spitting you out at the community-run Rooiberg Guesthouse, past the imposing Mount Rooiberg. In the early-morning light, your senses are inundated with colours, aromas and cheerful birdsong. The track weaves between rocks and boulders, over the sandy floor, up onto higher ground, back down into the river bed and up the other side again. You gain altitude steadily as you progress into the heart of the Goegap Nature Reserve, leaving the river behind you.

After an hour of this the time feels right for a tea break and so you stop in your tracks in the narrow river bed. Upon closer inspection of the environment you will be amazed by the diversity of the flora, particularly the succulents, surrounding you. Butter trees, those miniature baobabs, proliferate, as do a host of tiny plants competing for the limited moisture available.

Eksteenfontein

RICHTERSVELD BIODIVERSITY FACTS
- There are 2700 species in this area including almost 600 that exist nowhere else
- Only a few hundred of the giant Baster quiver tree (*Aloe pilansii*) remain on the remote mountain tops in the Richtersveld
- There are 29 lichen species, the most of any area in the world
- There are numerous species of lithops – tiny succulent plants resembling pebbles

Continuing along the track, you encounter short, sharp inclines, where you temporarily lose sight of the track below your bonnet, before it is once more revealed as you crest the rise and start your descent. After 20km the track leaves the river bed, continues along the bank and passes the Rooiberg Guesthouse, where you join the wide gravel road from Vioolsdrif bound for Eksteenfontein. We head for town, passing its name on a hillside, packed out in white rocks. In town the dominant feature is a huge roofed steel structure with no sides – the remains of an angora wool enterprise gone wrong. There are a few simple shops and a liquor store. A walk around town is an interesting experience. Visit the tourism office and museum and chat to the locals about what there is to do in and around town. Check out the Kom-Rus-'n-Bietjie Guesthouse in anticipation of your next visit, and maybe even get to watch traditional Nama dances.

Exiting town and arriving at a T-junction, we turn left towards Kuboes and Lekkersing, and immediately the road narrows and becomes rocky, undulating and interesting. At the next T-junction we turn right to Kuboes and drive almost due north into the mountains in the direction of Mount Wildeperderant ('Wild Horse Ridge Mountain'). The track drops into a wide flood plain with such dry silt that vast powdery clouds billow up beyond the vehicles as they pass by. Eventually you leave this silt field behind and the track leads up to the crest of a hill. As you descend this narrow winding track, the vast plain

down to Lekkersing reveals itself, providing yet another scenic aspect to this ever-changing landscape. To the right, a jumble of massive boulders is precariously balanced at the end of a short track. In the centre are two empty concrete dams. (Please resist the temptation to tip your rubbish into these dams, even if others seem to think it is all right to do so!) Around the edges are places to camp. This is Tierhoek, tonight's camp site.

A short stroll at sundown reveals the ruins of a building constructed against some boulders, using the natural rock as walls, thus saving on building materials. Up on the cliffs high above are the remains of an eagle's nest. The late afternoon light is wonderful for photographers. There is something for everyone here, belying its 'desert' description.

We make our camp fire beneath the overhang of a huge rock, sheltered from the evening breeze. A shooting star blazes a trail overhead, bringing a fitting close to a day in this dramatic and magical environment.

DAY 7

An eerie dawn breaks over the far-off hills, throwing shadows through the boulders of Tierhoek. The birdsong seems loud in the absence of the Orange River's flowing waters. The air is clear and the colours vivid. There's no need for rushing this morning, so bacon and eggs and toast and mushrooms seem like a grand idea – if the eggs have survived, that is!

We pack up and head out for the day's exploring. We make for the Bakkrans Caves, some 34km to the south on the Lekkersing road. You can make good time on this stretch, for although the twin tracks twist and turn through the low scrub,

EKSTEENFONTEIN
Eksteenfontein, named after Dominee Eksteen, is the gateway to the World Heritage Site known as the Richtersveld Cultural and Botanical Landscape, a vast 160,000ha area including the Richtersveld National Park. This small town is 50km from Lekkersing and 80km from Kuboes.

It has two community-run guesthouses. In the centre of town is Kom-rus-'n-Bietjie Guesthouse, a converted old mining shack where the local women offer self-catering accommodation. There is place for tents and caravans. A few kilometres out of town, Rooiberg Guesthouse also accommodates eight people.

If you give them a few days' notice, the women of Eksteenfontein will bake delicious fresh bread and prepare a traditional meal for your group.

the sand is firm and you can even use third gear! A myriad tracks crisscross the landscape, so good navigational skills are required to see you through to the desired destination. With experience you will realise that all these tracks eventually lead to the same place, so fear not.

A narrow gorge leads to the Bakkrans Caves, via tracks beneath the weathered cliffs. There are a number of eroded caves, the largest of which can easily shelter two or three vehicles. This is a popular spot among off-roaders, and children especially love playing around, investigating and generally having fun. Further along the track are some smaller caves, large enough for a hiker's tent and small fire, and there are some lovely camping spots on the flat should you wish to divert from our itinerary and spend a night here.

Camp at Bakkrans, day 6

The bird life in this small gorge is vocal and prolific, so spending a bit of time here is rewarding. Soaring hawks and Verreaux's eagles scour the landscape, sending mice and dassies (hyrax or coney) clambering for cover.

We backtrack to the entrance of the gorge and turn left to the west, driving more 'high-speed' sand tracks through low scrub for a further 22km, then crossing the main gravel road to Lekkersing, before we reach the Holgat River, another wide, dry watercourse.

Caution: Be extremely careful when planning to drive or camp in dry river beds as flash floods arise rapidly and unexpectedly. Don't fool yourself that you are safe because there are no rain clouds overhead. Flash-flood waters are often the result of downpours in catchment areas many kilometres away.

Follow the river bed for a few kilometres and look out for a decent spot to set up your last camp site. There are many small farms in this area and animals come to the wells and pumps for water, so don't go and settle right next to a drinking trough just because there are no animals around when you arrive!

It being the last night of the trip, we make a special meal to celebrate new friends, wonderful experiences and good times had over the previous week.

DAY 8

And so you arise after your last night in this special corner of South Africa. As the sun rises lazily and transforms night into day, you appreciate for one last time just how peaceful it is up here and you thank your lucky stars that you had the opportunity to spend just a small portion of your life in the Richtersveld,

along the Orange River and in a World Heritage Site.

Reluctantly you pack away one last time and say a quiet 'thank you' to the Northern Cape as you continue your drive down the Holgat River.

Along the way you can't help but notice the debris from various floods that have swept through, scouring the river bed of all vegetation and depositing trees, logs and branches against the more sturdy established trees or high up on the banks. The resilience of the flora is incredible, as within a few months of such a flood, the plants start to regenerate and even flourish.

About 10km before the river intersects with the tarred Port Nolloth to Alexander Bay road, the track leaves the river bed and heads north on a nice, firm sand twin track past the farms of Rooibank and Witbank, delivering you ultimately after 50km onto the main west-east gravel road from Alexander Bay to Kuboes (and the Richtersveld National Park), near the mining town of Brandkaros.

There is a camp site of sorts here at Brandkaros should you need one, but we prefer to continue along this wide gravel road to Alexander Bay and our journey's end. Beware of large mine trucks along this 32km section of road.

On arrival in Alexander Bay, report to the control boom offices and get permission to drive through to the mouth. This last section is thick sand, so lower your tyre pressures.

The bird life here is quite something to behold, especially the huge flocks of flamingo which browse in the shallows of the estuary. (The hill east of the gate is famous for the 26 species of lichens found there.)

A tea break and a stroll around the beaches at the mouth are a fitting end to this journey, which has taken us from Pofadder in the east, along the river and into the Richtersveld to this point, the westernmost edge of our country.

7 Kgalagadi Transfrontier Park – the place of great thirst

by Simon Steadman

TOP 10 ATTRACTIONS OF THIS TRIP

❶ Exploring the first formally declared transfrontier park in Africa ❷ Wide open spaces ❸ The red sand dunes ❹ The magnificent black-maned Kalahari lion ❺ Endless photographic opportunities ❻ Camping in the wild ❼ Spectacular thunderstorms in summer months ❽ Watching the nightlife around the water hole from the hide at Nossob Camp ❾ Sitting around the camp fire listening to the sounds of the wild ❿ Star-filled Kalahari skies

TRIP OUTLINE

We will start our adventure in Upington where we will meet at our guesthouse, stock up with last-minute supplies and fill our fuel tanks to the brim.

From there we head north to Twee Rivieren, the southernmost entrance to the Kgalagadi Transfrontier Park. There we will need to complete our border formalities for our visit to the Botswana side of the park later on.

We continue north through the park to Nossob Camp, situated in an area of the park renowned for its predator population. From Nossob we head east into the Botswana side of the park and to the Mabuasehube region, exiting the park at Mabuasehube and re-entering South Africa via the McCarthy's Rest border post before heading home via Kuruman.

SEE DETAILED MAP ON PAGE 76 ▶▶

APPEAL RATING

5/5

The Kgalagadi Transfrontier Park is a great place to experience the vast diversity of the Kalahari. From the red sand dunes, sun-scorched pans and dry river beds to the incredible bird life and wildlife, this unique park will provide you with a memorable Kalahari experience.

THE BEST TIME TO TRAVEL HERE

- December to April are the best months
- The rainy season is a great time to visit the Kalahari as this is when the landscape comes to life, offering spectacular scenery
- Thunderstorms are frequent but brief
- The sandy tracks become compacted after rain, making them easier to drive on
- There are no natural water sources in the Kgalagadi Transfrontier Park, so in the winter months the animals are forced to use the artificial water holes, making for excellent game-viewing

FAMILY-FRIENDLY RATING

3/5

- The game-viewing on the South African side of the park is more abundant than on the Botswana side, but in Botswana there's still enough game to keep the children interested
- The trip from Nossob to Mabuasehube is a long day's drive that may test the patience of younger children, but stopping frequently and enjoying the surroundings will make it easier
- As the camp sites are unfenced on the Botswana side of the park, it is always essential to keep a close eye on younger children and not let them stray from the fireside after dark

SELF-SUFFICIENCY RATING

4/5

Travellers need to be fairly self-sufficient on this trip and ensure that they carry ample supplies of fuel and water, especially for the Botswana side of the park as there are no facilities here.

- Fuel is available at Twee Rivieren, Mata Mata and Nossob camps but the supply can be a bit unreliable at times, especially during the busier periods such as school holidays
- The next fuel stop after Nossob is at Tshabong in Botswana, which is approximately 135km from the camp site in Mabuasehube
- There are clean ablution facilities at the camp sites on the South African side, with hot showers and flushing toilets
- The camps on the South African side have small shops that sell basic supplies
- Fresh bread is available to order at Nossob Camp – it is highly recommended
- The ablution facilities in Mabuasehube are basic, with only long-drop toilets and a cold shower
- The water is very brackish and is not recommended for drinking, so take enough drinking water along with you

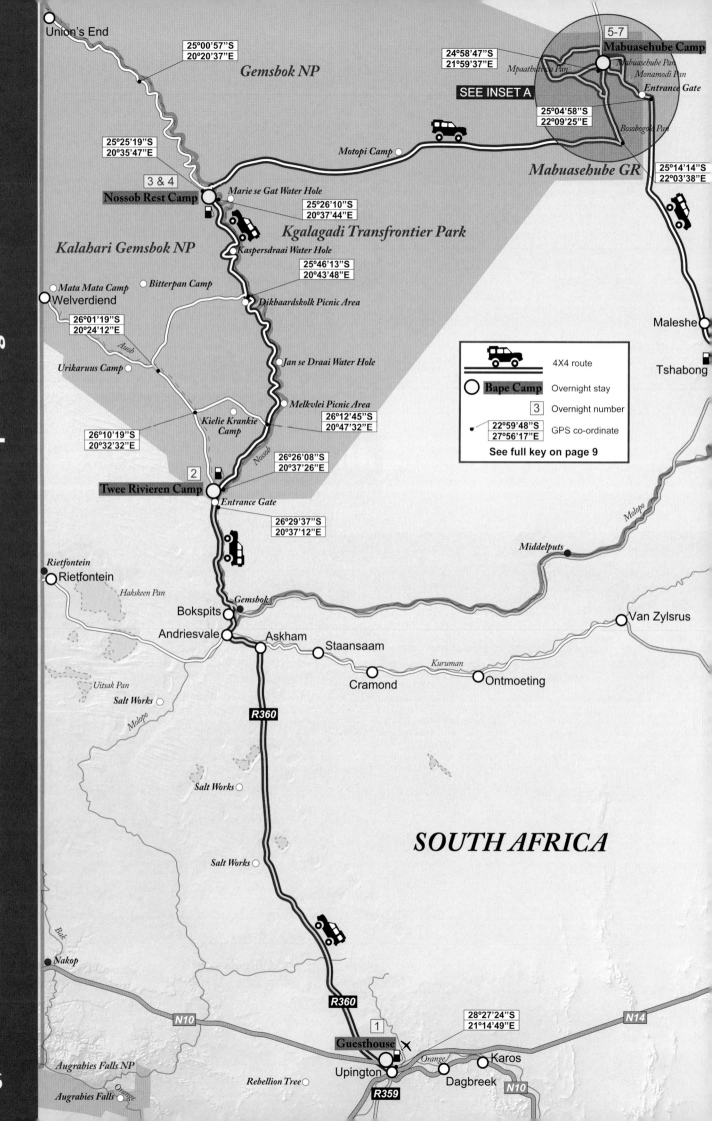

MAP 7 KGALAGADI TRANSFRONTIER PARK – the place of great thirst

Union's End

25°00'57"S
20°20'37"E

Gemsbok NP

24°58'47"S
21°59'37"E

5-7

Mabuasehube Camp

Mpaathutlwa Pan

Mabuasehube Pan

Monamodi Pan

Entrance Gate

SEE INSET A

25°04'58"S
22°09'25"E

25°25'19"S
20°35'47"E

Motopi Camp

Bosobogolo Pan

Mabuasehube GR

25°14'14"S
22°03'38"E

3 & 4

Marie se Gat Water Hole

Nossob Rest Camp

25°26'10"S
20°37'44"E

Kgalagadi Transfrontier Park

Kaspersdraai Water Hole

Kalahari Gemsbok NP

25°46'13"S
20°43'48"E

Maleshe

Mata Mata Camp

Bitterpan Camp

Dikbaardskolk Picnic Area

Welverdiend

26°01'19"S
20°24'12"E

Auob

Urikaruus Camp

Jan se Draai Water Hole

Tshabong

4X4 route

Bape Camp Overnight stay

3 Overnight number

22°59'48"S
27°56'17"E GPS co-ordinate

See full key on page 9

Melkvlei Picnic Area

26°12'45"S
20°47'32"E

Kielie Krankie Camp

26°10'19"S
20°32'32"E

Nossob

26°26'08"S
20°37'26"E

2

Twee Rivieren Camp

Entrance Gate

26°29'37"S
20°37'12"E

Molopo

Middelputs

Rietfontein

Rietfontein

Hakskeen Pan

Gemsbok

Bokspits

Van Zylsrus

Andriesvale

Askham

Staansaam

Kuruman

Cramond

Ontmoeting

Uitsak Pan

Salt Works

Molopo

R360

SOUTH AFRICA

Salt Works

Salt Works

Bak

Augrabies Falls NP

Nakop

N10

R360

28°27'24"S
21°14'49"E

1

N14

Guesthouse

Orange

Karos

Augrabies Falls

Upington

Rebellion Tree

Dagbreek

N10

R359

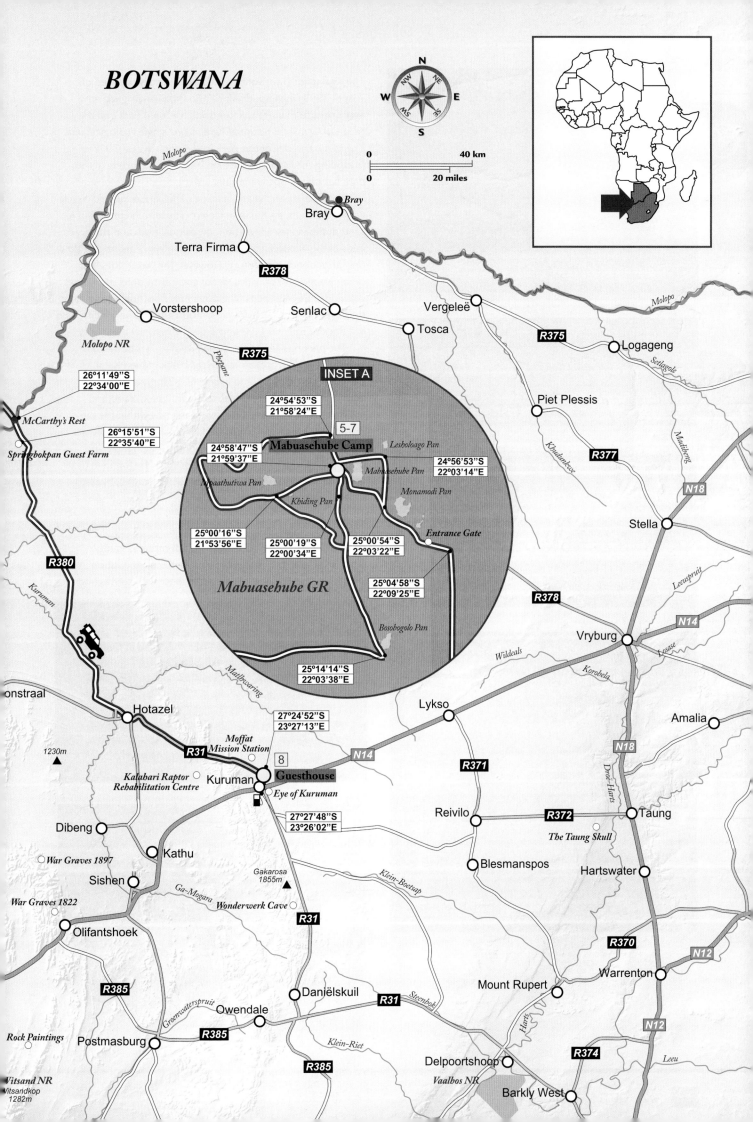

BOTSWANA

INSET A

5-7

8

26°11'49"S
22°34'00"E

26°15'51"S
22°35'40"E

24°54'53"S
21°58'24"E

24°58'47"S
21°59'37"E

24°56'53"S
22°03'14"E

25°00'16"S
21°53'56"E

25°00'19"S
22°00'34"E

25°00'54"S
22°03'22"E

25°04'58"S
22°09'25"E

25°14'14"S
22°03'38"E

27°24'52"S
23°27'13"E

27°27'48"S
23°26'02"E

Mabuasehube Camp

Mabuasehube GR

Lesholoago Pan

Mabuasehube Pan

Monamodi Pan

Mpaathutlwa Pan

Khiding Pan

Entrance Gate

Bosobogolo Pan

Guesthouse

Eye of Kuruman

Moffat
Mission Station

Kalahari Raptor
Rehabilitation Centre

Kuruman

Bray

Terra Firma

Vorstershoop

Molopo NR

Senlac

Tosca

Vergeleë

Logageng

Piet Plessis

Stella

Vryburg

Amalia

Taung

The Taung Skull

Reivilo

Blesmanspos

Hartswater

Warrenton

Mount Rupert

Delpoortshoop

Barkly West

Lykso

McCarthy's Rest

Springbokpan Guest Farm

onstraal

Hotazel

Dibeng

Kathu

Sishen

War Graves 1897

War Graves 1822

Olifantshoek

Postmasburg

Owendale

Daniëlskuil

Gakarosa
1855m

Wonderwerk Cave

Rock Paintings

Vitsand NR
Vitsandkop
1282m

1230m

Vaalbos NR

R378

R375

R375

R377

R18

R378

R14

R371

R372

R370

R12

R380

R31

R31

R31

R385

R385

R385

R374

R12

N14

N18

N18

N14

N12

Molopo

Molopo

Setlagole

Khudankave

Madibeng

Leeuspruit

Losase

Korobela

Wildeals

Droë-Harts

Harts

Leeu

Klein-Boetsap

Steenbok

Klein-Riet

Groenwaterspruit

Ga-Mogara

Kuruman

Phepane

Matlhoaring

0   40 km
0   20 miles

DAILY DRIVING DISTANCE AND TIME

Day 1	Meet in Upington		
Day 2	Upington to Twee Rivieren	252km	3hr
Day 3	Twee Rivieren to Nossob	160km	5hr
Day 4	Game drives in the park	100km	5hr
Day 5	Nossob to Mabuasehube	195km	8hr
Day 6-7	Game drives in Mabuasehube	75km	5hr
Day 8	Mabuasehube to Kuruman	355km	7hr
Day 9	Kuruman to home		

VEHICLE REQUIREMENTS

▶ Four-wheel-drive (low range not a necessity)
▶ Recovery points front and back
▶ Good ground clearance
▶ All-terrain tyres are an advantage but not a prerequisite

TRAILER-FRIENDLY RATING

4/5

A sturdy off-road trailer or caravan can handle this trip with relative ease, so bring it along if you want a bit more luxury.
▶ There are some stretches of fairly thick sand to negotiate, which can be tricky if using a trailer with small-diameter wheels
▶ Most of the roads in the park are good, solid tracks which will pose no problem at all to those towing

GENERAL WARNINGS FOR THIS ROUTE

The main thing to keep in mind on this trip is that you will be camping in unfenced camp sites in Mabuasehube, with the chance of having wild animals visiting your camp.

Here are some other things to remember and be prepared for on this trip:
▶ Protect yourself against the sun with sunblock and a wide-brimmed hat
▶ Use water sparingly to ensure it lasts the entire trip
▶ Keep yourself well hydrated
▶ Regularly check under your vehicle for grass and seeds that may have gathered there, especially near the exhaust manifold and prop shafts; vehicle burnouts are a real threat in the Kalahari and must be taken very seriously
▶ The Kalahari is a malaria-free area
▶ Local population is sparse, so criminal activity is low and unwanted attention is rare

The Kgalagadi Transfrontier Park was officially declared on 7 April 1999 when South Africa and Botswana signed an agreement to manage the Gemsbok National Park and the Kalahari Gemsbok National Park as one single ecological unit. The combined size of this park is an impressive 37,991km^2 (including the Mabuasehube region). Three-quarters of the park lies on the Botswana side.

Kgalagadi means 'place of thirst'. The park is located largely within the southern Kalahari Desert. The terrain consists of red sand dunes, sparse vegetation, occasional trees and the dry beds of the Nossob and Auob rivers. The rivers are said to flow only about once per century. However, the water does flow underground and provides life for grass and camel thorn trees growing in the river beds. The rivers may flow briefly after large thunderstorms, a cause for celebration among the wildlife, who will flock to the river beds and slake their eternal thirst.

The park has abundant, varied wildlife. It is home to large mammalian predators such as black-maned Kalahari lion, cheetah, leopard, and hyena. Migratory herds of large herbivores such as blue wildebeest, springbok, eland and red hartebeest also live and move seasonally within the park, providing sustenance for the predators. There are giraffe near the Mata Mata region of the park, but no elephant, rhino or hippo. More than 200 species of bird can be found in the park, including vultures and raptors such as eagles, buzzards, secretary birds and kori bustards.

DAY 1

The starting point for our Kgalagadi adventure is in the Northern Cape town of Upington. Our accommodation tonight will be in the form of a guesthouse with some good

UPINGTON

Upington was founded in 1884 and is located in the Northern Cape, on the banks of the Orange River. The town was named after Sir Thomas Upington, Attorney-General of the Cape. It originated as a mission station, which was established in 1875 and run by Reverend Schröder. The mission station now houses the town museum, known as the Kalahari Orange Museum. The museum is also the home of a donkey statue, which recognises the enormous contribution that this animal made to the development of the region during the pioneering days of the 19th century.

A fully equipped guide vehicle

Sign at Twee Rivieren

old-fashioned home cooking. Upington has plenty of fuel stations and all the major chain stores just in case you forgot to pack something and need some last-minute supplies.

We enjoy our last home-cooked meal as the group members get to know each other. From tomorrow, it's bush cuisine!

DAY 2

After a good night's sleep in a comfy bed, and a hearty breakfast, it's time to hit the road. We head into town to do some last-minute shopping and fill up with fuel for our journey to the southern entrance gate to the Kgalagadi Transfrontier Park, Twee Rivieren. Our drive today is a total of 252km on good tar roads. We leave Upington and head north on the R360 where the landscape becomes more and more sparse with each kilometre travelled. Some may say that this road can become boring but the feeling of freedom that the wide open spaces and seemingly endless tarmac bring is a great escape from city life. Just open the windows and enjoy the Kalahari air and feel the sun beating down upon the scorched earth. The sociable weaver nests built around telephone poles along this road are pretty impressive as well, and watch out for the odd jackal scampering across the road.

After around 190km on this road, we turn northwards and follow the R360 right up to the gate at Twee Rivieren. This next stretch of road used to be one of the worst roads in the country, with corrugations that would rattle you and your vehicle to pieces and test even those with the patience of a saint. However, this road has now been tarred all the way up to the gate, making a huge difference.

Once we reach the gate and all the normal check-in formalities have been completed, it's off to the camp site to set up camp for the night. Situated on the banks of the dry Nossob River bed, this is the park's largest camp and administrative headquarters. It has a reception, shop, fuel station, restaurant, information centre and swimming pool, and is the only camp with 24-hour electricity and cellphone reception. Activities and facilities are diverse, as are the animals and plants found both within the camp and in the surrounding areas. Accommodation options include chalets for those not wanting to camp.

After setting up camp, the next destination is the customs office across the road at Twee Rivieren where we will need to get our passports stamped for our entry into Botswana, even though we will only be entering Botswana in three days' time. With all the border formalities completed we can head out for a game drive and explore the dry river bed of the Auob Valley. The road network on the South African side of the park is fairly limited and is concentrated in the two river valleys – the north–south-oriented Nossob Valley and the northwest–southeast-oriented Auob Valley in the south.

Once back at camp, before gate-closing time, we enjoy our first night under the star-filled Kalahari sky and listen to the jackals calling in the distance. This is where the adventure really begins.

GEMSBOK (ORYX)

Gemsbok are light brownish-grey to tan in colour, with lighter patches at the bottom rear of the rump. Their tails are long and black. A dark-brown stripe extends from the chin down the bottom edge of the neck through the joint of the shoulder and foreleg along the lower flank of each side to the brown section of the rear leg. They have muscular necks and shoulders, and their legs have white 'socks' with a black patch on the front. Both genders have long, straight horns. Gemsbok are about 1.4m at the shoulder; males weigh 230–250kg and females 200–210kg. They live in herds of 10–40 animals, consisting of a dominant male, a few other males, and females. They can reach running speeds of up to 56kmph.

There are two 'types' of gemsbok: a northern and southern variety. The only difference is that the northern gemsbok have black-fringed ears while the southern ones have longer horns and more rounded ears. Southern gemsbok are more numerous and live in the Kalahari Desert of Southern Africa, while the northern variant can be found in Tanzania, Zambia, Kenya and parts of northern Namibia in the Khomas Hochland area. Gemsbok are mainly desert-dwelling and do not depend on drinking to supply their water needs, but many of the northern gemsbok live in open grasslands where water is readily available.

NOSSOB CAMP

Nossob Rest Camp is situated within the dry river bed of the Nossob. The camp is surrounded by tree savannah and is famous for spectacular predator sightings. Because of the sparse vegetation and concentration of animals in the dry beds of the Auob and Nossob rivers, Kgalagadi offers premium game-viewing all year round.

Nossob is especially renowned for predator-watching and for the seasonal movement of large herbivores such as blue wildebeest, springbok, eland and red hartebeest. Ground squirrel and suricate (meerkat) are another two of the park's more prominent species. You will have an excellent chance of seeing cheetah, leopard, brown and spotted hyena and the distinctive black-maned lion.

Nossob Camp and its surrounds exhibit a blend of bird species typical of the other camps, and have the added attraction of a wide variety of raptor species.

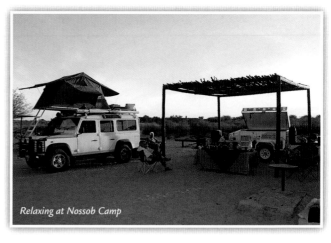

Relaxing at Nossob Camp

DAY 3

After an early breakfast, we pack up camp and head north through the Nossob Valley to our next port of call, the Nossob Rest Camp. It is advisable to fill up with fuel before leaving Twee Rivieren, jerry cans included, as the fuel supply at Nossob can be quite unreliable at times. While the tanks are being filled you can also deflate your tyres a bit to make the corrugated roads that we will be travelling on for the next few days a bit more tolerable.

The drive from Twee Rivieren to Nossob is a distance of 160km and the road is a good gravel road, but very badly corrugated. They do let the grader loose on these roads from time to time, but it doesn't take long for the corrugations to return again.

The journey will take us the best part of five hours to complete as there is a 40kmph speed limit and no need to rush. Rather enjoy the game-viewing and stops at the numerous water holes en route to see what may be lingering around. Some of the popular water holes worth visiting are ones like Jan se Draai, Kaspersdraai and Marie se Gat.

The Nossob Valley is host to a vast array of mammal species, such as gemsbok, springbok, eland and hartebeest. Brown hyena and black-backed jackal are found in abundance, as well as smaller species like bat-eared fox and Cape fox. Predators such as lion, leopard and cheetah are commonly seen in the Nossob Valley, so keep your eyes peeled.

There are a couple of picnic areas along the way (at Melkvlei and Dikbaardskolk) which also have toilet facilities and allow you to stretch your legs and enjoy a picnic lunch, but keep your wits about you as they are unfenced and who knows what's hiding behind those bushes?

We will aim to reach Nossob Rest Camp by late afternoon in order to give us enough time to set up camp and enjoy a sundowner at the water hole. We'll be here for two nights so you can make yourself quite comfortable. Inside the camp site there is a hide that overlooks the water hole at Nossob and can provide the patient visitor with some great animal encounters.

A busy water hole

LEEUDRIL

Make sure you keep all your food locked away – at Nossob Camp there is a problem with jackals that get through the fence and they can be quite cheeky when it comes to stealing a tasty meal!

DAY 4

An early rise and start to the day is advisable if you want to watch the lions walking down the road to the water hole or hopefully see a leopard playing with her cubs next to the road. The area around Nossob is renowned for its predator sightings and an early game drive will more often than not reward you with a quality sighting of at least one of the big cat breeds.

Once all the photos have been taken and camera batteries depleted, it's back to camp for a good hearty brunch followed by some serious relaxing around camp or by the swimming pool to escape the heat of the day.

Nossob Rest Camp has a predator centre which has some great photos and interesting information of these fascinating beasts. Other facilities at Nossob are a shop, reception, fuel station and swimming pool. A generator provides electricity for 18 hours per day. There is no cellphone reception at Nossob and you can now pack away the cellphone until we reach civilisation again on the last day of the trip.

When going on a game drive from Nossob, you can go either north or south when exiting the camp gate. This afternoon's game drive will be in the opposite direction we went for the morning game drive in order to see a different part of the park.

Exploring northwards all the way to Union's End is far too long a trip for a single day, being a 260km round trip. If you have an extra day, rather camp over so that you can take in and enjoy the countryside.

Besides the awesome predator sightings around Nossob, another highlight is the many raptor species found in the area. Species such as black-chested snake-eagle, southern pale

Mabuasehube Camp

chanting goshawk, gabar goshawk and bateleur are found in abundance, as well as the lanner falcon and greater kestrel. If you are lucky you will see a Verreaux's eagle-owl perched in a tree next to the road in the late afternoon.

Back at camp it's time to get the fire going and enjoy another refreshing sundowner after a day of rewarding game-viewing, Kgalagadi-style.

Nothing beats sitting by the fire, listening to the lions roaring in the distance while the meat sizzles away on the braai. A great way to end another tough day in Africa!

DAY 5

Today requires an early start as we've got a bit of a drive ahead of us. So after an early breakfast, we pack up camp and head north from Nossob for about 3km where we turn right and cross the dry Nossob River bed into the Botswana side of the park. Here we leave the corrugated gravel roads behind in exchange for some serious Kalahari sand tracks. The journey that lies ahead of us today is 195km of sandy twin-tracks through some spectacular Kalahari Sandveld, with a few small dunes along the way.

The concentration of game along this route is low and the scenery can become a bit monotonous at times, but it will be worth it in the end. Our destination today is our camp site in the Mabuasehube region in the extreme east of the Kgalagadi Transfrontier Park and, more specifically, the Mabuasehube Pan. But we'll get into that in more detail later.

There is a camp site called Motopi, located around halfway to our camp site at Mabuasehube Pan, and this serves as a good spot to stop for a lunch break and to stretch our legs before continuing through the sand until we reach the Bosobogolo Pan. It is here where we turn and head north via Mpaathutiwa Pan and eventually reach our camp site at Mabuasehube Pan. There are four camp sites at Mabuasehube Pan and they all overlook the pan, which has an artificial water hole, making game-viewing as simple as sitting in your camping chair with a pair of binoculars in one hand and a cold liquid refreshment in the other.

UNION'S END

Positioned at S24°54'55" and E19°59'59", Union's End is the northernmost boundary of western South Africa and a point where three neighbouring countries meet – Namibia, Botswana and South Africa. It is named for the extreme border of the Union of South Africa – a situation that ceased to exist in 1961, when the Union became a Republic – and is also the point where the Nossob River enters South Africa from Namibia.

There is a fence between Namibia and South Africa and between Namibia and Botswana, but no fence between South Africa and Botswana, because of the Transfrontier Park. Although the R360 runs almost all the way to Union's End in South Africa and the N39 meets up with it from the Namibian side, there is no border post here. The closest border control post is the Mata Mata post, some 110km to the south.

The camp sites in Mabuasehube are unfenced and have basic ablution facilities – each site has a cold shower and long-drop toilet. Keep an eye out at night for lions and leopards that like to drink from the drains and dripping taps next to the shower. I would advise keeping your shower times to daylight hours for this reason.

This part of the park will give you a different feeling than the South African side due to its being wild and remote. There are usually not many visitors here, making that feeling of solitude even more satisfying. The roads in Mabuasehube are sandy twin tracks which are easier to negotiate during the cooler times of the day but aren't really too challenging at all.

DAY 6

After yesterday's early start, a lie-in is on the cards this morning, as is a scrumptious breakfast of bacon and eggs while enjoying our view over the pan. Mabuasehube is lion country and one doesn't often leave here without having had a few quality encounters with these magnificent creatures. So once the breakfast has settled, it's time to go out onto the trail and to explore the many pans scattered around this area. The game-drive network in Mabuasehube is a series of tracks linking the many pans found here. It is on these pans where game congregates and where predators lie in wait. Most of the pans have artificial water holes to sustain the animals through the harsh dry season, making them ideal spots to sit and enjoy the exciting animal encounters that occur when animals get desperate for water. Some of the best pans for game-viewing are Mpaathutiwa, Mabuasehube and Monamodi pans.

The most common mammal species you will find in this part of the park are gemsbok, springbok, hartebeest, bat-eared fox, brown hyena, lion, leopard and cheetah. You will also find good opportunities to photograph birds of prey at the water holes as they enjoy a refreshing bath, while you cool off from the unrelenting Kalahari sun and enjoy a refreshing drink.

It is advisable to be back in camp well before sunset so that you have enough time for a quick shower and to get the camp fire going before the predators start to prowl after dusk. Lions and leopards are frequent visitors to the camp sites in

Mabuasehube, so don't stray too far from the fire. If you have to visit the toilet, make sure you take a torch with you and preferably someone close that you can post as a lookout.

Most of the time you would not even know you had a predatory visitor in your camp site. They are so quiet and stealthy, trying to go undetected while stealing a drink from your dripping tap. So keep having a look around with your torch or you could miss them. It's only once you've gone to bed and the camp site is quiet that they get a bit braver and will come closer and inspect all your camping gear, hoping to find some morsels of food left behind from dinner. Therefore it is essential to your self-preservation that you make sure you have been to the toilet before zipping up the tent and falling asleep to the calls of the wild all around you.

DAY 7

You'll be champing at the bit this morning to get out on a game drive after listening to all the lion activity during the night. An early-morning sunrise drive is a good idea if we want to find lions and, if we are really lucky, come across a pride still feasting on their kill from the night before. You normally don't have to drive far in 'Mabua' on a morning drive before you find something worthwhile. But that's no guarantee – this is Africa and she can be unpredictable. A visit to the neighbouring pans after circumnavigating Mabuasehube Pan is a good idea as this is where all the game congregates before moving off into the shade during the heat of the day.

As the sun gets higher in the sky, we head back to camp for a well-deserved brunch. After brunch, you can spend the next few hours relaxing around the camp site, reading a good book while keeping one eye on the water hole just in case you miss something.

Those with enough energy can head out on an afternoon game drive before enjoying another night around the camp fire in this magnificent piece of unspoilt wilderness.

DAY 8

Sadly today is our last day in the Kgalagadi as we pack up camp and head out of the park. Once all the gear has been packed up and the camp site is nice and clean, we head for the Mabuasehube gate, which is 25km from our camp site. There is still a chance for

Water hole at Monamodi Pan

Sunset over Mabuasehube Pan

THE KGALAGADI TRANSFRONTIER PEACE PARK

The merging of South Africa's Kalahari Gemsbok Park with the Gemsbok National Park of Botswana saw the establishment of Africa's first transfrontier park, opened in May 2000 by the presidents of the two countries. To date it is the only such park that is open in the true sense of the word – where tourists can travel freely across the international border within the parameters of the park.

Subsequent to its founding, it has become an even more popular destination for nature lovers and 4X4 enthusiasts willing to explore the off-road trails and experience the tranquillity of the Kalahari.

The park comprises some formal rest camps, 4X4 routes through the dunes and otherwise out-of-bounds areas, luxury lodges and community-run camp sites.

DAY 9

Unfortunately our Kgalagadi adventure has come to an end and it's time to head home, hopefully with lifelong memories and full memory sticks to keep us yearning for a return to this great thirstland.

After saying our goodbyes we hit the road for our respective homes and start planning our next adventure, which is hopefully sooner rather than later.

some more game-viewing as we pass the Monamodi pans on our way to the gate. Once out of the park, there is a stretch of thick sand to negotiate until we reach the town of Tshabong where we can fill up with fuel. From Tshabong we are back on tar roads for a while until we reach the McCarthy's Rest border post and cross back into South Africa. From the border we drive on a good gravel road for a distance of around 90km before hitting the tarmac again just before the town of Hotazel, where we can reinflate our tyres. From there it is only another 105km to Kuruman where we will rest our heads for the night. Kuruman has a number of good guesthouses and B&Bs where you can enjoy a hot shower and wash away the Kalahari sand.

Attractions worth visiting in Kuruman are the Moffat Mission Station, the Kalahari Raptor Rehabilitation Centre and the Eye of Kuruman – a natural fountain that delivers 20–30 million litres of crystal clear water every day.

As usual, the last dinner time spent together as a group is a bittersweet experience as those who were once strangers now depart as friends.

THE PEACE PARKS FOUNDATION

A Transfrontier Conservation Area is an area or component of a large ecological region that straddles the boundaries of two or more countries, encompassing one or more protected areas, as well as multiple resource use areas.

The mission of the Peace Parks Foundation is to facilitate the establishment of Transfrontier Conservation Areas (peace parks) and develop human resources, thereby supporting sustainable economic development, the conservation of biodiversity and regional peace and stability. The reinstatement of ancient migratory paths is a natural result of the enactment of the primary philosophies.

To quote Dr Nelson Mandela: 'In a world beset by conflict and division, peace is one of the cornerstones of the future. Peace parks are a building block in this process, not only in our region, but potentially in the entire world.'

There are currently ten transfrontier peace parks in Southern Africa.

8 Central Kalahari Game Reserve – a true African wilderness

by Simon Steadman

TOP 10 ATTRACTIONS OF THIS TRIP

❶ One of the last true wilderness areas left in Africa ❷ Wide open spaces ❸ Deception Valley and its large herds of game ❹ The magnificent black-maned Kalahari lion ❺ Endless photographic opportunities ❻ Camping in the wild ❼ Spectacular thunderstorms in summer months ❽ Solitude – Kalahari-style ❾ Sitting around the camp fire listening to the sounds of the wild ❿ Star-filled Kalahari skies

TRIP OUTLINE

The Central Kalahari Game Reserve was established in 1961 as a wildlife reserve and also as a sanctuary for the San people of Botswana to enable them to continue with their hunter-gatherer lifestyle. Mark and Delia Owens brought the magic of the Central Kalahari to the world in the mid-1980s with their book *The Cry of the Kalahari*. This husband-and-wife team spent seven years living in Deception Valley conducting research on the brown hyena in the area.

We will start our adventure in the north of the reserve, camping in Deception Valley, not far from where the Owens's camp was located. This region of the reserve is scattered with various pans that attract game after the summer rains, as well as the predators that follow them. While exploring the area, it is definitely worth visiting Sunday, Leopard and Deception pans as there is normally lots to see around these pans.

From Deception Valley we travel southwest to Piper's Pan which is always a good place for game-viewing as it has a permanent water hole – the ideal place to sit and watch the sunset and the animals that come down for a drink.

From Piper's Pan we travel right through the 'spine' of the reserve and through some San villages that are definitely worth a visit, down to the southern section of the reserve and on to the Khutse Game Reserve.

SEE DETAILED MAP ON PAGE 86 ▶▶

APPEAL RATING

5/5

The Central Kalahari Game Reserve is the second largest conservation area in the world, covering an area of 52,800km², surpassed only by the Selous Game Reserve in Tanzania. This vast wilderness area is a definite must for every nature lover. Nowhere else in Africa will you find the same wilderness atmosphere and solitude as you will in the Central Kalahari. This place really has got 'soul' and leaves an everlasting impression on everyone who experiences it.

THE BEST TIME TO TRAVEL HERE

- November to April are best
- The summer rains bring life back into the Kalahari with some spectacular thunderstorms and cloud formations
- Storms are frequent but brief
- Large herds of game gather on the grass-covered pans, attracting the predators that feed on these animals
- The dry winter months are not as good for game-viewing, as the herds disperse in search of water and grazing

FAMILY-FRIENDLY RATING

2/5

The Central Kalahari is for the serious bush lover – the experience is more about the vast open spaces and solitude rather than huge concentrations of game.

- The days where lengthy drives are necessary may not suit younger children
- As the camp sites are unfenced, it is always advisable to keep a close eye on younger children and not let them stray from the fireside after dark

SELF-SUFFICIENCY RATING

5/5

Travellers need to be completely self-sufficient on this trip and ensure they carry ample supplies of fuel and water.

- The last fuel stop is in Rakops, but it is recommended that you fill up in Mopipi in case Rakops has no fuel; you will need to carry enough fuel for around 1200km of travel to the next fuel stop
- There is no water at the camp sites within the reserve but you can get water at the reserve gates; this water, however, is not suitable for drinking
- The 'ablution' facilities at the camp sites consist of a long-drop toilet and a bucket shower that you fill with your own water

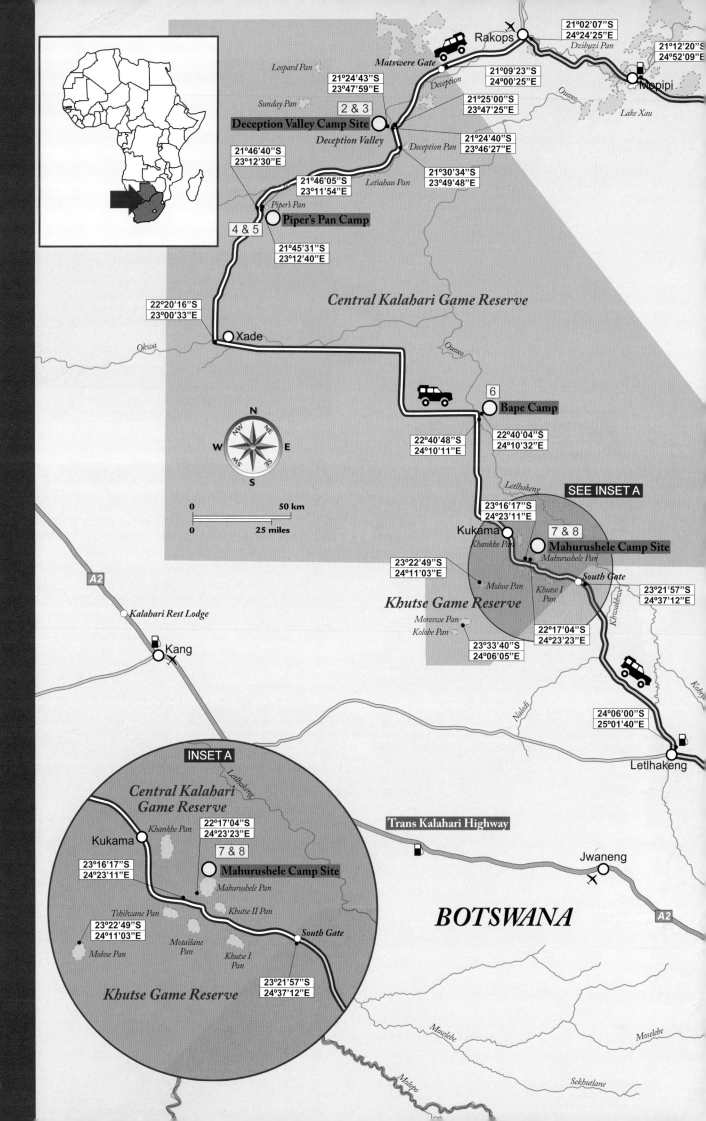

MAP 8 CENTRAL KALAHARI GAME RESERVE – a true African wilderness

Rakops

21°02'07"S
24°24'25"E

Dziburzi Pan

21°12'20"S
24°52'09"E

Mopipi

Leopard Pan

Matswere Gate

21°24'43"S
23°47'59"E

21°09'23"S
24°00'25"E

Deception

Sunday Pan

21°25'00"S
23°47'25"E

2 & 3

Lake Xau

Ouaxo

Deception Valley Camp Site

Deception Valley

21°24'40"S
23°46'27"E

Deception Pan

21°46'40"S
23°12'30"E

21°46'05"S
23°11'54"E

Letiahau Pan

21°30'34"S
23°49'48"E

Piper's Pan

4 & 5

Piper's Pan Camp

21°45'31"S
23°12'40"E

Central Kalahari Game Reserve

22°20'16"S
23°00'33"E

Okwa

Xade

Ouaxo

6 Bape Camp

22°40'04"S
24°10'32"E

22°40'48"S
24°10'11"E

Letlhakeng

SEE INSET A

23°16'17"S
24°23'11"E

Kukama

Khankhe Pan

7 & 8
Mahurushele Camp Site

Mahurushele Pan

22°17'04"S
24°23'23"E

23°22'49"S
24°11'03"E

Molose Pan

Khutse I Pan

South Gate

23°21'57"S
24°37'12"E

Khwaibrve

Moreswe Pan
Kolobe Pan

Khutse Game Reserve

23°33'40"S
24°06'05"E

24°06'00"S
25°01'40"E

Naledi

Kobye

Letlhakeng

A2

Kalahari Rest Lodge

Kang

INSET A

Central Kalahari Game Reserve

Letlhakeng

Kukama

Khankhe Pan

22°17'04"S
24°23'23"E

7 & 8

23°16'17"S
24°23'11"E

Mahurushele Camp Site

Mahurushele Pan

Tshilwane Pan

Khutse II Pan

23°22'49"S
24°11'03"E

Motailane Pan

South Gate

Molose Pan

Khutse I Pan

23°21'57"S
24°37'12"E

Khutse Game Reserve

Trans Kalahari Highway

Jwaneng

BOTSWANA

A2

Moselebe

Molopo

Moselebe

Sekhutlane

N NW NE W E SW SE S

0   50 km
0   25 miles

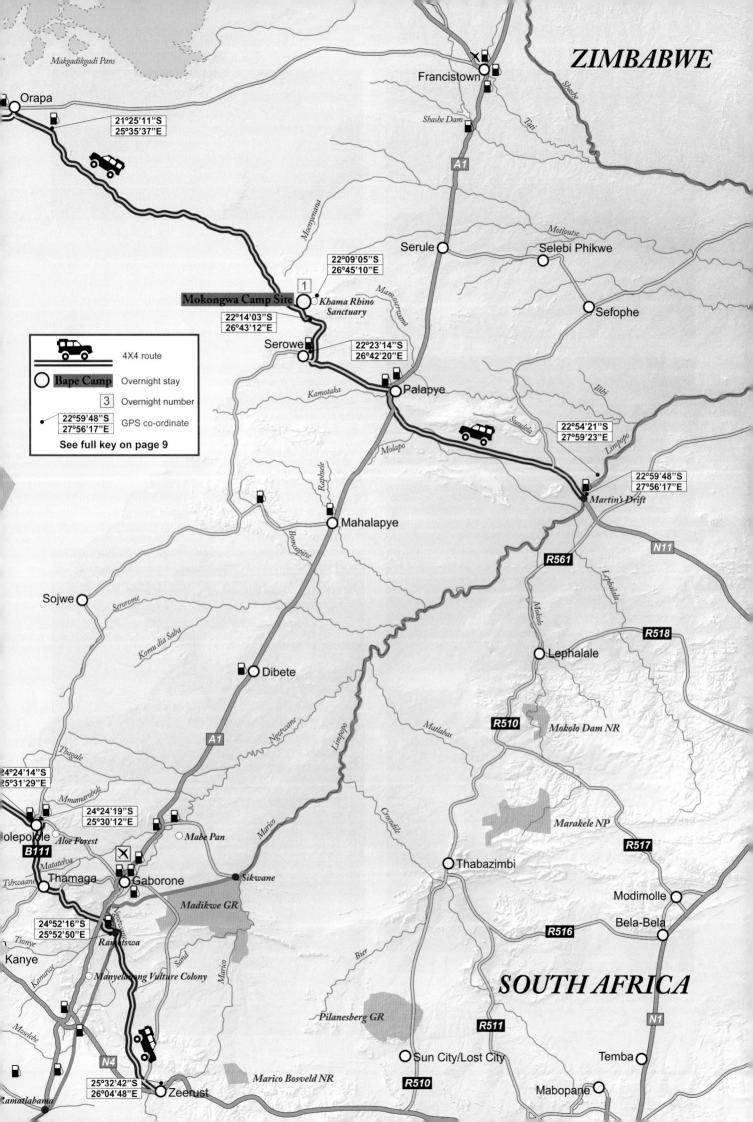

ZIMBABWE

Makgadikgadi Pans

Orapa

21°25'11"S
25°35'37"E

Francistown

Shashe Dam

Serule

Selebi Phikwe

22°09'05"S
26°45'10"E

Mokongwa Camp Site

1

*Khama Rhino
Sanctuary*

Sefophe

22°14'03"S
26°43'12"E

Serowe

22°23'14"S
26°42'20"E

Palapye

22°54'21"S
27°59'23"E

Molapo

22°59'48"S
27°56'17"E

Martin's Drift

KEY

4X4 route

Bape Camp Overnight stay

3 Overnight number

22°59'48"S
27°56'17"E

GPS co-ordinate

See full key on page 9

Mahalapye

R561

N11

Sojwe

Serorome

R518

Komu dia Saba

Lephalale

Dibete

Mokolo Dam NR

A1

R510

Matlabas

Marakele NP

24°24'14"S
25°31'29"E

R517

24°24'19"S
25°30'12"E

olepolole

Aloe Forest

Mabe Pan

Thabazimbi

B111

Matatelva

Modimolle

Thamaga

Gaborone

Sikwane

Madikwe GR

Bela-Bela

R516

24°52'16"S
25°52'50"E

Ramotswa

Kanye

Manyelanong Vulture Colony

Sand

SOUTH AFRICA

Pilanesberg GR

R511

N1

N4

Temba

25°32'42"S
26°04'48"E

Zeerust

Marico Bosveld NR

R510

Sun City/Lost City

Mabopane

Ramatlabama

DAILY DRIVING DISTANCE AND TIME

Day 1	Meet at Khama Rhino Sanctuary in Botswana		
Day 2	Khama Rhino Sanctuary to Deception Valley	390km	7hr
Day 3	Game drive in Deception Valley	100km	5hr
Day 4	Travel south to Piper's Pan	95km	5hr
Day 5	Game drives around Piper's Pan	50km	5hr
Day 6	Continue south to Bape Camp	255km	9hr
Day 7	Bape Camp to Khutse Game Reserve	85km	4hr
Day 8	Game drives around Khutse area	75km	6hr
Day 9	Depart Khutse for home		

VEHICLE REQUIREMENTS

- Four-wheel-drive with low range
- Recovery points front and back
- Good ground clearance
- All-terrain tyres an advantage but not a prerequisite

TRAILER-FRIENDLY RATING

4/5

A sturdy off-road trailer or caravan can handle this trip with relative ease, so bring it along if you want a bit more luxury.

- There are some stretches of fairly thick sand to negotiate – this can be tricky with a trailer
- Most of the tracks in the reserve are good, solid tracks which will pose no problem at all to those towing
- The longest we camp in one place is two nights, so keep in mind that you will be breaking up camp a total of five times on this trip

GENERAL WARNINGS FOR THIS ROUTE

The main thing to keep in mind on this trip is that you will be camping in unfenced camp sites with the chance of having wild animals visiting your camp. Here are some other things to remember and be prepared for on this trip:

- Protect yourself against the sun with sunblock and a wide-brimmed hat
- Use water sparingly to ensure it lasts the entire trip
- Keep yourself well hydrated
- Regularly check under your vehicle for grass and seeds that may have gathered there, especially near the exhaust manifold; vehicle burnouts are a real threat in the Kalahari and must be taken very seriously
- The Central Kalahari is a malaria-free area
- Local population is sparse, so criminal activity is low and unwanted attention is rare

KHAMA RHINO SANCTUARY

The Khama Rhino Sanctuary is situated just outside the town of Serowe and is a community based project officially established in 1992 and run by the Khama Rhino Sanctuary Trust. The sanctuary is dedicated to the rehabilitation of Botswana's rhino population which was in severe danger of being completely poached to extinction. The total number of white rhino currently at the sanctuary is 34, and there are two black rhino.

DAY 1

Khama Rhino Sanctuary near Serowe, Botswana, is our meeting place for this trip and is about a 170km drive from the Martin's Drift border post. This reserve is approximately 4300ha in size and one of the few places you can still see a white rhino in the wild in Botswana. Some of the other mammal species found here are zebra, blue wildebeest, giraffe, impala, kudu, gemsbok, steenbok, red hartebeest, leopard, caracal, brown hyena, bat-eared fox and African wild cat.

Mokongwa camp site is situated under large mokongwa trees and serviced by clean ablutions with hot showers. An afternoon game drive followed by sundowners at one of the pans is the ideal way to kick-start this adventure.

DAY 2

Today's drive is a total of 390km, of which around 90km is off-road, so we depart Khama Rhino Sanctuary after breakfast and head northwest to the town of Mopipi where

LAKE MAKGADIKGADI

Approximately three million years ago, strong easterly winds brought about the formation of elongated dunes which ran from east to west across the middle of the Kalahari Desert. During wetter times, these dunes channelled the flow of the great rivers of the area – the Okavango, Chobe, Zambezi and Limpopo – eastwards into the Indian Ocean.

About two million years ago, the formation of the fault known as the Kalahari-Zimbabwe axis, which runs from the Zimbabwe capital of Harare through its second largest city Bulawayo and ends in the eastern side of the Kalahari, created an enormous basin and forced these rivers to flow into and fill up the basin. Lake Makgadikgadi was thus created.

As the millennia passed, the lake was filled to capacity and began to overflow. About 20,000 years ago, as a result, it began to drain northwards and then eastwards. This caused the middle and lower Zambezi rivers to connect, resulting in the formation of Victoria Falls. With the water now able to flow out of the basin, Lake Makgadikgadi was able to drain partially and its average level decreased.

A drier climatic period followed, which caused an increase in evaporation and a decrease in the flow of the rivers that fed the lake. By about 10,000 years ago the drying of Lake Makgadikgadi was in an advanced stage. Sediment and debris from the Okavango River and windblown sand gradually filled the lake.

Today the only remains of Lake Makgadikgadi are the Okavango Delta, the Nxai Pan, Lake Ngami, Lake Xau, the Mababe Depression, and the two main Makgadikgadi pans of Sowa and Ntwetwe.

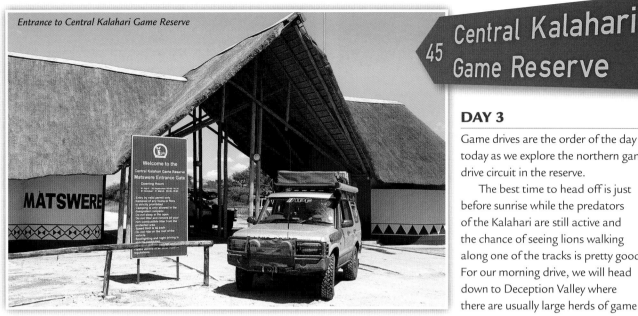
Entrance to Central Kalahari Game Reserve

MATSWERE

DAY 3

Game drives are the order of the day today as we explore the northern game drive circuit in the reserve.

The best time to head off is just before sunrise while the predators of the Kalahari are still active and the chance of seeing lions walking along one of the tracks is pretty good. For our morning drive, we will head down to Deception Valley where there are usually large herds of game such as springbok, red hartebeest and gemsbok. Cheetah are also regularly spotted in this area. From Deception Valley, we head to Deception Pan. The pan is situated next to Deception Valley and derives its name from the fact that during the hot summer months the mirages make it look as if the pan is full of water. There is usually good game to be spotted around Deception Pan and it is a popular hang-out for the few giraffe found in the reserve.

Time permitting, we can continue west to Letiahau Pan where there is a permanent water hole, before turning back to camp via the same route for a well-deserved brunch.

we will refuel and stop for a lunch break. At this point we are travelling just south of the Makgadikgadi pans, and from Mopipi we get a good look at Lake Xau. This lake used to be part of the great Lake Makgadikgadi that dried up around 10,000 years ago. You will see the landscape change dramatically in this area as the vegetation becomes more sparse and the horizons ever wider.

Depending on fuel availability, we can stop in Rakops for a quick top-up and then it's time to leave the tar behind for the next seven days. Just outside Rakops we turn off and stop to deflate our tyres for the sandy 50km drive to the Matswere gate, where we enter the Central Kalahari Game Reserve. After completing the formalities at the gate, we can fill up our water tanks for showering and dish-washing. This water is a bit brackish and not suitable for drinking.

The drive from the gate to Deception Valley is around 40km, and we cross some small sand dunes before we get our first sight of Deception Valley. Our camp site for the next two nights is situated right on the edge of Deception Valley and very popular with the local lion prides that regularly pass through on their way up the valley floor.

After setting up camp, there may be time for a quick drive down to Deception Valley to enjoy the spectacular sunset before heading back to camp to get the fire going and listen to the sounds as the bush around you comes to life.

DECEPTION VALLEY
TRACK VERY SLIPPERY
WHEN WET, DRIVE SLOWLY

DECEPTION VALLEY

Deception Valley is actually a huge fossil river bed that formed part of the ancient river system that flowed in this area around 16,000 years ago. It is the good grazing in this fossilised river bed that attracts the huge herds of game that congregate on the valley floor after the first summer rains every year. It is for this reason that a drive through Deception Valley is the highlight of any trip to the Central Kalahari – you are always likely to encounter such species as lion, cheetah, jackal, bat-eared fox, brown hyena and, if you're really lucky, one of the elusive leopards that live in the area.

Lion, Deception Valley

During the heat of the day, it is best to take a lesson from the Kalahari residents and relax under the shade of the acacia trees in the camp site or cool off with a cold shower before heading off for an afternoon game drive.

This time we will head north of our camp and visit Sunday Pan and Leopard Pan. There are tracks that follow the edges of the pans and it is always worth driving all the way around each pan just in case there are some lions lounging under the trees or a cheetah teaching her cubs to hunt. Other species to look out for in this area include bat-eared fox, brown hyena and black-backed jackal.

We will once again enjoy the sunset in Deception Valley, before heading back to camp for dinner and another enjoyable evening around the camp fire, listening to the symphony of activity in Deception Valley.

SPECIFIC KIT REQUIRED FOR THIS TRIP

- Camping gear (tent, bedding, chairs, table, etc.)
- Enough water for seven days
- A fridge/freezer as temperatures can soar in summer
- GPS with latest maps if you are going without an off-road guide
- Radiator seed net is a MUST
- Licensed VHF two-way radio
- Sense of adventure

ESSENTIAL REQUIREMENTS FOR THIS TRIP

- Puncture-repair kit, tyre-pressure gauge and compressor
- Kinetic strap or rope and tow strap or rope
- Spade or shovel
- High-lift jack or air jack
- Basic tools and basic spares for your vehicle
- Insect and lion repellent
- Basic first-aid kit
- Sunblock
- Camera with plenty of memory cards
- Binoculars

SEE FULL PACKING LIST ON PAGE 218 ▶▶

DAY 4

The smell of bacon sizzling must be one of the best smells to wake up to in the bush. After enjoying a scrumptious breakfast, we break up camp for our journey to Piper's Pan. The total driving distance to our camp site at Piper's Pan is around 95km and should take us the best part of five hours to complete. We head southwest through Deception Valley, driving the same route as we did on yesterday's morning drive. About 15km past Letiahau Pan, the track splits and we keep to the left to Piper's Pan, which is another 40km down this track.

There is no need to rush this drive today, but rather take it at a leisurely pace and enjoy the game sightings along the way. Stopping for a lunch break at Letiahau Pan is a good idea as it is just over halfway.

BLACK-MANED KALAHARI LIONS

The Kalahari lion is a subspecies that behaves and looks different from other lions as a result of its adaptation to the harsh Kalahari environment. Kalahari lions differ from other lions in the sense that they live in smaller prides, have larger home ranges and hunt smaller prey. Kalahari lions can also go without water for up to three months, surviving solely on the moisture obtained from their prey. They can cover up to 60km in a day while out looking for food. The Kalahari lion weighs less than other lions but the black mane makes it look more threatening.

We should reach our camp site in the late afternoon, giving us enough time to set up camp and head off to the water hole on the edge of the pan to sit and watch the sunset and whatever wildlife comes down to drink before night falls. It is only a few kilometres from our camp site, so we can spend a bit more time at the water hole, ensuring that we are back in camp before dark.

There are normally lions in this area due to the large concentration of game attracted here by the permanent water source, so you can expect to hear them throughout the night and possibly even have them in the camp site. This is what camping in the bush is all about!

DAY 5

A lazy day is on the cards today as our game drives will be done around Piper's Pan, so we will not have far to travel from the camp site. The game drive route in this area is very limited but the high concentration of game around the pan means that you don't need to travel far, as the game is literally on your doorstep. There is a track, approximately 7km in length, that runs around the pan and is definitely worth exploring. This track can be quite treacherous in the wet as it consists of black cotton soil. In the dry it still needs to be tackled slowly as the dry mud creates a very uneven, bumpy ride.

It is worth doing the drive in the early morning to try and catch a glimpse of some of those lions that kept you awake all night and that may still be on the prowl, or you may even see a brown hyena on its way back to the hungry family at the den. You never know what the Kalahari is going to show you and that is what makes it such a special place. You will encounter things here that you won't find in other places, and it's important to keep a lookout for the smaller creatures and birds and appreciate them as much as the bigger animals that everyone generally wants to see when venturing into the bush.

After your game drive, it's back to camp for a good, wholesome

Letiahau Pan

breakfast and then you can spend a few hours lazing around camp or take a drive to the water hole on the edge of the pan and sit there watching the animals come and go while enjoying a few chapters of your favourite book.

Piper's Pan sunrise

Once the sun starts to get a little lower in the sky, it's a good idea to fire up the trusty steed and head out on an afternoon drive around the pan before settling in near the water hole again for another special Kalahari sunset.

Enjoy all this game around you now, because tomorrow is a different story ...

DAY 6

Today is the day we like to refer to as 'The Test'. The reason for this is that your sense of humour, sense of adventure, patience and sand-driving skills are all going to be put to the ultimate test today as we head through the 'spine' of the reserve which is not known for its game concentrations as much as for its monotony.

Now that we have scared the living daylights out of you, we're going to tell you that it's not really that bad, and it is an integral part of traversing the second largest conservation area in the world. If tackled with the right attitude, it can be good

fun, and (once it is behind you) it gives you a really satisfying feeling of accomplishment.

The distance to be travelled today is a total of 225km to Bape Camp where we will be spending the night. We will need to pack up camp early in order to be on the road by 07:00 and if all goes well we should reach our camp site by the latest at 16:00, giving us enough time to set up camp before it gets dark.

So we say goodbye to Piper's Pan and the northern region of the reserve and we head south to Xade. This is the western entrance to the reserve and new ablutions have recently been built here so we can fill up our water tanks for ablution purposes. We wouldn't recommend drinking this water, even though the locals will tell you otherwise. This stretch from Piper's Pan to Xade is around 80km and will take approximately two-and-a-half to three hours to complete – the road is fairly good. It crosses a few pans that usually have some gemsbok and springbok around them.

Gemsbok – iconic inhabitants of the Kalahari

After a short stop for a toilet break and to fill the water tanks, we continue on our way, now heading due east through an ancient fossil river bed, following the course of the ancient Okwa River for a distance of another 80km before making a 90° right turn (the first of three 90° turns on this journey). We then head due south for another 30km where the road turns left (another 90° turn) and then, just before we reach our camp site at Bape, the third 90° turn is completed. You can see from the tracks going straight on for a few metres that many travellers before you have missed this last turn and have had to backtrack once they realised that the road had disappeared.

This section of the journey, from Xade to Bape, can become quite tiring and monotonous as the long, straight stretches of sandy tracks, with thick bush on either side, seem as if they will never end, so turn up the radio and enjoy the ride. (A radio also helps to drown out the sounds of thorn bushes scraping down the side of your vehicle!) This is the thickest sand that you will encounter on this trip and it's where you need to be on your game if towing a trailer or a caravan.

Bape Camp is really a 'transit' camp and one that is not used very often as most visitors to the Central Kalahari only visit the northern section in search of the big game and neglect this remote part of the reserve. There are no facilities at Bape, so you will need to make use of the 'bush ablutions' for this one night.

The silence and solitude you will experience in this part of the reserve is really something special and very hard to find in today's times of overcrowded camp sites.

Enjoy the silence!

DAY 7

After a peaceful night's sleep and a scrumptious bush breakfast, you will feel recharged and ready to hit the track again. No need to rush with the breaking of camp as today's journey is only 85km long and considerably easier than yesterday's.

Once the vehicles are packed and all the grass and seeds have been removed from the undercarriages, we continue our journey south to our camp site at Mahurushele Pan in the Khutse Game Reserve. (More about Khutse Game Reserve later.)

Today our journey will take us past a number of San villages, including Mothomelo and Kukama. These villages are home to the last few remaining San people still living their hunter-gatherer lifestyle within the reserve. It is definitely worth spending some time here to meet and interact with these unique inhabitants and get a glimpse of how they survive in such a harsh environment.

Just over 20km from Kukama you will cross a small dune and the Khankhe Pan will open up before you. This pan is situated in the northern part of the Khutse Game Reserve's road network, although it is actually within the boundaries of the Central Kalahari Game Reserve.

You will notice that the landscape and vegetation around Khutse are very different to that of the Central Kalahari. Khutse is a very unique part of the Kalahari, in the sense that it is part of an ancient river system that used to feed Lake Makgadikgadi to its northeast. The many pans and dry river valleys in Khutse are evidence of a much wetter period in this area's history. In fact, 'Khutse' actually means 'place where you can kneel down to drink'.

The main game-drive routes in Khutse are concentrated around the reserve's many pans which fill up with a thin layer of water after heavy rains. These lush grazing grounds then attract large herds of game to the pans. There are permanent (artificial) water holes situated at Molose and Moreswe pans in the far southwestern corner of the reserve.

We will be spending the next two nights camping at Mahurushele Pan. It has four camp sites and is nicely situated for access to the larger pans to the southeast as well as the Molose Pan and Moreswe Pan down south.

After setting up camp, it's always a good idea to go for a short afternoon drive to one of the nearby pans and enjoy the sunset before heading back to camp for a well-deserved dinner around the camp fire.

DAY 8

Khutse Game Reserve is one of the most popular of Botswana's reserves as it is easily reachable from Gauteng in a day, making it a popular destination for a long-weekend excursion. The reserve is fairly small at 2590km^2 and the roads within the reserve are good all year round.

Our game drive today will be a full day's drive and will take us down to the southern part of the reserve, stopping off along the way at the Molose Pan. There are normally lions in this area, and on quite a few occasions we have seen wild dogs enjoying the water hole during the heat of the day.

After spending some time at the water hole we continue to Moreswe Pan, crossing the Tropic of Capricorn en route. At Moreswe there is another permanent water hole and normally good game-viewing. There is a track that goes around the pan and to the smaller Kolobe Pan just beyond Moreswe. It's worth taking some time to explore all the tracks in this area as it is always full of game and the chances of sighting lion, wild dog and brown hyena are very good. There are four camp sites situated around Moreswe Pan and they make a good lunch stop, provided you can find a vacant one.

Wild dogs at Molose Pan

The Tropic of Capricorn

After lunch we make our way back to the northern part of the reserve, using the track that runs along the eastern side of the reserve up to the numerous pans in the north. On our way back to camp we will pass pans with names such as Khutse I, Khutse II, Motailane and Tshilwane until we reach our camp site at Mahurushele Pan to enjoy the last sunset of the trip and sit and ponder the many memorable experiences the Kalahari has provided over the last few days.

DAY 9

An early rise is called for as we break camp and begin the long journey home. The road to the gate takes us past the same pans as the day before when we were on our way back to camp, and it is a total distance of 28km from the camp site to the gate.

From there a good gravel road of 100km leads to Letlhakeng where we stop to refuel and reinflate our tyres. Fuel supplies in Letlhakeng can be unpredictable, so it's best to make sure you have enough fuel to get to Molepolole which is another 65km further on and has many fuel stations.

From Molepolole it's advisable to take the B111 to the right just as you come out of town; this way you will bypass the hustle and bustle of Gaborone, and the road is generally a lot quieter than the busy A12 that leads to Gaborone. If using this route, the Ramotswa border post is the best option as it is the quietest of the three border posts that feed Gaborone, and you are normally able to go through the border and back into South Africa in no time at all.

From the border we head to Zeerust where we say our goodbyes and hit the N4 highway for the last leg of the journey home to our hot showers and comfy beds, wishing we were back under those star-filled Kalahari skies and falling asleep to the sound of a male Kalahari lion roaring in the distance.

SOME TIPS AND ADVICE FOR CAMPING IN THE WILD

- Always sleep in a closed tent; do not sleep outside in unfenced camps
- Extinguish all fires before going to bed at night
- Do not throw any food or bones into the bush
- Do not feed animals – they are wild and need to stay that way
- Do not wander too far from your tent at night; always use a torch
- Do not take any food into your tent; keep it all in your vehicle
- Always leave the tap on the bucket shower open after using it, otherwise it will fill up with rain water and birds could drown in it
- Always check for snakes and scorpions under your tent before rolling it up

SOME TIPS AND ADVICE FOR TRAVELLING IN THE KALAHARI

- Always use a radiator seed net to prevent overheating
- Make sure you carry enough fuel and water
- Only make fires in the fire pits provided in each camp site
- Carry all your litter out of the reserve with you
- Regularly check under your vehicle for grass that may have gathered there
- You are only permitted to camp in designated camp sites
- Take all your firewood with you – you may not collect wood from the veld
- Throw some cold ash down the long-drop each day – it helps mask the smell
- Stay on existing tracks; off-road driving is not permitted
- Leave your camp site in the same condition that you would expect to find it

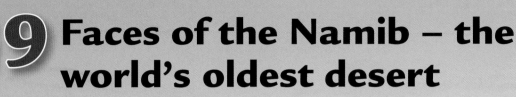

⑨ Faces of the Namib – the world's oldest desert

by Jurgens Schoeman

TOP 10 ATTRACTIONS OF THIS TRIP

❶ Driving the world's highest dunes ❷ The vastness and solitude of the desert ❸ Magnificent sunrises and sunsets ❹ Endless photographic opportunities ❺ Desert fauna and flora ❻ Diamond-mining history ❼ The *Eduard Bohlen* shipwreck ❽ Topnaar culture ❾ Sandwich Harbour ❿ Three meals daily, prepared by the guides

TRIP OUTLINE

The Namib is one of the greatest and most unique natural creations on earth. It is the smallest desert, but the world's oldest (80 million years), with the highest dunes offering an exceptional ecology. For many centuries the Namib was forbidden land for the general public as diamonds were mined in the *Sperrgebiet*. In June 2004 it became possible for tourists to visit this vast sea of sand, but only if accompanied by the concession holders who have permission to enter this sacred ground.

　　This six-night five-day experience commences at Solitaire and ends in Walvis Bay. The route follows the Kuiseb River along the old ox-wagon route before you negotiate the highest dunes on earth to reach the diamond-mining villages of Grillenberger, Holtsazia and Meob Bay. Then you drive north along the coast up to Walvis Bay where the tour ends.

SEE DETAILED MAP ON PAGE 96 ▶▶

APPEAL RATING

5/5

At first it is the adrenaline rush of crossing the world's highest sand dunes, but as the tour continues it becomes evident that the Namib holds much more in store for its visitors.

- The thrill of driving down a 150m-long slip face becomes addictive; the first couple of times your palms are sweaty, but then you and your vehicle will crave it
- The world's oldest desert is not just sand devoid of fauna and flora – an oryx on the horizon, a jackal keeping a safe distance from the convoy, small crawling creatures hiding in the sand and the occasional snake are surviving in these harsh conditions
- Home to the most southern *Welwitschia mirabilis* and the !nara melon
- Spectacular sunsets mesmerise you with changing colours of the sky
- Dunes from yellow to orange to cinnamon colours
- It is the world's largest sandpit and a wonderful playground for young and old alike
- The desert has an amazing history and there are lots of wonderful fables
- The solitude, vastness and freedom of the desert will recharge your soul
- You can only do this tour if accompanied by the concession holders, and the number of vehicles is strictly controlled

THE BEST TIME TO TRAVEL HERE

Because the Namib has such moderate temperatures and a pleasant climate, the Faces of the Namib tour can be enjoyed at any time of year. There are, however, seasonal sandstorms and strong winds, but these are relatively unpredictable.

- Optimum times to schedule a tour are from January to the end of April or the beginning of May
- September to December is also very pleasant in the desert
- June to August is recommended as third choice
- During the winter months (June–August) you may experience a warm east wind blowing in the desert
- At other times the prevailing wind is a southwesterly, beginning in September and blowing in from the chilly ocean until December

GENERAL WARNINGS FOR THIS ROUTE

It is only possible to do this trip in the company of the concession holder, and two guide vehicles will accompany the group. Vehicles are equipped with radios and we are all in contact with each other. If you follow the rules and listen to the guides there are no major warnings.

- To protect the environment, vehicles must drive in the leading vehicle's tracks
- Protect your eyes against the glare
- Take in plenty of liquids to stay hydrated
- Don't litter at all

MAP 9 FACES OF THE NAMIB – the world's oldest desert

C34

B2

Hotel Burg Nonidas

Vineta

Swakopmund

Old Railway Station

Goanikontes

C28

Walvis Bay

Old Rhenish
Mission Church

B2

6

22°58'50"S
14°29'11"E

Dune 7

Rooikop

Various Accommodation Options

Seal Colony

Walvis Bay

Sandwich Bay

Langewand

Sandwich Harbour

NAMIB DESERT

Schwartzekuppe
150m

Rooibank

Kuiseb

Swartbankberg 465
465m

Kuiseb

C14

Hamiltonberge
551m

Vogelfederberg
527m

Leeukop
648m

Kibmas

Namib Desert Research Station

Gobabeb

Kuiseb

Mirabib Camp Site
Hirabeb
841m

Tumas Viewpoint

Game Viewing Shelter

C28

Namib–Naukluft Park

Tirkas

Gauwib

Sewakop

Zaramkab

Onanis

Aurusib

C14

Rutile

Koedoe

Kuiseb

Kuiseb Canyon

Picnic Site
Gaub

C26

Rooiberg
1400m

Kamberge
1111m

Zebra Pan

Kaiseb

Rostock Ritz

Chgasib

Sphinx

KHOMAS HOCHLAND

Ruimte

Khomas Guest Farm

Kraaipoort

Katros

C24

C74

C19

Karoff

Arib

Diep

Betesba

Saagberg
1444m

Solitaire

1 Various Camps

Namib-Naukluft Lodge

23°53'18''S
16°01'35''E

Tsondab

Namib Rest Camp

Petrified Dunes

Sesriem

Sesriem Canyon

Mövenpick
Sossusvlei

Hot-Air Balloon Safaris
Kuiseb Desert Lodge

Tsauchab

Tsondabvlei

2 Kuiseb Canyon Camp

23°38'41''S
15°14'20''E

Namib-Naukluft Park

NE
N   SE
MN   S
NW   MS
W   SE
SW   S
E

20 km

10 miles

0

0

Bape Camp

4X4 route

Overnight stay

3 Overnight number

22°59'48''S
27°56'17''E   GPS co-ordinate

See full key on page 9

Sossusvlei

NAMIB DESERT

Wreck of the Shawnee

23°51'49''S
14°46'58''E

23°54'59''S
14°29'59''E

Conception Bay Camp

3

Black Cliff

Conception
Bay

Wreck of the Eduard Bohlen

24°11'38''S
14°38'10''E

Conception Water Camp

4 & 5

Holtsazia

Charlottenfelder

Leeukoppie Camp

4 & 5

Grillenberger

24°5'03''S
14°37'11''E

24°2'00''S
14°37'32''E

24°24'40''S
14°38'41''E

24°31'01''S
14°36'24''E

Msob Bay

Black Reef

24°32'00''S
14°41'12''E

Hollams Bird Island

FAMILY-FRIENDLY RATING

5/5

The Faces of the Namib tour is not just for testosterone-driven adrenaline junkies. If you enjoy five days of pure dune driving (with as many risks as possible), this one's not for you.

▶ The focus of this tour is to offer a truly unique experience … a one-of-a-kind desert adventure safari

▶ The emphasis is on inclusivity – that means a family-friendly atmosphere to suit adults and children alike, all activities taking place in the world's oldest desert

▶ The tour is geared towards combining the thrill of dune driving with an exploration of the Namib Desert's uniquely adapted ecosystem, as well as visiting sites of historic and cultural interest and spectacular scenic beauty

▶ As a family bonding experience, this tour is an absolute must; your children will spend five days playing in and exploring the world's largest sandpit

▶ Many children regard this as their best holiday ever

SELF-SUFFICIENCY RATING

5/5

Only concession holders may escort self-drive off-road tourists in this area, so all of the logistical and navigational preparation is done for you. There are capable and qualified guides with cooks and assistants ever-present to show you the ropes, keep you informed and prepare your meals for you. However, you still need to prepare yourselves and your vehicle well for a trip through the Namib.

▶ There is no fuel, no water, no firewood and no cellphone reception while you are on tour

▶ From Solitaire, the trip is approximately 550km long and you need to carry enough fuel for this distance – in the desert petrol engines (it varies from make to make) use one litre of fuel every 2.5 to 4km, and diesel-driven vehicles manage 4–5km per litre

▶ Your daily liquid consumption in the desert will be more than you are used to; make provision for 2 litres of water per day per person in your vehicle (excluding cool drinks or beer), and additionally you also need to carry 60 litres of water of which 40 litres can be used for showering and 20 litres for the communal kitchen

▶ Two bags of firewood are required for food preparation and for a nice camp-fire atmosphere

▶ At the overnight stops a camp shower and toilet will be set up; an eco-friendly chemical toilet is set up at each evening's camp and is available until shortly before departure the following morning

▶ No toilets are available during the day; should you have a call of nature, seek privacy behind a grassy dune knoll or behind the wheel of the last vehicle in the convoy

▶ Keep toilet paper in your vehicle for this purpose but dispose of it in a refuse bag in the car – under no circumstances should paper or any other refuse (sweet wrappers, cans, bottles, etc.) be left in the desert

▶ Juice and tea or coffee are provided during meals, but bring your own wine, beer and cool drinks, and if you like to nibble while driving or between meals, ensure that you pack enough snacks – there is no shop to satisfy any craving that you might have

The vastness of Namibia

DAY 1

You will be travelling from home to Solitaire in your own time. If you plan your itinerary carefully you might have time to take in one of Namibia's most visited attractions. Sossusvlei is about 66km past the Sesriem gate, which in turn is approximately 85km from Solitaire. The last 6km can only be traversed with 4X4 vehicles as this is where the concrete road ends and the deep, thick sand begins.

Sossusvlei is a clay pan, of roughly elliptical shape, covered in a crust of salt-rich sand. While the pan has been shaped over time by the Tsauchab River, the actual flooding of the pan is a rare event, and sometimes several years pass between one flood and the next. The river is dry most of the year, and even when it is not, it carries relatively little water to the vlei. The vlei is surrounded by high, iron-rich, orange-reddish dunes, partially covered by vegetation comprising grass, bushes and some trees. Sesriem is the entrance to Sossusvlei.

The groups assemble at Solitaire before nightfall. Solitaire is a small hamlet situated at the junction of the C14 and C24 roads near the Namib-Naukluft Park. Solitaire consists of a post office, fuel station and general dealer.

This will be your last chance to stock up on last-minute supplies and fuel. Remember, you need fuel for six days. It is advisable to arrive in Solitaire with your jerry cans filled … only top up your fuel tank.

Tonight you will have the opportunity to meet the guides and your fellow travellers. After a detailed briefing of what to expect during the next couple of days, you will be treated to a lovely meal around the camp fire. Tonight's accommodation is camping, but it's your last opportunity to upgrade to the luxury of a room. The camp ground has good ablution facilities with hot and cold water and flushing toilets.

DAY 2

We depart early from Solitaire and enter the Namib-Naukluft Park about 35km north of Solitaire – a restricted Namib area. This is the start of a unique adventure offering you aspects of the Namib seldom experienced by the 'normal' tourist. We cross the Namib plains more or less on the same ox-wagon route followed by early settlers, German *Schutztruppe* (on horseback and camels) and *transportryers* in the late 1800s.

THE KUISEB RIVER

Rising in the Khomas Hochland near Windhoek, the Kuiseb River is an ephemeral river that crosses the Namib Desert but no longer reaches the sea – it has been blocked by the northward movement of dunes.

The Kuiseb serves commercial farmers in its upper reaches, the Namib-Naukluft Park and the Topnaar community in the middle reaches, and the town of Walvis Bay along the coast. The river also provided water for Swakopmund and several mines in the past and, in the case of uranium mines and prospecting activities, continues to do so to this day. The Kuiseb can be called a typical Namib Desert river, with agriculture in the upper reaches and, in some cases, a dense human population near its mouth. The river valley forms a canyon, from where it leaves the escarpment to about the area of Homeb, and vegetation gradually increases as the river bed widens. Downstream of Homeb there is a flood plain of varying width, with fairly uniform perennial woody vegetation to where the river course peters out and is broken up by small sand dunes.

For much of the year it is typically dry, and is little more than a broad, sandy river bed, flooding only when sufficient rain falls in its catchment area. Normally it only flows for two or three weeks a year, reaching Gobabeb, from where it seeps into the sand before reaching the sea.

Although the river ends in the dunes near Walvis Bay, it may still force its way through the dunes to the sea due to heavy flooding. Records show that this happened in 1934, when it flowed for several months, and once again in 1963. What a sight that must have been! In 1997, the water almost reached the Walvis Bay salt works, but was diverted by a hastily bulldozed wall.

A total of ten woody plant species grow along the banks, and the sycamore and Namaqua fig can be found in the river bed. A bright green bush, salvadora, is also an important part of the Kuiseb environment, and the !nara occurs on the banks and extends well into the dunes.

Other non-woody plants grow in the sandy river bed and depend on moist conditions near the surface, but they die off annually as the water table drops.

More hardy species such as wild tobacco, castor-oil plant and bitterbos inhabit the river bed and flood plains, and some are infamous as invasive alien plants in Namibia.

The Kuiseb River generally flows each year at some time in January, February or March. Once it has stopped flowing, water remains in scattered pools, which in time gradually dry up. At the end of the rainy season, only the open water in the narrow regions of the Kuiseb Canyon remains.

The route leads to the Kuiseb River. The landscape gradually changes from the typical Namib plains into a colourful landscape of red sand dunes separated by grassy plains. The Kuiseb Canyon offers unique scenery. Its southern bank is formed by massive red sand dunes and the northern bank by pitch-black rock formations, while the river bed itself is overgrown with massive endemic trees. The red sand dunes south of the river reach heights of over 150m. The prevailing winds blow the dunes northward, but their movement is blocked by the river.

We proceed in a westerly direction along the edge of the canyon until we reach a spot were the dunes fall right into the

THE KUISEB CANYON

West of the Khomas Hochland, the Kuiseb River carves a spectacular feature called the Kuiseb Canyon as it enters the Namib-Naukluft Park, about 165km from Swakopmund and 230km from Windhoek. It is a wild landscape of badlands, crisscrossed by a maze of dry river courses that eventually make their way to the Kuiseb River.

Overlooking the canyon is Carp Cliff. The view from here is spectacular, especially in the late afternoon when the canyon walls take on a fiery orange shade as the last rays of the sun disappear over the horizon.

There are a number of game species to be seen here, and it is home to klipspringer and even leopard. Spotted hyena are often heard at night, and jackal make a good living from the herds of springbok on the plain. The canyon's upper reaches are uninhabited, but where the valleys broaden out, scattered Topnaar Khoi villages can be found on the north bank.

Kuiseb Canyon

river, near Homeb. Depending on the status of the river (which may be in flood), we will 'slip' into the river, enjoying its unique ecosystem. This includes a variety of trees and an abundance of birds. We will cross over onto the northern bank of the Kuiseb Canyon, enjoying breathtaking views. On the northern side of the Kuiseb you can see the southernmost examples of the *Welwitschia mirabilis* plant, endemic to the Namib Desert. Although the plant looks as if it has many leaves, it has in fact only two, shredded by the winds over the course of centuries. The plant's scientific name is a combination of the first European to describe it, an Austrian botanist named Friedrich Welwitsch, and 'mirabilis' which comes from Latin and refers to its marvellous ability to survive in harsh, apparently waterless conditions.

Here we will set up our first desert camp. The night is spent under the desert sky.

The desert camp has no facilities, but a camp shower (you provide your own water and the guides will heat it) and toilet will be erected for the night.

Distances differ from day to day but average about 100km per day. Please keep in mind that we take a lot of breaks for sightseeing purposes, for refreshment or photo stops, and also during more complex dune manoeuvres as drivers are carefully guided through challenging sections of dune terrain. After all, if we spent all our time sitting in a car seat, there'd be no opportunity to enjoy the WOW! factor of the world's oldest desert. The journey between rest camps thus usually lasts 6–8 hours. Departure time in the mornings differs from season to season, according to the distance to be covered and sites to be visited. However, guides generally encourage a departure time of no later than 09:00 and try to reach the next camp site by around 17:00.

VEHICLE REQUIREMENTS

- A 4X4 vehicle with high- and low-range gear functions
- Vehicles with a high ground clearance are recommended
- Recovery points in the front and back
- You do not need specialist tyres to do the tour; most of the standard tyres which 4X4s come equipped with are perfectly suitable for desert or dune terrain
- Tyres known colloquially as old 'Marie Biscuit' tyres are too narrow and will not do well
- New vehicles with too many technical gadgets may also be problematic; in this instance simpler is better, mostly because sand has the tendency to get into nooks and crannies and potentially jam sensitive mechanisms
- Modern so-called soft-roaders may cause problems

TRAILER-FRIENDLY RATING

No trailers should be brought on this tour. Desert tours cannot and should not be attempted with off-road extras such as trailers and caravans.

DAY 3

The Namib Desert follows the coast of Namibia for approximately 2000km. It varies in width from 80 to 200km. The most important climatic features of the Namib Desert are its sparse and highly unpredictable annual rainfall, which ranges from 5mm in the west to about 85mm along its eastern limits, and the regular sea fogs that arise as the cold Benguela Current from the south and west meets the hot desert winds from the north and east. The fog banks gather during the night, roll inland, and by 10:00 the sun has dispersed them, only for the same procedure to recur day after day. The moisture from the fog allows for the survival of many species, both plant and animal.

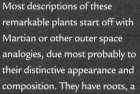

WELWITSCHIA BAINESII (OR WELWITSCHIA MIRABILIS)
Most descriptions of these remarkable plants start off with Martian or other outer space analogies, due most probably to their distinctive appearance and composition. They have roots, a short trunk (or stem) and two leaves. Amazingly, these two leaves are never shed and endure for many centuries. The plants are often thought to have more than just two leaves as they become split and shredded by the hectic desert winds.

Male and female plants bear pollen and ova in cones, and they exude nectar to attract insects to assist with pollination. In earlier years it was suspected that pollination occurred by wind, but the most recent research indicates that a particular species of wasp is the responsible agent.

Female cones mature in spring, nine months after fertilisation. The seeds are 35 x 25mm in size, with a papery wing to aid dispersion by the wind. There is a high rate of attrition as insects and small animals feed off them; however, they can survive for up to five years before they germinate, which is generally only after heavy rains have fallen.

The seeds rely on the dense sea-driven fog for their moisture. As a result, they are never found more than 150km from the coast. They occur in a long belt stretching from the Kuiseb River in the south up to Namibe in southern Angola.

Antelope and rhino chew the leaves for their juice during times of drought, and spit out the tough fibres. They also eat the soft part near the groove. This luckily does not damage the plants, as they simply grow out again from the meristematic tissue.

The core, especially of the female plant, was used as food for people in earlier times. It is said to be very tasty, either raw or baked in hot ashes, and this is how it got its Herero name, *onyanga*, which means 'onion of the desert'.

The plant was named after Austrian botanist, Friedrich Welwitsch, despite his recommendation that it be called *tumboa*, its native Angolan name. He came across the plants during his explorations of Angola in 1859. Thomas Baines encountered them in the Swakop River bed two years later and sent specimens to the gardens at Kew.

The initial species name *mirabilis* (remarkable) was changed to *bainesii* so as to honour both men involved in its European discovery.

Driving across the dunes

The objective of this trip is to drive across the desert from east to west while experiencing the dramatic changes in the environment. From Homeb, we head southwest into the sand sea. In the deep Namib, en route to Conception Bay, the massive dunes are negotiated.

As we proceed, the desert landscape keeps changing. You might think you already have the most beautiful and perfect desert picture ... until you cross the next dune and another awe-inspiring sight awaits you.

The dunes create a mosaic of interesting patterns and shapes. The crescentic dunes are about 20km wide and are formed by the strong southwesterly winds. The linear dunes in the interior are influenced by southwesterly and easterly winds and are separated by wide 'dune streets'.

The dunes are picturesque and colourful. The older ones are tinted red due to iron oxidation and small pieces of garnet. Younger dunes are greyer in colour. Your sand-driving skills will be improving as the dunes offer greater and greater challenges. The dune streets are massive, and the dunes themselves even more impressive. Most have a height in excess of 150m.

THE HOMEB SILTS

The area known as the Homeb Silts in the Namib Desert was researched by Dr Mary C. Bourke and various geologists with funding from the Smithsonian Institute.

Similar fine-grained terraces that represent past episodes of valley aggradation are found in many of the world's arid regions, like the Flinders Ranges of South Australia, the Anti Atlas Mountains in Morocco, and the Sinai Desert, although the sediment textures contrast markedly.

The terrace sequences of the Homeb Silts in the Kuiseb Canyon run along the northern boundary of the hyper-arid Namib Desert. Twenty-five-metre thick sequences of sand, silt and clay are preserved in channel and tributary mouth embayments and now stand up to 45m above the channel bed. These remarkable deposits have a well-preserved stratigraphy and their aspects are typical of slackwater environments. More recent research suggests that these slackwater deposits were paleo-stage indicators of large Pleistocene floods. The presence of similar vertically stacked, fine-grain deposits in at least three other river systems in northwestern Namibia suggest this occurred on a regional scale.

From http://www.psi.edu/about/staff/mbourke/bourkeprojects/Homeb1.html

RULES FOR SAND DRIVING

▶ Deflate tyres to at least 1 bar; if you're still battling, go to 0.8 bar

▶ Select a gear to keep momentum and speed instead of slow power

▶ Always expect a serious slip face on the other side of a dune when trying to cross it – rather do it over than overdo it

▶ When travelling along a dune slope at an angle, select the right gear to travel at a minimum speed of at least 40kmph in order to avoid sliding

▶ Never stop your car at an angle or on an incline as this will almost certainly get you stuck

▶ If you go down a slip face, engage low-range first or second gear to let your engine do the braking

▶ If stuck, engage low range to protect your clutch and go forward or backward gently without spinning your wheels; stay in the same track and don't try to make a new one

▶ Always stay 100% in the tracks

Your gear selections will depend on your vehicle's torque curve and engine power. Experiment on the 'not-so-serious' dunes in order to find the right gear for the more serious dunes.

Also remember that there is no slip face in the Namib Desert too steep to go down. The maximum angles are between 37° and 40°.

Tonight we enjoy our second night of desert camping in the dunes.

DAYS 4 AND 5

During the next couple of days we will see vast flocks of birds, drive past Cape fur seal colonies, visit the wreck of the *Eduard Bohlen* near Conception Bay and see various relics dating back to the diamond-mining era.

This part of the journey is something history buffs will particularly enjoy ... keep a lookout for ghost towns.

During the glory days of diamond mining, the settlements of Holtsazia, Charlottenfelder and Grillenberger were established between Conception Bay and Meob Bay. As no engine-driven land transport was available, ships from Swakopmund were used to bring supplies and equipment to these settlements. The cutter, *Viking*, also serviced Sandwich Harbour, Conception Bay and Meob Bay. It was inevitable that shipping casualties occurred. One such was the stranding of the *Eduard Bohlen* in 1909 near Conception Bay.

Ghost town

TRAVEL DOCUMENTATION

▶ South African citizens, including children, will require a passport, but no visa
▶ ZA sticker on your vehicle
▶ Vehicle registration papers (remember a letter of authorisation from the registered owner if the vehicle is not in your name)
▶ Proof of vehicle insurance
▶ Travel insurance that will cover emergency evacuation

SPECIFIC KIT REQUIRED FOR THIS TRIP

▶ Own snacks and refreshments (alcoholic beverages, cool drinks, etc.)
▶ Torch and batteries; a headlamp is recommended
▶ Camera and video camera (extra films or memory cards or tapes and batteries)
▶ Binoculars
▶ Sunglasses, hat and SPF lotion
▶ Clothing for very hot and very cold conditions
▶ Toiletries and towels; a rich lotion is recommended as your skin dries out quickly in the Namib, and a good lip balm and biodegradable body and hair soap (this is kinder to the environment) are also recommended
▶ Basic first-aid kit, prescription medication, over-the-counter medication (e.g. headache tablets, tablets for nausea, etc.), and mosquito or insect repellent
▶ Groundsheet on which to put suitcases, bedding, etc. while pitching or breaking camp or repacking vehicles
▶ Tent, folding chairs, bedding, etc.
▶ Cloth and windscreen cleaner
▶ Sand boards

ESSENTIAL REQUIREMENTS FOR THIS TRIP

▶ Q20 spray
▶ A second spare wheel (no. 6)
▶ Spade
▶ Tyre-pressure gauge
▶ Plastic bags to carry waste, e.g. empty cool-drink tins, toilet paper, etc. – everything you take into the desert you must bring out
▶ Brake fluid
▶ Gear oil
▶ Engine oil
▶ Fuses
▶ Spare V-belt set

SEE FULL PACKING LIST ON PAGE 218 ▶▶

THE *EDUARD BOHLEN*

The transport of supplies to the mining settlements along the Namibian coast was mainly done by ship from Swakopmund and by the cutter, *Viking*, that frequently visited Sandwich Harbour, Conception Bay and Meob Bay. Various shipping casualties occurred, such as when the *Eduard Bohlen* intended to off-load mining equipment and was lost at Conception Bay.

On 5 September 1909 the *Eduard Bohlen*, a 2272-ton passenger and cargo ship, was on a voyage from Swakopmund to Table Bay. The ship had cargo and 30 passengers on board. On this day the sea and coast were covered in thick fog. The 310.6ft ship lost its way and ran aground at Conception Bay, about 150km from Swakopmund, with no loss of lives. Attempts to salvage the ship failed. In the 1930s the wreck served to accommodate contract labourers working at the diamond mines. The wreck of the *Eduard Bohlen* is a desert icon and is a popular photographic subject. Today the shipwreck lies about 900m from the coast and is half-covered by shifting sand, a totally amazing sight to witness.

The remains of an ox-wagon near Grillenberger and surfboats at Meob Bay are examples of pre-World War I transport methods.

By 1913 a railway operated from Conception Bay to Conception Water. The settlements mostly consisted of prefabricated buildings. The foundations of only some of these are still visible, which makes it difficult to establish how large the settlements were and the number of people that lived there.

In November 1914 all the people in this area were requested to stop operations and return to Swakopmund. This order came as a result of an expected invasion of allied troops.

In all probability the first European to set foot on Namibian soil was Diogo Cão (or Diogo Cam), a Portuguese explorer, followed by Bartholomeu Dias two years later, on 8 December 1487. This date represents the holiday commemorating Mary's Conception, therefore the bay received the name *Santa Maria da Conceição* (Conception Bay).

Tonight we will be camping in the Conception Bay area – either at Leeukoppie ('Lion's Head') or at Conception Water, depending on our progress and/or the weather.

DAY 6

This is our last day in the desert and it includes driving the Langewand, a stretch of beach that can only be driven during low tide ... correct timing is therefore of the utmost importance. After Conception Bay the dune belt stretches right onto the beach and this is where our beach drive will start. There are only a few places on earth where you will see this natural phenomenon: dune massifs on your right and the ocean to your left.

After the beach drive the route heads back into the dunes. It will take us in a northerly direction towards Sandwich Bay.

Closer to the coast again you will pass the wreck of the *Shawnee* and drive around the salt pans of Sandwich Harbour.

Crossing the Langewand at low tide is critical

Although called Sandwich Harbour, it was never a harbour or even a port. It is a shallow lagoon lying about 80km south of Walvis Bay. The area was surveyed in the 1880s by the Royal Navy but was considered inferior to Walvis Bay and no development took place. Occasional sealing vessels used it as an anchorage and there were some temporary settlements used by seasonal fishermen catching snoek.

From Sandwich Harbour the trail enters an area known among locals as the 'Roller Coaster'. This is a series of massive 'roaring' slip faces, and driving down them is the ultimate roller-coaster ride. It also offers breathtaking views of Sandwich Harbour and the dune landscape en route to Walvis Bay.

The convoy will arrive in Walvis Bay during the early afternoon. The group will check in at our accommodation … tonight we will sleep in proper beds again! There will be time to get rid of some of the sand and dirt before the tour concludes over dinner.

DAY 7

It is now time for sad farewells, as each family departs for home under their own steam and once again following their own itinerary.

THE TOPNAAR COMMUNITY

The Topnaars are the custodians of the Namib Desert. Related to the Nama people, they are the longer-term residents of the Namib, where they live mainly in small villages scattered along the lower Kuiseb and around Walvis Bay.

There was once a time when the Topnaars were wholly dependant on the !nara melon for their income and food. Today they also practise small-scale stock farming, along with the collection, harvesting and processing of the !nara melon. The whole plant is utilised as a source of food for the Topnaars and their livestock.

!NARA MELON – *ACANTHOSICYOS HORRIDUS*

Another wonder of the Namib Desert is the interesting !nara melon, also known as butter-nut. !Nara is both the Nama and Damara name for the plant. The plants are commonly seen in and among the small dunes of Sossusvlei.

Fossil evidence indicates that the !nara existed some 40 million years ago, was probably utilised in the Stone Age, and is likely the sole reason why the desert communities survived in this harsh environment through to modern times.

These bright-green thorny plants grow continuously in order to keep above the blown sand that collects up against their stems. As the dunes become higher and higher, so the lengthening roots and the stem of the !nara stabilise the sand. Therefore, should you come across dead !nara plants, and there are several in the area, remember the National Parks' Environmental Code, and leave them where they lie.

The !nara is endemic to the desert along the west coast and grows only on sand dunes where subterranean water exists. It is common in many of the rivers leading into the Atlantic Ocean, in both Namibia and southern Angola.

The !nara has sharp, straight thorns and these protect it from browsers to a certain extent. Photosynthesis takes place through the thorns and stems, as it has no leaves to perform this function. Male and female flowers are borne on different plants. The male plant flowers throughout most of the year and the wax-like flowers are pale yellow or greenish. The female flowers appear similar to those of the male plants but have a small bulge, the ovary, below the petals.

Once a year the !nara produces a crop of round, spiky fruits, the size of a large orange. These fruits are highly nutritious and, quite remarkably, have sustained indigenous people of the Namib for centuries. The fruit is also eaten by gemsbok, jackals, hyenas, mice, porcupines and birds, and in the Skeleton Coast Park it forms a very important food source for the dune-dwelling lizard. The plant also shelters a wide variety of insects and reptiles, including snakes.

The !nara can live to 100 years old and the plants are most likely insect-pollinated.

The Topnaars still harvest the fruits annually. The seeds are allowed to dry and then bagged for sale in town or stored for their own use. They are considered to be a bit of a delicacy, and can be nibbled on – as they are, or even roasted and salted.

Walvis Bay area

10 Tanzania Wildebeest Migration

André van Vuuren

TOP 10 ATTRACTIONS OF THIS TRIP

❶ Vilanculos and the Bazaruto Archipelago in Mozambique ❷ Cahora Bassa Dam in Mozambique ❸ The shores and tranquillity of Lake Malawi ❹ Zanzibar Island and Stone Town ❺ Mount Kilimanjaro ❻ Ngorongoro Crater ❼ Wildebeest migration and the big cats of the Serengeti ❽ Kapishya Hot Springs and Shiwa Ng'andu in northern Zambia ❾ A microlight flight over the Victoria Falls from the Zambian side ❿ Chobe National Park in Botswana

TRIP OUTLINE

The route will take us through five African countries:

1. In Mozambique we will follow the main road from Maputo to Beira and will visit places like Casa Lisa, Maxixe, Vilanculos and Bazaruto Island. We will also stay over at Casa Msika and the Cahora Bassa Dam.
2. In Malawi we will explore Lilongwe, the political capital of Malawi, as well as the shores of Lake Malawi and the Livingstonia Mission near Rumphi.
3. We will spend the majority of our time in Tanzania where we will properly explore Zanzibar Island and the Northern Wildlife Circuit of the country.
4. On our way back we will visit Kapishya Hot Springs and Shiwa Ng'andu in Zambia and explore the Victoria Falls from the Zambian side.
5. Once in Botswana, we will explore the northern part of the Chobe National Park in our 4X4 vehicles before going on a three-hour sunset boat cruise on the Chobe River.

SEE DETAILED MAP ON PAGE 106 ▶▶

APPEAL RATING

5/5

Many wildlife enthusiasts will start to do 4X4 safaris and expeditions within South Africa and, as they gain experience and confidence, will venture further into neighboring countries like Namibia, Botswana and Mozambique. The ultimate destination and experience, however, remains an overland expedition to Zanzibar Island and the Ngorongoro Crater in Tanzania and to witness the Wildebeest migration when the big herds of gnus cross the Mara River in the northern part of the Serengeti National Park.

THE BEST TIME TO TRAVEL HERE

Although this safari to East Africa is not only about the migration of the wildebeest in the Serengeti, it undoubtedly remains the reason for this trip and one has to plan the dates with the migration in mind. Having witnessed the migration many times, in our experience we can recommend the following two time slots:

In March the wildebeest start to gather in the vicinity of Lake Ndutu and on the Naabi Plains. It is also calving season and all the animals are walking with their young. This phenomenon is referred to as the 'Birth of Life'. This is the wet season and the plains are green and lush. The trek will go through the Seronera area and the Grumeti River in the Western Corridor of the Serengeti before turning in a northerly direction towards the Masai Mara in Kenya.

The migrating herds will reach the Mara River towards the end of July, and that is the time of year when we offer our second annual safari to Tanzania. This is the dry season and winter time, but with the area being only 1–3 degrees south of the equator, temperatures are quite pleasant.

FAMILY-FRIENDLY RATING

3/5

In the past we have done this safari with children as young as eight years without any problems. There are days of many long hours of driving, but if the parents stimulate the children in the car, they will be fine. There is enough for children to do and experience to also give them a memorable trip.

Elderly people also manage on this specific safari. We quite often have guests in the 70–75 age bracket.

SELF-SUFFICIENCY RATING

3/5

- Fuel (diesel, leaded and unleaded petrol) is available all along the route; at times, especially in Zambia and Mozambique, refuelling points can be unreliable as well as far apart and we recommend a range of at least 700km per tank – a long-range fuel tank (or jerry cans) is advisable as fuel can be very expensive in certain areas
- We take all our fresh meat vacuum-packed from South Africa, but fresh supplies like bread, fruit and veggies, dairy products, etc. can be obtained in all the major Sentra stores; Shoprite are well represented in Africa
- One can stock up with drinking water from boreholes at most of the camp sites; bottled water is also freely available
- Most of the camp sites have hot-water showers and flushing toilets
- Travel light and do not pack everything that you think you will need – remember that you have to pack and unpack everything you take with you, and that it's extra weight to carry in your vehicle

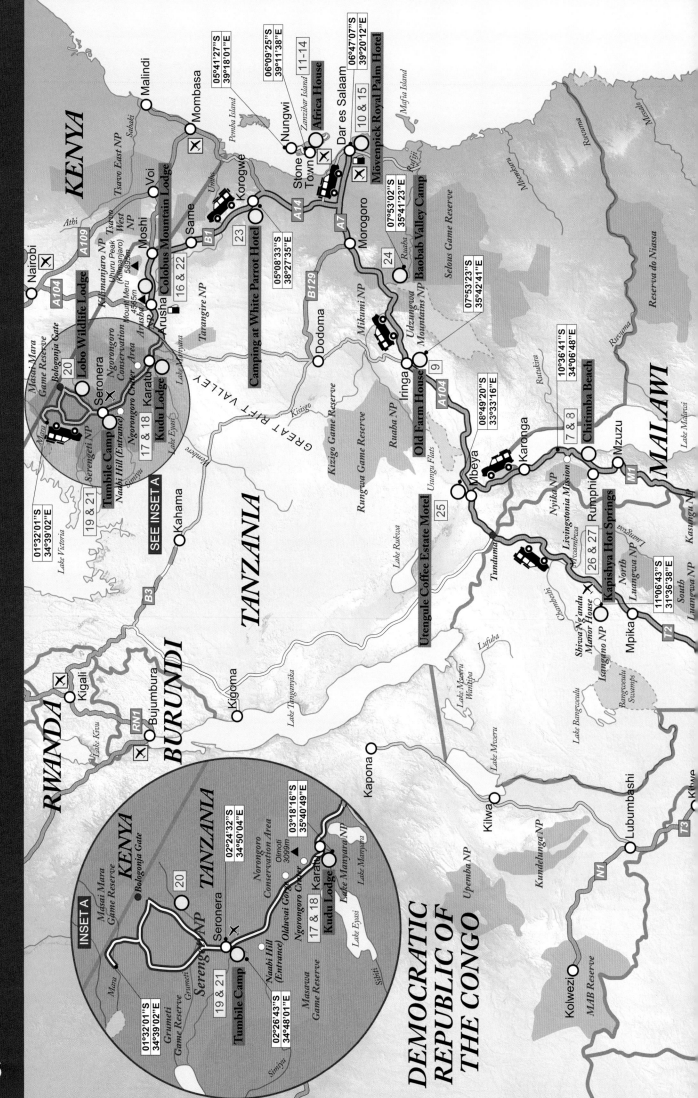

MAP 10 TANZANIA WILDEBEEST MIGRATION

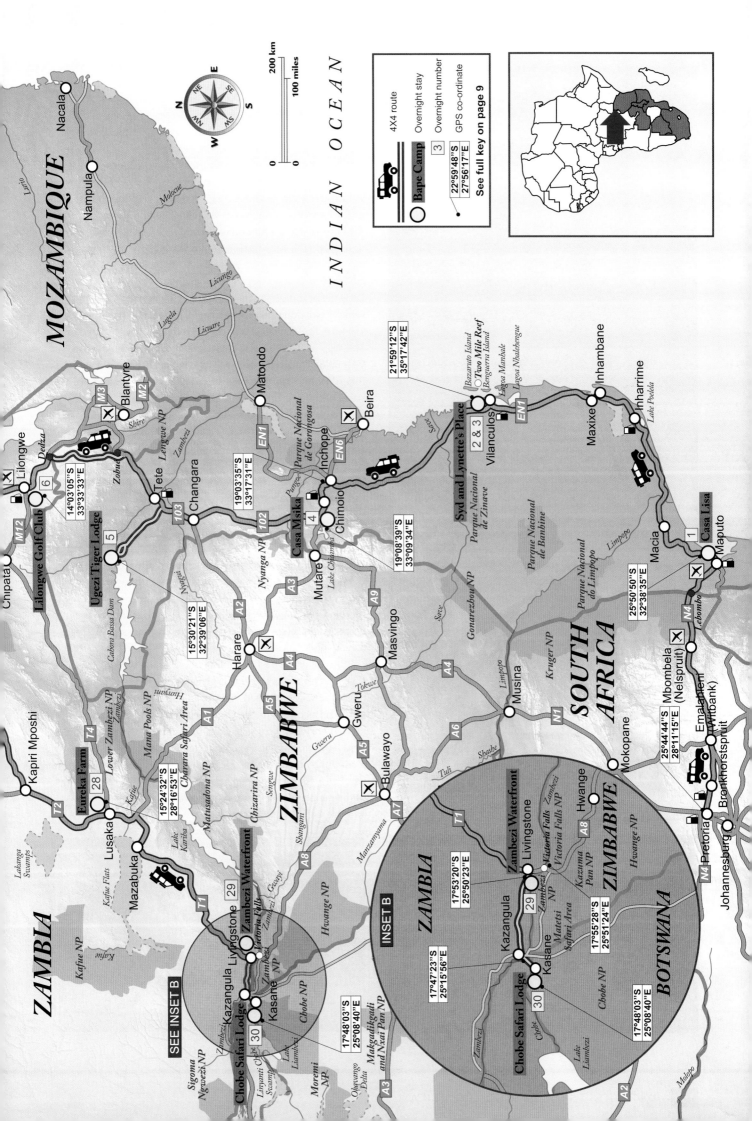

DAILY DRIVING DISTANCE AND TIME			
Day 1	Pretoria to Casa Lisa	600km	10hr
Day 2	Casa Lisa to Vilanculos	680km	10hr
Day 3	Vilanculos: Day at leisure		
Day 4	Vilanculos to Casa Msika	520km	7hr
Day 5	Casa Msika to Cahora Bassa	460km	7hr
Day 6	Cahora Bassa to Lilongwe	470km	9hr
Day 7	Lilongwe to Chitimba Beach	500km	7hr
Day 8	Chitimba Beach: Day at leisure		
Day 9	Chitimba to Iringa	510km	8hr
Day 10	Iringa to Dar es Salaam	500km	8hr
Days 11–15	Zanzibar Island (no driving)		
Day 16	Dar es Salaam to Arusha	640km	9hr
Day 17	Arusha to Karatu	160km	3hr
Day 18	Visit Ngorongoro Crater with chartered Game Drive Vehicles (no driving)		
Day 19	Karatu to Seronera	180km	5hr
Day 20	Seronera to Mara River	220km	6hr
Day 21	Mara River to Seronera	220km	6hr
Day 22	Seronera to Arusha	340km	5hr
Day 23	Arusha to Korogwe	360km	5hr
Day 24	Korogwe to Baobab Valley	450km	6hr
Day 25	Baobab Valley to Mbeya	520km	7hr
Day 26	Mbeya to Kapishya Hot Springs	400km	8hr
Day 27	Kapishya: Day at leisure		
Day 28	Kapishya Hot Springs to Lusaka	800km	10hr
Day 29	Lusaka to Livingstone	500km	7hr
Day 30	Livingstone to Kasane	90km	3hr
Day 31	Game drive in Chobe National Park	70km	Half day

VALUE FOR MONEY

It is 10,000km to the Serengeti and back, and the journey will take you through six African countries and 12 border posts. With lots of research and experience you can do it on your own, but we recommend that you use an experienced safari company and tour guide. The guide fee forms a relatively small percentage of the total cost of a safari of this nature and by using a guide you will definitely enhance the experience and add value.

Various routes can be taken, but we normally go up through Mozambique and Malawi to Tanzania and come back to South Africa via Zambia and Botswana.

DAY 1

The departure point is in Pretoria and everybody will meet at The Rose One Stop filling station between Pretoria and Bronkhorstspruit on the N4 to Mbombela (Nelspruit). You will be issued with a UHF radio before departing for the border post with Mozambique at Komatipoort. We have a connection at the border that we use to help smoothe the border procedure. We drive to Casa Lisa where we will overnight in the chalets and dine together with André van Vuuren, CEO of Explore Africa Adventures. He is a fully qualified and experienced safari guide and will do the introductions and briefing.

DAY 2

Early the next morning the convoy of 10 'dressed to kill' 4X4 vehicles (we don't take more than 10 vehicles on this safari) will leave for Vilanculos. We drive through cashew-nut country and stop at Macia to buy nuts to nibble on the long drive to Vilanculos. The day's route will take us via Lake Poelela at Inharrime and Maxixe where we will fill up with fuel and buy some of the best bread rolls – *pão* in Portuguese or *katkoppe* as they're commonly called in Afrikaans – in all of Mozambique. On arrival in Vilanculos we will drive straight through to our camp site, known to all as Syd and Lynette's Place, where we will stay for the next two nights. It is a lovely grassed and secured camp site with hot-water showers and flushing toilets, located close to all major places of interest in Vilanculos.

DAY 3

Today will definitely be the highlight of our visit to Vilanculos. The group will charter a lovely speedboat, called *Spanish Fly*, to take us to the Islands of the Bazaruto Archipelago. The Bazaruto Archipelago is a protected national park and the islands are pristine and undeveloped. The area offers unspoilt coral pink beaches, world-class deep-sea fishing, saltwater fly fishing, scuba diving and snorkelling.

We will cruise past Benguerra Island on our way to Two Mile Reef for the snorkelling experience of a lifetime. The internationally renowned diver, Jacques Cousteau, rated Two Mile Reef as one of the best snorkelling spots in the world. From there we will cruise to Bazaruto Island where we just chill on the beach, swim in the crystal-clear warm water and enjoy a picnic lunch on the beach. Depending on the tide we can also visit Pansy Island to pick up some pansy shells before returning to the mainland. The restaurants at Vilanculos are gorgeous and the seafood absolutely divine.

Luxury lodge on Ilha de Benguerra

Baobab at dawn

DAY 4

After breakfast and breaking camp we leave for Chimoio. We continue in a northerly direction until the road joins the EN6 that connects Harare with the important import/export harbour city of Beira. The majority of this section is not very busy. The road winds through lovely indigenous forests and countryside, and driving conditions are reasonably good. We stop at Shoprite in Chimoio to stock up with provisions and refuel the vehicles. There is an ATM and one can also change money if necessary.

Then it is on to Casa Msika, situated on the shores of Lake Chicamba, where we camp for the night. An old house was converted into ablutions with hot-water showers and flushing toilets. There is also chalet accommodation and a restaurant overlooking the lake with ice-cold 2Ms – one of the best local Mozambican beers.

DAY 5

Early in the morning we depart for Ugezi Tiger Lodge, which overlooks Cahora Bassa Dam. The last 120km to Cahora Bassa will take you through typical African countryside, with small villages situated between huge baobab trees. We normally arrive early enough to pitch camp before going on a scenic sunset cruise to the historic dam wall. We all sit down for a hearty dinner (bream, of course) before going to bed after another eventful day.

DAY 6

After an early breakfast of omelettes in the restaurant, we head for the Malawi border. On our way we refuel in Tete and cross the Zambezi River via one of the most spectacular suspension bridges in Southern Africa. Our expected time of arrival at the Dedza border post is 15:00. It is normally a song to go out of Mozambique into Malawi. (It's incomprehensible why border posts like Dedza and Ngoma can be so painless and why they give you such a hard time at Kaporo, Tunduma and Beit Bridge.)

Lilongwe is the political capital of Malawi and we usually arrive here at peak traffic hour. It is quite an experience to be exposed to the dominating Muslim religion of this city. The one night that we camp here is at the Lilongwe Golf Club.

DAYS 7 AND 8

After breaking camp, we stop at the 7-Eleven in town for some shopping, fuel and changing of money before leaving via Mzuzu for Chitimba Beach in the north. The road winds through beautiful lowveld countryside before descending to Lake Malawi – a view that will stay with you for ever. Arrival at Chitimba Beach is around 16:00 and we'll have ample time to pitch camp right on the beach of Lake Malawi where we stay for the next two nights – a well-deserved break after a few days of serious driving and border crossings. Chitimba is now under the management of a Dutch couple, Eddie and Carmen, and what a fantastic place it is to be. We will chill out, swim in the lake, enjoy cold Kuche Kuches with Eddie in his pub, sort out vehicles and kit, and also get some washing done. We take a 4X4 route to the historic Livingstonia Mission and the University of Livingstonia and enjoy the most fantastic views of Lake Malawi. The friendliness and productivity of the Malawian people make a great impression and will stay with you for many years to come. After three nights in this wonderful country everybody will be in love with the laid-back atmosphere and the words *Kaya Mawa*, a Malawian expression meaning 'maybe tomorrow'.

> **ACCOMMODATION CHOICES**
> On a month-long safari it is very hard on oneself to do only camping, but on the other hand it's very costly to use only lodges and hotels. The success of this tour lies in a combination of the above to ensure that everybody gets that essential break from camping at an affordable price. In addition, only the best accommodation is booked on Zanzibar Island, and we have hand-picked the best camp sites in the Serengeti to experience the Wildebeest migration at full blast.

DAY 9

As the sun rises over Lake Malawi on the final morning at Chitimba Beach, there is a definite air of excitement – today we cross the border into Tanzania and start to experience the mystique of this East African country that brought all of us together on this once-in-a-lifetime safari.

We enter Tanzania north of Karonga and travel to The Old Farm House at Iringa (also called Kisolanza Farm) where we camp in a

Camping at Lilongwe Golf Club

VEHICLE REQUIREMENTS

- When travelling with one vehicle on your own, it is advisable to use a 4WD vehicle with a low-range transfer case; when travelling with a group of other vehicles, a 4X2 vehicle with ample ground clearance would be capable of doing the whole trip
- Proper all-terrain tyres
- A well-organised packing system is advisable, as it is not pleasant to pack and unpack everything that you carry on a month-long safari
- We would recommend a built-in safe concealed somewhere in the vehicle

TRAILER-FRIENDLY RATING

To tow or not to tow is normally quite a personal as well as a debatable issue. It is possible to tow on this specific safari to Tanzania, but travellers have to take the following into account:

- You will tow over a distance of 10,000km through five different African countries and the cost of towing can add quite a lot to your total safari bill in terms of extra fuel and border-crossing fees (third-party insurance)
- The road between Ngorongoro Crater and the Serengeti is terrible and you have to take it very easy; some stretches in the northern part of Zambia have bad potholes and should be negotiated with great care
- Do not travel without a set of spare wheel bearings as well as the tools and knowledge to replace them at the side of the road

GENERAL WARNINGS FOR THIS ROUTE

- This is a malaria area, so visit your doctor or travel clinic and find out about malaria prophylactics
- You will also need yellow fever inoculation
- When going on your own, take extreme care at border posts not to be ripped off by officials, insurance brokers and money changers; we only deal with the people we know
- Research accommodation and camp sites properly as one can easily have a bad experience
- Stay calm and friendly at roadblocks and border posts
- Obey all park rules in Tanzania; read the fine print on the back of park permits
- Try not to change money with street bankers and fuel attendants at filling stations
- Keep to speed limits – trespassers have to pay heavy spot fines or bribes

colonial atmosphere for the night. The camp sites have some of the best ablutions in Tanzania, and chalet accommodation will also be available for interested parties. Mark and Nicola are hosts of note and after a gorgeous supper in their restaurant you go to bed with a head full of thoughts of the fantastic experience that awaits you.

DAY 10

After a full English breakfast, the convoy snakes from the highveld all the way down to the coastal flats. As we pass Morogoro on our way to Dar es Salaam, thoughts of ANC training camps come to mind and it is wonderful to see that this once hostile country has turned into a prime destination for South African adventure travellers and that the atmosphere can be so relaxed and friendly. Some 600km later we check into the five-star Mövenpick Royal Palm Hotel in Dar es Salaam and park the vehicles in the safekeeping of the security department. They allow us to connect the freezers in the vehicles to the power supply of the hotel where they will remain for the next three nights while we visit Zanzibar Island. Having packed in some goodies for our island adventure and after a typical East African barbecue buffet, we retire to the luxury rooms of the Royal Palm Hotel.

DAY 11

It feels a bit weird leaving our vehicles behind – our trusty homes on wheels – when we take an early-morning charter flight to Zanzibar. After a smooth landing in Stone Town, the group (by now good travel companions) enjoys lunch at the famous Mercury's Restaurant overlooking the docks. (The restaurant was named after Freddie Mercury who was born on the island.) We overnight at Africa House, once an old colonial English club and now restored to the finest detail of old Arabic architecture. Later, we stroll through the alleys of

House of Wonders

Dhow at sunset

Stone Town and visit the Anglican Cathedral Church of Christ, built on the site of the former slave market, before returning to Africa House for sundowners and supper on the deck overlooking the dhows coming back from their fishing trips.

ZANZIBAR

Zanzibar, an archipelago of two major islands and about 50 islets, is an island partner state in the United Republic of Tanzania. The two major islands, Zanzibar ('Unguja' in Kiswahili) and Pemba, are 35km off the coast of mainland Tanzania, framed by white beaches and surrounded by the crystal-clear waters and coral reefs of the Indian Ocean. A cosmopolitan mix of people comes together in the narrow winding streets of the capital, Zanzibar Town (Stone Town), where the architecture reflects predominantly Arab styles. Historically and culturally important places include the Palace Museum, the Old Fort and the House of Wonders, with its intricate latticed woodcarving.

The name 'Zanzibar' is derived from a combination of two Arabic words, *Zinj*, meaning 'black', and *barr*, the Arabic word for 'land', the result meaning 'Land of the Blacks'.

DAYS 12 TO 14

On our way to Nungwi village, located on the northern tip of the island, we visit one of the many spice farms, and watch 'Mr Batafly' (Khamimakame Pandu) and his breathtaking coconut-climbing and -harvesting demonstration. A visit to the island without including him and his 'Amabokoboko' song from the top of a 30m-high palm tree will definitely not be the same.

The next three nights are spent in luxurious seafront rooms, constructed on stilts standing in the turquoise sea. The Fat Fish and other restaurants are literally a stone's throw away.

We always organise a trip with our old friend Ali Baba (and some of his 40 thieves?) to Mnemba Island. Everybody who is interested will board a traditional East African wooden dhow to the Mnemba Atoll for a memorable snorkelling experience – we get to see the most beautiful soft and hard coral and all the tropical fish species we can dream of. Before returning to our resort, we enjoy a sumptuous seafood barbecue in true Robinson Crusoe-style, consisting of kingfish, barracuda, fresh fruit, rice and chapatis served right on the beach.

The next day is a day at leisure and everybody can go out to see the beauty of this wonderful place, enjoy the stunning views from their rooms, or relax on the snow-white beach of this tropical spice island.

DAY 15

After breakfast, our regular bus driver, Popo, takes us back to Stone Town from where we fly out to Dar es Salaam. Back in Dar Es Salaam we are reunited with our trusty 4X4s, which are then checked and prepared for the next day's journey. The evening meal in the restaurant of the Royal Palm Hotel ends a truly wonderful East African experience.

DAY 16

After a hearty breakfast, we commence our journey via Mount Kilimanjaro and Moshi to Arusha in the Northern Wildlife Circuit of Tanzania. Here we pitch camp at Colobus Mountain Lodge, our private camp site near the entrance gate to the Arusha National Park, in the foothills of Mount Meru and overlooking Mount Kilimanjaro.

DAY 17

This morning everybody has time in Arusha for shopping at Shoprite, exchanging money and refuelling before we continue our scenic journey via Lake Manyara to Karatu. We stop at Lake Manyara to take some great scenic pictures, buy the famous red bananas and visit a typical Masai curio market. In Karatu we pitch camp at Kudu Lodge for the next two nights.

Catch of the day!

SPECIFIC KIT REQUIRED FOR THIS TRIP

- It is a self-sufficient camping trip and you'll have to take full camping gear; be careful not to take all kinds of gadgets you can do without
- A dome tent or rooftop tent will do
- Camp table, chairs, kitchen and cooking utensils
- A 12V compressor-operated freezer (a dual-battery system is not necessary)
- Water container with at least a 40-litre capacity
- When you go with us on one of our safaris, a GPS is nice to have, but if you go on your own it is a necessity
- On our safaris we provide each vehicle in the convoy with a two-way radio
- We will be camping wild for two nights on the bank of the Mara River and for that it can be a good idea to pack a camp shower or similar device as well as a fold-up toilet chair
- When travelling alone, we recommend that you take along a full recovery kit – a winch is not necessary; on our safaris this is not necessary as the guide vehicle is fitted with all recovery equipment, winch and a solid tow bar

ESSENTIAL REQUIREMENTS FOR THIS TRIP

- Fire extinguisher
- 12V air compressor and tyre-pressure gauge
- 12V lighting
- Basic tool kit and spare parts
- Tyre-repair kit
- A 10m (minimum) extension cord with a British plug adaptor
- Basic first-aid kit and personal prescription medication (together with the prescription)
- Basic repair kit consisting of duct tape, cable ties, glues, wire, gas cylinder seals, etc.
- Insect repellent, insect killer and malaria prophylactics

SEE FULL PACKING LIST ON PAGE 218 ▶▶

THE NGORONGORO CRATER

This is the world's largest intact caldera. Located in an exceptional geographical position and forming a spectacular bowl of about 265km² with sides up to 600m deep, it is the stalking ground of around 20,000 to 30,000 wild animals at any one time. The crater floor consists of a number of ecological environments that include grassland, swamps, forests and Lake Makat, a central soda lake filled by the Munge River. All these various habitats attract a great diversity of animals that come here to drink, wallow, graze, hide or climb. Although animals are free to move in and out of this contained environment, the rich volcanic soil, lush forests and spring-source lakes on the crater floor tend to incline both grazers and predators to remain here throughout the year. The crater rim, over 2200m high, touches swathes of clouds for most days of the year, with cool high-altitude vapours that seem to bring a clean lightness to the air, and also a chill. These highlands wake up to a misty fog in most months, other than the high dry season during December and January. The crater has a totally self-contained and balanced ecosystem.

DAY 18

Ngorongoro, here we come! The group is collected in rented game-drive vehicles for a day's game-viewing in the crater. Ngorongoro is a fascinating and unusual conservation area that includes the phenomenon of the Ngorongoro Crater at its centre, and then extends through the Crater Highlands, in which local tribes are permitted to maintain their traditional lifestyles in as natural an environment as possible. This extraordinary volcanic landscape is rich and fertile, with stunning craters and lakes, and the high altitude creates a malaria-free microclimate.

DAY 19

This is the day that the group reaches the highlight of our safari as we approach Naabi Hill where the main entrance gate to the Serengeti is situated. (Some day when you think back to the road from Ngorongoro to Seronera, you will probably recall memories of the worst road you ever travelled!) We will set up camp in the heart of the Serengeti in Tumbile Camp, one of the public camp sites at Seronera. After pitching camp, we are treated to a game drive along the winding Seronera River, looking for resident predators such as a leopard pulling a fresh Thomson's gazelle carcass up a yellow-barked acacia

Lobo Wildlife Lodge

Wildebeest crossing the river

pitch camp. A little while later he usually joins us with his little tent and an AK-47 to 'protect' us for the night.

This is always the undoubted highlight of this East African adventure – camping wild on the banks of the Mara River, one degree from the equator, with the sound of the rapids and the bellowing of thousands of wildebeest still in your ears, and the satisfaction of knowing that you have seen a river crossing, one of the most spectacular phenomena on earth.

DAY 21

Before turning south again, we return to where the 'action' is – thousands of wildebeest gathering on the Mara airstrip and white-backed vultures feeding on the carcasses of those left behind. Memories are made of this.

Now it is time for the long journey back home. We stay one more night in Seronera, exploring the by now well-known Seronera Valley. This is our final night on these endless plains. The group around the camp fire is unusually quite as everyone absorbs the smells and sounds of the night for the final time.

DAY 22

After breaking camp, we tackle the road via Ngorongoro back to 'civilisation' – meaning a car wash at Captains in Arusha, an oil change with Henry at the BP Service Station in Nairobi Road, and a pizza and cold Kilimanjaro Lager at Players Gym and Bar. From the Explore Africa camp site in the foothills of Mount Meru we will most likely have a final farewell sighting of Mount Kilimanjaro.

DAY 23

The convoy leaves the camp site early in the morning on the way via Same to Korogwe where we

(fever tree), a lionesses hiding her cubs in-between the rocks of the Masai kopjes, or a huge herd of buffalo in the bed of the Seronera River. Who will ever forget watching the red sun setting behind an *Acacia tortilis* (umbrella thorn acacia) tree, while sitting with a group of good friends around a fire in an unfenced bush camp in the middle of the Serengeti?

SERENGETI SHALL NOT DIE

A quote from Bernhard Grzimek's book, *Serengeti Shall Not Die*:
'Would the animals be able to go on living here? Were there enough plains, mountains, river valleys and bush areas to maintain the last giant herds still in existence? We had already noticed that large herds of wildebeest roamed outside the present boundaries of the park, and it was intended to change the borders to lessen its area. Nobody can follow these huge regiments of wildebeest and enormous armies of gazelles, and no-one knows where the hundreds of thousands of hooves will march.'

DAY 20

We have very good friends and connections (in Arusha, in the Serengeti and with Tanganyika Bush Camps) with whom we have nurtured relationships over the years. They always provide our tour groups with very useful information about where the hot spots of the migration are at the specific time of our visit.

Depending on the time of year and the specific rainfall, and coupled with the migration pattern, we will probably drive in a northerly direction for about two hours before we reach Lobo Wildlife Lodge. Everybody goes for a quick comfort break while we get the latest information from our Tanzanian colleagues at the wildlife camp. From here we can either go to the Bologonja gate on the Kenyan border or head for the ranger post on the Mara River, where we hope to see thousands of wildebeest grouping tightly together and gathering in the late afternoon on the plains and banks of the river, and also to witness a river crossing through the Mara River.

We camp wild in the middle of the migrating herds on the bank of the Mara River. Our old friend and ranger, Mr Robert, always shows us some trees next to the rapids where we can

The long road back to Ngorongoro

spend the night. The road goes through huge sisal plantations planted by a company with the name of Mohammed Enterprises. You will also see the same in the Morogoro area. Together with subtropical fruit, coffee and tea, the production of sisal forms quite an important part of agriculture in Tanzania. The night is spent camping next to the White Parrot Hotel, which has reasonable facilities.

DAY 24

Today we continue southwards through the Mikumi National Park to the Baobab Valley on the banks of the Ruaha River. The area hosts a rich diversity of flora and fauna, some of which are endemic species adapted to the unique climate and natural formations of this region. The area is surrounded by protected wilderness such as Mikumi National Park and the Udzungwa Mountains National Park. The camp site among all the baobabs is really something special and a photographer's paradise.

Camp fire at Baobab Valley

DAY 25

Today we take the winding road up the Kalongo Gorge to the highveld of Tanzania and drive via Iringa to Mbeya where we stay in the luxury of the Utengule Coffee Estate Motel on the edge of the Great Rift Valley. After camping for nine consecutive nights, the group – especially the women – will be delighted to stay in a motel again.

DAYS 26 AND 27

The group will enjoy a hearty English breakfast on the verandah before the convoy climbs out of the Rift Valley towards Tunduma, probably still one of the most chaotic and time-consuming border posts in Southern Africa. The Customs and Immigration officials know us quite well and even the 'runners'

know that the Explore Africa groups will find their own way through this labyrinth quite easily. Probably the best thing about the Tunduma border post is the fact that you can turn your watch back one hour when you reach the Zambian side, and that will compensate for the lost time!

About 300km further we take the turn-off on the dirt road to Shiwa Ng'andu – a grand English-style country house estate in the Northern Province of Zambia. Its name is based on a small lake nearby, Lake Ishiba Ng'andu, which in the Bemba language means 'Lake of the Royal Crocodile'. The house itself is also known as 'Shiwa House'. It was the lifelong project of an English aristocrat, Sir Stewart Gore-Browne, who fell in love

THE BAOBAB

There is an African tale that tells the story that God once gave a beautiful, verdant tree to an elephant. The elephant was very happy to get it, so it planted it right away and watered it every day. The next day God gave a beautiful blooming tree to a lion. The lion, too, was charmed with the gift and took care of it with a lot of pleasure. The third day God gave a totally dried tree to a hyena. The hyena was surprised and didn't know what to do with it. And then it remembered – it pulled the tree out of the earth, turned it upside down and planted it again. It became much prettier and the hyena named it Baobab.

with the country after working on the Anglo-Belgian Boundary Commission that was responsible for determining the border between what is now Zambia and the Democratic Republic of the Congo. After his death, the estate was managed by one of his daughters, Lorna, and her husband, John Harvey. They had four children, who grew up on the estate. In 1991 Lorna and John Harvey were murdered in Lusaka by three men who were caught and convicted. They were ANC members living in exile in Zambia. The ANC disavowed any prior knowledge of this and condemned the murders, and although some property was stolen, possible motives remain a matter of speculation.

In the years following the murders the house fell into disrepair. Recently, Shiwa House has been partially restored under the name Shiwa Ng'andu Manor House and has opened five rooms for paying guests. An airstrip has been built for charter flights, and the estate's remote beauty is once more

Kapishya Hot Springs

accessible to visitors. The grave of Sir Stewart rests in the extraordinary African paradise he created. Lorna and John Harvey's sons, Charlie and Mark, have reintroduced wildlife, and established a large cattle ranch. Poaching is under control, and the estate is proving to be a significant source of employment in the area.

We stay with Mark and Mel Harvey at Kapishya Hot Springs for two nights. Mark has been known to tell the most interesting stories while lazing in the crystal-clear, sulphur-free natural hot springs, sipping on an icy cold Mosi Lager (the local Zambian beer).

DAY 28

Today we join up with the Great North highway at Kapiri Mposhi. This is the main road connecting the Copperbelt with Lusaka and the south. It is our longest stretch, being almost 800km to Lusaka. We stay over with Henry and Doreen van Blerk at Eureka Farm, and arrange with them to cook up a storm for us that evening. They boast 'the best showers in Africa'. There are also chalets available for those who do not want to pitch camp.

DAY 29

After breakfast we hit the final 500km in Zambia, travelling to the world-renowned Victoria Falls at Livingstone. Our drive takes us via Mazabuka, a large sugar-producing area, and locally called 'the sweetest place in the nation'. We pitch camp at the Zambezi Waterfront before we board a river boat for a sunset dinner cruise on the mighty Zambezi.

Victoria Falls

DAY 30

After breaking camp we visit the Victoria Falls, which is approximately 1690m wide and varies in height from 62m (Devil's Cataract) to 109m (Eastern Cataract). In comparison, the Niagara Falls is 968m wide and 45m high.

From Livingstone it is about an hour's drive to Kazangula where an extremely 'border-crossing-fit' group crosses the Zambezi on the Kazangula ferry into Botswana. We continue to Kasane, where we set up camp in the luxurious surroundings of the Chobe Safari Lodge, which has an outstanding camp site and ablutions, hot-water showers, a swimming pool and a charismatic pub overlooking the Chobe River.

THE GREAT RIFT VALLEY
This is a vast geographical and geological feature, approximately 6000km in length, which runs from northern Syria in southwest Asia to central Mozambique in East Africa. The main section of the valley in Africa continues from the Red Sea southwest across Ethiopia and south across Kenya, Tanzania and Malawi to the lower Zambezi River Valley in Mozambique. Many small lakes in Ethiopia and several long, narrow lakes, notably lakes Turkana and Malawi, lie on its course. Just north of Lake Malawi there is a western branch, which runs north, chiefly along the eastern border of the Democratic Republic of the Congo. This branch of the valley is marked by a chain of lakes, including lakes Tanganyika, Kivu, Edward and Albert. (Lake Victoria does not lie in the Great Rift Valley but between its main and western branches.)

DAY 31

Today, the end of this epic month-long safari will be celebrated in true African style with a morning game drive in the Chobe National Park and a three-hour sunset boat cruise on the Chobe River.

The Chobe is very proud of, and famous for, its abundance of elephants – the highest concentration to be found anywhere in Africa. The Chobe also boasts huge herds of buffalo, a rich bird life and, not least, exquisite sunsets – an African experience not to be missed.

This Explore Africa Adventures' journey to East Africa ends in true colonial style with a seated supper in the open-air restaurant of Chobe Safari Lodge. Spirits are high and, although everybody misses their loved ones back home after a full month on the road and wants to get home as soon as possible, it is with a sense of sadness that we bid each other goodbye. A strong feeling of camaraderie has built up among the members of the group and lifelong friendships have been formed.

Colourful cloth for sale

11 Northeastern Botswana – a drive on the wild side
by Andrew Brown

TRIP OUTLINE

Our rendezvous point for this trip, and its starting point, is Maun. This trip is structured around four primary destinations:

Moremi, both inside and outside the national park

Chobe National Park

The Hunters Road

Nxai Pan and Baines' Baobabs.

The route essentially follows a clockwise direction and is concentrated in the northeastern region of Botswana.

The intention when structuring this route was to lessen, as far as possible, the number of long days of driving that can so easily follow one another, day after day, in Botswana. This facilitates the opportunity to use time productively in each destination.

SEE DETAILED MAP ON PAGE 118 ▶▶

APPEAL RATING

We are often asked why Botswana is such a compelling destination. Those who have travelled with us on this trip now know the answer to that question. The areas of Botswana that are covered in this chapter all bestow upon the traveller an implicit feeling of adventure, coupled with a compelling sense of awe and admiration for the pristine and unspoilt wilderness through which one travels. At times, it is possible to transport oneself back in time to the late 1800s and early 1900s when traders and hunters would ply their respective trades in the towns that are now the developed centres of Maun, Kasane and Kazungula while en route to the northern or southern regions of the country then known as Bechuanaland. Some of history's most famous explorers, among them Dr David Livingstone and Thomas Baines, left their indelible mark on the country. Here are a few very good reasons for undertaking this particular journey:

▶ Botswana is really the last remaining destination reasonably accessible to South Africans and, for that matter, international self-drive tourists, which can provide a completely wild and unspoilt experience
▶ The areas that we will visit are places where game runs free, unfettered by fences
▶ The raw beauty of the grasslands, pans and woodlands is awe-inspiring and is preserved to be as it was hundreds of years ago
▶ Botswana arguably holds the top spot for variety and proliferation of game and bird species
▶ The night skies display so many stars that it makes it difficult to find all but the most prominent of constellations
▶ Interesting and variable driving conditions

THE BEST TIME TO TRAVEL HERE

▶ July to October is the best time
▶ This route is probably best driven in the dry-season months between May and October – you will definitely not want to struggle with the black cotton soil which is prevalent on the Hunters Road and turns into a boggy morass during the wet season
▶ The days are pleasantly warm to hot in the June to October period, although you may be surprised to find that you need to get out an extra fleece or two in the evenings during June, July and August
▶ The summer months bring high temperatures and rain; during the months of October, November and December in particular temperatures of upwards of 35°C are not uncommon throughout the country
▶ Rainfall is higher in the Chobe Waterfront area than elsewhere, but throughout the entire region the wettest months are between November and April
▶ During the dry months game is attracted to the rivers and water holes and this generally leads to a more rewarding game-viewing experience
▶ Some of the parks, particularly Moremi, can be frustratingly difficult to negotiate in wet conditions; therefore it would be best to travel this route in the months of July, August or September

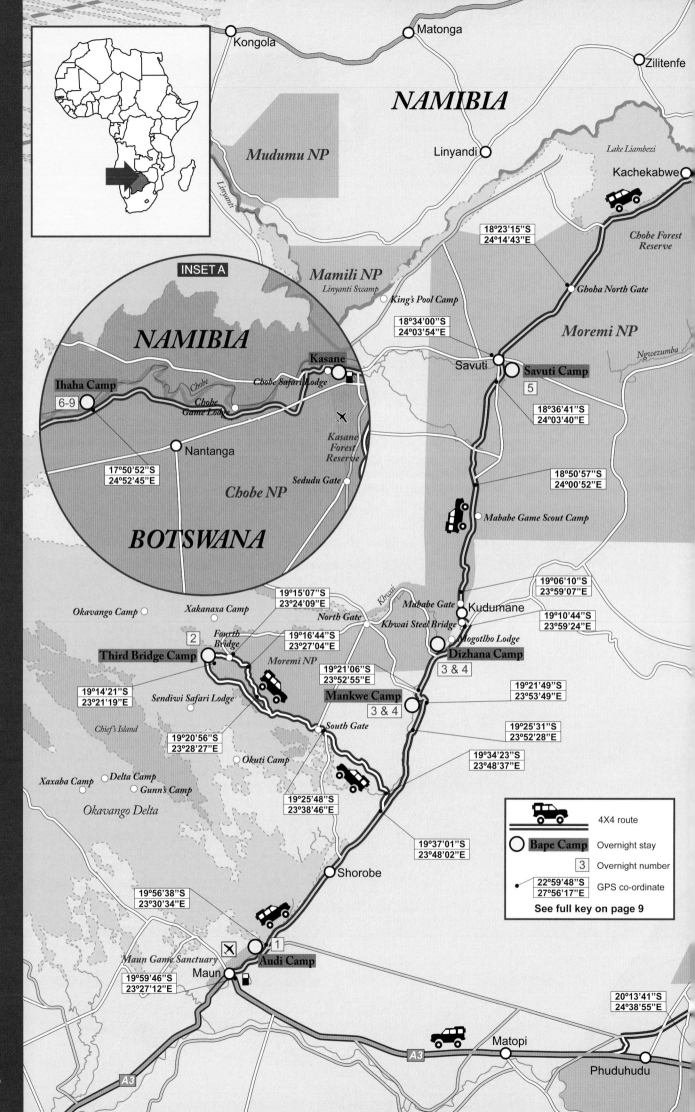

MAP 11 NORTHEASTERN BOTSWANA – a drive on the wild side

NAMIBIA

Kongola

Matonga

Zilitenfe

Mudumu NP

Linyandi

Lake Liambezi

Kachekabwe

Chobe Forest Reserve

| 18°23'15"S |
| 24°14'43"E |

Ghoha North Gate

Mamili NP

Linyanti Swamp

King's Pool Camp

| 18°34'00"S |
| 24°03'54"E |

Savuti

Moremi NP

Savuti Camp

5

Ngwezumba

INSET A

NAMIBIA

Kasane

Chobe Safari Lodge

Ihaha Camp

6-9

Chobe Game Lodge

Chobe

| 17°50'52"S |
| 24°52'45"E |

Nantanga

Kasane Forest Reserve

Sedudu Gate

Chobe NP

BOTSWANA

| 18°36'41"S |
| 24°03'40"E |

| 18°50'57"S |
| 24°00'52"E |

Mababe Game Scout Camp

Okavango Camp

Xakanaxa Camp

| 19°15'07"S |
| 23°24'09"E |

Khwai

Mababe Gate

Kudumane

| 19°06'10"S |
| 23°59'07"E |

North Gate

Khwai Steel Bridge

| 19°10'44"S |
| 23°59'24"E |

Fourth Bridge

2

| 19°16'44"S |
| 23°27'04"E |

Mogotlho Lodge

Dizhana Camp

3 & 4

Third Bridge Camp

Moremi NP

| 19°21'06"S |
| 23°52'55"E |

| 19°21'49"S |
| 23°53'49"E |

| 19°14'21"S |
| 23°21'19"E |

Sendiwi Safari Lodge

Mankwe Camp

3 & 4

| 19°25'31"S |
| 23°52'28"E |

Chief's Island

| 19°20'56"S |
| 23°28'27"E |

South Gate

| 19°34'23"S |
| 23°48'37"E |

Okuti Camp

Xaxaba Camp

Delta Camp

Gunn's Camp

| 19°25'48"S |
| 23°38'46"E |

Okavango Delta

| 19°37'01"S |
| 23°48'02"E |

Shorobe

| 19°56'38"S |
| 23°30'34"E |

Maun Game Sanctuary

| 19°59'46"S |
| 23°27'12"E |

Maun

1

Audi Camp

Legend	
	4X4 route
○ **Bape Camp**	Overnight stay
3	Overnight number
•— 22°59'48"S 27°56'17"E	GPS co-ordinate
See full key on page 9	

| 20°13'41"S |
| 24°38'55"E |

A3

Matopi

Phuduhudu

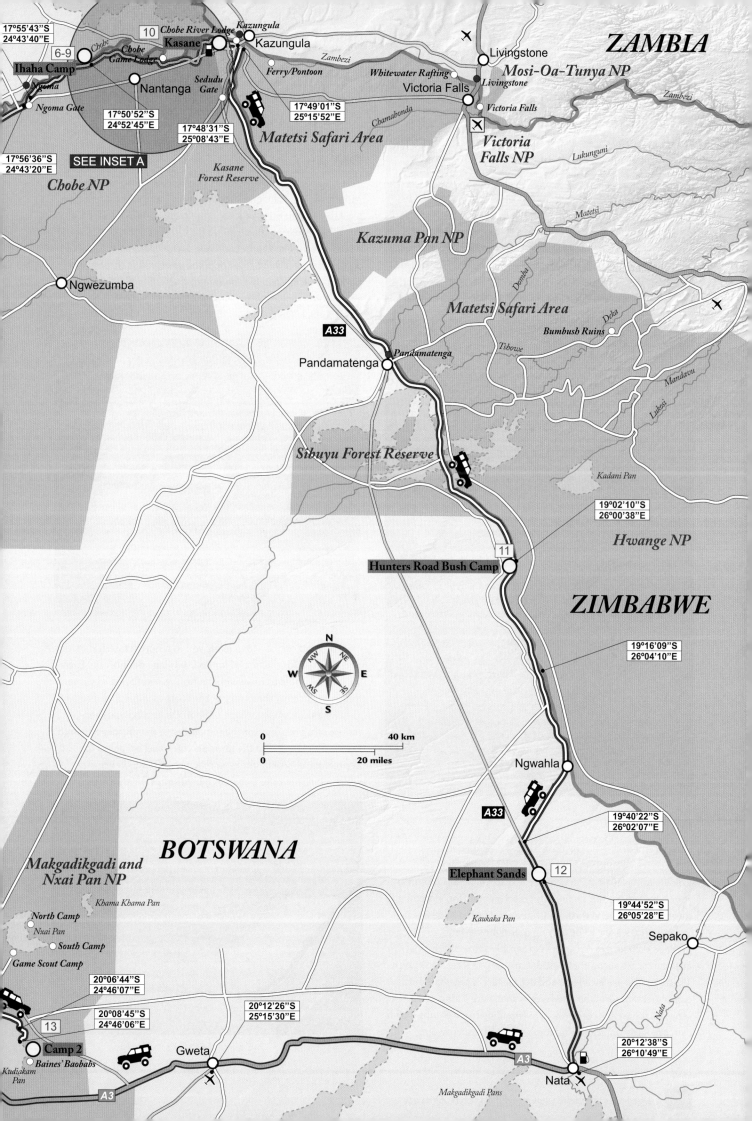

FAMILY-FRIENDLY RATING

3/5

▶ Apart from a river cruise in Chobe, there is not very much to keep young children entertained for the entire duration of this trip (of course, not all children are the same and those with an interest in wildlife will be thrilled by the never-ending variety of mammals, reptiles and birds that are sighted)

▶ Some of the driving days are quite long and the roads are rough in places, leading to long spells of rocking and rolling which can become uncomfortable, particularly for those occupying the rear seats

▶ This trip is built around camping but there are alternatives to a life under canvas in some of the places visited

SELF-SUFFICIENCY RATING

3/5

You will need to be fully independent and self-sufficient on this trip. While the towns of Maun, Kasane and Nata all provide good shopping opportunities, the days spent bush camping require that you are fully equipped. The following should be considered:

▶ At times you will be travelling quite some distance from easily accessible mechanical assistance, so your vehicle will need to be reliable and well maintained to obviate stressful mishaps

▶ Basic distances between fuel stops do not exceed 400km but allowance needs to be made for game drives in the national parks and other extraneous excursions; to be safe, carry sufficient fuel for a range of 600km

▶ A comprehensive selection of food is available in Maun, Kasane and Nata, but replenishment in-between is unlikely

▶ You can normally find adequate firewood at the roadside, either purchased from local traders or scavenged

▶ Water must generally be regarded as undrinkable but is suitable for washing, etc. (bottled water is available all over the area, there is a drinking water supply at Audi Camp in Maun – fill up your tank – and some of the hotels and lodges in Kasane will allow you to fill up from their supply if you ask nicely)

▶ Not all of the camps have flushing toilets and hot-water showers, so be prepared to do it bush-style (dig, do, burn and bury!)

DAY 1

Prior to embarking on the route that is described in this chapter, you should visit the office of the Department of Wildlife and National Parks where it is advisable to confirm your bookings and to secure day-visitor permits for Moremi and the eventual crossing through Chobe en route to Kasane.

As you are likely to be staying overnight in Maun, or perhaps even longer if you wish to sample some of the local attractions, we recommend Audi Camp if you intend to camp. The amenities are excellent, and decent fare is served in the camp's restaurant. One downside is that Audi Camp often serves as a base for commercial overlanding truck groups which can, on occasion, lead to a bit of noise and overcrowding.

Maun provides an excellent base from which to explore the southern end of the Moremi National Park, take in a mokoro cruise, enjoy a light aircraft flip over the Delta, or simply shop for the provisions that you will need for your onward journey.

DAY 2

This is a day full of choices, as once you are through the Moremi South Gate entrance you have some route alternatives available to you on your journey through to Third Bridge Camp. For the purposes of this trip, we have selected the 'direct' route which is most likely to be passable over a greater period of time during the year. During wet periods, when roads through the park may be impassable, be sure to enquire at the entrance gate whether you will be able to reach Third Bridge.

WELCOME TO THIRD BRIDGE NO SWIMMING

Crossing Third Bridge, day 2

The road out of Maun leads you in a northeasterly direction and is tarred for the first 47km to the village of Shorobe. Even so, it is advisable to drive with caution as livestock and game frequently occupy the centre of the road as if it is their property!

Once through the village of Shorobe, it is advisable to reduce tyre pressures for the remainder of the journey to South Gate. After the end of the tar road you travel on gravel for approximately 20km until you reach the Buffalo Fence, at which point the road becomes a bush track. Within just a

MAUN

Maun is the main stepping stone for those wishing to visit the Moremi National Park. Originally established in 1915, it has over the past two decades become a vibrant and well-developed town which boasts an international airport. Virtually everything you could require for a fly-in self-drive safari is available here or, for that matter, anything that you may need for your own vehicle in preparation for the trip.

Using Maun as a base, you will be able to enjoy many of the attractions of the area including flights over the Okavango Delta, mokoro trips on the Delta, and so on. There are plenty of good retail outlets, curio shops, restaurants and a fully functioning commercial centre.

Travelling through Moremi, day 2

kilometre of starting on the bush track you see the turn-off to South Gate. The gate entrance is a further 33km along the track from this point.

Sightings of elephant, warthog, giraffe, zebra and antelope are common along this route from Maun to South Gate, which makes it an interesting drive.

The layout of the roads in this park offers a wonderful variety of vegetation, ranging from dense, tall mopane woodlands to the open spaces and grasslands of the Khwai River flood plain.

Your reward for taking this journey is the vast array of game that you will see alongside the river and at the many water holes, particularly in the dry winter months. The birders will not be disappointed either.

If you are undertaking this journey in the dry season, once in Moremi you will encounter well-defined tracks, although the sand can be soft in a number of places.

One route option is to enter at South Gate, travel slowly through to Third Bridge and set up camp. The following day you can proceed to Fourth Bridge and return to South Gate via an interesting loop which eventually joins up with the track that you entered on in the morning. Alternatively you could travel via Fourth Bridge to the North Gate entrance if this is navigable. This exit point provides you with a beautiful drive along the northern side of the Khwai River. However, for the purposes of the route plan under discussion in this chapter, you will follow the road back to South Gate.

As a point of interest, we are perpetually amazed at the frequency of encounters with overseas tourists in rental 4X4s in Moremi. Invariably, even if their vehicle is well equipped and fit for purpose, their level of expertise and bushcraft is woefully inadequate. They are normally travelling alone (i.e. without a second vehicle) and have very little idea of navigation or time versus distance, and even less knowledge of emergency repairs.

DAY 3

Once you have completed the challenge of deciding which route option to take back to South Gate, you will find yourself back on the gravel road that takes you northeast to the Mababe Gate and Chobe National Park.

A worthwhile excursion before entering Chobe entails a couple of nights' stay at either Mankwe Bush Camp or Dizhana, the Mababe community camp. We have camped at both these venues and it is important to understand the difference between the two. Mankwe is a long-established bush lodge which has beautiful camp sites. The camp site names – Camel Thorn and Mopane – denote the particular vegetation prevalent in each site. Mankwe Bush Lodge has good infrastructure, including lodges, a swimming pool and bar. The camp sites are equipped with bucket showers and flushing toilets.

On the other hand there is Dizhana, which is preferred by many. This is a community-run camp site, although the nearby Mogotlho Lodge assists the Mababe community with the overseeing of the management of the camp. The camp sites are pleasantly positioned and have an ablution block with hot water provided via a donkey boiler. The downside is that the cleanliness and degree of preparation of the camp for visitors can be unreliable. At the time of our last visit the staff had 'run away', which resulted in us having to clean up the camp after the previous visitors. Help was obtained from the Mogotlho Lodge but to find the camp unprepared was an unwelcome inconvenience. However, Dizhana possesses a charm of its own and the decision to stay at either camp is well rewarded.

The road up to Mankwe is good gravel and you will make good progress. The lodge is situated approximately 2km off the main road. Even if you are staying at Dizhana it is worth paying Mankwe a visit. There is a track that runs to the north through their concession area, but do not use this route without permission.

From Mankwe to Dizhana it is a short drive of approximately 17km along the good gravel road that you turned off to visit Mankwe. The turn-off to Dizhana is not well signposted but a white-painted half-tyre marks the spot. You should arrive at Dizhana by mid-afternoon.

DAY 4

While travelling through this area you cannot afford to miss the delights that are offered by Moremi and the Khwai River areas. You can choose to retrace your steps to the road that takes you to the South Gate entrance of the reserve or, as an equally enjoyable alternative, you can follow the track that runs

Crossing the Mankwe Pole Bridge

DAILY DRIVING DISTANCE AND TIME

Day 1	Rendezvous in Maun		
Day 2	Maun to Third Bridge Camp, Moremi National Park	150km	6hr
Day 3	Third Bridge Camp to Dizhana, or Mankwe	146km	6hr
Day 4	At leisure, Moremi and Khwai River		
Day 5	Dizhana to Savuti Camp, Chobe National Park	120km	5hr
Day 6	Savuti Camp to Ihaha Camp, direct route, or	141km	5hr
	Savuti Camp to Ihaha Camp, alternative route via Kasane	249km	9hr
Days 7–9	At leisure, Chobe National Park	120km	6hr
Day 10	Ihaha Camp to Kasane	45km	3hr
Day 11	Kasane to the Hunters Road Bush Camp	186km	8hr
Day 12	Hunters Road Bush Camp to Elephant Sands (Nata district)	99km	5hr
Day 13	Elephant Sands to Baines' Baobabs	257km	5hr
Day 14	Baines' Baobabs to Maun	174km	3hr

VEHICLE REQUIREMENTS

- ▶ Four-wheel-drive with low-range transfer case
- ▶ Recovery points front and back
- ▶ Good ground clearance
- ▶ Proper off-road tyres
- ▶ Rear diff-lock or traction control an advantage

TRAILER-FRIENDLY RATING

This trip is trailer-friendly, but it is worth noting that soft sand and mud create considerable strain on the towing vehicle, so be sure that your vehicle has sufficient power and torque to keep you out of trouble.

5/5

Elephants at the Khwai River, Moremi

alongside the northern side of the Khwai River. At this point, in fact, the river forms the northern boundary of the Moremi National Park. The track eventually terminates at Moremi's North Gate entrance. During our last visit, in September 2009, a fair amount of nifty navigation was required to locate this track. The obvious route had altered quite a bit from the time of our previous visit two years earlier due to the difficulty in crossing the Khwai River at the traditional position. (We had to cross the river over the Mankwe Pole Bridge, which was, to say the least, showing signs of serious overuse.) Anyhow, these days, once you find the new steel bridge that crosses the river just outside Mababe village on the main track, the route is fairly obvious.

We have followed the Khwai River route on a number of occasions and it never disappoints. It is one of the better days of the trip and really does make you feel privileged to be able to visit such pristine wilderness that remains completely untouched by commercial enterprise.

Highlights of the game-viewing in this area are giraffe, elephant, zebra, various antelope, and diverse bird life. The riverside area is extremely pretty and offers the photographic enthusiasts some wonderful compositions.

DAY 5

The completion of the bridge across the Khwai River has certainly simplified this particular leg of our journey. You are no longer faced with the perilous plunge into the murky waters of the river where the unsuspecting have found themselves stranded and flooded after descending into a hidden hole. (Our first-ever crossing of this river was at night and was a most intimidating driving experience.)

The bridge is situated close to the village of Mababe and is on the main gravel road leading to Mababe Gate, the southernmost gate of the Chobe National Park.

Once you have completed the formalities and have passed through the Mababe Gate, the wonder of the Chobe National Park becomes immediately apparent. The track that takes you to Savuti is well defined but the depressions left by vehicles struggling with the muddy conditions of the wet season will ensure that you travel slowly. This is a good thing, actually, as you will then have time to see all the game and bird life that abounds here.

The journey from Dizhana to Savuti should be easily accomplished in under six hours, which will provide ample time for you to set up camp and relax. You may even feel inspired to take a late-afternoon game drive.

DAY 6

Once again there are some alternatives to choose from for the drive to Ihaha Camp. One route takes the eastern, longer and less-used route from Savuti, but is more interesting than the other, which follows the western side of the reserve from Savuti and exits at Ngoma Bridge at the extreme northwestern corner of Chobe. If your intention is to travel directly to Ihaha without entering Chobe via Kasane, then the western track would make more sense.

Generally the routes can be classified as follows: the western route is shorter but frequent stretches of deep sand

Final stretch before Ngoma Bridge

DAYS 7 TO 9

The Chobe National Park is one of Southern Africa's most enchanting destinations and deserves to be traversed slowly. Patience is always rewarded and the longer you spend there, the more productive your game-viewing will be.

Ihaha camp site is well maintained and well equipped. Located at the water's edge alongside the Chobe River, there are numerous shady camp sites as well as clean ablution and wash-up facilities with solar water heating.

You will not be allowed to enter Ihaha unless you have a confirmed and pre-paid booking.

Using Ihaha as a base, you will find it very conveniently situated as it affords easy access to the primary game-viewing routes through Chobe National Park.

DAY 10

This is a very short drive. Unfortunately, to travel from Ihaha to the Hunters Road without a stop-over in Kasane will compromise the Hunters Road experience and, to be fair, you will miss a lot of fun in Kasane.

The 33km to Kasane can easily be lengthened by doing some extended game-viewing. Our suggestion, however, is to time your arrival in Kasane for midday. After checking into your camp site (we recommend Chobe Safari Lodge, but there are several others listed on the internet), hit the town to stock up on fuel and other provisions so that you have enough time to get to one of the boat stations for a sunset cruise. To avoid disappointment it is advisable to pre-book these trips.

Whenever we visit Chobe we never miss the opportunity to take in a sunset river cruise. The observing of game such as hippo, crocodile, elephant, the full spectrum of antelope, jackal, giraffe and buffalo is just so different when viewed from the water. Very often you will catch sight of a lion (or lions) relaxing in the riverine bush during the late afternoon.

From a birding perspective, let us whet the appetite of those readers who enjoy birding with a small sample of good sightings: various raptors, white-fronted bee-eaters, African skimmers, yellow-billed storks, African jacana, lesser jacana, pied kingfishers, little bee-eaters, black heron, black-winged stilt, to name but a few.

For the photographically minded, excellent wildlife shots and beautiful sunsets are the order of the day.

If you wish, you can extend your stay in Kasane and take a day trip to Victoria Falls. This wonderful attraction can be viewed either from the Zambian side of the river or the Zimbabwean side. Whichever you choose, you will have a very fulfilling day. A flight over the falls in a helicopter or microlight aircraft is a truly mind-blowing experience.

DAY 11

The Hunters Road is not a track that you want to hurry. While it is theoretically possible to drive the section covered in this chapter in a single day, there really is no logical reason why you would wish to do this.

This track is still one of Botswana's gems and its real charm lies in the fact that it is little known and passes through pristine wilderness areas, most notably the Sibuyu Forest Reserve. Rather bizarrely, for most of the two-day journey along this

can slow your progress considerably. On the other hand, the eastern route is longer but the road condition is, under normal circumstances, firmer and can lead to the journey being quicker. It is worth checking with the management at Savuti Camp before departure to establish which route would be best. We have taken the eastern route and lost a lot of time negotiating wash-aways and vegetation encroaching on the track.

Before making a final decision on route selection, another consideration will be whether your stocks of fuel, water and provisions are sufficient for your stay at Ihaha. If not, a visit to Kasane for shopping will need to be part of your itinerary and it would therefore make sense to enter Chobe National Park via the Sedudu gate close to Kasane.

Whichever route you elect to follow, an early start is recommended to ensure that you have enough time for game-viewing and, if required, shopping in Kasane.

If you choose to take the direct route from Savuti along the western track you will, shortly after passing through Ngoma gate, take a left turn to the north which, after 24km, brings you to Ihaha camp site. Alternatively you can follow the tar road to Kasane for approximately 50km. After 30km, at Nantanga, you will meet the intersection with the road from Savuti which is

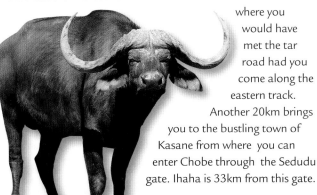

where you would have met the tar road had you come along the eastern track.

Another 20km brings you to the bustling town of Kasane from where you can enter Chobe through the Sedudu gate. Ihaha is 33km from this gate.

CHOBE NATIONAL PARK

The northern section of the park, now referred to as the Waterfront area, was during the middle of the last century a thriving timber centre. The remains of some of the logging structures are still evident in the Serondella region. Prior to that, the area was well trafficked by hunters and explorers travelling through the region.

Chobe was first declared a game reserve in 1961 and was subsequently proclaimed as a national park in 1968.

The Chobe National Park measures some 10,698km² in extent.

GENERAL WARNINGS FOR THIS ROUTE

Other than a general warning to be vigilant in the towns, where muggings are not uncommon, you should pay particular attention to the following guidelines:

▶ Sun-protection creams, hats and long-sleeved shirts are necessary
▶ Protect eyes against glare
▶ Hydrate regularly
▶ This is a high-risk malaria area – prophylactics and general precautions against being bitten must be taken
▶ Remember that wild animals are dangerous – even in the camp sites and at picnic sites in the national parks the animals abound
▶ On occasion we hear reports of harassment by officials, police and military, but in our experience the only officials who have behaved oddly were those manning the veterinary cordons – they hoped to acquire some fresh meat from unsuspecting travellers
▶ Unless absolutely essential, avoid driving at night – in the towns you will encounter some extremely odd driving habits and vehicles with poor lights, and on the open road all manner of mammals, donkeys and cattle occupy the roadway and are almost impossible to see except with powerful driving lights; even then, they run in front of you from the side of the road (this cautionary note applies equally to the main highways and to the minor roads)

SPECIFIC KIT REQUIRED FOR THIS TRIP

▶ Full camping gear, bedding, tents, table and chairs
▶ Full kitchen and braai utensils
▶ Water reserves for five days (5 litres per person per day minimum)
▶ A fridge in the vehicle is a minimum requirement, and one with a separate freezer compartment would be useful
▶ GPS, a working knowledge of GPS navigation and either the Shell Tourist Map of Botswana or the Info Map as a backup
▶ Licensed 29MHz radio
▶ Radiator seed net in spring months

ESSENTIAL REQUIREMENTS FOR THIS TRIP

▶ Compliance with Botswana road traffic requirements for towing (a ZA sticker on the trailer and the tow vehicle)
▶ Puncture-repair kit, tyre-pressure gauge and compressor
▶ Kinetic strap or rope and tow strap or rope
▶ Spade
▶ High-lift jack or inflatable airbag – one in the group is sufficient
▶ Basic tools and basic spares for your vehicle
▶ Lighting
▶ First-aid kit catering at least for sores and cuts, contusions, fractures, burns, hay fever, sore eyes, headaches, nausea, bites and stings

SEE FULL PACKING LIST ON PAGE 218 ▶▶

THE HUNTERS ROAD

What is now known as the Hunters Road began life in the late 1800s as a wagon track along which supplies and trade goods were moved between the Witwatersrand in South Africa and the Zambezi River at Kazungula.

Perhaps inspired by the reported exploits of Dr David Livingstone, the Zambezi became a place of particular interest to hunters, explorers and traders at that time. Before long the Hunters Road was a well-known arterial route from the south to the Zambezi at Victoria Falls and Kazungula.

It is documented that circa 1870 an Englishman by the name of George Westbeech established a trading store in Pandamatenga. Old George was obviously doing well as he fairly quickly expanded his operations to include two other stores in Kazungula and Leshomo. The old wagon route was progressively upgraded and became known as the Hunters Road. The present-day track follows the original route.

Aside from the game, the vegetation varies dramatically in the form of mopane forests, acacias and broad-leafed woodland. The views from some parts of the track bring home to the modern traveller just how the African continent must have looked in the days of Mr Westbeech's entrepreneurial enterprises.

Note: At the time of going to print there were rumours that the government intended to de-gazette the Hunters Road. This will mean that it will no longer carry the status of a public road. Anyone wishing to utilise this route would be well advised to check beforehand with the relevant authorities or, failing that, local businesses such as Elephant Sands.

route there are two tracks running more or less side by side – one on the Zimbabwe side, the other on the Botswana side – separated by not more than 20m.

Although progress is slow, this track is relatively easy to drive in the dry season, but not recommended in the wet season. The black cotton soil in the pans becomes like quicksand when wet, making the track virtually impassable.

A further word of caution to anyone considering this route (if you can find it) is the presence of poachers coming over the border from the Zimbabwe side. We were advised that they can be ruthless if apprehended and the 'safety in numbers rule' most definitely applies.

Access is gained near the Botswana-Zimbabwe border post at Kazungula. Once you have located the track, the route takes you through the Kasane Forest Reserve. Here, the birders and the tree-spotters will be in their element. At this stage the track

Roadside camp, Hunters Road

is good. Be alert for a couple of twists and turns and be careful not to stray across the border onto the Zimbabwe track.

Follow the track without taking any turn-offs and you will eventually cross the Kazuma Pan. From the pan it is about a further 24km to the border post at Pandamatenga. You will by now have travelled on a variety of road surfaces ranging from firm gravel to bush tracks and a firebreak.

The route south from Pandamatenga becomes even more interesting. The track continues to be variable in terms of driving surface, and fairly long stretches of this section are driven on recently formed firebreaks. Stay alert on these as often you will hit pockets of deep sand which can bring you to an unscheduled stop quite easily.

In places, for example in the section through the Sibuyu Forest Reserve, the track is overgrown and sometimes difficult to follow. If you do not have a GPS with the Hunters Road included in the map set, you will have to follow your instincts.

There are several places to make camp at the roadside. We have a particular favourite which is situated close to a water hole – a very beautiful but wild camp site. As there is always evidence of recent elephant activity all around the area, we are always careful to ensure that our tents are not pitched across tracks made by elephant heading to the water hole. Please also remember that there is an ever-present fire risk in this area, and you must under no circumstances leave your camp fire unattended or unextinguished before retiring for the night.

DAY 12

The track south continues in much the same vein as the previous day. You will be pleasantly rewarded by sightings of a vast variety of game and birds. It is worth noting that for much of the drive on the Hunters Road, Zimbabwe's Hwange National Park is your neighbour across the international boundary line. As you progress you will pass a number of interestingly named pans such as Jolley's Pan, Hendrick's Pan, Stoffel's Pan and others that give you good cause to wonder at how they got their names.

Eventually, and probably with some sadness, you will reach a turn-off at Ngwahla. This is situated 149km south of Pandamatenga. Do not expect to see a signpost – it is unlikely that there will be one. Follow this track for 23km to join the main tar road to Nata.

To reach Elephant Sands, which is situated approximately 50km north of Nata, simply turn left on the tar road and head south for about 10km, at which point you will see signs directing you to the place.

The camp sites at Elephant Sands work on a first come, first served basis, and the ever-helpful Ben Moller or one of his colleagues will make sure that you are looked after properly. If your travelling companions are in need of a bit of TLC, Elephant Sands has cottages, and a fine dining experience awaits you in the restaurant.

DAY 13

Baines' Baobabs are situated in the Makgadikgadi and Nxai Pan National Park. From Elephant Sands you will retrace your route to the Nata Road (A33) and turn south in the direction of Nata, which is approximately 50km from where you turned

Sunset over Baines' Baobabs

onto the tar. This road carries a vast amount of heavy traffic and has over time fallen into a nightmare of potholed disrepair. Efforts are now being made to repair (or rebuild) the road; nevertheless, caution is required.

Nata provides a good opportunity to refuel and stock up on provisions en route to Nxai Pan via Gweta. In Gweta you can take a detour south to visit the extremely large and impressive Green's Baobab and Chapman's Baobab. If you intend to take this detour, be advised that to visit both will be a three-hour excursion which, if not well planned, will result in a late arrival at the Nxai Pan entrance gate. However, the detour, particularly to Chapman's Baobab, is well worth the effort.

From Gweta continue west along the tar road in the direction of Maun. After 68km you will arrive at the very impressive new entrance to the Makgadikgadi and Nxai Pan National Park. The drive to Baines' Baobabs follows a sand track in a northerly direction from the entrance gate. This is usually very sandy in the dry season but becomes extremely difficult in the wet season. After 19km there is an obvious junction where you turn to the right and follow the track in an easterly direction. (If you were to continue north at this point, you would come to the Nxai Pan and the public camp site known as South Camp.) After the right turn, the road is a sand track but the compacted sand is normally very corrugated. After crossing a couple of small pans you will come to the very large and obvious Kudiakam Pan. The baobabs are situated here.

It is essential that you arrive at Baines' Baobabs in time for the quintessential sunset photographs. There are three official camp sites at Baines' Baobabs, but there are no amenities other than a long-drop toilet at each one. Our favourite is Camp 2 at which you pitch your tent under another huge baobab. The morning sunrise behind your own personal baobab trees is a truly memorable experience.

DAY 14

Today you will have plenty of time to explore the area around the baobabs and even travel up to Nxai Pan if you so wish.

The journey to Maun involves retracing your tracks to the entrance gate and to the main tar road (A3), at which you will turn right to complete the journey west to Maun, some 138km along the road.

12 Angola – scenic inland and coastal splendours

by Jurgens Schoeman with Dolf Els

TOP 10 ATTRACTIONS OF THIS TRIP

❶ The magnificent Leba Pass between Lubango and Namibe – waterfalls, cantilevered hairpin bends, numerous dramatic rock formations and breathtaking views ❷ The spectacular Tundavala escarpment near Lubango, a photographer's dream ❸ The Kalandula Falls on the Lucala River in the Malanje province; other falls are at Hunguéria, Huíla and Binga ❹ Pedras Negras de Pungo Andongo, or the Black Rocks at Pungo Andongo – enormous formations ❺ Lake Arco, a beautiful inland lake near Tombua ❻ Iona National Park, with its fascinating rock formations and ancient *Welwitschia mirabilis*, is home to the legendary Himba people ❼ The marble statue of Cristo Rei overlooking Lubango ❽ Humpata, with its rich cultural and historic legacy of the South African Dorsland Trekkers ❾ A multitude of *Welwitschia mirabilis* and baobab trees ❿ Drive on expansive beaches under sandstone cliffs, enjoy panoramic views, secluded spots, or visit quaint little fishing villages

TRIP OUTLINE

This 15-night, 16-day tour is an expedition. We will drive through towns and cities, but mostly through large parts of remote and untouched countryside. The itinerary serves as an indication of the route, but due to bad road conditions and unforeseen events the day-to-day programme may be adjusted and overnight camp sites changed at the discretion of the guide.

The tour commences at the northern Namibian town of Ruacana and ends back at the Ruacana border post. We follow an inland route via Cahama, Lubango, Humpata, Catata Nova, Huambo, Cela, Quibala, Dondo, Cacuso, Uaco Cungo and Pedras Negras to Luanda.

The return trip follows the coastal route from Luanda via Porto Amboim, Sumbe, Lobito, Benguela, Dombe Grande, Dombe Grande Pass, Lucira, Bentiaba, Baia das Pipas, Baba, Mucuio, Namibe, Flamingo Lodge and Tombua. The final leg takes us back via Namibe to Lubango and onwards to the Ruacana border post where the tour ends.

SEE DETAILED MAP ON PAGE 128 ▸▸

APPEAL RATING

★
5/5

Angola is a beautiful country with a natural splendour peculiar to its own uniqueness, despite its war-torn history. Large parts of this remote and undiscovered country are still untouched. It's a country of contrasts with an ever-changing landscape that varies from desolate desert dull to lush subtropical green; from Karoo kopjes to blue granite mountains; from thick tropical rainforest to grassy plains; and from dry river beds to rushing rivers and dramatic waterfalls.

During this 16-day expedition, you'll drive through twisty bends on mountain passes, on dirt tracks in the bush, on roads with the occasional patch of tar, and over narrow, patched-up bridges, but also on spanking new tar roads and over newly engineered bridges. In the rural areas the Portuguese influence is still visible in the remains of churches and colonial houses.

Tourist facilities are just about non-existent and you can pitch your tent under the stars every night. Although signs of a rapid recovery are everywhere, with the infrastructure being rebuilt at an astonishing pace, Angola is still a challenge, requiring patience and tenacity. This tour reflects the breathtaking scenery, which is in stark contrast to the poverty and scars of a debilitating civil war of 27 years.

The tour will show you spectacular hidden geographic gems that very few visitors have seen before. Among them are huge, bizarre rock formations, deep gorges, stunning waterfalls and amazing caves carved through the underbelly of mountains over millions of years. You'll drive through forests of towering baobab giants, but also through stunning vistas where numerous ancient *Welwitschia mirabilis* plants lie scattered across the plains. You'll have the opportunity to relax on pristine white beaches, try your luck at catching that elusive big fish, or enjoy the solitude of a dry river bed under a starry sky. All in all, you can anticipate an amazing experience that will overwhelm your senses and warm your soul. This trip will be among the greatest travel experiences of your lifetime.

THE BEST TIME TO TRAVEL HERE

The best time to visit Angola is during the cooler, drier months from the middle of April to October. The rainy season lasts from November until about February/March in the south and from September to April in the north. Travelling off the main roads is much easier during the dry season. The country is much greener during the wet months, with lots of photographic appeal because of the crisper colours, but more difficult to travel because of muddy roads and rivers being in flood. The wet conditions will have an impact on bush camping as well.

GENERAL WARNINGS FOR THIS ROUTE

!

▶ It is advisable to do this trip in the company of an experienced guide who is proficient in Portuguese and knowledgeable about areas where landmines still pose a danger; our guides are highly experienced in travelling around Angola
▶ Vehicles are fitted with radios and are in contact with each other; if you follow the rules and listen to the guide there are no major dangers
▶ You need to take preventative measures against malaria as Angola is a high-risk malaria area

MAP 12 ANGOLA – scenic inland and coastal splendours

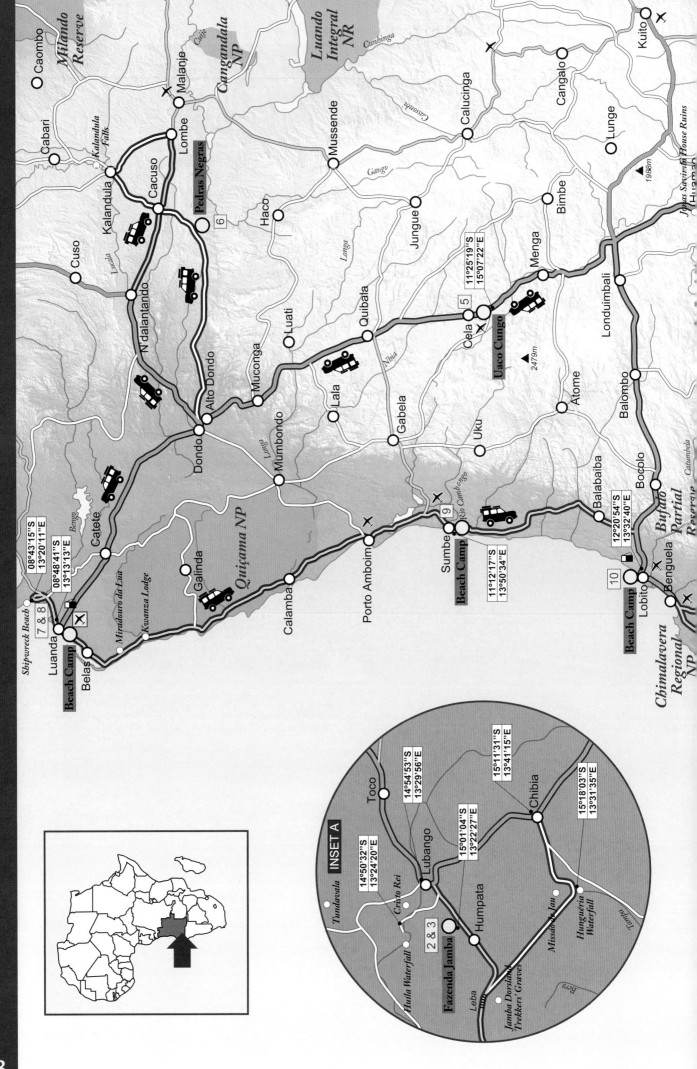

Caombo
Cabari
Cabari
Milando Reserve
Combo
Caiije
Kalandula Falls
Malanje
Cangandala NP
Lombe
Pedras Negras 6
Cacuso
Kalandula
Cuso
N'dalandando
Haco
Lucala
Lucala
Alto Dondo
Muconga
Dondo
Longa
Mumbondo
Longa
Catete
Bengo
Galinda
Miradouro da Lua
Kwanza Lodge
Quiçama NP
Calamba
Porto Amboim
Luanda
Shipwreck Beach
Beach Camp 7 & 8
Belas

08°43'15"S 13°20'11"E
08°48'41"S 13°13'13"E

Luati
Quibala
Nhia
Lala
Uku
Gabela
Rio Cambongo
Sumbe
Beach Camp 9

11°2'17"S 13°50'34"E

Mussende
Gango
Jungue
Cela 5
Uaco Cungo
Menga
2479m
Atome
Balombo
Balabaiba
Bocolo
Bufato Partial Reserve
Lobito
Benguela
Chimalavera Regional NP
Beach Camp 10

11°25'19"S 15°07'22"E
12°20'54"S 13°32'40"E

Luando Integral NR
Canhinga
Calucinga
Cangalo
Lunge
Bimbe
Kuito
Jonas Savimbi House Ruins (Huambo)
1998m
Londuimbali

128

INSET A
Toco
Lubango
Tundavala
Cristo Rei
Huila Waterfall
Chibia
Humpata
Fazenda Jamba 2 & 3
Leba
Jamba Dorsland 'Trekkers' Graves
Missão da Jau
Humguéria Waterfall
Tchivo
Bero

14°50'32"S 13°24'20"E
14°54'53"S 13°29'56"E
15°11'31"S 13°41'15"E
15°01'04"S 13°22'27"E
15°18'03"S 13°31'35"E

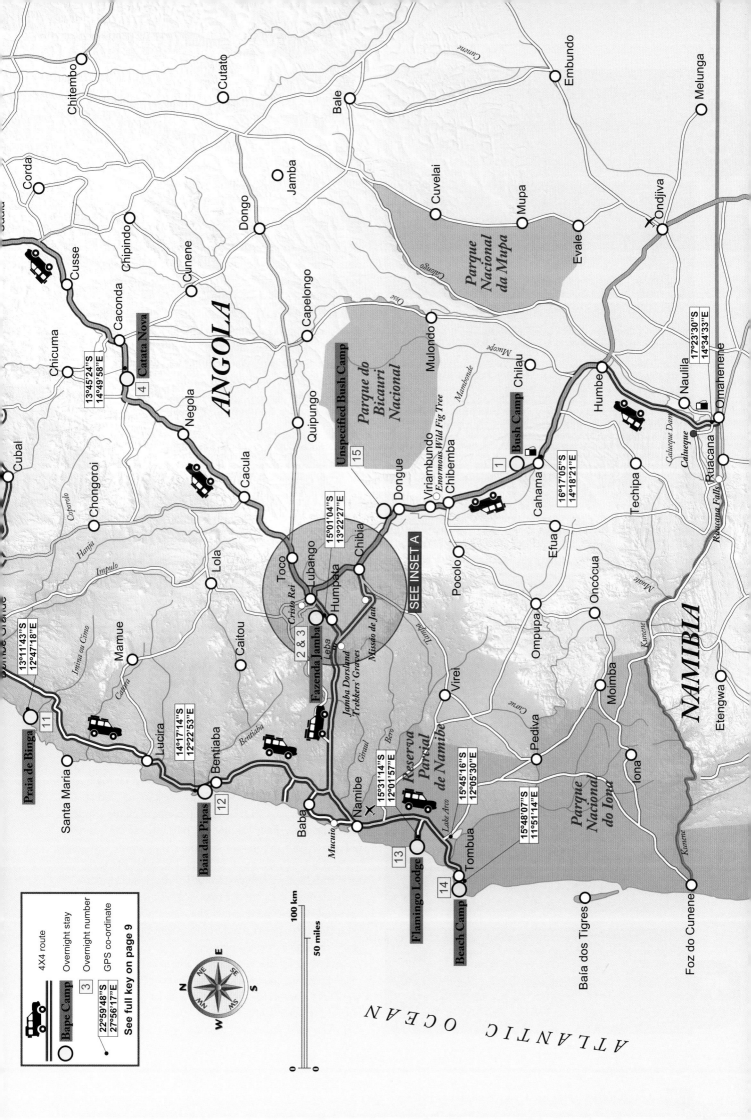

Day 1	Calueque border post to Cahama	250km	7hr
Day 2	Cahama to Humpata	300km	8hr
Day 3	Sightseeing around Lubango and Humpata	50km	4hr
Day 4	Humpata to Catata Nova	600km	8hr
Day 5	Catata Nova to Uaco Cungo	500km	8hr
Day 6	Uaco Cungo to Pedras Negras	300km	8hr
Day 7	Pedras Negras to Luanda	300km	8hr
Day 8	Spend the day in Luanda	50km	6hr
Day 9	Luanda to Sumbe	250km	5hr
Day 10	Sumbe to Lobito	300km	5hr
Day 11	Lobito to Praia de Binga	350km	5hr
Day 12	Praia de Binga to Baia das Pipas	300km	5hr
Day 13	Baia das Pipas to Flamingo Lodge	180km	5hr
Day 14	Flamingo Lodge to Tombua	250km	7hr
Days 15 and 16	Tombua to Ruacana	600km	8hr

Distances differ from day to day due to weather and road conditions, but average out to about 300km per day. We take a lot of breaks for sightseeing purposes and for refreshment or photo stops. The journey between rest camps usually lasts 6–8 hours. Departure time in the mornings differs from season to season, according to distance to be covered and sites to be visited. However, guides generally encourage a departure of 09:00 and try to reach the next camp site by around 17:00.

VEHICLE REQUIREMENTS

- A 4X4 vehicle with high- and low-range gear functions
- Vehicles will need to have a high ground clearance
- Recovery points in the front and back
- Recovery equipment such as tow ropes and shovels
- You need tyres suitable for any type of terrain
- Basic vehicle spares, such as fan belts, fuel filters, radiator pipes, etc.
- Provision must be made for a strong roof rack on your vehicle
- Two reflective triangles
- Please make a note of your vehicle's immobiliser security code, and bring spare batteries for the immobiliser
- Spare set of car keys
- Service your vehicle thoroughly before departure
- Make sure that your engine number and chassis number are clean and easily seen for border-crossing checks

TRAILER-FRIENDLY RATING

No trailers. Road conditions at times will not allow safe travel with off-road extras like trailers and caravans. However, a tour package comprising only trailer-friendly routes is available on request.

You will be travelling in your own time to Ruacana, where the group gets together. Tonight you will have the opportunity to meet the guides and your fellow travellers. You will receive a detailed briefing of what to expect during the next couple of weeks while enjoying a superb prepared dinner at one of the lodges. You will be camping tonight, but have the option to upgrade to a room should you prefer this. The camp ground has ablution facilities with hot and cold water.

DAY 1

Depart from Ruacana to the Omahenene-Calueque border post where we will cross the border into Angola. We proceed to the town of Cahama, one of the hot spots of the war where South African troops fought tough battles. We visit a former Cuban base with its underground bunkers before entering the town. In town, we drive past a memorial (in the shape of a jet fighter) honouring Angolan and Cuban soldiers, and view the abandoned military tanks and armoured vehicles, remnants of the bloody war that tore the country apart for 27 years. Just north of Cahama on the road to Lubango is a striking memorial, located at the site where the Cubans had their headquarters. A total of 117 Cuban graves lie scattered next to the memorial, some still with a simple, weather-beaten wooden cross as a headstone.

We set up our first bush camp a few kilometres north of Cahama and spend the night under the Angolan sky. (There are no shower or toilet facilities.)

Day 1, en route to Cahama

DAY 2

We drive north to Lubango and Humpata on a tar road and stop at an enormous wild fig tree next to the road at Viriambundo village to take a group photo of all the vehicles under the tree's shady canopy. In Chibia we visit the beautiful old church with its two identical spires, built by the Portuguese and still in use by the local residents. The luxury of the tar road soon ends, and we navigate our way through muddy pools and waterways on a red dirt track. We visit the breathtakingly beautiful Hunguéria Waterfall. The water thunders down a sheer cliff into a pool carved from the light-brown rock and visible through a cave-like entrance.

At Jau we visit the remnants of a flour mill and the magnificent aqueduct built by the Dorsland Trekkers. A seminary complex (Missão do Jau), with its large church, was built at the site in 1942. The school buildings, surrounding a large courtyard and central fountain, were added later.

Tonight we pitch our tents in a camping site on Fazenda Jamba, the strawberry farm near Humpata managed by a South African couple, Garry and Erica Davidson. Nearby is one of the Dorsland Trekkers' historic graveyards. We have hot showers and flushing toilet facilities and a lovely braai lapa.

DAY 3

Today we visit some of the sights in and around Humpata and Lubango. We drive the stunningly beautiful Leba Pass and spend some time savouring the magnificent view from the lookout point at the top. The pass is the gateway to the coastal plains and the city of Namibe on the Atlantic coast. We make our way all the way down and back again through the 88 twists, 36 of which are the hairpin bends for which the Leba Pass is so well known, all of them situated within a stretch of 35km. This breathtaking feat of engineering is said to have been designed by a Portuguese woman. From the plateau, at an altitude of 1845m, we go all the way down to sea level.

Humpata offers a rich cultural and historic legacy of the South African Dorsland Trekkers, who left the Transvaal Republic in 1874 to establish a farming community on the fertile plateau around the town. Friction between them and the Portuguese gradually grew – over language, schooling and religious issues – and by 1928 the entire community had moved on to Outjo in the then South West Africa. We visit remnants of their farmsteads, the memorial erected for the commemoration festival in 1957, and graveyards where the names of families like the Van der Merwes and Bothas are carved into the simple tombstones.

We also visit the serene, white marble statue of Cristo Rei (Christ the King) high up on the escarpment overlooking the city of Lubango. It is one of three in the world and is a smaller version of the famous Corcovado statue in Rio de Janeiro. The third one is in Lisbon. The statue was built between 1945 and 1950. The serene figure still has bullet marks on the face and parts of the fingers on the outstretched left hand are missing – scars left behind by the war.

We stop at the Huíla Waterfall, a short drive outside the city. Like all of Angola's stunning waterfalls, this has a charm of its own. We also visit the incredible gorge at Tundavala, a few kilometres outside Lubango. This spectacular escarpment, with its beautiful rock formations and stunning volcanic fissure, offers breathtaking views. Stand at the lookout right at the edge of the vertical cliff and look down into the narrow ravine, so deep that the bottom is barely visible. The view of a sheer drop to sea level 2300m below is a photographer's dream, with the vast green plateau stretching 130km to the coastal town of Namibe. But there is also a macabre side to this beautiful natural gem. It is said that, during the war, deserters and opponents of the ruling faction were either shot at this site and their bodies thrown over the edge, or forced to jump!

DAY 4

We leave the dirt tracks behind for now and follow the tar road north to Huambo. The road cuts through numerous small villages like Toco, where the wreck of an armoured personnel carrier still lies at the roadside. Like so many other wrecks of military vehicles across the country, it is the local children's favourite playground.

Larger towns, like Caconda, still have playgrounds built by the Portuguese, now in a sad state of disrepair. Caconda's

Twists and turns of Leba Pass

SELF-SUFFICIENCY RATING

4/5

You need to prepare well for a trip through Angola, as you will travel approximately 4500km.

▶ It could happen that fuel stations do not have any fuel, especially in smaller towns; each vehicle must carry enough fuel to be able to cover a distance of 800km between fuel stops

▶ You will be required to take along 40 litres of drinking water per vehicle as Angolan tap water and ice are not safe to drink; drinking water is available at specific well points along the route (make provision for showering and cooking as well)

▶ Firewood is available along the inland route, but not everywhere along the coast – carry bags of wood and/or charcoal for food preparation and for a great camp-fire atmosphere during the coastal part of the trip

▶ Camping during overnight stops will be mostly in the bush or on the beach, with no shower and toilet facilities

▶ Bring your own food supplies, snacks, tea/coffee and juice, wine, beer and cool drinks; fresh fruit, vegetables and *pão* (bread rolls) can be bought at roadside markets along the route, and additional food supplies are available from stores in towns and cities

FAMILY-FRIENDLY RATING

5/5

The Angola Tour offers a truly unique experience to all participants, being a one-of-a-kind adventure safari. Our emphasis is inclusivity – that means a family-friendly atmosphere to suit adults and children alike.

▶ Our tour takes you to very remote and undiscovered territory – it is geared towards combining the thrill of 4X4 driving with an exploration of many of Angola's closely guarded secrets

▶ As a family bonding experience, this tour is an absolute must; you and your family will spend almost three weeks exploring a remote and largely undiscovered African country with manifold geographic attractions

TRAVEL DOCUMENTATION

▶ South African citizens (including children) require a valid passport, as well as a visa

▶ You need an invitation letter to apply for an Angolan visa

▶ International driver's licence

▶ ZA sticker on your vehicle

▶ Vehicle registration papers

▶ Proof of vehicle insurance

▶ Travel insurance that will cover emergency evacuation

▶ Yellow fever inoculations are compulsory

▶ Take at least eight certified copies of your passport, insurance, vehicle registration papers, etc., in addition to the original documents

playground still boasts a concrete slide resembling a giraffe, but that's about all that's left. The ruins of the Hotel Turismo at the top of the traffic circle tell a story of former glory and a tourism trade from an era long gone.

The road from Cusse is a reminder of what it was like travelling in post-war Angola before the Chinese and Brazilians started rebuilding the infrastructure. It used to be a tar road in a former era, but it is difficult to spot any sign of tar now – there are more potholes than road surface! The locals have created a new dirt track next to the 'tar road' – bad as it is, it's still much easier to drive.

Tonight's bush camp is situated just a few hundred metres from the road.

DAY 5

On the road to Caála we encounter some of the notorious patchwork bridges still scattered around the country. These narrow structures are a mosaic of steel plates, iron bars, sections of train tracks, logs and whatever was available to create a passable roadway across the bridge. You have to navigate your way slowly across these precarious structures to avoid the many gaping holes. We stop at one of the numerous open-air roadside markets where fresh produce is on offer. However, stay away from the stalls laden with dried fish where the sudden wave of an arm will send clouds of flies into the air!

We visit the Capella sa do Mento, a beautiful little church on a hillside outside Caála, about 20km from Huambo. Caála's main street, like that of many similar towns, is a series of huge potholes. A long stairway leads up to the church entrance. The church is surrounded by 15 small arches, each with a painting depicting the Stations of the Cross along the Via Dolorosa. It is said that the South African Recces (Special Forces) hid under the church's floorboards while on an operation during the war.

In Huambo, former stronghold of the UNITA leader, Dr Jonas Savimbi, we visit the ruins of his house at the edge of the town. Savimbi lived in his luxury 'White House', complete with marble steps, when he established his capital here in Huambo during the civil war. The house was severely damaged in an attack by government forces during one of the the bloody battles that raged in the town.

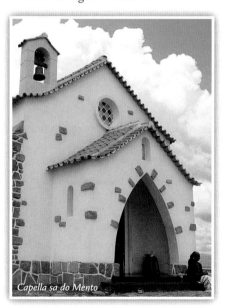
Capella sa do Mento

We leave Huambo and drive past massive blue-grey granite rock formations on our way to Cela, where we visit the beautiful church at the foot of the mountain. This town played an important role during the South African military campaign in 1975 and was also involved in battles later on during the civil war. Pockmarks where bullets struck indiscriminately are still visible on the walls and the spires.

We make our bush camp a few kilometres outside Cela.

DAY 6

We drive through Quibala, another of the towns that suffered heavily during the war, with the devastation and scars still evident. Several buildings in the town were flattened by heavy bombardment. Political slogans on some of the walls still sing Savimbi's praises. The ruins of an old Portuguese fort sit atop a huge granite rock at the entrance of the town.

The road from Alto Dondo to Dondo is in a bad state, but work on a new road has already commenced. The landscape is changing again, with more and more impressive granite hills and huge baobab trees along the route. The winding road climbs up to the escarpment through lush green tropical forests. Numerous wrecks along the road are testimony to the reckless driving of some of the Angolan drivers. Fresh fruit and vegetables are available at the many small markets along the road.

We take the turn-off at Lombe to visit the magnificent Kalandula Falls on the Lucala River in Malanje province. This is one of the largest waterfalls by volume in Africa, and it is fortunately still untouched by tourist facilities. Stand at the edge of a sharp precipice and watch the thundering waters cascade down the rock faces into a narrow gorge 105m below. Chances are good that you'll see a spectacular rainbow to complete the picture.

Kalandula Falls

The next stop will be the amazing rock formations called Pedras Negras, also in Malanje province. Tonight's bush camp will be in the shadow of Pedras Negras.

DAY 7

Today we explore the fascinating Pedras Negras de Pungo Andongo, or 'Black Rocks at Pungo Andongo'. These impressive rock formations are 35km from Cacuso on the road to Luanda. Some of them look like massive prehistoric monsters sleeping in the lush vegetation; others resemble a huge human head or a

monster frog lurking in the trees. The route now takes us to the capital, Luanda, where we'll spend the night.

DAY 8

We spend the day in Luanda, exploring the bustling city where the *zungueiras* operating amid the chaotic traffic are a part of the scenery. These colourful citizens sell their wares – everything from ice-cold cool drinks to wiper blades (which are fitted on the spot!) – on the streets. The majority of their customers are those caught in the slow-moving traffic.

We visit 'Shipwreck Beach' where more than 40 large fishing vessels were stranded by their owners when they had to flee the country during the political upheavals of the 1970s. We visit the impressive Freedom Monument on the outskirts of the city where the country's freedom struggle is depicted in a series of plaques, the last one featuring the important sitting of the International Court of Justice in The Hague. We drive past the futuristic monument that houses the graves of former President Agostinho Neto and his archenemy, Dr Jonas Savimbi, and visit the local fish market.

Tonight's camp is just off a beach renowned for the sea turtles that nest in the vicinity.

DAY 9

We are now on the return leg of our journey, which will take us south along the coastal route. We visit Miradouro da Lua, or 'Viewpoint of the Moon', a massive crater resembling a lunar landscape with spectacular erosion patterns carved into the sandstone cliffs. On the way to Sumbe we'll make a detour to the Kwanza Lodge on the bank of the Kwanza River, close to the river mouth. Optional activities include a cruise up the river. We cross the Kwanza over the modern bridge and the landscape changes again. By the time we reach Porto Amboim, the lush green scenery has become an almost dry, semi-stone desert.

We visit Sumbe, formerly known as Nova Redondo, a coastal town with historical links to South Africa's 1975 military campaign. The famous Pink House of the Portuguese governor of Nova Redondo province at the time, which was used as the headquarters of Battle Group Bravo, still stands today. Numerous mud houses line the hills on the outskirts of the town.

A few kilometres from Sumbe we visit one of Angola's hidden geographical treasures that very few visitors have seen. The Rio Cambongo carved its way through the underbelly of the mountain over millions of years, resulting in a chain of huge caves tunnelling through the mountain from one side to the other. It is quite an experience to walk through the cavernous belly of the mountain!

We proceed to a lovely deserted beach a few kilometres outside of town, where we will camp tonight.

Camping on the beach, day 9

DAY 10

We continue along the coastal route to Lobito. The numerous mud houses on the hills on the outskirts of the town resemble those at Sumbe. Lobito was an important harbour town, as it was tied to the Benguela railway line. It was also a major holiday town that housed a community of rich Portuguese families. We visit the sprawling open-air market on the outskirts of the town, and the open-air display of old steam tractors and locomotives.

We stock up at the large Shoprite before heading to our beach camp right next to the fabulous open-air Zulu Restaurant on the Golden Mile peninsula. Huge mansions from a former era of wealth and glory still line the peninsula – some old and derelict, others with new owners and a new coat of paint.

Tonight's beach camp offers the opportunity to dine at the open-air Zulu Restaurant.

DAY 11

We leave Lobito via the impressive new 438m bridge over the Catumbela River. Our next stop is Benguela, where we visit the huge Cine Kalunga, an open-air amphitheatre cinema from the 1960s, with chairs laid out in traditional style, surrounded by a beautiful garden. However, feature films are seldom shown now. The theatre is mostly used for parties and fashion shows.

We proceed to Dombe Grande. The landscape changes to semi-desert and we drive the rocky Dombe Grande Pass, which resembles the rocky desert of the Kaokoland. We follow a rocky track up the escarpment and stop at the edge overlooking the magnificent Praia de Binga with its long half-moon of white sandy beach between the blue ocean and the rocky mountains. A derelict fishing village from the Portuguese era nestles in one corner. This beautiful place is our camp site for tonight.

DAY 12

Today we visit some pretty little seaside villages where monster oysters and crayfish are usually to be found for sale on the beach. We stop at Lucira's old fishing factory from a bygone era, where the locals still spread fish on rows of wooden frames to dry in the sun. The dried fish is then stacked in layers that form huge square blocks with interesting patterns created by the alternating layers of different fish species. We visit the breathtakingly beautiful pinkish-orange sandstone cliffs at Bentiaba, with its narrow fissure carved out by the wind.

Tonight's beach camp will be at Baia das Pipas, where we'll camp right on the beach.

Sandstone cliffs at Bentiaba

DAY 13

The landscape is now mainly desert, scrub and savannah, with an arid coastal strip. The isolated beaches are ideal for fishing. We travel through some very beautiful sandstone formations to Baba fishing village and stop right at the edge of the cliffs to look at the clear turquoise water and the fishermen far below readying their nets for the next catch. We continue to Mucuio where the derelict pink mansion near the beach was once the grand home of the Portuguese harbour master. We visit the dusty fishing town of Namibe, formerly known as Moçâmedes, and drive the tar road south on our way to Flamingo Lodge, a fishing paradise. The 23km of sand track in a dry river bed leading to the coast will test your stamina and that of your vehicle, as it is a heavily corrugated track for most of the way. But everything is forgotten once you've reached the rustic lodge perched high on a sandstone cliff, where the hosts will greet you with an ice-cold beer. Flamingo, an angler's dream, is in the middle of 70km of uninhabited coastline with large fish populations, especially garrick. Those not wanting to try their hand at landing the big one could explore the spectacular sandstone canyons in the vicinity.

TEN NATIONAL PARKS, BUT VERY LITTLE WILDLIFE

The thousands of game species that roamed Angola's 10 national parks some four decades ago, among them a number of endangered and protected species, have been all but wiped out by the country's long civil war, land mines, poaching and hungry locals. Iona National Park was once known as an animal paradise. Today you'll find only a few roaming springbok.

Conservation efforts are slowly beginning to take shape, with authorities battling to reintroduce species that once roamed the country's parks. Elephants, antelope and other species are being reintroduced in the Quiçama National Park in the Kwanza River Valley. More rehabilitation programmes will follow. The rare giant sable antelope, unique to Angola, has also survived the ravages of war and is slowly growing in numbers again.

Tonight you have the option of camping among the sand dunes next to the basic ablution facilities (with hot water and flushing toilets), or you could rent one of the comfortable wooden cabins. Dinner will be a delicious seafood meal at the lodge's open-air restaurant.

DAY 14

After relaxing and enjoying the legendary fishing at the lodge, we drive onwards to Tombua. En route we stop at the vast former Cuban base with its numerous interlinked underground bunkers. It is said that Fidel Castro's elite 50th Brigade was stationed here during the final years of the war. A few kilometres further along the tar road is the turn-off to the breathtakingly beautiful inland Lake Arco. We follow the scenic road through the canyon to the parking area with its large shady trees. From there it is a short walk through the stunning rock formations surrounding the lake to a viewpoint with beautiful views.

The last stop before we head for home is Tombua, Angola's southernmost town. It is another of Angola's neglected little towns that was charming and picturesque in its heyday. The Art Deco cinema building in the middle of the town is still impressive, despite the broken windows and peeling paint. The streets, like those of many similar towns, are pockmarked with large potholes.

DAYS 15 AND 16

The last two days will be spent travelling back to the border post at Ruacana. We'll backtrack to Namibe and Lubango before heading for the border. After crossing the border it is time for sad farewells. You will be responsible for your own travel arrangements from there onwards.

13 Liuwa Plains, western Zambia

by André van Vuuren

TOP 10 ATTRACTIONS OF THIS TRIP

❶ Chobe National Park in Botswana ❷ Kabula Tiger Lodge ❸ One night's wild camping between Kabula and Kalabo ❹ Crossing the Luanginga River by hand-driven pontoon ❺ The calving season of the wildebeest in Liuwa Plains ❻ A visit to King's Pool in Liuwa Plains ❼ The ponds and the bird life in the vicinity of Liuwa Palm ❽ The ferry crossing at Mongu ❾ A cold Mosi Lager (Zambian beer) in the shebeen at Kalangola after the third and final primitive ferry crossing ❿ Farewell dinner at Nata Lodge

TRIP OUTLINE

The route will take us through northern Botswana, eastern Namibia and southern Zambia. In Botswana we will explore the northern part of the Chobe Game Reserve in our 4X4 vehicles, viewing the abundant wildlife, before going on a three-hour sunset boat cruise on the Chobe River.

We will enter Namibia at the Ngoma border post with Botswana, probably scenery-wise one of the most beautiful but also one of the most efficient border posts in Africa. We then travel through typical Namibian countryside in the Caprivi Strip before visiting the town of Katima Mulilo.

We will spend three days in the Liuwa Plain National Park. The park has a long history of animals and humans co-habiting. There are currently 432 villages in and around the park, with close to 20,000 inhabitants. Many of these people's ancestors were placed here by previous kings (*litungas*) to protect the park and the wildlife. This was regulated by a complex set of traditional laws and systems, all of which are documented, some as early as 1902. Many of these laws are still intact.

SEE DETAILED MAP ON PAGE 138 ▶▶

APPEAL RATING

5/5

A safari to Liuwa Plains in western Zambia is probably one of the more adventurous safaris that Explore Africa Adventures has on offer.

- Abundant wildlife – animals as well as birds
- Vast herds of calving wildebeest during migration season
- The legend of the lone lioness, Lady Liuwa
- Flooding of the plain
- Ferry crossings, river cruises and tiger fishing

THE BEST TIME TO TRAVEL HERE

- The wildebeest herds congregate on the plains during November
- The plains are accessible by vehicle from June to December
- For the adventurous, it is possible to access the park by canoe and on foot from February to May – contact the park beforehand to arrange boats and guides

FAMILY-FRIENDLY RATING

3/5

- We have done this safari before with children as young as eight years without any problems; there are days of long hours' driving, but if the parents stimulate the children in the car they will be fine – there is enough for children to do and to experience to give them a memorable trip
- Elderly people also do fine on this specific safari; we quite often have guests on this safari in the age bracket 70–75
- During the dry month of November the family-friendly factor would be much higher than during the wet, flooded months – camping in wet tents with mud underfoot is often impossible and never fun

SELF-SUFFICIENCY RATING

3/5

- Fuel (diesel, leaded and unleaded petrol) is available all along the route up to Katima Mulilo – you can pay for fuel in Botswana with a MasterCard or Visa credit card, and the filling stations in Katima accept Petro and Garage cards as in South Africa; once in Zambia the only fuel will be available in Mongu and sometimes in Senanga (they only accept Zambian kwacha – you can draw kwacha at the ATM in Mongu by using a Visa credit card); the distance from Katima to Mongu is around 700km and from Mongu back to Katima Mulilo 1000km – a long-range fuel tank (or jerry cans) is advisable as fuel can be very expensive in western Zambia
- We take some pre-cooked dinners and meat from South Africa, but no fresh meat – sometimes they will confiscate raw meat on the Namibian side at the Ngoma border post; one can buy good-quality meat in Katima Mulilo, and fresh supplies like bread, fruit and veggies, dairy products, etc. can be obtained in Kasane, Katima and Mongu; bottled water is also freely available in these bigger towns
- Prepare for one night's wild camping in the teak forest on the fringe of the Barotse Flood Plains; most of the other camp sites have hot-water showers and flushing toilets

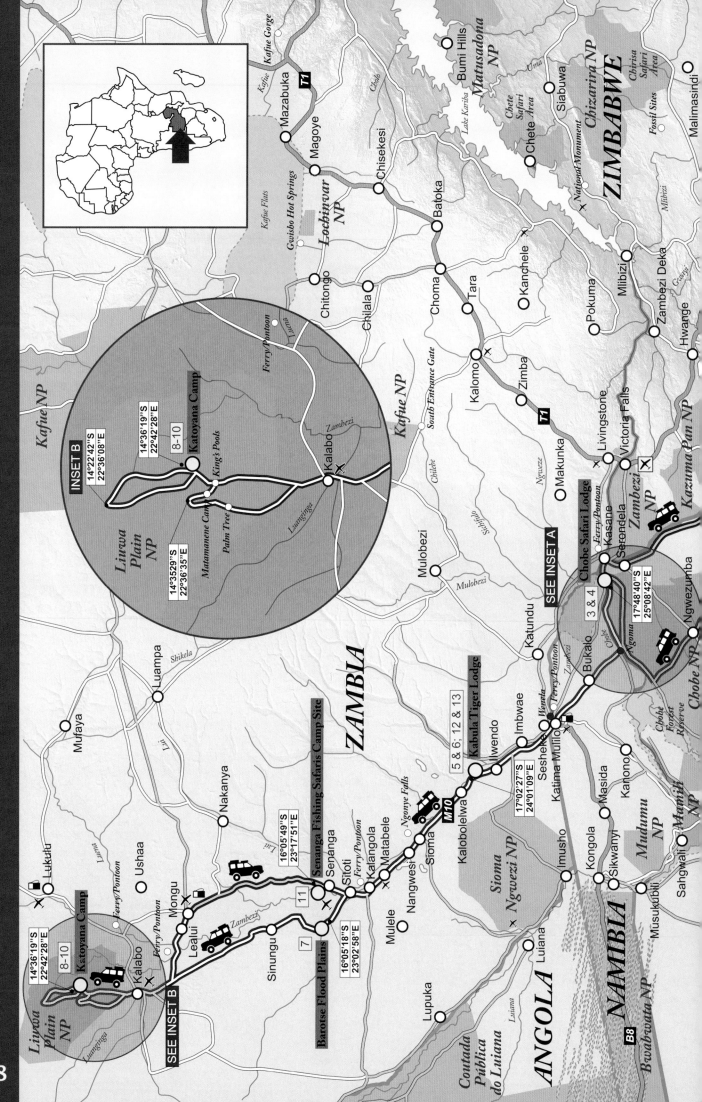

MAP 13 LIUWA PLAINS, WESTERN ZAMBIA

138

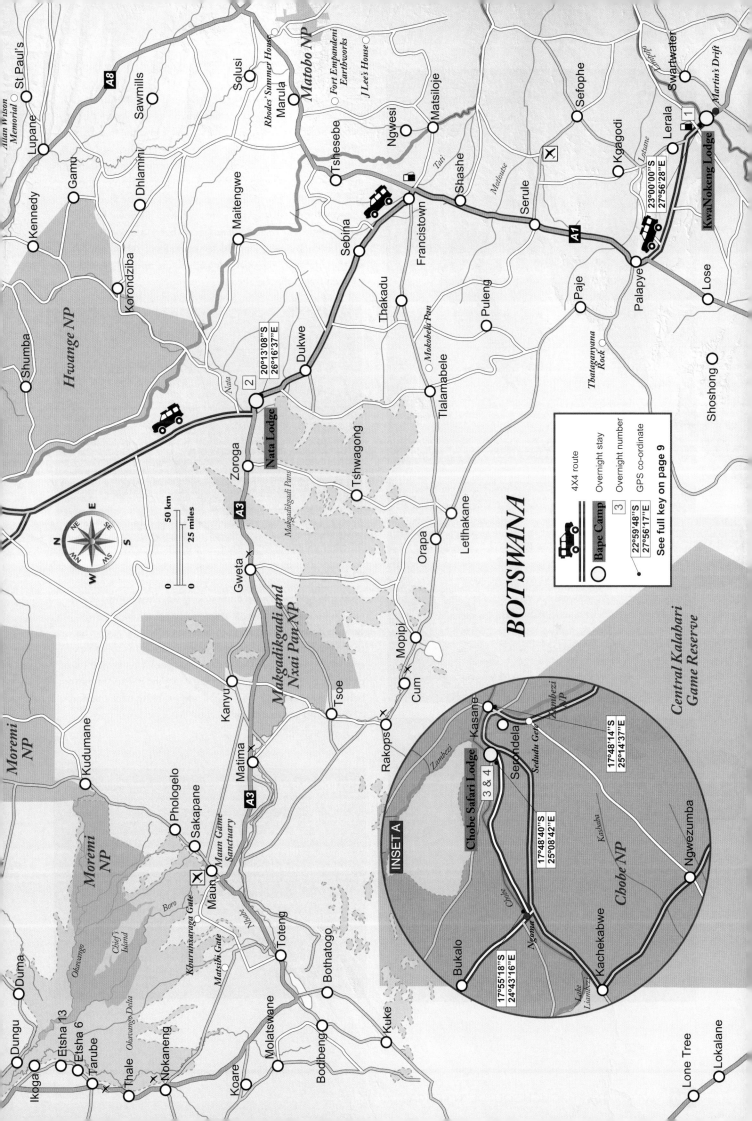

Allan Wilson Memorial ○
St Paul's ○

Lupane ○
Gamu ○
Kennedy ○
Dhlamini ○
Sawmills ○

A8

Shumba ○
Korondziba ○

Hwange NP

Maitengwe ○
Solusi ○
Marula ○
Rhodes' Summer House

Matobo NP

Fort Empandeni Earthworks ○
J Lee's House ○

Ngwesi ○
Matsiloje ○
Matsiloje ○

Sefophe ○
Swartwater ○
Martin's Drift

Kgagodi ○
Lerala ○
☐1

23°00'00"S
27°56'28"E

KwaNokeng Lodge

Tshesebe ○
Shashe ○
Serule ○

✗

Sebina ○

Francistown ○

A1

Palapye ○
Lose ○

Dukwe ○
Thakadu ○
Mokobela Pan
Puleng ○
Paje ○

20°3'08"S
26°16'37"E
☐2

Nata Lodge

Shoshong ○

Zoroga ○
Tshwagong ○
Tlalamabele ○
Thataganyana Rock ○

A3

Orapa ○
Letlhakane ○

BOTSWANA

50 km
25 miles

0
0

Gweta ✗
Makgadikgadi and Nxai Pan NP

Mopipi ○
Cum ○ ✗

Kanyu ○
Tsoe ○

Rakops ○ ✗

Central Kalahari Game Reserve

Moremi NP

Kudumane ○

Pbologelo ○
Sakapane ○

A3

Matima ○ ✗

Maun ○ ✗
Maun Game Sanctuary

Moremi NP

Okavango Delta
Chief's Island
Boro
Nhabe
Khurunxaraga Gate
Matsibi Gate

Toteng ○
Molatswane ○

Bothatogo ○
Bodibeng ○
Kuke ○

Dungu ○
Duma ○
Ikoga ○
Etsha 13 ○
Etsha 6 ○
Taruhe ○
Thale ○
Nokaneng ○
Koare ○

4X4 route
Bape Camp
○ Overnight stay
③ Overnight number
GPS co-ordinate

22°59'48"S
27°56'17"E

See full key on page 9

INSET A

Kasane ○
Seondela ○
Setudu Gate
Zambezi NP

Chobe Safari Lodge
③ & ④

17°48'14"S
25°14'37"E

17°48'40"S
25°08'42"E

Zambezi
Chobe

Bukalo ○
Ngoma ○

17°55'18"S
24°43'16"E

Kasbaba
Lake Liambezi

Kachekabwe ○
Ngwezumba ○

Chobe NP

Lone Tree ○
Lokalane ○

DAILY DRIVING DISTANCE AND TIME

Day 1	Pretoria to KwaNokeng Lodge	370km	5hr
Day 2	KwaNokeng Lodge to Nata	422km	5hr
Day 3	Nata to Kasane	300km	4hr
Day 4	Game drive in Chobe	100km	Half day
Day 5	Kasane to Kabula Tiger Lodge	175km	9hr
Day 6	Leisure day at Kabula Tiger Lodge		
Day 7	Kabula Tiger Lodge to Barotse Flood Plains	150km	8hr
Day 8	Barotse Flood Plains to Katoyana Camp (Liuwa)	150km	10hr
Day 9	Game drive in Liuwa	100km	
Day 10	Game drive in Liuwa	100km	
Day 11	Katoyana Camp to Senanga	228km	9hr
Day 12	Senanga to Kabula Tiger Lodge	155km	7hr
Day 13	Leisure day at Kabula Tiger Lodge		
Day 14	Kabula to Nata Lodge	475km	8hr

VEHICLE REQUIREMENTS

- It is essential to use a 4WD vehicle with decent ground clearance and a low-range transfer case – the sand is just too soft and deep for a 4X2 vehicle (if one has had rain before traversing the flood plains, a 4X2 vehicle will not be able to cross between Senanga and Mongu)
- Proper all-terrain tyres
- A well-organised packing system is advisable, as it is not pleasant to pack and unpack everything that you carry every time you need something
- We recommend a built-in safe hidden somewhere in the vehicle for passports, cash and important documents

3/5

TRAILER-FRIENDLY RATING

To tow or not to tow is normally quite a personal as well as a debatable issue. It is possible to tow on this specific safari to Liuwa Plains and we've had off-road trailers as well as caravans before. Travellers have to take the following into account:

- We will go through three different African countries (Botswana, Namibia and Zambia) and the cost of towing can add quite a lot to your total safari bill in terms of extra fuel and border-crossing fees (third party insurance)
- The driving conditions in November (according to us, the best time to visit Liuwa Plains) will vary from very deep and soft sand to mud and cotton soil on the Kalabu to Mongu stretch
- Do not travel without a set of spare wheel bearings as well as the tools and knowledge to replace them next to the road

DAY 1

André Van Vuuren, Director of Explore Africa Adventures and fully qualified safari guide, will meet you at the Martin's Drift border post with Botswana and we will spend the first night of our journey of discovery in the camp site at the KwaNokeng Lodge on the Botswana side (chalet accommodation is also available for those who do not want to pitch camp on the very first night of their safari – reservations can be made via Clinton@botsnet.bw). We normally have a sit-down buffet dinner under the huge *mashatu* (jackal berry) tree on the wooden deck overlooking the Limpopo River, where André will do the briefing of the upcoming adventure and set the scene for the two weeks that lie ahead.

Tented accommodation at KwaNokeng Lodge

DAY 2

After taking down camp and packing up, we will meet at the KwaNokeng Caltex filling station where we will fill up the vehicles before leaving via Francistown for Nata Lodge. The roads are good and we normally make good time to arrive early enough to plunge into the crystal-clear pool after having set up camp. Sitting around the camp fire while the red sun is setting behind the mokolwane palms will always bring back memories of this camp site on the fringe of the Makgadikgadi pans.

VALUE FOR MONEY

This is a 4000km round trip from Gauteng that takes you through Botswana, Namibia and Zambia. With lots of research and overlanding experience you can do this trip on your own, but we recommend that you use an experienced safari company and tour guide. The guide fee forms a relatively small percentage of the total cost of a safari of this nature and by using a guide you will definitely enhance the experience and add value. The learning fee when doing this safari on your own will be very close to what the guide fee would be.

Explore Africa Adventures has offered safaris to Liuwa Plains for the past 10 years and, as previous owners of Kabula Tiger Lodge, we know the area, its people and their culture extremely well.

DAYS 3 AND 4

We leave early in the morning for Kasane, a 300km trip to our stay-over venue at Chobe Safari Lodge, which is located on the lush banks of the Chobe River. This is a really beautiful camp site with clean, serviced ablutions, hot-water showers, swimming pool and a characterful thatched pub overlooking the Chobe River.

The Chobe National Park is proud of (and famous for) its abundance of elephants, the highest concentration to be found anywhere in Africa. Chobe is also famous for its huge herds of buffalo and for its rich bird life. A game drive into the park is always rewarding, and the earlier you enter via the Sedudu gate, the more time you will have to explore the park before returning to Chobe Safari Lodge to board the sunset boat cruise which leaves at 15:00. The photographic opportunities from the boat are exceptional. You are likely to see elephant, hippo, Cape buffalo, crocodile and giraffe, as well as various antelope, including sable, coming down to the river to drink. The flood plains are the only place in Botswana where the puku antelope can be seen.

Elephants in Chobe

Birding is excellent. Large numbers of southern carmine bee-eaters are spotted in season. African fish eagles are also present, and African spoonbills and various species of ibis, stork, duck and other waterfowl flock to the area when it is in flood.

After probably one of the best buffet dinners to be had in Botswana, we will spend the night in the private camp site at Chobe Safari Lodge.

DAYS 5 AND 6

From Botswana we enter into Namibia at the Ngoma border post, and we will refuel and stock up with provisions in Katima Mulilo. From here we travel via the Wenela border post to Kabula Tiger Lodge, a total distance of 175km. The last 30km could be tough going, depending on the condition of the road, and this makes for a long day. Our expected time of arrival at Kabula is in the early afternoon, as much time is spent in Katima Mulilo doing the shopping, refuelling the vehicles and, of course, crossing through two border posts.

Make sure you have enough money – in Namibia you have to pay a Cross Border Charge (CBC), and entry into Zambia is quite expensive too. There are third-party insurance costs as well as a carbon tax, a council levy and a road toll.

Kabula Tiger Lodge was developed by Explore Africa Adventures, and for the next two nights we will stay in our

GENERAL WARNINGS FOR THIS ROUTE

- This is a malaria area – take malaria prophylactics
- When going alone, take good care at border posts not to be ripped off by officials, insurance brokers and money changers (we only deal with people that we know)
- Research accommodation and camp sites properly as one can easily have a bad experience
- Stay calm and friendly at roadblocks and border posts
- Obey all park rules in Liuwa Plains
- Keep to speed limits in Botswana – trespassers have to pay heavy spot fines or bribes
- Take enough foreign currency – you can get pula at your bank in South Africa or at the Bureau de Change at KwaNokeng Lodge at the Martin's Drift border post, and you can change kwacha at the Sesheke border when you enter Zambia (you pay the ferries with local currency)

SPECIFIC KIT REQUIRED FOR THIS TRIP

- This is a self-sufficient camping trip and you'll have to take full camping gear; be careful not to take all kinds of gadgets you can do without – they just take up extra space
- Either a dome tent or rooftop tent will do
- Camp table, chairs, kitchen, braai goodies and cooking utensils
- 12V compressor-operated freezer (a dual-battery system is not a necessity)
- Water container with at least a 40-litre capacity
- When you go with us on one of our safaris, a GPS is nice to have but if you go on your own it is definitely a necessity
- On our safaris we provide each vehicle in the convoy with a two-way radio
- We will be camping wild for one night in the teak forest on the fringe of the Barotse Flood Plains and for that it can be a good idea to pack a hot-water camp shower or similar device as well as a fold-up toilet chair – these can also be of use in Kwale Camp as they only have cold-water showers
- When travelling alone, we recommend that you take along a full recovery kit – a winch is not necessary (on our safaris this is not necessary as the guide vehicle is fitted with all recovery equipment, winch and a solid tow bar)

ESSENTIAL REQUIREMENTS FOR THIS TRIP

- Fire extinguisher
- 12V air compressor and tyre-pressure gauge
- 12V lighting
- Basic tool kit and spare parts
- Tyre-repair kit
- Minimum of 10m extension cord with a British plug adaptor
- Basic first-aid kit and personal prescription medication (together with the prescription)
- Basic repair kit consisting of duct tape, cable ties, glues, wire, gas cylinder seals, etc.
- Mosquito repellent, insect killer and malaria prophylactics

SEE FULL PACKING LIST ON PAGE 218 ▶▶

exclusive camp site on the banks of the mighty Zambezi River (chalet accommodation will also be available at additional cost – visit www.kabulalodge.com for more details).

Although tiger fishing is the main activity at Kabula, other adventures could include a ride in an authentic mokoro (dugout canoe) in search of a Pel's fishing-owl's nesting site, and later perhaps an exotic island walk or a visit to a nearby cultural village. A sunset cruise on the Zambezi is a magnificent experience, accompanied by the sounds of the wild, which only Africa can provide.

DAY 7

Today we once again need to make an early start, as we have a long hard day of driving through thick sand, lots of bush and maybe even some mud. We will traverse the M10 all along the western bank of the Zambezi River, passing through the little rural villages of Kalobolelwa, Sioma, Nangwesi and Matabele. North of Matabele we will cross a small flood plain with a very suspect Double-Double Bailey Bridge before getting to Kalangola and Sitoti.

Here we will not take the ferry to Senanga, but instead we take an alternative route and turn away from the M10 in a northwesterly direction, heading for Kalabo on a small sand track that winds through some of the most beautiful indigenous kiaat and mzauli forests. This is real 4X4 stuff.

We will drive round until about 16:00 when we will start to look for a suitable place to pitch a bush camp next to the road to spend the night. In days to come, when thinking back on your safari to Liuwa Plains, this night's free camping will be one of the many highlights that will always come back to you as a fond memory.

DAYS 8 TO 10

As dawn breaks on another early African morning, we break camp and continue our journey towards the little town of Kalabo, a distance of some 300km from Kabula Tiger Lodge. On arrival in Kalabo, you have to go to the offices of African Parks Conservation where a very friendly and helpful tourism

WILDLIFE IN LIUWA

In addition to the blue wildebeest, Liuwa Plain National Park has a diversity of animal species, including tsessebe, zebra, red lechwe, oribi, reedbuck, lion, spotted hyena, wild dog, leopard and cheetah.

The diversity of grasses and plant species forms an integral part of the park's ecosystem. *Echinocloa stagnina* and *Vossia cuspidate* are grasses that are vital for herbivorous grazing. Copalwood (*Guibourtia coleosperma*), silver cluster leaf (*Terminalia sericea*), Zambezi teak (*Baikiaea plurijuga*) and weeping wattle (*Peltophorum africanum*) are species which make up most of the wooded islands found in the park.

The park boasts an abundance of bird species, particularly in the flooding season, including grey crowned and wattled cranes, marabou stork, great white pelican and brown-headed parrot, as well as migratory birds such as the Horus swift. The presence of endangered species (such as the wattled crane) and vulnerable species (like the southern ground-hornbill and martial eagle) makes this an important conservation area for birds.

LADY LIUWA

This is the extraordinary and moving true story of how one lone lioness turned to humans for companionship, who in turn tried to find her a family of her own.

It all began in 2004, when Namibian filmmaker Herbert Brauer arrived in Liuwa Plain National Park to make a wildlife documentary. As he began filming the animals from his open-topped truck, he noticed a single lioness in the distance, watching his every move. Local rangers told him that her entire pride had been slaughtered by poachers five years earlier, but Lady had somehow managed to survive, and was now the last lion left in the national park.

'I found it remarkable that she would attempt to seek the company of humans, especially as her own pride had been slaughtered by poachers – hence her enforced solitude.'

From then on, the lioness appeared to be waiting for him as he went about his work. She began tentatively following the filming truck, sitting at a distance and watching as they focused their cameras on the wildlife. Then one day she made an extraordinary move. Bounding up towards the truck, she suddenly dropped down and rolled over onto her back, purring deeply. 'I was so shocked,' says Herbert, 'that it took me a couple of seconds to realise what I was seeing. Here was a wild animal who was greeting us with an unheralded display of friendship.'

But Herbert quickly realised that there was more to this behaviour than a simple show of affection. Lady was lonely – and the film crew was her only company. 'She began to follow us each day,' he says, 'and would sit happily nearby watching us complete our filming. You could sense her contentment that she had found company at last.'

'It's the most unnatural thing in the world for a lion to be relaxed with humans around. Her only experience of humans had most certainly been a violent and destructive one – with memories of the poachers who had killed her pride. But despite this, she was willing to trust and accept us.'

Then one night, as Herbert and his crew relaxed outside the tents in their camp, they heard a noise in the bushes. Slowly but surely, Lady walked towards them. To a man, everyone froze. But Lady appeared oblivious to the tension. She simply stopped 10 yards away from Herbert, dropped down on her vast stomach, and purred deeply.

'As soon as I saw her, I was strangely unafraid,' he says. 'I somehow sensed that Lady had come into camp just to find me. When she dropped down and relaxed, we all realised that she just wanted to be near us.'

And so an extraordinary ritual began. By day, Lady would roam the wilds, always on the lookout for the film crew. At night, once they had returned to camp, she would creep in and settle down to sleep just yards from their tent. Humans had become her only comfort and, despite every wild instinct in her body, loneliness was driving her closer and closer to the only friends she knew.

The story goes on to tell of how Brauer set about the task of reintroducing male lions into the park as her only chance of companionship and motherhood.

Read more at http://www.dailymail.co.uk/femail/article-1233172/How-lonely-lioness-love-little-help-friends.html#ixzz160t4IIOJ

officer will assist with issuing the park permits and other necessary documentation.

After completion of these formalities, we cross the Luanginga River on a very old and dilapidated hand-driven pontoon. The ferry can only take two vehicles (or one car plus a trailer) at a time. Once all the vehicles in the convoy are safely on the other side, we will head for our main destination of the trip, the Liuwa Plains. This is one of Africa's last hidden secrets and we will spend the next three nights in our own exclusive tented bush camp pitched at Katoyana on one of the beautiful tree islands.

This is serious, uncommercialised Africa and a once-in-a-lifetime experience for most people. The park is open to visitors for self-drive and camping from 1 June to 31 December, and there is a limit of 25 vehicles at any one time. We will have two full days to explore Liuwa Plains and to be part of this wildlife paradise. We will drive from pond to pond and will see thousands of wildebeest with their newborn young, and there will be numerous sightings of wattled cranes, grey crowned cranes, oribi, a clan of 10 hyenas and huge flocks of rock pratincole (*Glareola nuchalis*).

But to many people, the main attraction of the plains does not lie in any of the above, but rather in tracking and finding the legendary lone lioness, 'Lady Liuwa' – undoubtedly the highlight of any safari!

Finding Lady Liuwa and her two new male companions is really not an easy task. In the Serengeti there are 4000 lions and almost a thousand game-drive vehicles patrolling the plains. If you want to see predators in the Serengeti, you simply look for a concentration of vehicles and – bingo! In Liuwa there are now only three lions, no game-drive vehicles and a thousand tree islands that can provide shelter. It's like looking for a needle in a haystack.

We saw Lady Liuwa for the first time before there were camp sites in the park. The Explore Africa group were camped at the workshop in Matamanene when she walked through the camp. Two years later we saw her again between Matamanene and the Palm Tree, and in November 2010 we were fortunate to meet her again, together with her two beautiful new male companions, in a big tree island 2km northeast of Matamanene.

Njoka Bridge

DAY 11

After an early breakfast we take down camp, do a final game drive in the park and return via the ferry to Kalabo. Remember that there are no refuse facilities in the park and so the rule applies that what you take in, you have to bring out with you again. You can leave all refuse bags at the workshops of African Parks opposite their offices and they will gladly destroy your refuse for you.

When leaving Kalabo, some good news and some bad news will be waiting for you. The good news is that we will be driving on a good tarred road. The bad news is that this heavenly

feeling will only last for about 30km before we will be dumped onto one of the worst sections of roads of this entire safari.

Crossing the Barotse flood plains was never easy. The Chinese tried to build a road between Kalabo and Mongu over the plains but it was washed away a couple of times before it was completed, and now it is worse than ever – terrible when dry and impossible in the wet season.

We drive past the village of Lealui, the capital of the Barotse Kingdom, to the ferry 25km west of Mongu. Here we cross to the eastern bank of the Zambezi River. Do not miss the *vetkoek* on sale at the many reed stalls on both sides of the river at the ferry point.

In Mongu we stop to refuel the vehicles and replenish our supplies at the well-stocked local Shoprite before leaving for Senanga, where we will be spending the evening camped at the Senanga Fishing Safaris camp site. It is slightly more than an hour's drive on a good (new) tarred road.

Liuwa, a beautiful area of vast flooded plains

TIGER FISH OF THE ZAMBEZI

There are several species of the tiger fish family, all of which are particularly prized as gamefish. These African fish are found in many rivers and lakes on the continent and are fierce predators with distinctive protruding teeth.

The southernmost species is *Hydrocynus vittatus*, commonly found in the Zambezi River and in the two biggest lakes along the Zambezi – Lake Kariba in Zambia and Zimbabwe, and Cahora Bassa in Mozambique.

Tiger fish can be considered Africa's equivalent of the South American piranha, though they belong to a completely different family, as they are famous for their ferocity when hunting. They have razor-sharp interlocking teeth and streamlined, muscular bodies built for speed. Tiger fish are aggressive predators.

A tiger fish has a gas-filled sac in its body, which it uses as a sound receiver. This transmits vibrations from the water, enabling it to detect any animals nearby and respond accordingly. A school of juveniles can tackle animals of almost any size, including any land animals that stray too close to the water's edge. Adults tend to travel in smaller groups of four or five, but they are no less dangerous. Even an individual can take down prey as large as itself. When food is scarce or the competition for food is too great, tiger fish may resort to cannibalism. This is particularly common in the dry season.

Being aggressive predators, they put up a great fight, making them popular with sport fishermen.

DAY 12

After having a steaming cup of coffee on the fishing jetty, we take down camp before crossing the Zambezi flood plain again to Kalangola where we have to do another ferry crossing from the eastern bank to the western bank of the Zambezi River. The ferry is called the *Fernando Pavaroti*.

Kalangola is quite an interesting little trading-post town and it is worth spending some time here before getting back on the (by now well-known) M10 for the final leg to Kabula Tiger Lodge, 120km further to the south. On our way we will stop for lunch at the Ngonye Falls.

Also known as Sioma Falls, being just outside the village of Sioma, these beautiful falls mark the transition point of the Zambezi River's flow from Kalahari sand flood plain to basalt dyke – the latter eventually contributing to the magnificent gorges of the Victoria Falls.

The horseshoe-shaped Ngonye Falls are most impressive due to the sheer volume of water that cascades over the staggered 20m drop. An interesting aspect is that the river flows underneath the rock on either side of the falls. It's quite remarkable to stand upon the rock, feeling and hearing the underground flow.

Directly below the falls are several rapids that make for a good day's white-water rafting, offered by the nearby Maziba Bay Lodge.

Sunset cruise at Kabula Tiger Lodge

DAY 13

By now Kabula Tiger Lodge will feel as if it is your home from home in Barotseland – one of our guests once said over the two-way radio when driving into the lodge that 'it is good to be back at Moon Base Alpha'.

The day is spent at leisure – the washing of dirty vehicles and clothes will receive the attention of the more-than-willing camp staff. In the meantime we can go tiger fishing or just relax in the beautiful surroundings of the lodge for the last time.

A sunset boat cruise is always a great way of ending your final day in Barotseland.

DAY 14

From Kabula we head south for Nata in Botswana, where we set up our last camp (alternatively you may opt for the creature comforts offered by the lodge accommodation at your own cost).

This Explore Africa adventure to Barotseland will end, as do all our other safaris, in true colonial style with a sumptuous seated supper in the open-air restaurant of Nata Lodge.

BAROTSELAND

Barotseland is a region in the western part of Zambia, and is the homeland of the Lozi people, or Barotse. Its heartland is the Barotse flood plain on the upper Zambezi River. Barotseland is still an old African kingdom and the traditional monarch of Barotseland is called the *litunga*, meaning 'keeper (or guardian) of the earth'.

Barotseland is a very poor region – it has only one tarred road into the centre, from Lusaka to the provincial capital of Mongu, and lacks the kind of state infrastructure projects found in other provinces. Electricity supplies are erratic, relying on an aging connection to the hydroelectric plant at Kariba.

14 Zimbabwe – a journey of the unexpected

by Andrew Brown

TOP 10 ATTRACTIONS OF THIS TRIP

❶ Varied off-road driving conditions – corrugated gravel, bush tracks and river crossings; easy to moderate in the dry season but technically challenging in the rainy season ❷ Experiencing the hope and optimism displayed by the residents with whom you come into contact ❸ Enjoying the colonial atmosphere of Troutbeck Inn ❹ Wide open spaces and dense mopane forests ❺ The history and construction of Kariba Dam ❻ Photographic opportunities ❼ Birders' paradise ❽ Exceptional game-viewing ❾ Seeing the beginnings of a return to normality in the national parks and witnessing first-hand the passion and enthusiasm that the staff have for the challenges that face them every day ❿ The location of the camp sites Hlaro, Mana Pools and Mandavu Dam

TRIP OUTLINE

After entering Zimbabwe via Mozambique at Sango, the scheduled primary destinations are the southern section of the Gonarezhou National Park (Mabalauta), followed by the northern section of Gonarezhou (Chilojo Cliffs area). From there the route visits the Eastern Highlands (Troutbeck Inn in the Nyanga district) and then Mana Pools. From Mana Pools the itinerary takes in Kariba and then the Hwange National Park.

This is an anticlockwise route around the country, visiting four national parks and Kariba. The varied driving, scenic beauty and remoteness of some areas visited all contribute to this being a well-balanced overlanding trip. While the driving is never 'hard core', some tracks you will encounter require concentration, and a vehicle with good ground clearance is a prerequisite.

At journey's end the logical exit point from Zimbabwe is Plumtree, which eliminates the tedious Beit Bridge border control and facilitates a relatively stress-free and speedy passage.

SEE DETAILED MAP ON PAGE 148 ▶▶

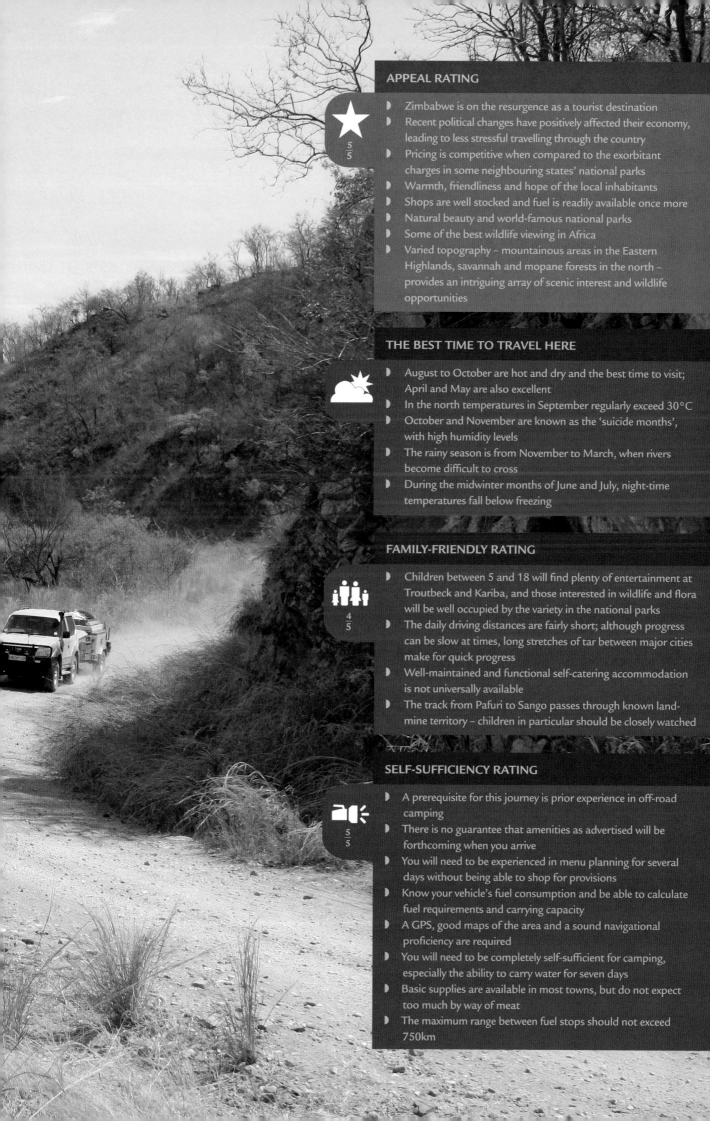

APPEAL RATING

5/5

- Zimbabwe is on the resurgence as a tourist destination
- Recent political changes have positively affected their economy, leading to less stressful travelling through the country
- Pricing is competitive when compared to the exorbitant charges in some neighbouring states' national parks
- Warmth, friendliness and hope of the local inhabitants
- Shops are well stocked and fuel is readily available once more
- Natural beauty and world-famous national parks
- Some of the best wildlife viewing in Africa
- Varied topography – mountainous areas in the Eastern Highlands, savannah and mopane forests in the north – provides an intriguing array of scenic interest and wildlife opportunities

THE BEST TIME TO TRAVEL HERE

- August to October are hot and dry and the best time to visit; April and May are also excellent
- In the north temperatures in September regularly exceed 30°C
- October and November are known as the 'suicide months', with high humidity levels
- The rainy season is from November to March, when rivers become difficult to cross
- During the midwinter months of June and July, night-time temperatures fall below freezing

FAMILY-FRIENDLY RATING

4/5

- Children between 5 and 18 will find plenty of entertainment at Troutbeck and Kariba, and those interested in wildlife and flora will be well occupied by the variety in the national parks
- The daily driving distances are fairly short; although progress can be slow at times, long stretches of tar between major cities make for quick progress
- Well-maintained and functional self-catering accommodation is not universally available
- The track from Pafuri to Sango passes through known land-mine territory – children in particular should be closely watched

SELF-SUFFICIENCY RATING

5/5

- A prerequisite for this journey is prior experience in off-road camping
- There is no guarantee that amenities as advertised will be forthcoming when you arrive
- You will need to be experienced in menu planning for several days without being able to shop for provisions
- Know your vehicle's fuel consumption and be able to calculate fuel requirements and carrying capacity
- A GPS, good maps of the area and a sound navigational proficiency are required
- You will need to be completely self-sufficient for camping, especially the ability to carry water for seven days
- Basic supplies are available in most towns, but do not expect too much by way of meat
- The maximum range between fuel stops should not exceed 750km

MAP 14 ZIMBABWE – a journey of the unexpected

148

ZAMBIA

ZIMBABWE

BOTSWANA

Kafue Flats
Mazabuka
Mana River Mout
Kafue Gorge
15°44'35"S
29°23'12"E
8-13
Nyamepi Camp
Gwisho Hot Springs
Chirundu
Lochinvar NP
Fossil Forest
T2
Marongora
Makuti
16°11'19"S
29°09'42"E
Fort Monze
and Cemetery
T1
14-17
Makuti
Travel Lodge
Caribbea Bay Resort
16°30'17"S
28°57'30"E
Kariba
Carara Safari Area
16°35'25"S
29°05'08"E
16°32'09"S
28°48'17"E
Choma
Lake Kariba
16°48'28"S
29°06'03"E
Tashinga Camp
Matusadona NP
17°05'15"S
29°03'07"E
Bush Camp
18
Chete Safari Area
Siabuwa
17°11'18"S
28°28'39"E
Sanyati
Ngweze
17°41'40"S
27°25'53"E
Madzivazido
Zambezi
18°00'16"S
27°09'29"E
Binga
National
Monument
Chizarira NP
Chirisa Safari Area
Sessami
Livingstone
Mlibizi
Zambezi
Sebungwe
Seoni
Mosi-Oa-Tanya NP
Victoria Falls
Victoria Falls NP
Mlibizi
Umi
Victoria Falls
Deka
18°07'56"S
27°04'20"E
Fossil Sites
Zambezi NP
18°20'49"S
26°30'11"E
Kamativi
Sengwa
A8
Kazuma Pan NP
Hwange
Lutope
Cross Roads
18°29'17"S
26°55'15"E
Kana
ZIMBABWE
Sinamatella Camp
Matetsi Safari Area
19
Dete
Gwayi River
Mandavu Dam Camp
22
Shangani
Allan Wilson Memorial
Mbaze Pan Sanctuary
20 & 21
Hwange Main Camp
Godfrey Huggins Bridge
Shumba
Lupane
Nkayi
Crossroads
SEE INSET B
Noel Hunt Bridge
Gwei
18°43'49"S
26°57'03"E
Hwange NP
A8
Bembesi
20°09'10"S
28°34'56"E
Moffat's Old Mission
Nsiza
A5
BOTSWANA
Dhlo Dhlo Ruins
Makgadikgadi Pans
Natta
Tsholotsho
Khami Ruins
20°23'29"S
28°30'27"E
Insiza
Fort Rixo
Memoria
20°32'41"S
27°43'44"E
20°22'32"S
28°19'23"E
Bulawayo
Mbalabala
INSET B
Rhodes'
Summer House
Mzilikazi Memorial
Filabu
18°20'49"S
26°30'11"E
Plumtree
A7
Matobos Hills Lodge
Hwange
Manzamnyama
Siloxwane Cave
Kamativi
A8
Plumtree
Matobo NP
Matetsi
Safari Area
Sinamatella Gate
Cross Roads
18°29'17"S
26°55'15"E
Mangwe Fort
20°29'42"S
28°29'15"E
Gwanda
19
Sinamatella Camp
Gwayi
River
Cave of Hands
Mandavu Dam
Picnic Site
18°35'07"S
26°18'55"E
Dete
Hwange Gate
20 & 21
18°40'24"S
26°20'15"E
Francistown
A1
Shumba
Tshompani Dam
22
Nyamandhlovu
Viewing Platform
Hwange Main Camp
Tati
Shumba
Picnic Site
Hwange NP
18°43'49"S
26°57'03"E
Serule
Motloutse
Tuli Safari Area
Selebi Phikwe
Tuli

Bape Camp   Overnight stay

3   Overnight number

22°59'48"S
27°56'17"E   GPS co-ordinate

4X4 route

See full key on page 9

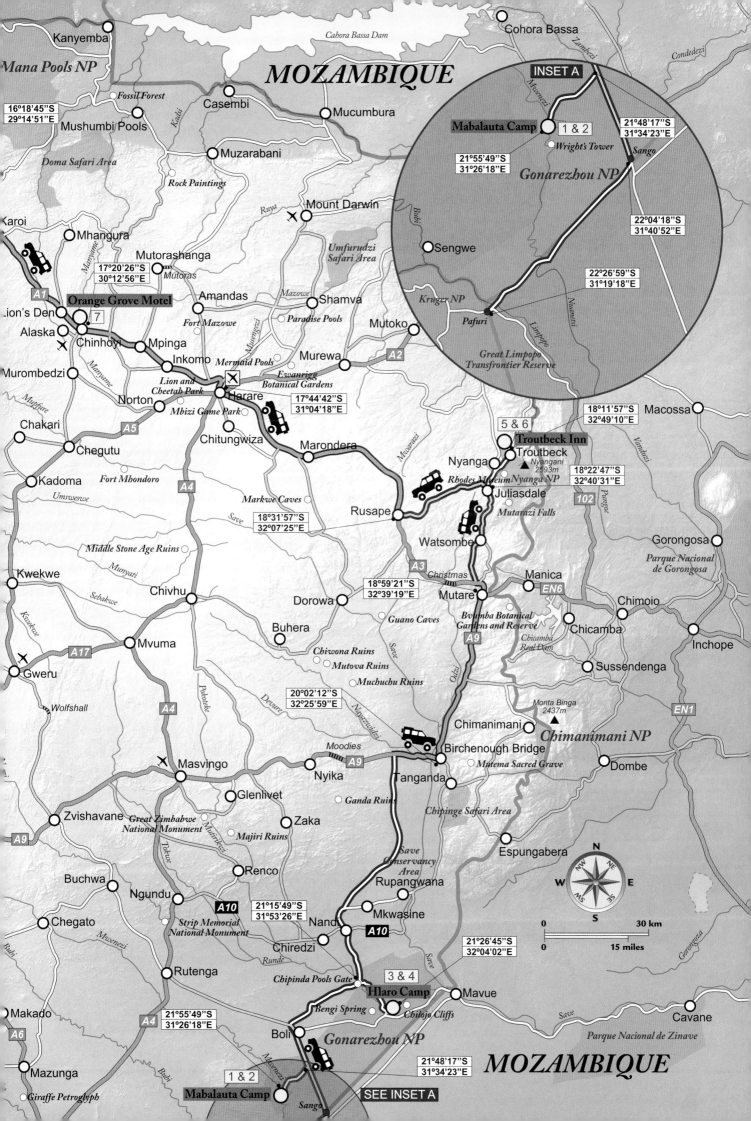

DAILY DRIVING DISTANCE AND TIME

Day		Distance	Time
Day 1	Travel from Punda Maria to Mabalauta, Gonarezhou National Park	155km	9hr
Day 2	At leisure around Mabalauta		
Day 3	Travel from Mabalauta to Hlaro Camp, Gonarezhou National Park	148km	6hr
Day 4	At leisure in Chilojo Cliffs area		
Day 5	Hlaro Camp to Troutbeck Inn	491km	8hr
Day 6	At leisure, Troutbeck Inn		
Day 7	Troutbeck to Chinhoyi, including buying provisions in Harare	398km	8hr
Day 8	Chinhoyi to Mana Pools	275km	6hr
Days 9–13	At leisure, Mana Pools National Park		
Day 14	Mana Pools to Kariba	167km	4hr
Days 15–17	At leisure, Kariba		
Day 18	Kariba to bush camp outside Matusadona	212km	7hr
Day 19	Bush camp to Sinamatella	396km	10hr
Day 20	Sinamatella Camp to Mandavu Dam Camp (long route)	54km	4hr
Day 21	At leisure, Mandavu Dam area		
Day 22	Mandavu Dam to Hwange Main Camp	106km	5hr

VEHICLE REQUIREMENTS

- ▷ Four-wheel-drive with low-range transfer case
- ▷ Recovery points front and back
- ▷ Good ground clearance
- ▷ Proper off-road tyres
- ▷ Rear diff-lock or traction control an advantage

TRAILER-FRIENDLY RATING

5/5

This route is trailer-friendly, and purpose-built off-road trailers will be fine.

- ▷ The route is generally on Grade 2 dirt roads and tracks with some long stretches of tar
- ▷ In Gonarezhou and along the route from Kariba to Hwange there are steep inclines and declines, so braked axles are essential

DAY 1

An early departure from Punda Maria is recommended as two border crossings and negotiating the Limpopo River lie ahead.

The journey through the Kruger National Park to Pafuri follows a tar road for most of the way, but once across the border, you have a short drive on a sandy track to the river. En route you pass through an impressive fever tree forest which provides welcome shade while you reduce tyre pressures in preparation for the river crossing.

Before launching into the water, take time to walk all possible lines across the river to be able to select the most favourable line to cross.

The track up to Chicualacuala is a mixture of sand and gravel but the driving is fun as it runs alongside the railway line for most of the distance. The ever-present signs demarcating areas still considered to be landmine hazards bring a grim reminder of the bloody conflicts that have taken place in this part of Mozambique. The remains of a water supply pipeline and other related infrastructure can be seen along the route, but there is little evidence that this pipeline is working.

The border formalities on the Mozambican side are no problem, but at Sango, on the Zimbabwean side, the normally quiet immigration post can become very crowded on Thursdays. The problem is caused by 'Thursday shopping day', with people returning by the busload after a cross-border shopping spree. (Don't use Sango on a Thursday afternoon.)

Once the border formalities have been completed, you turn right onto a tar road which you follow for approximately 30km, at which point you will find the turn-off to the Gonarezhou National Park. A few twists and turns and you soon arrive at Mabalauta, the southern entrance to the park. After checking in, the trip to the camp site is less than a kilometre.

Mabalauta Camp

GONAREZHOU HISTORY

The Gonarezhou National Park is a park of two halves and its name means 'The Place of Many Elephants'. It is likely that there were a great many more elephants at the time it received its name than there are nowadays, but you will still see plenty.

Together with the Kruger National Park, Gonarezhou forms part of the Great Limpopo Transfrontier Park, resulting in the free migration of animals throughout the area.

In the southern part of the park the topography tends to be relatively flat, while the northern area of the park is hillier and is famed for the Chilojo Cliffs.

Crossing the causeway to Chipinda Pools

As you sit with your sundowners by the camp fire in the evening you should be able to look back on an eventful but satisfying day's travel.

DAY 2

The Gonarezhou National Park is split into two halves, simply referred to as the northern and southern areas, respectively.

Your base in the southern area will be Mabalauta, named after a species of hardwood tree found in the area. The camp site, positioned adjacent to the Mwenezi River, is well maintained and spotlessly clean. If there is no water in the ablution block, arrange with the camp manager to have a drum of water delivered so that you can bucket-flush the toilet.

According to Zimparks, the area hosts lion, leopard, cheetah, buffalo, giraffe, zebra and many species of large antelope, with nyala and the rare suni also resident. While game is not abundant in the south, you should have good sightings of impala and elephant – and birders will not be disappointed.

There are some very pleasant drives out of Mabalauta. Although fairly corrugated, the driving is easy. A worthwhile drive takes you south to Wright's Tower, where there is a picnic site, a hide and a viewpoint offering spectacular views over the Mwenezi River.

DAY 3

To reach the northern area of Gonarezhou, the route takes you out of the park to Boli, whereafter you re-enter at the Chipinda Pools gate. This road is gravel and corrugated in places, but the driving is easy. Shortly before arriving at the entrance gate, stop and inspect the broken bridge over the Runde River – it was washed away in the floods of 2000. The route to the Chipinda Pools gate now detours across a couple of low-level causeways. These are easily negotiated in the dry season but could be problematic during the wet season, when you would probably have to enter the park through the northern gate via Chiredzi.

You will be warmly welcomed at the gate by a helpful receptionist who will direct you to either the Chipinda Pools Camp, close to the reception area, or one of several exclusive camps located at the side of the Runde River below the Chilojo Cliffs. There are a number of exclusive camps to choose from in this area of the park. Hlaro, Fishans, Directors and Chilojo camps all provide spectacular views of the Chilojo Cliffs.

From the gate, follow the track to the north of the river to Hlaro Camp, approximately 35km from reception. This track is rough in places, which makes the formal enforcement of the 40kmph speed restriction unnecessary. Allow two hours for this leg of the journey as you will want to stop along the way to take in the views, and you have to cross the Runde River to gain access to the southern bank, where the camp is situated.

On the way through to the Chilojo Cliffs area it is worth visiting the Chipinda Pools main camp to enjoy lunch by the river. You will find clear evidence of hippo activity close to the riverside camp sites. Elephant droppings in the camp provide a timely reminder that you are in a wild part of the country.

Hlaro Camp is equipped with a long-drop toilet but no water or other amenities. Plenty of shady trees make life comfortable during the day's heat. The Runde River runs alongside this camp site and you should see plenty of game activity from the comfort of your camp chair. Sundowners, with the reddish-orange hues of the Chilojo Cliffs just across the river, are special in this beautiful place.

DAY 4

Game drives from Hlaro are usually productive with good sightings of elephant, impala, hippo and kudu – and birders are well rewarded for their patience too. The river bed is covered by the spoor of numerous mammals, and pods of hippos bask on a nearby sandbank.

For an afternoon excursion, visit the Chilojo Cliffs viewpoint – a must-do activity on any itinerary through this area. The red sandstone cliffs are a well-known feature of the park, and a track takes you onto the top of the cliffs from where you can enjoy the breathtaking view across the lower flood plain of the Runde River. On a clear day it is possible to see the confluence of the Runde and Save rivers some 30km to the east. Look out for two nesting Verreaux's eagles on the cliffs.

Chilojo Cliffs

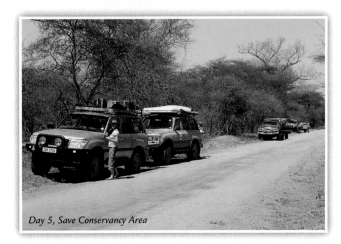

Day 5, Save Conservancy Area

The cliffs are particularly beautiful when viewed from the camp site at sunset – they take on a reddish-orange hue, making for great photographs.

Crossing the Runde River

DAY 5

The destination on this day is Troutbeck Inn in the Nyanga region of the Eastern Highlands. This is a fairly long day as the drive from Hlaro Camp to the entrance gate will take you a minimum of one-and-a-half hours.

Leaving Gonarezhou through the north gate of the park, you could follow the gravel road via Nandi and Mkwasine to join the A10 highway and on to Rupangwana, where you turn north onto the highway to Mutare via Birchenough Bridge. However, the gravel road leading to the A10 is a much more enjoyable drive. By following the gravel road, rather than taking the A10 highway all the way from Nandi to Birchenough Bridge, you have a more interesting day. The road passes through Mkwasine, which lies in the heart of the sugar belt. As you travel between Nandi and Mkwasine, you will notice the run-down condition of the once productive sugar-cane farms.

As always, the road surface is corrugated in places and, if travelling in convoy, it will become a bit strung out due to the dust. Your decision to take this route will be rewarded, however, as the drive passes through the Save Conservancy Area with a fair amount of game and bird life along the way. The track north of Mkwasine, where dense mopane forests and numerous varieties of acacia trees abound, is particularly pleasant.

This gravel road joins up with the A9 about 35km west of Birchenough Bridge. The bridge was completed in 1935 although it was altered to accept a wider carriageway in 1984. At the time of construction it was, at 329m, the third longest single-arch suspension bridge in the world.

From Birchenough Bridge the route to Troutbeck Inn is tarred all the way. As you leave the town follow the A9 north to Mutare, which is reached after about 145km. Be alert for speed traps as you negotiate the sometimes chaotic traffic in this town. Mutare provides a good opportunity to refuel. After following the Harare road (A3) for a short distance, take the right turn to Juliasdale, which is reached after 88km. Continue north towards Nyanga. After 20km, shortly before reaching the town, there is a well-signposted right turn to Troutbeck.

The delightful Troutbeck Inn, developed by Colonel Alfred MacIlwaine, has not lost any of its charm despite the hardships of the past decade, and it is reassuring to see that the fire in the reception still burns. Legend has it that the fire was first lit when the hotel opened in 1951 and has not gone out to this day. Well, that's what they say!

After several days of bush camping, you'll really appreciate a hot shower and a couple of nights in a soft bed. If, on the other hand, you are hardened camping purists, there are a number of camping sites in the area and also in the nearby Nyanga National Park.

DAY 6

The Nyanga National Park offers visitors a multitude of activities, including trout fishing, hiking, sightseeing and bird-watching. Mount Nyangani, at 2593m the highest point in Zimbabwe, is located in the park and presents a pleasant, moderately strenuous climb to its summit. The views of the surrounding area from the summit of Mount Nyangani make the climb worthwhile.

A number of impressive waterfalls are within easy reach. The Mutarazi Falls are the highest in Zimbabwe and reputedly the second highest falls on the African continent.

'Culture vultures' may be interested in visiting the Rhodes Museum, which is housed in a section of Cecil Rhodes's Summer Lodge.

DAY 7

Leaving the comforts of Troutbeck Inn, a sense of excitement builds at the prospect of moving on to the next destination, Mana Pools. The route is tarred all the way to the overnight stop in Chinhoyi and backtracks along the road to Juliasdale. Following the signposts to Rusape, you connect with the main road (A3) after approximately 100km. Be very alert on this stretch of road as there are a number of narrow switchbacks in which trucks habitually cut across the apex of the bend. Evidence of previous accidents lies scattered all over the slopes below the road at these places.

You will pass through the once economically strong areas of Mashonaland East where massive grain silos now stand as monuments to what once was.

Even if you do not intend overnighting in Harare, it is still well worth pausing for a couple of hours to stock up on essentials (such as tonic and Zambezi beer) and take advantage of the best shopping you will encounter on the entire trip.

It is advisable to call at the Zimparks office (difficult to find as it is out of town) to confirm your onward bookings at Mana Pools. This office is the only facility where you are able to book an exclusive camp in Hwange. This cannot be done at the Hwange park offices.

Again, be continually alert for the innumerable trucks that traverse the country on this arterial route to the north of Harare and be careful not to delay your departure from Harare too long or you risk driving the last hour or so in the dark en route to Chinhoyi. This is not recommended.

There is a decent overnight camp site behind the Orange Grove Motel in Chinhoyi. The ablutions are clean and there is electrical power until they turn off the generators. Hopefully you'll cope with the neighbouring dogs barking throughout the night, an insomniac cockerel, and the droning noise of a thousand trucks on the nearby Route A1.

DAY 8

From Chinhoyi you follow the main A1 northwards. This road is heavily populated with large trans-continental trucks travelling between Harare and the Zambian border. Accidents involving trucks and light vehicles are a daily occurrence. Stay vigilant!

After travelling through Karoi and Makuti, you are required to call at the Zimparks office in Marongora to pay park entrance fees. This office works efficiently and it should not take you long to get to the park entrance gate and onto the 80km road up to the Mana Pools Camp.

Much has been said about the poor condition of this road. It is badly corrugated – you will probably start out at about 30kmph, then try 40kmph and then 50kmph until you realise that there is no speed that you can travel at safely without being shaken to pieces. Our advice is to reduce tyre pressure, proceed slowly and enjoy the scenery, arriving at Mana Pools after approximately two hours.

Mana Pools consists of a main camp site (Nyamepi) situated on the southern bank of the Zambezi River, and several exclusive camps to the west and east of Nyamepi. It is possible to pre-book specific sites at Nyamepi, each site accommodating two or three camping units.

Eastern Highlands

MANA POOLS NATIONAL PARK

Mana Pools is a world-renowned UNESCO World Heritage Site. The name derives from the Shona word for 'four', referring to the four pools (inland from the Zambezi River) that were formed thousands of years ago as the river cut its way through the area. These four pools are rejuvenated each year during the rainy season.

Mana Pools boasts the largest populations of hippo and crocodile in the country.

One of the biggest attractions of this park is that you are allowed to leave your vehicle freely, either in the company of a guide or unaccompanied.

The remoteness of this true wilderness area takes you back in time to when the African continent was pristine, and it will leave an indelible mark on your memory.

As the exclusive camps are remote and private, they offer no amenities whatsoever, other than a long-drop toilet, and you are limited to two camping units per site. The sites are not close together so a group of more than two vehicles will be split up if you elect to use the exclusive camps.

The prime camp sites on the edge of the river bank are protected by large fig trees that provide welcome shade from the 38°C temperature. Large mammals are regular visitors to the camp, and elephants regularly wander through it, seemingly uninterested in either your presence or your antics.

Camping in this wild environment is awesome and one of the really great experiences of the whole journey. However, be warned that there have been numerous incidents at Mana Pools of unwary campers having unpleasant, sometimes fatal, encounters with the local wildlife. A resident pack of hyena makes no secret of its presence, and buffalo also frequent the camp. Lion are not uncommon visitors either, particularly at night.

Elephant encounter, Mana Pools camp site

DAYS 9 TO 13

The time you spend on game drives is normally very productive here as the vegetation is not very dense and large areas of the park are accessible, open grassland. The view site at Mana Mouth is positioned at the confluence of the Mana and Zambezi rivers, which makes for good sightings of crocodile, hippo and water birds.

The days at Mana Pools quickly fall into a pattern. An early-morning game drive, back to camp for breakfast, a few household chores, a short nap, lunch, another short nap, and an evening game drive before returning to camp for a wonderful meal with friends around the camp fire. Mana Pools creates a relaxed ambience between you and your surroundings and you can expect wonderful sightings of all the usual culprits (elephant, buffalo, lion, impala, kudu, zebra, a myriad bird life, etc.). If you are lucky, you may even see a pack of wild dogs.

Although Mana Pools camp is well managed, it suffers from the effects of a shortage of funds, and basic services are intermittent; the rule is to carry out your own rubbish. The roads in the park are in need of maintenance, being rutted and potholed in many places.

The ablutions in the Main Camp are kept clean, but problems with water supply can cause congestion during peak times, especially school holidays.

DAY 14

Eventually, and with heavy hearts, the day dawns when it is time to leave Mana Pools – but many magic experiences and locations lie ahead.

The road out of Mana Pools is the same one by which you entered, and the corrugations are no less annoying in this direction than they were on the way in!

After exiting the park at the junction with the A1, you backtrack about 25km or so to Makuti. At the intersection with the road to Kariba town you find the Makuti Travel Lodge, a fascinating survivor from the distant years of colonial Rhodesia. A quaint sign hanging in the bar advertises 'Free Beer ... Tomorrow'.

The tar road to Kariba snakes its way down the escarpment and into town where you'll find a host of camp sites – or you can elect to stay in time-share cottages at the Caribbea Bay Resort. Now we are talking luxury – blow-dry and manicure, fresh bream in the restaurant, and a beautiful pool to combat the 40°C temperature. With apologies to purists who may think overlanding is severely compromised by the presence of luxury, we maintain that three days at Caribbea Bay are really restful and always prove to be a worthwhile interlude on a long trip such as this.

For those who simply cannot bring themselves to sleep anywhere except under canvas, there are several camp sites in Kariba. The MOTH camp site is usually well maintained.

Looking across the Zambezi to Zambia

Luxury at Caribbea Bay Resort

DAYS 15 TO 17

Kariba is an interesting, if not unusual, town. Established when the dam was constructed in the late 1950s, the town has prospered from the burgeoning fishing industry and, of course, tourism. Sadly, the events of recent years took their toll on the town as tourism numbers dwindled to almost nothing. Being situated far from the main centres of Harare and Bulawayo made it impossible for locals to visit in the days when fuel was in short supply and probably resulted in Kariba being even more negatively affected than other tourist centres. The famous ferry which plied between Kariba and Mlibizi was closed for business several years ago. Prior to that, you would be lucky to get a booking unless you booked several months in advance. The good news is that the ferry is now running again (only one vessel, not two as before), so it is possible with good planning to travel down the lake instead of taking the drive to the south of the lake via Binga.

The dam wall is easily accessible, and the collage on the Zimbabwean side provides interesting statistics about the dam.

It is easy to imagine that you are sitting by the sea when you are at the lakeside. From most vantage points land is not visible on the opposite horizon, and the numerous kapenta boats out on the lake complete the illusion of a marine setting rather than a freshwater lake.

KARIBA DAM

The Kariba Dam was designed to generate hydroelectric power for Zambia and Zimbabwe. The dam wall, the southern power cavern and the generation station were constructed between 1956 and 1959 by Italian contractors. The northern power cavern was undertaken in 1977.

In Kariba's old town, where the construction workers and staff were housed, stands an open-sided Roman Catholic Church. Within the church a monument commemorates the workers who died during construction. Each one is listed by name.

The dam boasts some impressive statistics. The lake is over 280km in length and 32km at its widest point, with a surface area of 5580km^2. At maximum retention level it contains 180.6 billion cubic metres of water. Mean daily evaporation is 23 billion litres.

The well-documented Operation Noah initiative (to rescue the mammals, reptiles and birds that became marooned on the islands that the rising waters created) was launched as the dam began to impound in 1959. Continuing through to 1963, this operation saved the lives of more than 5000 animals.

The turn-off onto the required track is located some 20km back along the road to Makuti. A reliable GPS with good mapping, if not an experienced guide, is needed to ensure that you take a series of left and right turns correctly. At one particular point you travel beneath the power lines carrying electricity generated by Kariba's turbines to other distribution centres elsewhere in the country. The track is obviously used as a service road.

Eventually the track enters the lower levels of the escarpment and then climbs gradually along a well-made but rough track to the top. The scenic quality of this track cannot be overstated. Although the route is widely condemned as being rough and slow going, once you are in the groove you

DAY 18

From the busy town of Kariba our next destination is tranquil Hwange. While it is technically possible to do this in a single day, it is unlikely that you would want to as, quite apart from the poor condition of the road in many places, the journey deserves your spending some time along the way admiring the scenery and observing rural life in Zimbabwe.

The Zambezi downstream of Kariba Dam

cannot help but enjoy the experience. Unsurprisingly you encounter very few vehicles during this entire day. Those that you do are invariably 4X4 overlanders, like yourself, or the occasional hunting vehicle.

Along the way you cross dry rivers, climb out to the top of the next hill and once again descend down into a valley and another dry river.

Eventually, after about four hours, you come to an intersection with the Karoi–Binga Road. You turn right here onto what appears to be a well-graded gravel road. This does not last long and you soon encounter potholes, corrugations and dongas, slowing your pace.

Unless you intend going up to Tashinga in the Matusadona National Park, which is normally about three hours' drive from the Karoi road, there are no other formal places to camp in this area, so try to find a place to bush camp close to the entrance to the park.

That evening one tends to talk excitedly of the day's journey.

DAY 19

Your journey today will take you from your bush camp to Hwange National Park. The road conditions are much the same as those of the previous day, and you will pass through several villages where you again witness life in rural Zimbabwe. The road gradually improves as you approach the tar road to Binga, and you should be able to make good progress over the last 80km to the turn-off.

At the tar road you can turn right towards Binga, which is some 18km off the road to the north, to visit this little lakeside town. Fuel is normally available here should you need to top up your tanks.

A left turn here takes you along the tar road which joins the main road (A8) at Cross Roads. At times you will find yourself wishing for the gravel road that you have just left rather than the potholed tar! Generally speaking, this is much easier on the suspension than the track known as the Karoi road.

Along the way you pass the turn-offs to Mlibizi (where the Lake Kariba ferry operates) and Deka. At Cross Roads you turn right and follow the A8 for 50km to the town of Hwange.

It will probably be mid-afternoon when you reach Hwange, providing ample time to refuel and for a bit of grocery shopping (there is a reasonably good Spar) before setting out for the national park. A short way back along the A8 you will find the turn-off to the Sinamatella entrance gate of the Hwange National Park.

Interestingly, the road to the park entrance gate passes through a very large coal mine which provides fuel for the Hwange power station.

As always, there will be a cheerful warden at the Sinamatella office to check you in, and you will camp in a beautiful camp site on the edge of an escarpment overlooking the plains below. Again the ablutions are only partly functioning but, as has been the case at all the parks, there are obvious signs of improvement. The camp workers and management are trying to achieve so much with so little.

There are several cottages for hire, but only a few are functional. There is, however, a refurbishment programme in progress.

DAY 20

If you wish, you can make today a very short drive as the distance to the next camp, Mandavu Dam, is only 17km. Alternatively, you can do a game-drive loop which eventually becomes a 54km journey. This track is badly eroded in places and gives the trailer-towers a bit more of a challenge.

You will be pleasantly surprised on arrival at Mandavu Dam picnic site where, by prior arrangement with the Harare office, you can obtain permission to camp. By way of explanation, in Hwange National Park you can arrange to camp, at extra cost, in what are generically called 'platform sites'. These are effectively hides on stilts that have been erected in open veld next to water holes or small dams. The idea is that you set up camp around the platform and then, if you wish, sleep in the elevated platform.

These platforms are a good option, but very basic. Needless to say, the wildlife around the water hole will be very exciting at night. Don't sleep with your feet hanging out of the tent – you might lose them!

The Mandavu Dam picnic site differs greatly from the platforms, as the hide and ablution buildings are constructed of stone, not timber. Set at the edge of Mandavu Dam, the hide is a substantial structure of stone and thatch and is perched on the bank of the dam about 2m above the water. The camping spots are level and neatly tended by the camp staff. The ablutions are generally pristine and a donkey boiler provides continuous hot water to the shower. Several trees offer welcome shade.

Sunset over Mandavu Dam

Elephant, Hwange National Park

DAY 21

Game-viewing in this area of the Hwange National Park requires some patience, but it will be rewarded with good sightings of elephant, buffalo, impala and other large antelope. Of course, lion, leopard and cheetah are resident throughout the park, and sightings of these are not uncommon.

Perhaps the most enjoyable experience at Mandavu Dam is to sit in the hide and just watch life go by. Large herds of elephant, buffalo, giraffe, zebra, kudu, eland and waterbuck just simply come to visit and, once they have satisfied their thirst, continue on their way in sedate contentment.

DAY 22

This is the final day of the trip and a time to reflect on the experiences, sights, scents and sounds of the previous three weeks' travelling through this beautiful country and its friendly, peace-loving people.

You rise early, shortly after dawn, and sit, coffee in hand, in the hide at Mandavu Dam feeling, about as relaxed as is possible. In front of you, about 5m away, a hippo bathes in the water. Two crocodiles glide slowly across the dam, presumably in search of the perfect spot to turn some unsuspecting mammal into breakfast. You catch sight of a colony of yellow-spotted hyrax. A bit further away, on the bank of the dam, four zebra come to the water to drink. There is a proliferation of birds, most notably dozens of Meves's starlings in their bright blue plumage.

You come to the conclusion that all the mammals, birds, reptiles and insects that are sharing this moment with you are just doing their thing, just like you are.

And so the trip ends as you make your way through Hwange to Main Camp before heading home.

Modern-day Zimbabwe is full of unexpected but wonderful surprises. With a correct and respectful appraoch to the country's officialdom, Zimbabwe will be kind to you and freely offer up its delights with few hassles and at an affordable cost.

Footnote: For those travelling south from Hwange via Bulawayo, the Matobo National Park is well worth a visit. Stunning scenery, perennial streams and unusual rock formations set the scene. Within the park there are a number of accommodation options. The Matobos Hills Lodge has beautifully appointed rooms, and wonderful food cooked over an open fire in the lapa. The Plumtree border post is an easy two-hour drive from here.

EXCLUSIVE CAMPS

The exclusive camps throughout Zimbabwe's national parks give you sole right to the facility for the full time of your booking.

They are also described as 'undeveloped camps', as they have no amenities other than a long-drop toilet, but offer a secluded and private camping experience to those who can manage without a formal infrastructure.

In Mana Pools in particular, the exclusive sites are fairly small and accommodate only two camping units per site.

15 Southern Mozambique – tropical paradise on Africa's eastern coast

by Hugo Potgieter

TOP 10 ATTRACTIONS OF THIS TRIP

❶ Tropical atmosphere and rustic camp sites ❷ Varied off-road driving conditions – jungle tracks, coral sand, sand dunes and dirt roads from moderate to technical ❸ The taste, affordability and diversity of local cuisine and seafood; amazing off-the-beaten-track Portuguese restaurants ❹ Varied activities and fun for the entire family ❺ Beauty of the tropical jungle and coastal forest reserves ❻ Pristine coastal bays and coral-reef systems ❼ Photographic opportunities and cultural history of the area ❽ Snorkelling (almost aquarium-like conditions), diving and fishing paradise; very good diving infrastructure and facilities ❾ Long and deserted beaches with clear air, blue skies and lukewarm ocean ❿ Friendly and helpful local people

TRIP OUTLINE

From the city of Maputo – including its famous fish market, botanical gardens, old castle and a steel house designed and built by French engineer Gustave Eiffel – we progress north up the coast to Manhica, previously known as the heart of the cashew and orange production district.

Then we continue to Xai-Xai, where the wide Limpopo River basin is 10km wide and the backstreet restaurants are well worth a visit. We go further northwards to the town of Inhambane, a quaint colonial town where a strong Portuguese influence exists all around and a trip on a dhow sailing vessel across the bay to the town of Maxixe is a 'must-do' experience.

We explore the many coastal bays south of Inhambane, with their rustic camp sites or luxurious developments, and set up a base camp at Paindane, from where we easily access the surrounding area's attractions.

Circling southwards back to Maputo, we commence the more challenging 4X4 part of the trip to Ponta Malongane and Ponta do Ouro, encountering numerous coastal bays and sand dunes en route. South of Maputo the area is sparsely populated, comprising the Maputo Elephant Game Reserve and a few secluded bays, all protected by dense coastal foliage. The tour ends far too quickly at the Kosi Bay border with South Africa.

SEE DETAILED MAP ON PAGE 160 ▶▶

APPEAL RATING

5/5

- The allure of Mozambique's warm, azure blue sea and coral reefs
- Sandy tracks winding through tropical jungle, coconut palms and coastal bays
- Friendly Portuguese villages with lovely markets to browse around
- Rustic camp sites with direct off-road access to the beach
- Tasty and affordable foods – freshly baked *pão* (bread rolls), spicy peri-peri chicken, prawns and *couta*, not to mention ice-cold *cerveja* (Dois M and Laurentina beers) and cashew nuts
- Diversity of the landscape and the rich architecture of old Portuguese villages
- Adventure activities, from swimming with dolphins and whale sharks to scuba diving and big-game fishing
- Romantic sunsets make for great memories and photo opportunities

THE BEST TIME TO TRAVEL HERE

- March to April and October to November are best
- The peak summer months are hot and humid, although best for game-fishing, scuba diving, bird life and tropical fruit; mosquitoes are most active during warm summer months and early February rains
- Twice a year (February and August) the changes in trade winds create tropical cyclone and storm conditions, causing major river systems to flood
- For snorkelling, good availability of cashew nuts, prawns and fresh fish, March–April is distinctly the best time to visit
- The winter months are cool and fine and October–November is pleasant too

FAMILY-FRIENDLY RATING

4/5

- Mozambique has plenty to attract and entertain a wide range of ages; good communications with your tour guide should create the correct expectations
- Malaria, cholera and other tropical diseases are a real danger, so the elderly and infants especially must be watched
- Consult your doctor or travel clinic with respect to malaria preventative options and required inoculations
- Bear in mind that hospitals are very far apart, so think carefully before bringing children younger than 18 months into this area
- The elderly could suffer from the extremes of temperature
- Although this is mainly a camping trip, alternative accommodation is available at all of the places where we stay
- Pleasure craft such as boats and rubber ducks add to your enjoyment of the Mozambique experience

SELF-SUFFICIENCY RATING

3/5

At all times you will be within three hours' drive of help should an emergency situation arise.

- Fuel is available along the route
- Local markets sell vegetables, fruit (in season), canned food, cleaning materials, utensils, cool drinks, beer and spirits
- Potable water is available at most of the camps, except in Maputo, where it is recommended that you boil the water and/or use sterilisation tablets or fluids
- All camps have hot showers and flushing toilets
- All camps have 220V electricity; a 20m electric lead is useful

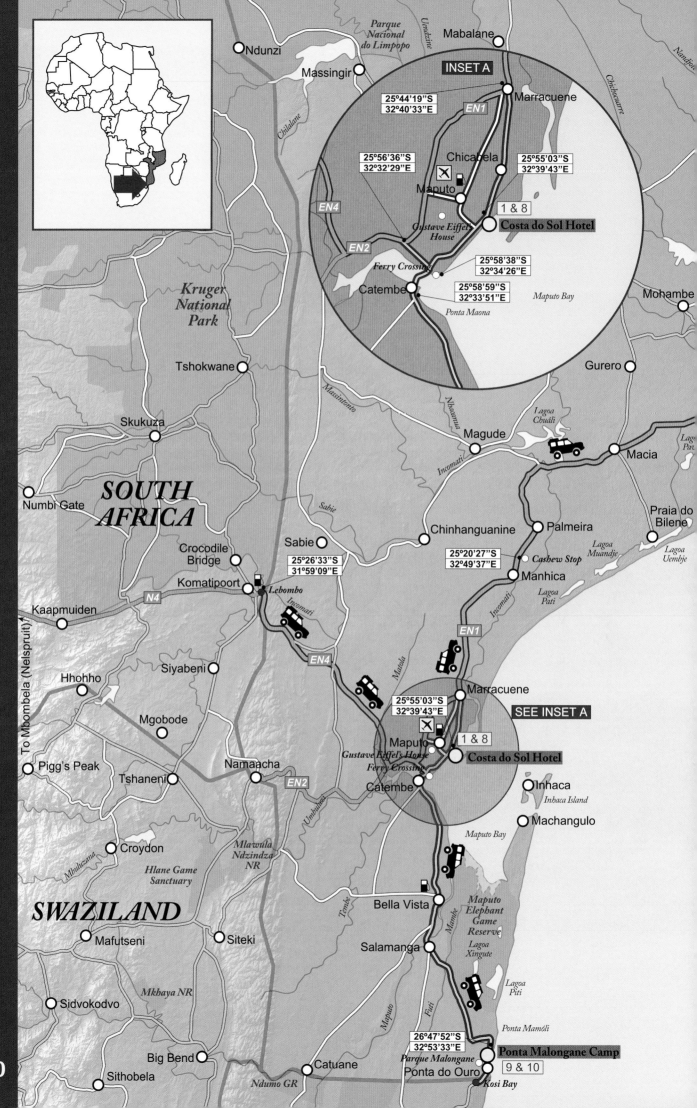

Ndunzi

Massingir

Parque Nacional do Limpopo

Mabalane

Chichocuarre

Nandon

INSET A

25º44'19"S
32º40'33"E

EN1

Marracuene

25º56'36"S
32º32'29"E

Chicabela

25º55'03"S
32º39'43"E

Chidane

Maputo

EN4

1 & 8

Costa do Sol Hotel

EN2

Gustave Eiffel's House

Ferry Crossing

25º58'38"S
32º34'26"E

Catembe

25º58'59"S
32º33'51"E

Ponta Maona

Maputo Bay

Mohambe

Gurero

Kruger
National
Park

Tshokwane

Massintonto

Nhaozuia

Incomati

Lagoa Chuáli

Magude

Macia

Lage Pati

Skukuza

Sabie

SOUTH
AFRICA

Numbi Gate

Chinhanguanine

Palmeira

Praia do Bilene

Lagoa Muandje

Lagoa Uembje

Crocodile
Bridge

Sabie

25º26'33"S
31º59'09"E

25º20'27"S
32º49'37"E

Cashew Stop

Incomati

Manhica

Lagoa Pati

Komatipoort

N4

Lebombo

Incomati

Kaapmuiden

EN4

EN1

Matola

Siyabeni

To Mbombela (Nelspruit)

Hhohho

Mgobode

25º55'03"S
32º39'43"E

Marracuene

Maputo

SEE INSET A

1 & 8

Costa do Sol Hotel

Pigg's Peak

Namaacha

EN2

Gustave Eiffel's House
Ferry Crossing

Catembe

Inhaca

Inhaca Island

Tshaneni

Umbuluzi

Machangulo

Maputo Bay

Croydon

*Mlawula
Ndzindza
NR*

Mbuhzana

*Hlane Game
Sanctuary*

Tembe

Manhe

*Maputo
Elephant
Game
Reserve*

*Lagoa
Xingute*

SWAZILAND

Mafutseni

Siteki

Mkhaya NR

Bella Vista

Salamanga

*Lagoa
Piti*

Sidvokodvo

Maputo

Futi

Ponta Mamóli

26º47'52"S
32º53'33"E

Ponta Malongane Camp

9 & 10

Big Bend

Catuane

Ndumo GR

Parque Malongane
Ponta do Ouro

Kosi Bay

Sithobela

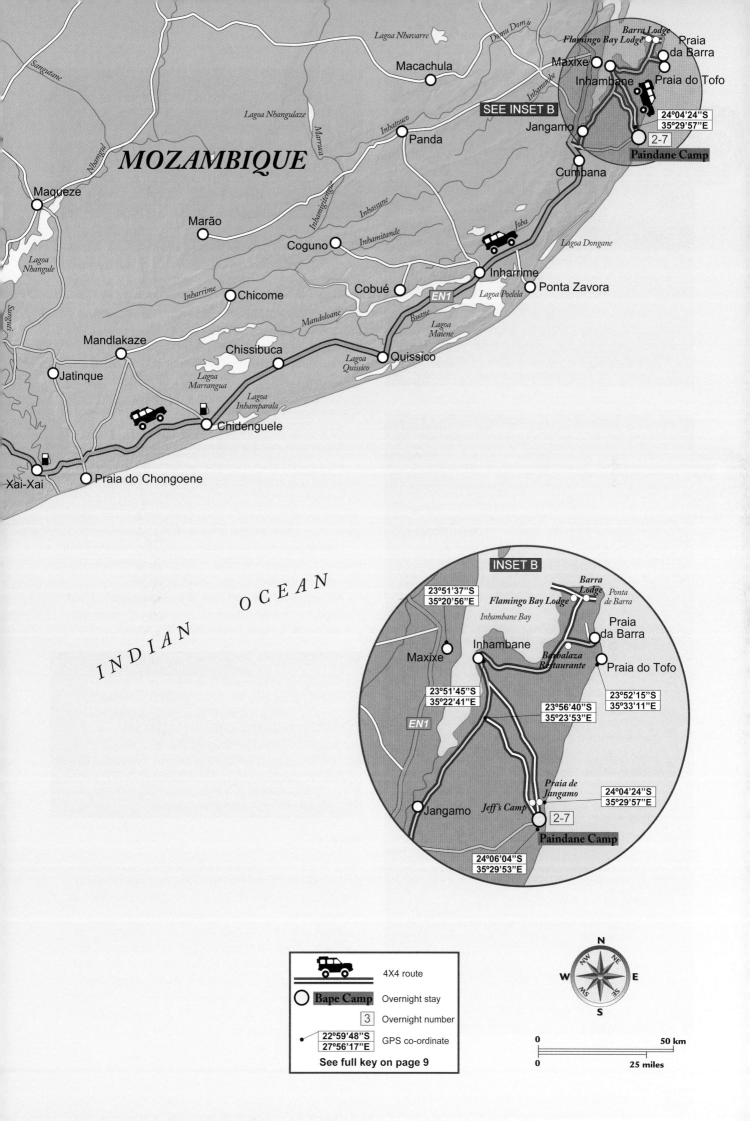

DAILY DRIVING DISTANCE AND TIME

Day		Distance	Time
Day 1	Explore Maputo	20km	5hr
Day 2	Maputo to Inhambane	500km	10hr
Day 3	Explore coastal tracks	30km	4hr
Day 4	Explore Inhambane markets	30km	4hr
Day 5	Explore Tofo	30km	4hr
Day 6	Explore Paindane reefs		4hr
Day 7	Explore Maxixe (dhow trip)	30km	6hr
Day 8	Inhambane to Maputo	500km	10hr
Day 9	Maputo (ferry, 4X4 track) to Ponta Malongane	150km	10hr
Day 10	Explore coastal forest and Ponta do Ouro	30km	4hr
Day 11	Exit at Kosi Bay	20km	2hr

GENERAL WARNINGS FOR THIS ROUTE

- Sun protection – creams, hats and long-sleeved shirts; wear a T-shirt or thin wet suit when snorkelling
- Protect eyes against glare
- Hydrate regularly
- This is a malaria area – consult your doctor or travel clinic and pack insect repellent and malaria prophylactics
- Tropical hygiene requirements apply, e.g. wash hands regularly, and wash all fruit and vegetables in mild disinfectant solution prior to consumption
- Consider all east-flowing rivers to contain crocodiles and still-standing waters to harbour bilharzia
- In the bush beware of snakes
- In the sea beware the poisonous scorpion fish, stonefish and bluebottles; wear gloves when snorkelling
- Petty crime exists in the border zone and the major cities, but criminal activity is low in camp sites with security arrangements in place
- Best practice recommendation is to take out all-risk insurance on your valuables
- Upgrade trailer axles as 10" wheels are unsuitable for any part of this tour
- Comprehensive travel insurance for each person
- Vehicle and trailer insurance for outside the borders of South Africa
- Do not break away from the convoy as there are no rescue or recovery services should you get lost
- Adhere to all traffic regulations at all times as fines are high
- All passengers and drivers must wear seat belts at all times
- Army and police roadblocks still occur – be polite, remove dark glasses and keep your seat belt on during the entire conversation
- Beach sand becomes hot during the day, while coral rocks are razor-sharp for bare feet – always wear suitable footwear or sandals

GETTING THERE BY PLANE

Most international flights to Mozambique land at Maputo. Local airlines operate domestic flights within Mozambique.

Taxis ply the route from the airport to town, and hotels generally send their buses to meet flights. Local SIM cards can be bought at the shop near the exit of the terminal, where there is also a bank.

There are direct flights a few times a week from Maputo to Inhambane Airport and on to Vilanculos, further to the north.

The usual meeting point for this Mozambican trip, and for your safety and comfort in Maputo, is at the Costa do Sol Hotel in Maputo, where a pre-trip briefing session will be held on the evening prior to departure. All confirmed off-road travellers will receive a comprehensive information pack covering the finer details of the trip, with GPS waypoints, camp-site maps, check lists and many practical hints and tips.

Many people come from all over and join the trip at pre-arranged stopping points throughout South Africa and Mozambique, but for most the planned assembly point is 4km before Mbombela (Nelspruit) at Hall's Farm Stall and Shell Service Centre. This is an ideal opportunity for refuelling, filling up fresh-water tanks and buying any last-minute necessities.

About 2km before the border post we have another scheduled stop at the BP Lebombo Village on the left, to top up fuel tanks and jerry cans. Given that fuel prices fluctuate between South Africa and Mozambique, consult with your tour guide about where it's best to fill up. Provided your passport and vehicle papers are all in order, the border procedure itself is quick, with only one form to be filled in on the South African side and another form on the Mozambican side.

At the hotel all off-road vehicles are securely parked, and after check-in you can explore the beach area at leisure and assume the Mozambican pace of life before dinner.

COSTA DO SOL

Costa do Sol Hotel and Restaurant is 10km from the centre of Maputo on the Marginal coastal road. The hotel offers exquisite views of the palm-dotted beach and open sea. The original hotel, with its Art Deco architecture, has been in operation for many years under family management. It remained open throughout the civil war, making it something of a Maputo landmark. It boasts a long-standing tradition of good service, excellent food and value for money, for both tourists and business people.

DAY 1

We start the city tour by visiting the fish market, botanical gardens, Gustave Eiffel's model house, the Maputo railway station (built between 1913 and 1916), the old Fortaleza de Maputo, and the Laurentino beer brewery.

Maputo has well-stocked shops such as Shoprite where familiar South African goods can be purchased, including fresh South African meat. The fish market has a great diversity of seafood and gives a new meaning to the term 'large prawns'. Buy and save some in your freezer for the first day of camping, but bear in mind that prawns and fish are generally available and cost less further north.

Eiffel's House, Maputo

Alexandre Gustave Eiffel's house of steel (*Casa de Fierro*) provides a rare photo opportunity of this ingenious design that has stood the test of time. It is a well-preserved national monument. The nearby botanical garden has many old trees and a statue of Samora Machel that is worth seeing.

Enjoy lunch and dinner back at the hotel; alternatively, you could follow your off-road tour guide to another exciting spot on the coast.

The afternoon is the perfect opportunity to check vehicles for the rest of the trip and to make sure that all two-way radios are working.

After a stroll on the beach, a lazy evening on the hotel balcony ends this beautiful first day.

DAY 2

Today's objective is to get to Inhambane and set up base camp at Paindane. The overall distance is 500km, starting with slow conditions through the busy suburbs of Maputo, then 220km of good road to Xai-Xai, followed by 64km of poor road out of Xai-Xai, 220km of good road to the Inhambane junction, and ending with a 40km off-road section prior to reaching camp. An early departure is required.

Leaving the city of Maputo behind us, we stop for cashew nuts on the side of the road between Manhica and Palmeira – this is considered the cashew nut and orange district of Mozambique. (Note that the roadside vendors disappear during the early afternoon.)

MAPUTO

Formerly Lourenço Marques, the capital has an estimated population of 2.5 million people (2010). It is a port city on the northern banks of the Tembe River on the Indian Ocean, from where coal, cotton, sugar, chromite, sisal, copra and hardwoods are exported. The city manufactures cement, pottery, furniture, shoes and rubber, and has a large aluminium-smelting plant called Mozal.

Post-war recovery is accelerating in the city, and trading is showing signs of returning to normal. Buildings are being repaired or rebuilt and infrastructure renewed. Informal trading continues in large open markets.

Between 1544 and the early 1700s numerous forts and trading stations were built on the southeastern banks of Maputo Bay, but these were subsequently destroyed. The current city of Maputo developed around a Portuguese fortress completed in 1787 on the northern banks.

INHAMBANE

The capital of Inhambane Province is one of the oldest settlements on the east coast of Mozambique. It is a sleepy historic town known for its colonial architecture. The settlement owes its existence to a deep inlet into which the small river of Matamba flows. Two sandy headlands protect the harbour and form a sandbank. The town of Maxixe is located across the bay. Dhows traded here as early as the 11th century. Muslim and Persian traders were the first outsiders to arrive in the area by sea and traded pearls and ambergris. The area became well known for cotton spinning and production by the Tonga people. Some time before the Portuguese came to this town, the Karanga had invaded Inhambane and appointed a number of local chieftains who dominated the Tonga cotton workers and took the rewards of their trading with the Muslims.

When Vasco da Gama rounded Africa in the late 15th century he called into Inhambane to replenish stocks and to explore the land. He took an immediate liking to Imhambane and named it *Terra de Boa Gente*, or 'Land of the Good People'. In 1505 a ship sent by Francisco de Almeida was shipwrecked south of the town, but the Portuguese gained access to the ship after approval from the Karanga chiefs. Later, the sons of the shipwreck survivors landed on Mozambique Island to survey the situation. The Portuguese eventually established a permanent trading post at the settlement in 1534. In 1560, Inhambane was chosen as the site of the first Jesuit mission to East Africa.

Having passed a few towns, we now enter the wide basin of the Limpopo River on our way to Xai-Xai, located on the opposite bank. This basin is almost 10km wide, with the actual river stream normally flowing at the northern bank of the river where a majestic bridge crosses the stream. The flotsam bears testimony to the horror of severe flooding that sometimes occurs here. A toll booth on the opposite bank collects toll for southbound vehicles, but this changes from time to time.

In Xai-Xai (about 220km from Maputo) we stop at a Portuguese restaurant for lunch and to refuel before we head off north to Inhambane.

As we leave Xai-Xai, the condition of the tar road is very bad, and roadworks are in progress (2010) to rebuild a 45km section – take care when overtaking, especially the buses (see the goats on the roof carriers!), most of which crab due to skew axles. Approximately 65km from Xai-Xai, at the turn-off to Praia do Chongoene, a beautiful old church stands on a hill on the left side of the road – it is worth stopping to photograph it.

Just past Chidenguele, the beautiful coconut palm trees and lush green tropical vegetation starts, providing ongoing good photo opportunities. The coconut plantations stretch for over 200km to the north; the number of trees owned indicates the financial status of the owner.

As we exit Quissico, a major town (with a hospital) on the EN1, a stop on the seaward side of the road is advised to admire the beautiful back-to-back lagoons that run parallel to the shoreline. Support the roadside store, with its colourful tables set under an open pergola next to the road. Some 40km further we cross the Inharrime River that forms a very large lake, called Lagoa Poelela, on both sides of the road. It is a

VEHICLE REQUIREMENTS

▶ Four-wheel-drive with low-range transfer case
▶ Recovery points front and back
▶ Good ground clearance
▶ Proper off-road tyres and spare wheel
▶ Rear diff-lock or traction control an advantage
▶ A dual battery system when using in-vehicle 12V fridge/ freezers
▶ Blue and yellow Mozambique towing triangle in front of towing vehicle and on back of trailer, obtainable from AA stores
▶ Mozambican third-party insurance for vehicle and trailer, obtainable at AA offices or Outdoor Warehouse
▶ ZA sticker on back of both the towing vehicle and trailer
▶ Two green road safety (waistcoat) jackets
▶ Two red emergency triangles
▶ Original registration papers of the vehicle and trailer (if the vehicle or trailer is not registered in your name, then you also need a letter from the registered owner or company authorising you to take this vehicle or trailer out of South Africa and into Mozambique)

TRAILER-FRIENDLY RATING

This trip is suited to those who like to tow their pleasure craft and creature comforts with them.
▶ The main highway (EN1) is constantly being upgraded, but there are badly potholed sections where larger trailer wheels are essential
▶ Between camp sites the dirt roads and soft sandy tracks are Grade 2–3
▶ The return sand-track section (south of Maputo) has shallow water holes (ex-war machine-gun dugouts) in the road where braked axles are an advantage
▶ 10" rims or wheels on trailers are not suitable; take along a spare double set of trailer axle bearings, U-bolts, circlips and axle grease for your trailer
▶ Service your trailer before the trip

freshwater lake and its waters flow into the chain of lagoons seen earlier at Quissico.

Approximately 13km further on, we pass the turn-off to Ponta Zavora. Zavora Lodge is a favourite camp site for many, located about 18km from the EN1 and 180km from Xai-Xai. At Ponta Zavora the coral reef in front of the camp forms an aquarium-like round hole, about 2m deep, with sea turtles and a plethora of tropical marine fish inside and with excellent game-fishing around the tip of the reef. Prepare to do battle with mosquitoes here!

Stop at Cumbana to buy a bag of local charcoal. These bags are large, so strap yours somewhere on your roof-rack or trailer. This is also a good opportunity to buy reed mats for the camp – these are ideal for using on the beach as well as for keeping sand out of your tent.

We continue north on the EN1 towards the junction where the road to Inhambane splits off from the EN1. This is a major junction and well signposted. The road from there onwards

is potholed, so watch out, especially when getting on and off some of the narrow bridges. Just 3.5km from the junction, take the dirt road to the left (signposted as Jangamo) and follow it to the circle in the little town of Jangamo where you will reduce your tyre pressure. Depending on your vehicle and tyres, 1 bar is recommended as a maximum. Exit the town and follow the middle track (as shown in Tracks 4 Africa) that goes just south of Shalomoe Dam, to the Paindane camp site. The northern track also goes there, but goes over several high ridges and takes longer. The sand trail through the coconut forest (after turning off the main road to Jangamo) is neither difficult nor long, but it does provide a good sand-driving experience and the opportunity to employ sound off-road driving procedures and bush convoy etiquette, such as 'do not proceed into an obstacle until the vehicle in front of you has cleared it completely' and 'you are responsible for the vehicle behind you'. This is especially pertinent for newer off-road travellers. Take care when driving through the small villages, as curious onlookers gather to see the convoy.

MONEY MATTERS

The metical (plural: meticais) is the currency of Mozambique, abbreviated as MZN or MTn (Note: MZM, used for the previous issue of meticais, is still in use by some banks). From 1 July 2006, new banknotes were issued in denominations of 20, 50, 100, 200, 500 and 1000 meticais.

Exchanging money in Mozambique can be done at any of the banks. Credit and other bank cards are not widely accepted, mostly due to lack of land communications infrastructure, but can be used at some banks in Maputo. At the time of publishing, the fuel stations, camp sites and restaurants mentioned in this chapter did not accept credit or other electronic bank cards.

After registration, proceed to the allocated camp site (a *barraca* or *casita* site), set up camp and start preparing dinner.

Note: Certain forms need to be completed by the driver of each vehicle, payment details need to be verified, and passports recorded and held overnight in the office safe.

Camp options in Mozambique are generally as follows:
▶ A standard camp site includes generator power which is provided from 10:00 to 20:00 (some camps have now converted to Mozambique grid power).
▶ A *barraca* is a camp site containing a thatch-roofed wooden structure with a concrete floor, wash basin and open-

A barraca *camp*

sided walls, and one usually camps around the structure, although you can also 'camp' under the roof if it rains.

- A *casita* is very similar to a *barraca*, but has its own bathroom and small kitchen.
- A chalet is what you would expect – a walled and roofed sleeping structure, possibly with its own kitchen and bathroom, depending on the version of luxury you choose.

The first night of camping on the coast next to the warm ocean is always a great experience – you marvel at the phosphor which sometimes lights up the breakers, while the sound of surf always puts you into a good sleep. You're probably tired from a long day on the road and setting up camp, but there are two beach restaurants outside the camp offering tasty and affordable food.

There is not much trouble by way of tropical insects at Paindane. However, given that it is a malaria area, best practice is to use insect repellent at night, even if you cannot see or hear insects, and to ensure that your tent has fully functional mosquito mesh in all windows and doorways. Prevention is better than cure.

DAYS 3 TO 7

During our extended stay at Paindane, we go on day trips to explore the region's coastal coves and bays at our leisure, and soak up the warmth, food and pace of this coastal idyll.

In Mozambique the sun rises very early, so early in the morning we drive down the ramp on the south side of the camp, within the approved beach driving section behind the reef, or enjoy a walk along the beach or a fantastic snorkel in the rock pools – low tide offers the best snorkelling results.

Vossie Vosloo's professional Dive Shop is located on the beach at Paindane, and here you can sign up for fantastic snorkelling or scuba diving, whale-shark and dolphin tours. Vossie has all the required scuba-diving equipment for rent, as well as good boats, and he knows the best local diving spots. The ocean tours for whale-shark and dolphin spotting and snorkelling are popular and suitable for the entire family.

Every day the locals bring freshly baked *pão* (Portuguese rolls), prawns and fish caught overnight to the camp site, and you can buy these with confidence (take a small pocket scale with you).

After a healthy brunch in camp, we head off in our vehicles (there's no packing up as this is our base camp for a few days) northwards along the coastal track to visit neighbouring Jeff's Camp and Jangamo, where we stroll on the beach and sample the wares (and an ice-cold drink) at Rosie's Beach Restaurant. (Jangamo is connected to Jeff's Camp via the beach-drivable section.) On the way to Jeff's, we stop at the local bread baker's hut for a demonstration on how the dough is prepared and the *pão* is baked on coconut husks.

Each evening around the camp fire, we 'review and confirm' the events planned for the next day, and we can also add in spur-of-the-moment events or plans. There's no pressure. Be sure to ask what the plans are if you were out on the beach until late for sundowners!

During one of the day trips, we explore many of the coastal sandy tracks and bays towards Inhambane. In the town of Inhambane we visit the large market, where you can buy anything from fresh fruit and vegetables to canned foods, cleaning equipment, etc. Inhambane's market is also a good

place to exchange rands for meticais. We also visit the depot that sells bulk cool drinks, beer and the famous cinnamon-flavoured Mozambican rum (Tipo Tinto).

During the war, the railway yard and hangar in Inhambane were maintained by loyal workers who pitched up for work every day, despite receiving no pay. Now, many years later, the old and rusty steam locomotives and railcars can still be seen and photographed – a rare opportunity in these modern times.

Follow the signs to Tofo and the airport to get to the Barra Peninsula. At Bar Barbalaza Restaurante, the dirt road to Barra splits off to the east. The dirt road to the coast (Barra Peninsula) turns north at the junction near the beach dune. This road section is sometimes awash with pools of sea water during high tide, as you are now driving north on a narrow peninsula with sea on the right (over the coconut-covered sand dune) and with a lagoon on the left, behind thick mangroves. We stop at Barra Lodge for lunch upstairs at the beach café overlooking the beautiful turquoise sea.

After lunch and browsing around the Barra Lodge area, we head further north to stop at Flamingo Bay Lodge. Here one walks on raised wooden walkways through the mangroves deep into the lagoon area to visit Flamingo Bay Lodge for a photo opportunity. Besides the grandeur of the lodge built on stilts and with a swimming pool that seems to extend into the lagoon, it has astonishing rows of reed chalets on stilts further out into the lagoon. All are interconnected with raised wooden walkways, and golf carts ferry guests around. Spectacular sunset photos can be taken here.

The day trip to Maxixe starts by driving along the coastal track to Inhambane Pier. After a brief negotiation with the captains regarding a return fee, the dhows depart from

Barra Lodge

SPECIFIC KIT REQUIRED FOR THIS TRIP

- Full camping gear, bedding, tents, table and chairs
- Full kitchen and braai utensils
- LPG cylinder gas refills are available in local markets; gas cartridges are only available in major cities
- Water reserves for three days (2 litres per person per day minimum)
- A fridge/freezer in the vehicle is a necessity
- GPS and trig survey maps if you are going without an off-road guide
- Licensed working 29MHz radio
- Recovery kit
- Standard South African boat safety kit (if applicable)

ESSENTIAL REQUIREMENTS FOR THIS TRIP

- Puncture-repair kit, tyre-pressure gauge and compressor
- Kinetic strap or rope and tow strap or rope
- Spade
- High-lift jack – one in the group is sufficient
- Basic tools and basic spares for your vehicle, e.g. spare radiator hoses and fan belts
- 220V/12V rechargeable light for your tent and one headlamp per person are recommended
- First-aid kit catering at least for sores and cuts, hay fever, sore eyes, headaches, nausea, upset stomach, malaria emergency treatment, bites and stings
- Passports with a minimum of two blank pages, and valid for at least three months after return (non-South African passport holders require a visa, obtainable from Mozambican embassies)
- Snorkelling equipment such as mask, fins and gloves
- Scuba-diving equipment, fishing tackle and boating equipment as appropriate

SEE FULL PACKING LIST ON PAGE 218 ▶▶

Inhambane, using oars until they reach deeper water where they raise their colourful patched sails, to the delighted cheers of the passengers. These dhows glide silently across the calm bay to the opposite side of the lagoon, where we come to a busy market at Maxixe after a short walk up the slipway. For lunch, we visit a really good Portuguese restaurant on the northern side of the pier bank in Maxixe. It has large trees overhanging the eating areas, with a beautiful view across the bay towards Inhambane. Tasty, fresh *couta* and prawns and Portuguese steak rolls are their speciality. The return trip to Inhambane later in the afternoon is normally under a fresh sea breeze. Be prepared for some light but warm sea spray.

DAY 8

A very early start is required to pack up the camp site (we may do some of this on the previous evening) and depart for Maputo. The route takes us back along the EN1 with its familiar and fascinating scenery. We stop regularly for photos, to stretch our legs or just to take a break from the driving. Formal fuel and meal stops are co-ordinated via the two-way radios.

We see everything (and more) that we saw on day two, only in reverse order. Just before Maputo we leave the EN1 to drive an off-road section along the coast until we get to our overnight spot back at the Costa do Sol Hotel in Maputo.

DAY 9

We're all up for an early-morning departure with the objective of crossing the bay by ferry boat, stopping for lunch at Bella Vista and driving the sand tracks past the Maputo Elephant Game Reserve to our camp at Ponta Malongane near Kosi Bay. Here we also say goodbye to any 4X2 participants.

Leaving the hotel after an early breakfast ensures that we catch the early ferry and make camp by nightfall. We drive along the seafront to the pier and, after purchasing tickets, load the vehicles onto the ferry to cross Maputo Bay and the Tembe River mouth to Catembe, on the southern shore of the bay.

Driving onto the ferry

The ferry ride is an unforgettable experience, a kind of 'must do', as it is a true African event and great fun. At Catembe, a beehive of activity for vehicles, traders and people, we drop our tyre pressure for the hardened mud corrugations on the drive to Bella Vista. After rains, this section is far worse to travel as the mud is quite deep and very slippery, but even when dry and hard, the pace is slow. Interestingly, you will see experimental rice paddies along this road.

Time permitting, we'll have lunch at Bella Vista Restaurant – its architecture resembles a typical open-air Portuguese pergola-style restaurant. All food is cooked on a charcoal fire in the kitchen, located off to the side of the seating area. This draws much interest from off-road travellers. The general meal

MAPUTO'S FERRY

The new ferry was launched in 2009 to transport passengers and cargo between Maputo and Catembe on the other side of Maputo Bay. Named *Mpfumo* (the traditional name of the city of Maputo), it has the capacity to carry 250 passengers, 10 cars and four light trucks with 10–15 tons of cargo. *Mpfumo* is part of a batch of six new boats purchased in December 2008 by the government on an investment budgeted at 16.4 million US dollars to improve transport on the main water crossings in the country. (The sum also includes rehabilitation of docking infrastructures.) The other five vessels are currently operating in other parts of the country.

Sand tracks at Ponta Malongane

available here is peri-peri chicken, salad, rice and chips, and the waiters will come around to the table before the meal with a jug of water and a towel, stopping to wash and dry each person's hands. There is a small market next door and they also sell *pão* bread and fresh vegetables. Fuel is available at Bella Vista.

From Bella Vista we will be soft-sand driving southbound past the elephant game reserve to Ponta Malongane. Due to the old machine-gun dugouts that were located in the sand-track roadway during the war, now mostly full of water, progress is slow and we only reach our destination by late afternoon. This provides for a good off-road driving challenge.

Some 16.5km from Bella Vista is the town of Salamanga, with its Hindu temple and shrine, and this is followed by a final police control point. (Police control points further south, other than the border post itself, are uncommon.)

Approximately 10km further we reach the junction with the elephant park and here we turn south. After a further 28km of soft-sand track we take the turn-off eastward to Ponta Mamóli. Leaving the savannah grassland conditions, you will notice the approaching coastal forest. Approximately 6km further along there is a sandy track turning off south and leading to Parque Malongane at Ponta Malongane. There are many dead-end sidetracks running through the thick foliage – these lead either to subsistence farming communities or deserted huts.

Parque Malongane has good restaurant facilities and also a beautiful treetop thatched bar that overlooks the coastal forest onto the sea. They have good diving facilities and an equipped dive camp. There are a wide variety of tropical and coral reefs to dive, but snorkelling is difficult due to wave action. The swimming and body-surfing is just great at the beach, just over a dune from the camp.

DAY 10

We explore Ponta Malongane and Ponta do Ouro. The rustic environment of Ponta Malongane, with its beautiful forest-canopy rooftop bar, restaurant and long tropical beach, will help you to relax completely – a truly unforgettable experience. The sandy track leading towards Ponta do Ouro takes you along the coastal forest, past a freshwater lake and a large inland sand dune. In Ponta do Ouro and just outside the gate of the Ponta Malongane Camp, there are large informal trading stores for those last-minute curio purchases. In Ponta do Ouro there is also the original Bar Barbalaza, founded by the deceased Portuguese major of this little town, and famous for its crab-meat meals.

DAY 11

Sadly, we have come to the end of our exploration of southern Mozambique. An early departure is required in order to complete the border crossing as soon as they open their gates, and to enable those who need to travel long distances to get under way. Fortunately, the border is not far from Ponta Malongane – about 13km of sand track.

Border crossings at Kosi Bay are painless and take only a few minutes. The border officials will, however, check you for possession of tropical fruits, and items such as avocados will be confiscated – and for good reason: we support this initiative to protect our own fruit orchards from diseases.

After crossing the border, we say our goodbyes and all off-road travellers leave for home.

GENERAL AND SAND-DRIVING TIPS FOR MOZAMBIQUE

▶ It is wise to refuel whenever you have the opportunity as you never know whether the next town will have fuel or not

▶ Beach driving is against the law except for approved and clearly demarcated areas; at some locations, you can launch and retrieve a boat but must remove the vehicle and trailer from the beach after the process

▶ Avoid swampy or beach-sand driving in areas that show a whitish salt line – this indicates quicksand

▶ Coral sand is less compact than normal beach or desert sand; wet sand is more compact than dry

▶ Stay on existing tracks to avoid damage to the ecology

▶ Lowering tyre pressure lengthens the footprint and aids flotation

▶ Thick sand requires momentum – keep moving

▶ Select the correct gear before water crossings, as changing gears midstream will bring you to a dead stop

▶ Don't brake when stopping, as a wall of sand will arise in front of the wheels; rather roll to a stop and reverse a metre or so before pulling away

▶ Stop facing downhill if possible for an easier restart

▶ Try to climb and descend dune faces at 90° to avoid roll-overs

16 Transkei Wild Coast

by Philip Sackville-Scott

TOP 10 ATTRACTIONS OF THIS TRIP

❶ Long stretches of unspoilt beaches interspersed with rivers **❷** Lush green countryside **❸** Opportunity to photograph rural lifestyles in action **❹** Generally the driving is easy, but you can find challenges if you like **❺** Dwesa Nature Reserve **❻** Fishing and the availability of seafood **❼** Frontier War history **❽** Hole in the Wall **❾** Cultural heritage **❿** Proximity to coastline throughout

TRIP OUTLINE

The section of the South African Eastern Cape coastline halfway between Port Elizabeth and Durban is known as the Wild Coast. As the crow flies from start to finish, this trip is only around 230km; however, the actual distance that you will travel is much greater.

It is important to understand the lie of the land if you are to come to grips with navigating around the Wild Coast sections of the former Transkei homeland. One look at a topographical map will indicate the vast mountainous region of Lesotho to the west and a myriad rivers and streams that drain off these mountains away to the sea in the east.

SEE DETAILED MAP ON PAGE 170 ▸▸

APPEAL RATING

5/5

▶ Wonderful climate for most of the year, but can get cold during the winter months
▶ Plentiful long sandy beaches with warm sea water for swimming
▶ Experience rural Xhosa cultural sites
▶ Lush vegetation and stunning scenery
▶ Good old-fashioned family holiday with many adventure options such as kayaking, fishing, mountain biking, surfing and body-surfing

THE BEST TIME TO TRAVEL HERE

There is something to interest and entertain everyone all year round.
▶ The region experiences summer rainfall, making this the best time to see running waterfalls
▶ Summers can be hot, but due to the proximity to the coast and the plentiful rivers, there's always somewhere to cool off
▶ From April to September the weather is warm enough to make it an appealing escape from the cold Cape and Highveld winters

FAMILY-FRIENDLY RATING

5/5

▶ There are so many options for families travelling on this route that you are guaranteed to find plenty to keep all ages happy
▶ The beaches are absolutely pristine and a wonderful playground for all
▶ The camping sites are comfortable and generally well appointed
▶ This is predominantly a camping trip, although alternative accommodation is available at most (but not all) places along the route

SELF-SUFFICIENCY RATING

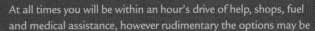

2/5

At all times you will be within an hour's drive of help, shops, fuel and medical assistance, however rudimentary the options may be
▶ Fuel is available along the route, so no long-range capacity is necessary
▶ You should stock up with food at East London as only the basics will be available in the rural general stores
▶ Fresh water is available along the way at holiday resorts and hotels
▶ Camp sites have hot running water and flushing toilets
▶ Cellphone reception is available, if sporadic, all along the route, especially on higher ground

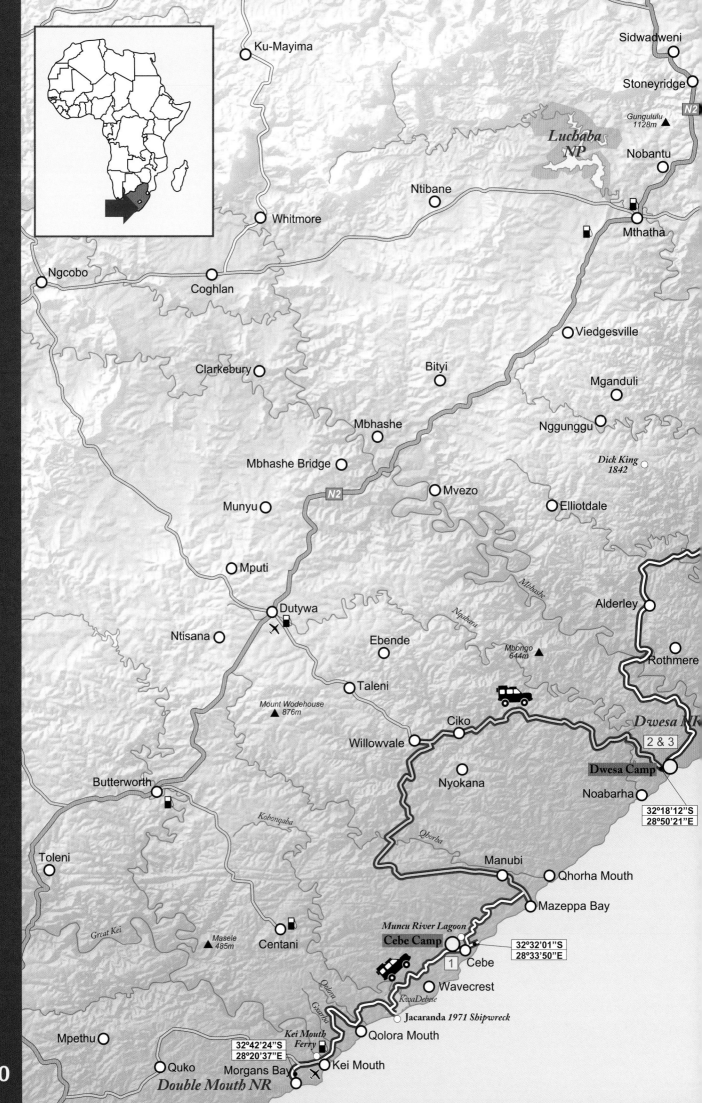

MAP 16 TRANSKEI WILD COAST

Ku-Mayima

Sidwadweni

Stoneyridge

Gungululu
1128m ▲

N2

Luchaba
NP

Nobantu

Ntibane

Whitmore

Mthatha

Ngcobo

Coghlan

Viedgesville

Clarkebury

Bityi

Mganduli

Mbhashe

Ngqunggu

Mbhashe Bridge

Dick King
1842

Munyu

Mvezo

Elliotdale

N2

Mputi

Mbhashe

Alderley

Ntisana

Dutywa

Ebende

Nqabara

Mbongo
644m ▲

Rothmere

Mount Wodehouse
▲ 876m

Taleni

Ciko

Dwesa NR

Willowvale

Nyokana

2 & 3

Dwesa Camp

Noabarha

Butterworth

32°18'12"S
28°50'21"E

Kobongaba

Toleni

Manubi

Qhorha Mouth

Qhorba

Mazeppa Bay

Great Kei

Masele
485m ▲

Centani

Muncu River Lagoon

Cebe Camp

32°32'01"S
28°33'50"E

1

Cebe

Wavecrest

KwaDebese

Jacaranda 1971 Shipwreck

Qolora

Mpethu

Gxarha

Kei Mouth
Ferry

Qolora Mouth

32°42'24"S
28°20'37"E

Quko

Morgans Bay

Kei Mouth

Double Mouth NR

170

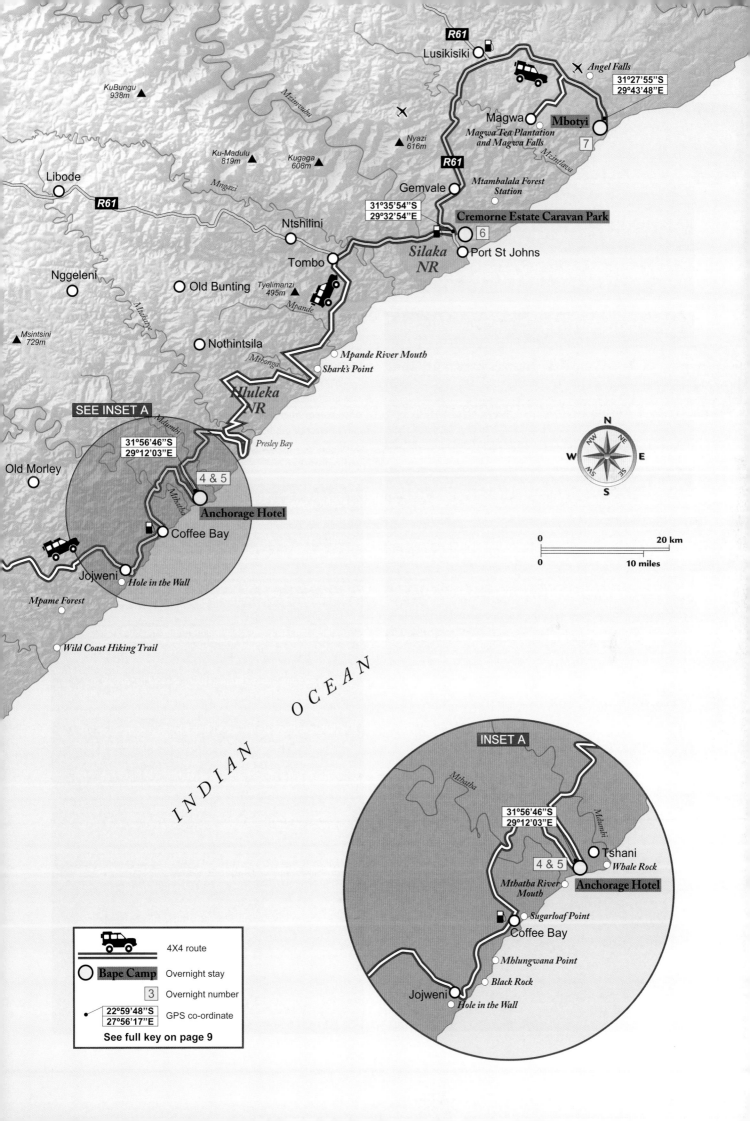

KuBungu 938m ▲

Libode

R61

Nggeleni

Msintsini 729m ▲

Old Morley

Ku-Madulu 819m ▲

Kugaga 608m ▲

Mzimvubu

Nyazi 616m ▲

Ntshilini

Old Bunting

Tyelimanzi 495m ▲

Tombo

Mpande

Nothintsila

Mthonga

Mpande River Mouth

Shark's Point

Hluleka NR

SEE INSET A

Mdumbi

31º56'46"S
29º12'03"E

Presley Bay

Anchorage Hotel

4 & 5

Coffee Bay

Jojweni

Mthatha

Hole in the Wall

Mpame Forest

Wild Coast Hiking Trail

R61

Lusikisiki

Angel Falls

31º27'55"S
29º43'48"E

Magwa

Mbotyi

Magwa Tea Plantation and Magwa Falls

7

R61

Gemvale

Mtambalala Forest Station

31º35'54"S
29º32'54"E

Cremorne Estate Caravan Park

6

Silaka NR

Port St Johns

Msinhlava

INDIAN OCEAN

N
NW NE
W E
SW SE
S

0 ——— 20 km
0 ——— 10 miles

INSET A

Mthatha

31º56'46"S
29º12'03"E

Mdumbi

4 & 5

Tshani

Whale Rock

Mthatha River Mouth

Anchorage Hotel

Sugarloaf Point

Coffee Bay

Mhlungwana Point

Black Rock

Jojweni

Hole in the Wall

Key

🚙 4X4 route

⬤ **Bape Camp** Overnight stay

3 Overnight number

•— 22º59'48"S 27º56'17"E GPS co-ordinate

See full key on page 9

DAILY DRIVING DISTANCE AND TIME

Day 1	Morgans Bay to Cebe	70km	9hr
Day 2	Cebe to Dwesa	175km	8hr
Day 3	Dwesa day at leisure		
Day 4	Dwesa to Anchorage Hotel	18km	7hr
Day 5	Anchorage Hotel day at leisure		
Day 6	Anchorage Hotel to Port St Johns	160km	7hr
Day 7	Port St Johns to Mbotyi	100km	3hr
Day 8	Mbotyi to home		

VEHICLE REQUIREMENTS

- ▶ Four-wheel-drive with low-range transfer case
- ▶ Recovery points front and back
- ▶ Good ground clearance
- ▶ Proper off-road tyres with high profile for rocky ground
- ▶ Rear diff-lock or traction control would be an advantage, especially if towing

TRAILER-FRIENDLY RATING

5/5

- ▶ This trip is suited to all types of camping trailers and even the heavy off-road caravans will cope – as long as the tow vehicle has sufficient engine capabilities
- ▶ There are some tight twists and turns and steep ascents and descents, but nothing with a high difficulty rating
- ▶ There is generally an alternative route should this be necessary
- ▶ The limited manoeuvrability with a large trailer could cause delays

QUEUE FOR FERRY STARTS HERE

Typical Transkei view, day 1

The group gathers the afternoon before at the Morgans Bay caravan park where introductions and last-minute preparations are made and the scene is sketched for the coming week's exploration of the fantastic Wild Coast. The amenities of the caravan park and its setting are wonderful, located as it is alongside a beautiful stretch of flat Inchara River frontage under shady trees and only 50m from the beach.

After a hearty session of socialising around the braai fires and having made new friends, we turn in, with the sound of crashing waves wafting over our ears – not for the last time on this trip.

DAY 1

Leaving the caravan park, we initially make our way inland before turning east towards the mouth of the Great Kei River, 5km away. This is the last opportunity for a while to fill up with fuel, before we board the nostalgic pontoon ferries that transport two vehicles at a time across the broad river.

Ferry crossings are such a dramatic way of plunging you straight into holiday mode as they conjure up romantic images of trans-continental travel from days gone by. However, one can't help but get butterflies in your stomach as you inch your darling 4X4 onto the ramps and aboard the ferry, hopefully without mishap.

NONGQAWUSE'S VISION

During the time of the worst suffering and devastation of the most bitter frontier wars, a young Xhosa girl named Nongqawuse was born near the Gxarha River. These wars had killed many Xhosa and their cattle and seen many grain fields burned. To make things worse, the remaining cattle contracted a lung disease from a herd of white-owned cattle, and the grain fields were infected, killing off the grain before it could ripen. Some blamed witchcraft for these troubles, but many Xhosa blamed the British who took their land and destroyed their traditions and beliefs.

One day during 1857, Nongqawuse went to a river pool where three spirits appeared to her in a vision. She told her people that the spirits had told her a new day would come for the Xhosa. The ancestors would rise from the dead and they would bring new cattle with them. The witchcraft would stop and the land would be full of new grain. The sun would set in the east and a whirlwind would come and blow all the whites into the sea.

But first the Xhosa had to do something very important – they had to kill all their cattle and destroy all their grain.

This message spread rapidly throughout the whole of the Xhosa nation, with other young girls claiming to have received the same message. The king believed he had received the vision too, but not all of the people believed the vision and were against the idea of destroying the only food they had left. The people who did believe were afraid that if everybody did not kill their cattle, the prophecy would not come true.

Almost all of the Xhosa people destroyed their animals and used all their grain to make beer, which they drank. But the promises of the spirits did not come true. Instead, thousands died of starvation. The nation was weak and vulnerable and the British easily crushed them in battle and took more land.

To this day, many blame the continued poverty and desolation of the area on the effects of Nongqawuse's terrible vision.

Heading towards The Gates, day 1

Once all vehicles are safely across, you proceed over a wide flood plain before the track rises up the first of many green, rolling hills to the turn-off onto a narrow track on the right-hand side. This twin track takes you down, via a twisty cross-axled route, to cross the Gxarha River. After a few hundred metres you will pass the pool and waterfall where the Xhosa Prophetess of Doom, Nongqawuse, is said to have received her fateful vision. (For details, see text box on page 172.)

The track then turns southeast again, towards the mouth of the Qolora River, in the first of numerous such navigational sequences. In order to proceed up the coast, it is necessary to track inland to a suitable fording place before returning back to the shoreline and continuing.

We pull in near the Qolora Mouth to view the well-known Trennerys Hotel and enjoy a light lunch at Seagulls.

On the move once more, we aim our vehicles away from the coast and head towards The Gates, a wonderfully picturesque rock pool on the Qolora River, where 6m-high rock cliffs stand guard like sentinels over the course of the river. It's a great spot for a picnic or a swim.

The track then proceeds over a small bridge and loops first inland and then seawards again towards the spot on the beach where the remains of the *Jacaranda* are still to be found.

Having taken our photos like the good tourists we are, we resume our journey in a northeasterly direction via the marshy KwaDebese and over numerous streams and river valleys to the Cebe community-run camp on the Muncu River Lagoon. The scenery is typical Transkei – rounded hills with shortly cropped, lush grass interspersed with river valleys running down to the seaside. Coastal forests and estuaries with crab-encrusted mangroves characterise the wonderful wide river mouths. There is so much to see and appreciate.

The camp site at Cebe is under shady trees alongside the southern river bank, but the lack of amenities and constant badgering by locals wishing to be employed as camp mamas or fishing gillies lead us to spend just the one night here and rather press on to Dwesa.

SHIPWRECKS OF THE WILD COAST

This hostile stretch of rocky, rugged coastline has been the demise of many a seagoing vessel over the centuries. The fast-flowing Mozambique Current and frequent gale-force winds combine to create heavy seas and freak waves. The stormy conditions that spring up, often without prior warning, are of such tenacity as to present a stern test to boat-builder and sailor alike.

The disappearance of the SS *Waratah* (1909), Australia's 'Titanic', is the most mysterious maritime tragedy associated with this area. While en route from Durban to Cape Town, she disappeared with 211 lives lost.

Two ships reported sighting the *Waratah* after she had sailed from Durban, where she was seen making heavy work of the rough seas and stormy winds at the time. A passenger report earlier described the ship as 'top heavy', which may be a clue to her going down.

To this day, no trace of her wreck has been found.

The *Grosvenor* (1782) is probably the most famous ship to flounder on this coast. She was a British East Indiaman on her way back from India, when a combination of foul weather (in the form of onshore gales) and inaccurate maps saw the ship run aground at Lambassi Bay. One hundred and thirty-six of the 150 aboard made it safely ashore; however, only six made it back to Port Elizabeth. A further 12 survivors were found by an expedition sent up from the Cape.

Only a few cannon and coins of the reputed treasures aboard were ever recovered.

The *Jacaranda* (1971) was a Greek freighter that went aground on the beach at Qolora Mouth, due to engine failure. The ship's captain, his wife and crew all made it safely ashore.

What is left of the wreck is still visible an hour's walk up the beach from Qolora.

The Greek-owned *Oceanos* (1991) sank in heavy seas off the coast near Hole in the Wall. The liner had left East London that afternoon with 576 passengers and crew aboard when it sprang a leak.

Shockingly, the Greek captain and crew abandoned ship, leaving the remaining passengers to fend for themselves! Fortunately the entertainment staff sent out an SOS, thereby preventing a huge loss of life. The rescue operation that ensued involved the South African Air Force, and many passengers were airlifted from the deck of the sinking ship, while others were rescued from lifeboats by ships answering the distress calls. The operation was a resounding success and a real tribute to all of those involved. No lives were lost.

DAY 2

Following the coastline some 2km inland, the track winds this way and that around hills and across streams until, after a two- to three-hour drive, it spits us out at Mazeppa Bay. Here we can experience rural Transkei at its best, with cattle ranchers on horseback and donkeys drawing home-made trailers and carts. We pass typical rondavels (round thatched huts), brightly decorated. Beware of the cattle, sheep, goats and even a few pot-bellied pigs roaming the countryside, all this to the continual chorus of 'sweeeeeeeeeeets!' from the semi-clothed children who literally appear out of nowhere and come sprinting down the hillsides as the vehicles approach.

Mazeppa Bay is a lush setting of subtropical plants and palms growing on the dunes above the broad sandy beach.

GENERAL WARNINGS FOR THIS ROUTE

There are moderate safety concerns on this trip due to the continual presence of local inhabitants. Pilfering is not uncommon and the pleas for 'sweeeeeeets' regularly ring through the valleys. As always in wilderness areas, you need to be bush-wise and take basic precautionary measures.

- Sun-protection creams, hats and long-sleeved shirts
- Eye protection against glare
- Hydrate regularly
- The weather at the seaside can change rapidly; wet-weather clothing and warm clothing and bedding are essential as backup, even during summer months
- Malaria-free throughout
- No large predators on this route
- The local population is all around you most of the time; criminal activity is a possibility, so don't leave possessions out at night or during the day when off at the beach
- People in rural areas and especially the children don't often see tourists travelling through their villages and farmlands, so they can be curious
- With children demanding sweets and adults offering to work on your camp sites, there is likely to be some unwanted attention; treat these situations with empathy and communicate your decisions with good humour

SPECIFIC KIT REQUIRED FOR THIS TRIP

- Full camping gear, bedding, tents, table and chairs
- Full kitchen and braai utensils
- Water reserves for two days (5 litres per person per day minimum)
- A fridge in the vehicle would be useful
- GPS with Tracks 4 Africa loaded and trig survey maps if you are going without an off-road guide
- Licensed radios for inter-vehicle communications
- Comprehensive tyre-repair kit

ESSENTIAL REQUIREMENTS FOR THIS TRIP

- Coastal Management enforce a 1000m proximity limit to the high water mark. Two permits are required to enter this zone for this route – one available in Grahamstown, the other in Mthatha from the offices of DEA. Contact edwina.oates@deaet.ecape.gov.za. for further information.
- Puncture-repair kit, tyre-pressure gauge and compressor
- Kinetic strap or rope and tow strap or rope
- Spade
- High-lift jack or inflatable airbag – one in the group is sufficient
- Basic tools and basic spares for your vehicle
- Lighting, 12V or gas
- First-aid kit catering at least for sores and cuts, sunburn, sore eyes, headaches, nausea, bites and stings

SEE FULL PACKING LIST ON PAGE 218 ▶▶

MAZEPPA BAY

Mazeppa Bay is named after a ship, the *Mazeppa*. The ship, captained by a CJ Cato, was on its way to Delagoa Bay from Port Natal in 1842 and was in search of a British man-of-war to rescue the garrison which had been besieged by the Boers. Captain Cato steered into the bay for shelter and ran aground. Legend has it that the ship's ruins are buried under the sand dunes at Mazeppa Bay.

Mazeppa Bay is not only renowned for its fishing, but for its prolific bird life too. Many walks can be enjoyed in the area, and in particular the walk to the Manubi Indigenous Forest, where the plant life is delightful.

A small island sits just off the beach, with a quaint suspension bridge providing access. (Apparently this bridge was a holiday project for a group of mechanical engineering students to improve the local fishermen's access to their best fishing spot.)

Having enjoyed a most scenic picnic lunch on the slopes of a green hillside with the most amazing sea views, we pack up and head for Dwesa.

Describing a giant arc, we travel inland searching, in vain as it turns out, for a short cut over the Qhorha River to avoid the long detour via Willowvale before turning towards the seaside once more and finding the stunningly beautiful Dwesa Nature Reserve. Wisely, we take the opportunity to refuel at Willowvale and top up on provisions at the local general dealer. (This unexpected 120km detour could have caught us out as far as our fuel reserves were concerned.)

The afternoon's drive from Willowvale takes us along a mountainous, winding and undulating gravel road passing the now familiar sights of huts and animals, happy, waving, screeching children, and lush greenery interspersed with streams and river crossings.

Along the way we pass a sign indicating the direction to the grave of King Hintsa – an unusual casualty of the Frontier Wars with the Brits.

Indigenous forest surrounds the lush green, grassed camp sites. The sites are huge and the whole group settles in for our first two-night stay of the trip. The only downside of the widely spread-out sites is that we have a fair walk to the ablution facilities, which are reached via a short suspension bridge. Another factor to be considered here is the presence of swarms of monkeys that chatter away in the trees, planning, I'm sure, their plundering of our possessions while we are relaxing at the beach tomorrow!

Camping at Dwesa

174 4X4 ROUTES THROUGH SOUTHERN AFRICA

DAY 3

Thankfully we can all sleep in today, after the extended drive of yesterday. After a good, wholesome breakfast, washed down with a good, strong espresso, we decide what to do for the day. On a previous trip, one of the party was trying to drum up support for a nature walk, when we got a report from park management that unfortunately, due to rhino culling, we would be unable to access the inland sections of the park, but must stay along the coast.

'Excuse me, rhino culling? In a South African game reserve?' It was emotionlessly explained to us that the six white rhino here are not indigenous to this area and so a contract has been awarded to a professional hunter to shoot them.

'As opposed to relocating them?' we ask. Apparently the financial benefit in selling the contract to Korean hunters is far more beneficial to the system than the cost of capture and relocation.

Enjoy a day on the beach near Dwesa

This 2009 incident seems even more ridiculous in the light of the more recent poaching spree that devastated our rhino population during 2010.

The day is spent hiking, enjoying the beach and lagoon setting, or simply relaxing in the camp site, reading or just plain chilling. On the morning's walk we cross a lovely stretch of pristine beach, round a stunning headland followed by a river mouth, another stretch of pristine beach, headland, river mouth, beach ...

Climbing up a grassy hillside just above the beach, we discover plenty of animal droppings and we even find the bathing spot of the soon-to-be-deceased white rhino. We then enjoy a refreshing swim in the sea, before hiking back to camp once more.

At tonight's camp fire, we can be creative when it comes to our bush cuisine. Home-baked breads, healthy stir-fries and interesting salads contrast with the more usual chops, sausage and foil-baked potato.

KING HINTSA

On 12 May 1835, during the Frontier Wars, Hintsa, king of the Xhosa nation, was shot and killed by George Southey while allegedly attempting to escape from British forces. This escape came about while Hintsa was accompanying British forces to recover raided cattle.

During this period there were attempts to form an alliance between the Xhosa and the British; however, Hintsa resisted and maintained that he was interested only in peace with the British, not subservience.

He was adamant in this to the point that he did not support those Xhosa chiefs who acted against the British. However, the British suspected him of colluding with these chiefs and it was in this regard that Sir Harry Smith, accompanied by Southey and a mixture of military and civilian forces, approached the kraal of Hintsa in order to recover looted cattle. They then insisted that Hintsa accompany them to the kraals of the chieftains they claimed had looted cattle. It was during this journey that the British claim Hintsa had attempted to escape. They claimed that as they approached the Rarabe River, they noticed Xhosa warriors moving in the undergrowth.

When they suspected Hintsa was leading them into an ambush, the king took off on his horse. Despite a warning shot having been fired, Hintsa raced off, and only after he was wounded twice and dismounted did he ask for mercy. It was then that Southey, one of the claimants regarding cattle theft, shot and killed the Xhosa king.

What followed is still under much dispute – some historians claim that Hintsa was beheaded and his head taken back to Scotland as a souvenir, others claim that his body was left whole to be recovered by his compatriots. What is certain is that his royal bracelets and jewellery were stolen and his ears cut off for souvenirs.

The plot thickens, though, as in 1996, a Chief Gcaleka arrived at the Inverness HQ of a Highland Regiment, claiming that the spirits had directed him to reclaim the skull of King Hintsa, or peace would never come to South Africa. The laird of a nearby estate called him up to say that he had the skull Gcaleka was looking for. The skull was duly handed over, but its authenticity was never tested, nor disputed!

King Hintsa's grave is near Cebe in the Eastern Cape.

ARCHAEOLOGICAL HISTORY IN THE EASTERN CAPE

One of the first dinosaurs to be identified, the Blinkwater Monster, comes from the Eastern Cape. It was discovered and identified near Fort Beaufort.

The Eastern Cape is the area where some of the oldest dwelling sites of modern human beings have been discovered, as well as some of the oldest, if not the oldest evidence of cultural activity in the world. This is the Klasies River cave site in the Tsitsikamma which has been dated back 125,000 years. At this site evidence has been uncovered that includes a grave where the skeleton was in a foetal position and surrounded by cowrie shells, indicating that the body was buried with some ceremony. Where there is ceremony, there is culture – and this is the earliest proven evidence of cultural activity to be found on earth.

All along the coastline of the Eastern Cape there are a number of sites left by the Later Stone Age people, often erroneously called the Strandloper people. These sites consist mostly of middens – mounds where their rubbish, usually containing mussel and other shells, was thrown.

Rock art, too, is prolific. Interestingly, some sites show scenes such as ox-wagons and soldiers in red uniforms. These are indications of a society under stress and this period can also be described as 'Apocalyptic Rock Art'.

King Hintsa's Grave 2 km

DAY 4

This is a long day in the car as you make your way inland almost to Elliotdale before turning eastwards and heading for Hole in the Wall. En route, we stop at the Mbhashe River for a late-morning snack before resuming our journey on dusty gravel roads, which eventually become tar roads, with the optimistic speed limit of 60kmph – optimistic owing to the proliferation of potholes.

Nearing Hole in the Wall and Coffee Bay, one senses a more active commercial presence, with numerous backpackers' establishments, bush pubs, pizza dens and the like advertised colourfully at the intersections. There are adventure activities too, such as hiking, kayaking, horse trails and boat trips.

A short drive takes us down to Hole in the Wall (or as close to it as we are allowed to go these days), which remains an impressive sight. A short walk over a rocky beach gets us down to sea level, where we really get an idea of the scale of this natural phenomenon.

Hole in the Wall

We pull into the Ocean View Hotel for a toastie and lager. It's a brilliant place, with slackpackers and other general holiday-makers, such as ourselves, passing through.

Leaving here, a 10-minute drive sees us crossing the Mthatha River before arriving at the Anchorage Hotel, where we set up camp for the next two nights. On our arrival, orders are placed for oysters and crayfish with the hotel staff, who will even clean and prepare this wonderful seafood for you if you so wish.

On a previous trip an interesting debate had raged over the inter-vehicle radios around the reason for the broken glass pieces embedded in the mud on the crown of the thatch-roofed

COFFEE BAY

Coffee Bay is named after coffee shrubs which began to grow after the 1863 wrecking of a ship carrying a cargo of coffee. The trees never grew successfully and eventually died, but the name stuck.

Coffee Bay is also known as Tshontini, the name of a dense wood found here.

HOLE IN THE WALL

Second to Table Mountain, this ranks as the next most recognisable geographic feature of the South African coastline. Although many times smaller, it is no less dramatic in its visual appeal as it stands sentinel at the mouth of the Mpako River.

The feature, some 260 million years old, comprises multiple layers of rock strata of different consistency, such as sandstone, mudstone and shale, with a layer of dolerite in-between. The constant wave action on the softer strata above the dolerite allowed them to be eroded away, which caused the massif to be separated from the mainland and was also responsible for creating the hole, the dolerite in effect acting as a giant lintel.

The rumbling sound of approaching waves is amplified as the waves enter the hole, explaining its local name of *esiKhaleni*, meaning 'place of sound' in the Bomvana language. It received its English name 'Hole in the Wall' from a Captain Vidal of the British Admiralty survey vessel, the *Barracouta*, which was sent to survey the coast from Keiskamma to Lourenço Marques. The ship's log describes 'two ponderous black rocks above the water's edge, upwards of 80 feet above its surface, exhibiting through the phenomenon of a natural archway'.

According to local legend, the Mpako River's passage to the sea was blocked off by a huge cliff, causing it to be dammed up and forming a huge lagoon as a result. Upon a certain day, the god-like sea creatures spied a beautiful maiden who lived beside this lagoon and were so taken by her splendid beauty that they tried to woo her.

The sea gods enlisted the help of a huge fish to bash a hole straight through the cliff through which they then swam so that they could have access to the lagoon. The maiden was taken away through the hole to live out to sea with the sea gods for ever.

huts. (The mud is used to seal the apex of the thatch to prevent water leaking in.) The one argument was that it was to prevent owls from perching on your hut, which is a bad omen according to traditional beliefs. The other was that it was used to bind the mud, allowing it to set firm. A Xhosa-speaking member of our party eventually stopped and asked a local woman the real reason. She explained that it was purely decorative, although the practice has the secondary benefits of binding the mud and keeping owls at bay. Sometimes bits of wood or colourful plastic are substituted.

Interestingly, just inland from where we travelled during the day lies the small village of Mvezo, the birthplace of Nelson Mandela. A commercial hike commemorates his daily walk to school at Qunu, where he still owns a house.

DAY 5

We really appreciate this further day at rest on our Wild Coast journey of discovery. Some walk along the beach to the mouth of the Mthatha River, while others fish, or swim, or revisit Hole in the Wall, before returning back to camp for some Cobb-baked bread and a pot-bread.

After a brief nap, we enjoy another beach walk, this time in the other direction, which isn't quite as picturesque, but the swim is worth it nonetheless.

Back at camp, after a refreshingly hot shower, we gather around the camp fire to enjoy the wonderful seafood fare, as prepared by the hotel staff.

Contrasting modes of transport

DAY 6

And so we set off early for the mouth of the nearby Mdumbi River before continuing our coastal exploration to Presley Bay and arriving at lunch time at the Mtakatye River, which resembles a private concession of sorts. We stop just outside and enjoy a picnic lunch in pleasant surroundings with a great view over the sea and river mouth.

Continuing after lunch, we cross the Mthonga River and call into the Mpande River mouth, before veering inland, for the last time, to pick up the tarred R61. This road passes through fairly mountainous terrain before levelling out alongside the Mzimvubu River as it lazily snakes its way into Port St Johns, or 'PSJ' as it is known to the locals. Here we settle into the Cremorne Estate caravan park, before spending the afternoon at leisure, touring this iconic if run-down Transkei town.

MAGWA FALLS AND TEA PLANTATION

The Magwa Falls are located in the heart of Pondoland near Lusikisiki in the Eastern Cape. It is a curtain-type waterfall that drops 144m into a slot-type canyon that was formed by seismic activity. Extreme caution is always advised here, as there are no guard barriers.

The Magwa Tea Plantation on which the falls are located has been steeped in political controversy ever since its questionable origins back in the 1970s by the then Transkei homeland government. Three clans living on the site had to be forcibly removed, with army backing, and relocated to seven neighbouring villages. This move boomeranged on the company when it was the subject of a successful land claim in 1998, in terms of which the claimants are now the owners of the estate.

Unfortunately, mismanagement and fraud nearly ran the estate into the ground and it then became heavily reliant on considerable financial shoring up from government. Without subsidisation, the estate is unprofitable. An ironic twist is that tea is not a viable crop in South Africa by virtue of a Southern African Development Community (SADC) agreement to import tea from Kenya and Malawi.

MBOTYI – THE PLACE OF BEANS

Of all the beautiful riverine estuaries in the Pondoland region of the Eastern Cape, Mbotyi is not only the most beautiful, it also has a colourful, eccentric history.

Take the story of the two original owners of the Mbotyi Trading Store, Johannes Victor Kottich and Jack Barber. Barber was the Robinson Crusoe of Mbotyi. After being wounded in World War I he met the love of his life, Sally Barnes, a nurse in a French military hospital. After he proposed to Barnes, Barber arranged for her to travel by ship from Boston to Mbotyi. Calculating when the ship would pass, he made a signal bonfire. Barnes arrived by ox-wagon and after landing got involved in the community, nursing the sick and the infirm. After Barnes died, Barber died in a cottage blaze.

Kottich was a recluse living in a tiny shack overlooking the sea. Apparently he was a morphine addict who established a fictitious pharmacy in Lusikisiki in order to secure a regular supply of drugs. He was also supposed to have made contact with German U-boats during World War II.

More recently, notorious ex-policeman turned bank robber, André Stander, stayed in a rondavel in Mbotyi while fleeing the police. He pretended to be an American until eventually he was identified, whereupon he disappeared. Shortly afterwards he fled to Fort Lauderdale in the United States, where he was shot dead.

DAY 7

And so, the last day of the trip is upon us. What lies ahead today is a drive up to Lusikisiki, a largish town, to visit the Magwa Tea Plantation and the magnificent Magwa Falls, before ending off this truly memorable trip at Mbotyi, the shiniest jewel in a jewel-encrusted crown, if only for its remote setting. It is distinctly noticeable how the scenery is starting to resemble that of the KwaZulu-Natal coastline, and this is due to the fact that we are travelling further and further northwards towards that region.

Around midday we have seen all that we have come to see, visited all the sites and taken plenty of images that we will take home with us. Enduring friendships have been forged around numerous camp fires. Many misconceptions of life in rural South Africa have been clarified.

We all leave the Transkei greatly enriched.

DAY 8

This final day sees each family making their way home at their own pace and according to their own agenda. Decisions have to be made for the first time in a week. That is the beauty of organised tours – you don't have to think about anything more than what to cook for supper!

(Based on a trip by the author with Cederberg 4x4.)

17 Great Limpopo – Soutpansberg and mythical Venda lore

by Dave van Graan

TOP 10 ATTRACTIONS OF THIS TRIP

❶ Stunning views from the mountain over the plains below ❷ Varied off-road driving 'obstacles' – from easy to moderate to technical – and varied driving conditions, including sand, rock, mud and some water crossings too ❸ Indulge your passion for stargazing ❹ The opportunity to hone your overlanding skills, especially on the drive to the bush camp at Tshirovha Waterfall ❺ Experience tropical rainforests and other ecosystems ❻ Birders' paradise – more than 540 species have been identified in the region ❼ Butterflies are in abundance, and at night moths of all colours and sizes fly around the lights ❽ Experience the Venda culture, legends, myths and folklore ❾ Rivers and waterfalls ❿ Get to know the history of the area

TRIP OUTLINE

The Soutpansberg is the northernmost mountain range in South Africa – 100km north of Polokwane and 100km south of Musina. The range starts near Vivo in the west and continues for 210km to the Kruger National Park in the east. At its widest point, the mountain can be up to 60km wide, and it is 15km at its narrowest point. The altitude ranges from 250m above sea level to Hanglip, which attains 1719m (the second highest peak), and Letjuma which, at 1748m, is the highest point of the Soutpansberg.

The Soutpansberg range covers a mere 5% of the ground area of South Africa; however, it is a 'living mountain' in that the region boasts 30% of the tree species found throughout the country. Due to the size of the mountain there are many different ecosystems, making it a very popular venue for nature lovers. The ecosystems range from tropical rainforest to dry bushveld, where you will find baobab (*Andasonia digitata*) and mopane (*Colophospermum mopane*).

The Soutpansberg geological system has an approximate age of 1700 million years. The main rocks forming the mountain are sandstone, quartz sandstone and quartzite. There are a few igneous intrusions, mainly dolerite. To the north and south of the mountain are mineral-rich areas, but the mountain itself is poor in minerals.

There are many routes in this area and sometimes a 4X4 vehicle is the only means to visit some of the sites.

SEE DETAILED MAP ON PAGE 180 ▶▶

APPEAL RATING

5/5

The name of the Soutpansberg was derived from the salt pans that are situated on the northwestern side of the mountain, near the village of Waterpoort. The salt was used to trade with the tribes of Mapungubwe and Great Zimbabwe. The Soutpansberg is the home of the Venda people, and quite a few of the places we'll be visiting are shrouded in Venda legend and folklore.

- The inclines, declines and gravel mountain routes will need the driver's constant concentration
- Some areas are very remote and the vehicle and equipment must be in good condition
- With the wide variety of ecosystems in the Soutpansberg, there are birds, butterflies, trees and plants that are unique to the area
- The Venda legends and stories will thrill visitors and make them look over their shoulders at night
- The dark, spooky forests, waterfalls and mountain vistas will make even a novice photographer look good
- The whole family will find enjoyment from at least one aspect of this trip
- For those wanting to get away from technology, signals for mobile networks may be sparse or non-existent in most areas
- San rock paintings

THE BEST TIME TO TRAVEL HERE

- The area may be visited all year round, but summer can be extremely hot on the northern side of the mountain, whereas winter is normally mild
- From April to August is a good time to escape the cold for a few days (plenty of pensioners flock to Tshipise during the winter to escape the cold weather normally associated with the Highveld – these travellers have been given the name 'the swallows'); night temperatures very seldom go below 12°C and day temperatures are around 25 to 30°C
- The best months are usually April and May, just after the rains, as the bush will still be lush and green and some of the migratory birds will still be around
- The drier months will make river crossings easier as the rainfall can be very high on the southern side of the mountain and flash floods occur regularly to the north; however, the waterfalls are less spectacular in the drier months
- Serious 4X4 drivers prefer the wet months as they get ample opportunity to get stuck and use all their recovery equipment

FAMILY-FRIENDLY RATING

4/5

- Small children might find the travelling boring, but we stop regularly at places of interest to alleviate the boredom
- The birds of prey soaring the warm air currents en route are a point of great entertainment for children and grown-ups alike
- Nwanedi and Tshipise are both any child's dream, with their swimming pools and playgrounds
- Adults and the elderly should see and experience enough to keep them interested
- There are plenty of sites to keep any photographer entertained
- This is a camping tour, but at some overnight stops alternative accommodation (such as rooms and chalets) is available
- There are outdoor activities to satisfy everyone in the family

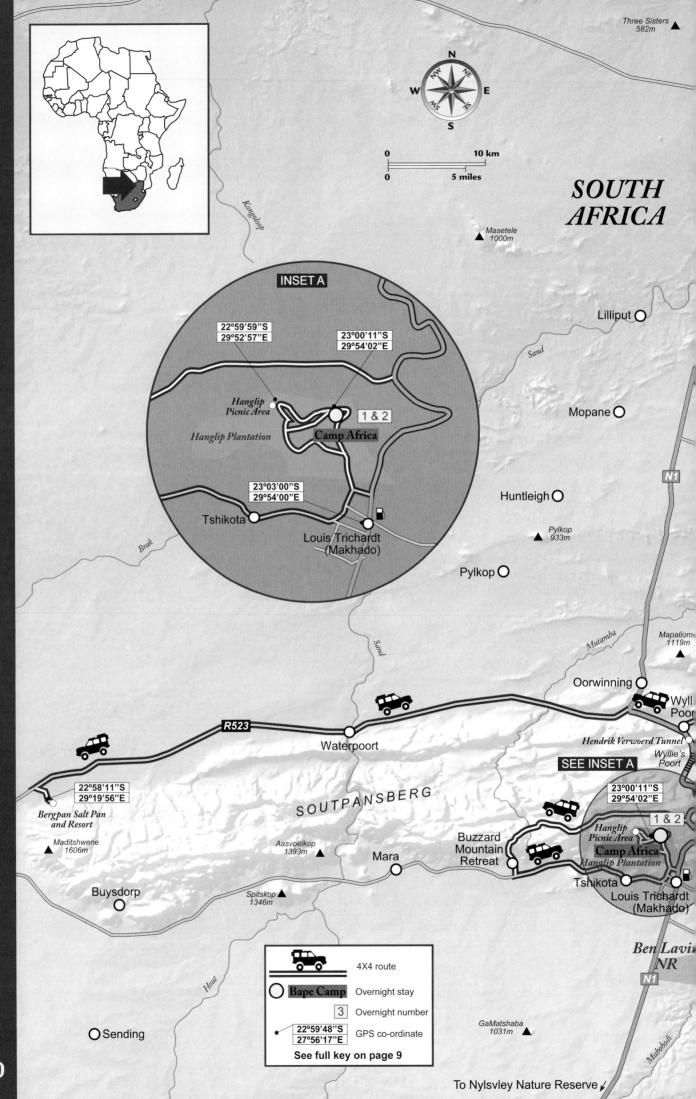

MAP 17 GREAT LIMPOPO – Soutpansberg and mythical Venda lore

INSET A

22°59'59"S
29°52'57"E

23°00'11"S
29°54'02"E

Hanglip
Picnic Area

1 & 2

Hanglip Plantation

Camp Africa

23°03'00"S
29°54'00"E

Tshikota

Louis Trichardt
(Makhado)

SOUTH
AFRICA

Three Sisters
582m

Masetele
1000m

Lilliput

Mopane

Huntleigh

Pylkop
933m

Pylkop

Kongolop

Sand

Brak

Sand

Mutamba

Mapaliom
1119m

Oorwinning

Wyll
Poor

R523

Waterpoort

Hendrik Verwoerd Tunnel

Wyllie's
Poort

SEE INSET A

23°00'11"S
29°54'02"E

1 & 2

Hanglip
Picnic Area

Camp Africa

Hanglip Plantation

Tshikota

Louis Trichardt
(Makhado)

22°58'11"S
29°19'56"E

Bergpan Salt Pan
and Resort

Maditshwene
1606m

SOUTPANSBERG

Aasvoëlkop
1393m

Mara

Buzzard
Mountain
Retreat

Buysdorp

Spitskop
1346m

Ben Lavi
NR

N1

GaMatshaba
1031m

Sending

	4X4 route
Bape Camp	Overnight stay
3	Overnight number
22°59'48"S 27°56'17"E	GPS co-ordinate

See full key on page 9

N

NE

E

SE

S

SW

W

NW

0   10 km

0   5 miles

To Nylsvley Nature Reserve

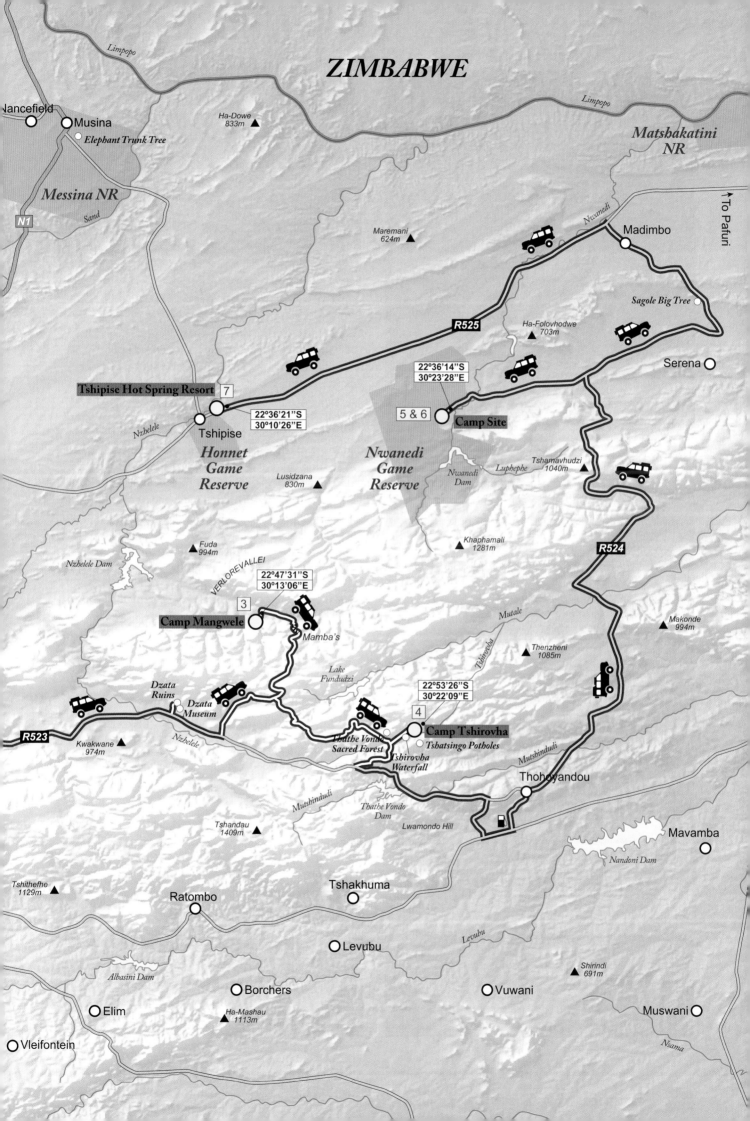

Day 1	Arrive at Camp Africa, Louis Trichardt (Makhado)		
Day 2	Explore Buzzard Mountain Retreat	60km	8hr
Day 3	Camp Africa to Camp Mangwele	180km	9hr
Day 4	Camp Mangwele to Tshirovha	50km	10hr
Day 5	Tshirovha to camp at Nwanedi Game Reserve	150km	10hr
Day 6	At leisure and exploring Nwanedi Game Reserve	20km	6–7hr
Day 7	Nwanedi to Tshipise Hot Spring Resort	90km	7hr
Day 8	After breakfast depart for home at own pace		

SELF-SUFFICIENCY RATING

3/5

▶ Although you get the feeling that you are far out in the bush, we are no more than an hour and a half from 'civilisation'; there are medical facilities in Thohoyandou, Louis Trichardt, Tshipise and Musina.

▶ The water at Camp Africa is very good, clean fountain water and everybody can fill their tanks before we depart; we can refill along the way, if needed

▶ The guide vehicle will carry firewood and we can replenish along the way (if you travel alone it is preferable to bring wood and charcoal along with you, just in case)

▶ Fuel is available along the way, but we suggest you fill up in Louis Trichardt before driving to Camp Africa on day 1

▶ All camps have flushing toilets and hot showers except the camp at Tshirovha Waterfall, which is a bush camp with no facilities – a swim in the pool below the falls washes away the dust (a kettle of warm water can also do the trick), and there is plenty of bush around the camp to do your cat-type ablutions in private

▶ Make sure your bedding is comfortable and bring an extra blanket just in case we get caught in a cold front

▶ Dinners are provided by Masazane Expeditions, but you provide your own breakfast and lunch (we also supply all the pots, pans and gas)

ARCHAEOLOGY

The world's oldest datable rock, a piece of granite gneiss almost 4000 million years old, is situated in the Messina Nature Reserve.

Dinosaur fossils that date back some 180 million years were found near Mapungubwe.

Hanglip

DAY 1

Camp Africa is situated in the Hanglip Plantation, 6km from Louis Trichardt (Makhado), and is surrounded by both pine and indigenous forests. Louis Trichardt is 400km north of Pretoria. Birding, hiking and mountain biking are some of the activities that attract people to this area. There are some farm animals at the camp to entertain the young ones.

Camp Africa is the base camp for Masazane Expeditions, and all their Trans-Africa expeditions start from here. The camp can accommodate at least 10 vehicles camping on the wide stretch of grass. There are also five huts with four beds in each hut (bedding is included), accommodating a further 20 people. There is a well-stocked, lively bar where plenty of travel stories are swapped and jokes are told. A fully equipped kitchen and fridge/freezer facilities are also available to guests. There are braai areas inside and outside, and electricity can be arranged for camping vehicles that carry fridges.

If approaching Louis Trichardt from the south, birders may want to stop and visit Nylsvley Nature Reserve. Take the N1 and follow the turn-off at Kranskop towards Modimolle. In Modimolle, take the road to Mookgophong (R101). At the Boekenhout station sign, 43km from the toll plaza, turn right. The Nylsvley entrance is 8km further, 1km past the railway line on the left. Nylsvley is a Ramsar site with a list of 191 woodland species.

FLORA, FAUNA AND AGRICULTURAL SNIPPETS

Due to the fact that the Soutpansberg lies north of the Tropic of Capricorn, the climate is perfect for the cultivation of avocado, pineapple, litchis, bananas and a variety of nuts. There is even a tea plantation near Thohoyandou. Bee-keeping is very popular due to the variety of trees and plants, and there is always some species flowering in the bush.

Leadwood trees can become very old and it has been established that some are over 1000 years old. The dead trunk of a leadwood tree can stand erect for up to 50 years.

The Bonsmara cattle breed originated at Mara Agricultural Centre, west of Louis Trichardt.

There are 48 different gecko species and 48 different snake species in the Soutpansberg area.

DAY 2

The area that we will explore today starts from Louis Trichardt and the first section will be west of the town on a farm called Buzzard Mountain Retreat. Although this farm is mainly a cattle farm, the owner loves his land and some game species were introduced for game-viewing purposes. The section of this farm that we drive is a long, winding road that takes us up into the mountain where we can enjoy fabulous views to the south over the plains. The ecosystem is varied and starts with typical bushveld species such as sickle bush to an almost fynbos-like ecosystem that reminds you of the Cape region. We will see some of the larger specimens of cycads that are indigenous to the Soutpansberg (*Euphorbia soutpansbergensis*), as well as the *Encephalartos transvenosus* cycad, also endemic to the area. A variety of birds of prey can be seen here, where they nest and hunt for dassies (hyrax).

Some sections can be difficult to drive and 4X4 low range is the only way to slowly climb higher and higher into the mountain's upper reaches. It can be rough going after the rainy season, with deep ruts that cross the road. Make sure that safe following distances are maintained between vehicles so that, if needed, the vehicle in front will have space to reverse and try again in the event of a cross-axle situation.

Eventually, we will meet the Bluegumspoort road that will take us back to the Hanglip Plantation (the name 'Bluegumspoort' is derived from a row of bluegum trees that was planted early in the 20th century). We then drive through a section of rainforest to the hiking hut where there are once again wonderful views to enjoy. The Hanglip peak is close by and on a clear day it provides really good photo opportunities.

The convoy prepares to go into the mountains

Tropical birds such as narina trogon, purple-crested turaco, Knysna turaco and African paradise-flycatchers are often seen here. Crested guineafowl are also found near the picnic area. Sightings of leopard, caracal, chacma baboons, bushbuck and red duiker are possible. A wide variety of ferns can be seen along the way, and old man's beard moss hanging from the trees gives the place an eerie feel. We usually enjoy a light sundowner before driving slowly back to Camp Africa for a well-deserved dinner. Later we relax around the fire where jokes are told and all the 4X4 obstacles are 'driven' again.

MOPANE WORMS AND TREES

These large, spiny and hairless worms subsist mainly on the leaves of the mopane tree (*Colophospernum mopane*). The mopane moth (*Gonimbrasia belina*) has a wingspan of 125mm. The worms are a sought-after source of protein for the local people. They are consumed raw, dried or cooked.

The worms' distribution is consistent with that of their favoured host, and they are found in a broad band in the northern regions of South Africa and stretching into Zimbabwe, Botswana and Namibia.

A substantial trade in mopane worms exists through the region.

THE SAUSAGE TREE – *KIGELIA AFRICANA*

This exceptional tree is found in the eastern parts of Southern Africa, from KwaZulu-Natal in the south all the way to Tanzania.

The fruits are unpalatable but are often ground and added to traditional beer brews. The wood is soft but tough, and when dry it is easy to work to a smooth finish. Due to its strength, it is popular for making yokes, oars and canoes.

Although the trees offer good shade, the fruits are big and heavy. Some fruits can grow up to 500mm in length and weigh up to 4kg. If one is in the way of a falling fruit it could cause serious injury. It is not a good idea to set up your camp under a sausage tree!

DAY 3

An early start is required, so today we will leave Camp Africa at 08:00 after a satisfying breakfast. The next section is along the Soutpansberg Pass, which is part of the N1, towards Musina, taking a short break at the Hendrik Verwoerd tunnels. We are now on the warm, dry side of the mountain where majestic baobab trees can be seen; other trees that occur here are marula, leadwood and knobthorn.

We follow the Waterpoort road that will eventually lead us to the salt pans. (The area around Waterpoort is the home of ZZ2, the biggest tomato producers in Africa.)

A local guide will give us a talk on the workings of the salt mine. The salt occurs as a result of water flowing from the mountain into

MINING ACTIVITIES IN THE REGION

The Venetia Mine, between Alldays and Musina, is the flagship operation of De Beers and one of the biggest opencast diamond mines in the world, producing 8.52Mct.

Because the mine is situated in an ecologically sensitive area, De Beers invested R17 million on environmental engineering projects such as burying the 35km-long water pipeline and installing state-of-the-art dust, noise and lighting reduction systems.

The Tshikondeni Mine is a high-grade coal mine situated in the northeast of Venda near Masisi. The mine was developed by ISCOR in the 1980s to assist the small former homeland of Venda to become more self-reliant. Today there is a modern village with a primary school, shops and sports facilities.

Adjacent to the Tshikondeni Mine is Makuya Game Reserve (18,000ha), which borders on the Kruger National Park. Big game such as elephant, lion, buffalo and hippo can move freely across the Levubu River between the two parks.

VEHICLE REQUIREMENTS

▶ Four-wheel-drive with low range
▶ Recovery points front and back
▶ Good ground clearance
▶ Proper off-road tyres
▶ Rear diff-lock or traction control will be an advantage
▶ Seed net

TRAILER-FRIENDLY RATING

3/5

▶ There is one section, called Mamba's Pass, that is difficult with a trailer (but we have towed off-road trailers and off-road caravans along the whole route before) – it is a slow crawl up the mountain with loose gravel and rocks underfoot; low range and a steady foot on the fuel will get you through without any problems (it is sometimes necessary to pack rocks in the erosion ruts that form after heavy rains)
▶ There are other short inclines and declines along the way, so braked trailer axles are definitely an advantage
▶ We camp at Camp Africa on days one and two – we will leave the trailers at the camp on day two
▶ On day six we have a rest day, and once again the trailers stay at the camp while we do some game-viewing
▶ Most of the route is on good gravel or tar roads

GENERAL WARNINGS FOR THIS ROUTE

▶ The area is a low-risk malaria area – we suggest that you cover up between dusk and dawn and use a good insect repellent (the risk is lower during the dry months)
▶ Odourless insect killer to spray your tents and vehicle (burning mosquito coils will also help)
▶ Take special care with children in terms of malaria
▶ Consult with your doctor before venturing into malaria areas
▶ Wear boots or closed shoes at night to prevent stings by scorpions (the cooler, drier months are less dangerous and you are less likely to encounter malaria or scorpions)
▶ The camp at Nwanedi Game Reserve is notorious for the arrogant baboons and monkeys that try to steal food from unsuspecting campers, so close all vehicle windows, doors and tents, and keep foodstuffs sealed and stored away
▶ Crocodiles do occur in some rivers and dams in Venda – if in doubt, rather stay out of the water
▶ Sun-protection creams, hats and long-sleeved shirts are recommended, as are sunglasses
▶ There are no large free-ranging predators on the route
▶ The local people are friendly and keep to themselves, but keep your doors locked when leaving the vehicle alone
▶ No quad bikes are allowed in any of the Komatiland Forestry areas
▶ Bring along your binoculars
▶ Keep an eye on the children at swimming pools and other open water; they should always be supervised
▶ Never dive or jump into dark water pools – there may be rocks under the surface
▶ Always keep in the tracks – we do not want to damage the environment

a small lake. The high temperatures and low rainfall in the area allow the water to evaporate. Over millennia, the salt concentration became so high that eventually the whole lake was filled with salt. We usually have lunch at the mine under some big shady trees before setting off towards Dzata Ruins and Museum.

Dzata, meaning 'Good Place', was one of the first places where the Venda people settled after leaving Mapungubwe. Dzata Ruins is the site of a Venda royal village dating back to AD1400. Iron furnaces dating back to AD1250 are found at Tshimbubfe. A local guide will share his knowledge of Venda culture and history.

After an informative visit to the ruins, we continue the drive to our overnight stop at Camp Mangwele. This camp is a community project and all the buildings have been built by the members of the community themselves. The camp is situated in the Verlorevallei ('Lost or Forgotten Valley') and is very basic, although there are flushing toilets and hot showers. The small stream that runs through the camp is popular with the young (and young at heart) for getting rid of the day's dust and sweat.

We are now in rural Venda and the people are very traditional in their ways. They still eat mopane worms when in season. It is not uncommon to see women catching grasshoppers, which they cook and eat with *pap* (maize meal porridge). The Venda people make an alcoholic drink from the sap of palm trees. The juice is left to ferment and after some time it becomes a very potent local 'beer'. They also distil the beer, which then becomes a type of *mampoer* (a tequila-like spirit) that is called *totot*. Beware: *totot* is a very strong drink with a very high alcohol content.

Start of Mamba's Pass

Lake Fundudzi

DAY 4

Today we do some more serious 4X4 driving, following a mountain track called the Mamba's Pass. (The history of the pass is not known but it appears that some civil engineering knowledge was needed to build it; there are both supporting and rock walls, suggesting that, at some stage, it was a government project.) You can almost imagine you're in the Southern Cape as there is plenty of fynbos around. There are beautiful views of the Nzhelele Dam in the distance.

We are now on the northern side of the mountain and, because it is generally hotter and drier than the southern side, we can expect totally different plants and trees. We

A SHORT HISTORY OF THE VENDA PEOPLE

The Ba Venda are a Bantu people living in Southern Africa. The Mapungubwe Kingdom emerged in the 9th century when, according to historical studies, King Shiriyadenga, the first king of Mapungubwe and Venda, united two tribes and formed the Vhavgona or Vhavhenda.

As with most of the other tribal peoples of Southern Africa, the Venda migrated southwards from Central Africa. They are regarded as the last black group to have crossed the Limpopo River, and they first settled in the Soutpansberg.

Venda history is closely related to the history of their successive sub-chiefs, especially those who were descended from their legendary ancestor, Thoho-ya-Ndou (or 'Head of the Elephant').

Thoho-ya-Ndou's kraal was called Dzata ('home'), and its remains are now a heritage site. Dzata had great significance for the Venda because they buried their chiefs facing in its direction.

Today there are 26 sub-chiefs who trace their origins to the great man, while a few others are descended from tribes that were later incorporated with the Venda.

There was an important social division in Venda society between commoners, called *vhasiwana*, and the children of chiefs and their descendants, known as *vhakololo*.

One of the most interesting and distinct groups of people who later joined the Venda were the African Semites known as the Lemba. The Lemba are believed to be the descendants of Semitic traders who entered Africa around AD696, or descendants of the Lost Tribe of Israel. DNA tests confirm they are indeed descendants of an ancient Jewish people. They keep to themselves, only marry within their own group and sometimes refer to themselves as Vhalungu, which means 'non-Negroid' or 'respected foreigner'.

Original Lemba beads are treasured to this day and used in divination and other magical ceremonies. The Lemba were very good traders and artisans, famous for their metalwork and pottery.

Venda culture is an interesting mix, in many ways culturally closer to the Shona people of Zimbabwe while also displaying strong affinities to the Lemba, Lobedu and North Sotho. Trade, warfare and intermarriage with Tsonga, Lobedu, Zulu, Swazi and other people have inevitably left their imprints on Venda culture.

The Venda appear to have incorporated a variety of East African, Central African, Nguni and Sotho cultural characteristics. For example, they forbid the consumption of pork, a prohibition that is common along the East African coast. They practise male circumcision, which is common among many Sotho, but not so among most Nguni peoples.

Venda culture is built on a vibrant mythical belief system, which is reflected in their artistic style. Water is an important theme to the Venda and there are many sacred sites within their region where the Venda conjure up their ancestral spirits.

SAN ROCK ART

The rock art of Limpopo province is not as well known as that in other areas in the country but, to date, 700 sites have been found and research is ongoing. There are two types of rock art, namely engravings and paintings.

So far 41 sites have been discovered in the Soutpansberg itself, but due to the sensitivity of the rock art, most of the sites are out of bounds to visitors. One of the sites that does permit visitors, by appointment only, is Medike Mountain Reserve. Reservations are made by e-mail (medike@mweb.co.za).

practised, the offerings are left at the side of the lake – there are still crocodiles in the lake. The local guide will tell you more stories about the lake.

Next we drive through the Thathe Vondo Sacred Forest where the guide will once again share his knowledge about Venda legends and folklore. For instance, it is believed that a white lion protects this forest and that the early Venda kings were buried there. No ordinary person is allowed in the forest to hunt or collect firewood. (One wonders if this practice was the start of a type of game reserve to protect the animals and plants in the region.) If time allows, we can visit a viewpoint that overlooks the tea plantations, Thathe Vondo Dam and Lwamondo Hill. This hill is also part of the Venda legends – the hill and the baboons living there are considered sacred because the baboons warned the people when their enemies were climbing up the hill to attack. It is believed that the baboons could tell friend from foe.

The next section follows a route that winds its way past a dam, a small waterfall and through a pine forest to our overnight stop at the Tshirovha Waterfall. The waterfall is surrounded by pine forest on the one side and indigenous forest on the other. This camp has no facilities and will give everybody

are sometimes rewarded with sightings of klipspringer and Verreaux's eagles. Slowly, in low range, we drive to the top of the mountain where the track joins a public road that takes us to the viewpoint above Lake Fundudzi.

Although it is not very big, Lake Fundudzi is the only true lake in South Africa. It was formed when a landslide partially blocked the Mutale River. The Venda believe that a sacred white crocodile and a white python live in the lake. In the past, young maidens were offered to the crocodile, but this practice was stopped a few years ago. Although the ceremony is still

Tshirovha Waterfall

SPECIFIC KIT REQUIRED FOR THIS TRIP

- Full camping gear, bedding, tents, tables and chairs
- Crockery and cutlery
- Drinking water for three days (water for washing is available at all the camps)
- A fridge/freezer can make life a little more luxurious in the bush
- Liquid refreshments and ice
- GPS (with Tracks 4 Africa) is a must if you want to travel without a guide
- Licensed 29MHz radio
- A pair of comfortable walking shoes
- A jacket or jersey

ESSENTIAL REQUIREMENTS FOR THIS TRIP

- Leather gloves to wear when setting up camp, collecting firewood, changing tyres and doing recoveries
- Puncture-repair kit, tyre-pressure gauge and compressor
- Kinetic and tow strap or rope.
- Bow and D-shackles
- Spade
- Inflatable air jack if your vehicle is not high-lift jack compatible (the guide vehicle is equipped with a high-lift jack and winch)
- Basic tools and spares for your vehicle
- Lighting – headlamp, a good torch and a lamp for your tent
- Toilet paper (white gold)
- Their favourite toys and games to occupy your children en route
- First-aid kit with plasters, bandages, disinfectant and medication for headaches, pain, nausea and diarrhoea
- Take enough personal medicine to last the whole trip
- Antihistamine tablets and creams for bites and allergies

SEE FULL PACKING LIST ON PAGE 218 ▶▶

THE CICADA BEETLE

There around 2500 species of cicada beetle in the world, of which 150 are found in South Africa. Different species are associated with different species of trees. The cicada that prefers mopane trees can take up to 17 years to mature.

Cicada males are responsible for the shrill, deafening noise that one often hears in the bush. They suck the sap from their favoured tree stems via a long proboscis. In some cultures they are regarded as a delicacy.

GEOGRAPHY

The Soutpansberg is the gateway to the rest of Africa. From here one can enter Botswana, Zimbabwe or Mozambique.

The major rivers are the Levubu, Mutale, Mutamba, Nzhelele, Limpopo and the Sand rivers. All the rivers are tributaries of the Limpopo River basin.

There are a few dams in the area, namely Nandoni Dam, Albasini Dam, Nzhelele Dam and Nwanedi Dam, where fishing, canoeing, boating, birding and even skiing will keep the outdoor lover occupied.

The highest average rainfall in the mountain (near Levubu) is 1874mm and the lowest (around Waterpoort) is 367mm.

an idea of what it is like to live like the explorers of yesteryear. This is a typical situation that one can expect on long African overland expeditions where bush camps are set up along the way. The pool at the waterfall is large enough to swim in and is very popular with children.

DAY 5

We need to start early and leave camp by 08:00, straight after breakfast. Our first stop will be at the Tshatsingo Potholes (also known as the 'Place of Execution'), also a part of Venda folklore. The water from the Tshirovha River flows into a large pothole with an underwater outlet. The Venda believe that if a criminal is thrown into the pothole and appears alive on the other side, that person is innocent of any crime, but if the person should die, he or she was guilty as charged – no chance of an appeal in this system!

We drive along gravel roads to Thohoyandou (it means 'the head of the elephant' in Venda) where we can replenish our stocks and refuel the vehicles. We follow a gravel road through the hills and valleys to Nwanedi Game Reserve. Stunning mountain vistas are the order of the day. We will arrive late in the afternoon at our overnight camp and set up camp under large shady trees. There are huts available for those who prefer a more luxurious stay.

Tshatsingo Potholes

DAY 6

Nwanedi Game Reserve lies at the confluence of the Nwanedi and Luphephe rivers. The reserve was proclaimed in 1979 by the former Venda homeland administration.

THE BAOBAB – *ADANSONIA DIGITATA*

The baobab is called the 'Tree of Life' with good reason, as it is capable of providing shelter, food and water for both animal and human inhabitants of the African savannah regions.

The cork-like bark is fire-resistant and is used for cloth and rope. The leaves are used for condiments and medicines. The fruit, called 'monkey bread', is rich in vitamin C and edible. The tree is capable of storing hundreds of litres of water, which is tapped in dry periods.

Mature baobab trees are frequently hollow, providing living space for numerous animals and humans. Trees are even used as bars, barns and more.

Radiocarbon dating has measured the age of some baobab trees at over 2000 years.

For most of the year, the tree is leafless, and looks very much as if it has its roots sticking up in the air. There are several legends offering explanations of how the tree came to be stuffed in the ground upside down, so that it could no longer complain.

There are also numerous superstitions among native African people regarding the powers of the tree. Anyone who dares to pick a flower, for instance, will be eaten by a lion. On the other hand, if you drank water in which the seeds have been soaked, you'd be safe from a crocodile attack.

Baobabs are actually succulents and consist of 80% moisture. They are pollinated by bats and bushbabies.

Big Tree, Sagole

Tshipise is a holiday resort with plenty to offer visitors old and young. There is a hot spring and quite a few swimming pools with hot water. There are large lawns where the children can play all sorts of games. Clean ablutions and other facilities make this resort the ideal place for a family breakaway. There is a game reserve adjacent to Tshipise. For those who need to replenish their stocks, there is a liquor store, butchery, bakery and restaurant in the small Tshipise Shopping Centre. Rondavels of different sizes are available, but it is essential to pre-book or you will miss out.

DAY 8

The tour ends after breakfast. Those who want to stay a few more days must make their own arrangements with the Tshipise Resort booking office. Visits to places like Mapungubwe National Park and other easily accessible places of interest in the area can be arranged.

As today is a rest day, we suggest a drive along the moderate 4X4 route through the reserve. Our advice is that at least two vehicles travel together on the game drive, to assist each other if necessary. The noise of a large convoy of vehicles will chase away all the animals and only the occupants of the first few vehicles usually see any game.

There are giraffe, white rhino, kudu, bushbuck, impala, klipspringer, monkeys, mongoose, African civet, leopard and many other species. Birding can be very rewarding, for beginners and experienced birders alike. There are plenty of waterfowl and other bird species along the rivers and dams. Other activities available are hiking, fishing, swimming or just relaxing in the camp. The energetic can tackle the long staircase to the top of the dam wall – beautiful views from the top make the climb worthwhile. It is a good idea for someone to stay in camp to guard against the marauding baboons and monkeys. The early risers can have a cup of coffee with rusks and then drive out to do some game-viewing. The group sometimes clubs in and enjoys a brunch at around 11:00.

DAY 7

Because of the easy route today, we rise a bit later and only leave our camp at 09:00 and drive via the Big Tree near Sagole to the Tshipise Resort. The Big Tree is truly a spectacular baobab tree with a circumference of 43m at the base and roots that are up to 2km long. It is estimated that the tree is older than 3000 years. From the Big Tree, we drive through mopane bushveld to connect with the Tshipise–Pafuri road. Those interested in touring the Kruger National Park, and even Mozambique, may break away from the group at this point and travel through the Pafuri border control post. During the winter it is quite simple to cross the Limpopo River and then drive via Mapai to Vilanculos.

18 Tracing the Molopo River – one of Africa's ancient rivers

by Philip Sackville-Scott

TOP 10 ATTRACTIONS OF THIS TRIP

❶ Varied off-road driving conditions – sand and rock ❷ Varied off-road driving tests – easy to moderate to technical ❸ Opportunity to hone your overlanding skills for that Namibia trip ❹ Wide open spaces ❺ Photographic opportunities ❻ Birders' paradise ❼ Clear air and blue skies ❽ Interesting cultures ❾ Unusual wildlife ❿ Hospitable people

TRIP OUTLINE

We follow the lower course of the Molopo from the Middelputs border post to its junction with the Orange River.

The Molopo River rises from a spring at the eye of Mafikeng, flows above ground for a few hundred kilometres and then discharges into a series of pans in southwestern Botswana, before emerging as a surface flow just before reaching the Orange River at Riemvasmaak.

There is a theory that the course of the Molopo was altered by the Morokweng impact event, where an asteroid of 3–6km in diameter struck the earth 0.8 million years ago. The impact split the river in two, diverting some flow into the Kuruman River, which also sources from a spring, the eye of Kuruman.

From Mafikeng the Molopo forms a significant portion of our northern border with Botswana as it continues to the west, reaching the Kgalagadi Transfrontier Park at the Bokspits border post, 60km south of Twee Rivieren. Here, in the Kalahari basin, it receives the Nossob River tributary and turns south towards Augrabies, where it joins the Orange 50km downstream from the falls. It is 960km in length and last flooded over 100 years ago.

SEE DETAILED MAP ON PAGE 190 ▶▶

APPEAL RATING

5/5

The Kalahari has intrigued explorers, adventurers and travellers for centuries due to the strange juxtaposition of prolific life on the one hand and semi-desert and arid conditions on the other.

▶ The soft red dunes provide for some exhilarating driving experiences
▶ The remoteness requires overlanding skills and vehicle preparedness
▶ The diversity of the landscape holds the whole family's attention
▶ The unspoilt vastness of the place is humbling
▶ The contrasting colours of red dunes, clear blue sky and khaki-coloured grass thrill the senses, while oddities like lone camel thorn trees provide alluring photo opportunities

THE BEST TIME TO TRAVEL HERE

▶ This is a region of extremes – the winters are freezing cold and the summers are boiling hot
▶ August–October and March–April are the best times
▶ During midwinter, temperatures drop to -8°C at night, with water freezing in pipes, although the days are pleasant at around 22°C; in summer expect 45°–50°C
▶ The spring and autumn months are moderate, but August to October is when the veld starts to awaken

FAMILY-FRIENDLY RATING

3/5

▶ There is plenty to attract and entertain all ages on this route
▶ Children in the 4–10 age bracket could get bored spending many hours in a vehicle; those younger than four would probably sleep in the car
▶ The elderly could suffer from the extremes of temperature
▶ Although ours is a camping trip, alternative accommodation is available at all of the places where we stay

SELF-SUFFICIENCY RATING

3/5

At all times you will be within an hour's drive of help, so although comprehensive planning and the selection of equipment are critical to your comfort, they aren't critical to your survival.

▶ Fuel is available along the route, so no long-range capacity is necessary
▶ A comprehensive selection of food is available in Upington and Kakamas, with basic replenishment in-between
▶ Water can be undrinkable at some camps
▶ All camps have hot showers and flushing toilets

GENERAL WARNINGS FOR THIS ROUTE

There are no major safety concerns on this trip; however, you need to be bush-wise and take basic precautionary measures.

▶ Use sun-protection creams, hats and long-sleeved shirts
▶ Protect eyes against glare
▶ Hydrate regularly
▶ Malaria-free throughout
▶ No large predators on this route, unless you divert into the national parks
▶ Local population is sparse, so criminal activity is low and unwanted attention is rare

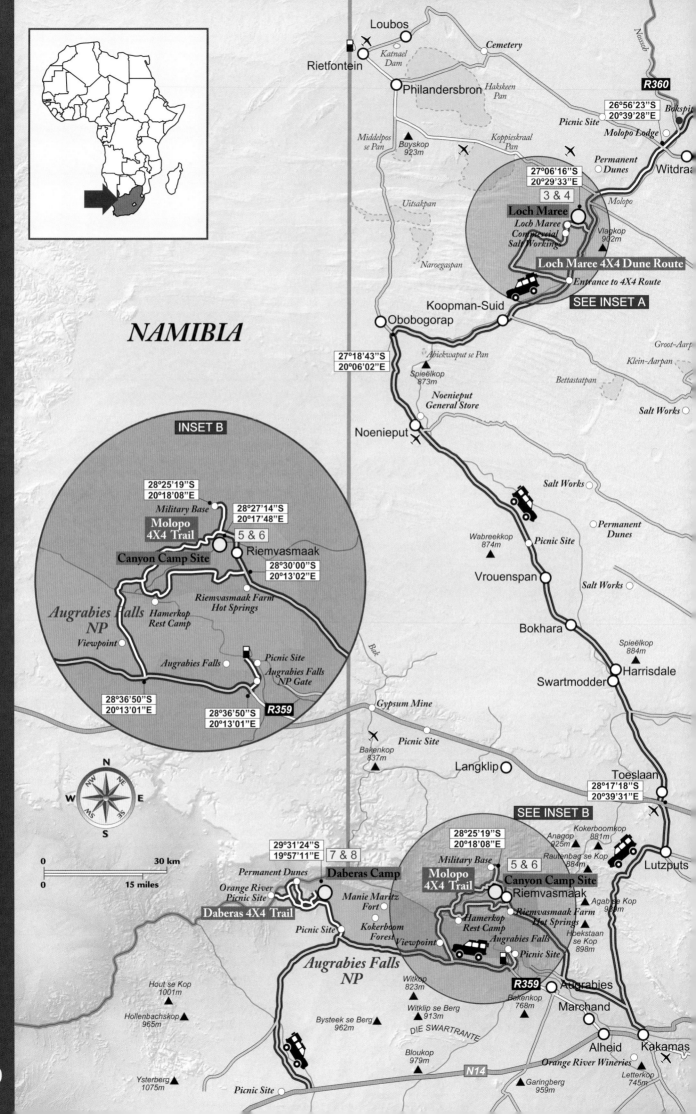

MAP 18 TRACING THE MOLOPO RIVER – one of Africa's ancient rivers

NAMIBIA

Loubos

Rietfontein

Philandersbron

Cemetery

Katnael Dam

Hakskeen Pan

R360

Middelpos se Pan

Buyskop
923m

Koppieskraal Pan

26°56'23"S
20°39'28"E

Bokspit

Picnic Site

Molopo Lodge

27°06'16"S
20°29'33"E

3 & 4

Witdraa

Uitsakpan

Permanent Dunes

Loch Maree

Loch Maree Commercial Salt Working

Vlagkop
902m

Molopo

Naroegaspan

Loch Maree 4X4 Dune Route

Entrance to 4X4 Route

SEE INSET A

Koopman-Suid

Groot-Aarp

Obobogorap

Abiekwaput se Pan

Klein-Aarpan

27°18'43"S
20°06'02"E

Spieëlkop
873m

Bettastatpan

Noenieput
General Store

Salt Works

Noenieput

INSET B

Salt Works

28°25'19"S
20°18'08"E

Military Base

Molopo
4X4 Trail

28°27'14"S
20°17'48"E

5 & 6

Riemvasmaak

Permanent Dunes

Wabreekkop
874m

Picnic Site

Canyon Camp Site

28°30'00"S
20°13'02"E

Riemvasmaak Farm Hot Springs

Vrouenspan

Salt Works

Augrabies Falls NP

Hamerkop
Rest Camp

Bokhara

Spieëlkop
884m

Viewpoint

Augrabies Falls

Picnic Site
Augrabies Falls
NP Gate

Harrisdale

Swartmodder

28°36'50"S
20°13'01"E

28°36'50"S
20°13'01"E

R359

Bak

Gypsum Mine

Bakenkop
837m

Picnic Site

Langklip

Toeslaan

N

NW NE

W E

SW SE

S

28°17'18"S
20°39'31"E

SEE INSET B

0   30 km

0   15 miles

28°25'19"S
20°18'08"E

Anagop
925m

Kokerboomkop
881m

29°31'24"S
19°57'11"E

7 & 8

Military Base

5 & 6

Rautenbag se Kop
884m

Permanent Dunes

Daberas Camp

Molopo
4X4 Trail

Canyon Camp Site

Lutzputs

Orange River
Picnic Site

Manie Maritz
Fort

Riemvasmaak

Agab se Kop
955m

Daberas 4X4 Trail

Kokerboom
Forest

Riemvasmaak Farm Hot Springs

Picnic Site

Hamerkop
Rest Camp

Hoekstaan
se Kop
898m

Hout se Kop
1001m

Viewpoint

Augrabies Falls

Picnic Site

Hollenbachskop
965m

Augrabies Falls NP

Witkop
823m

R359

Bakenkop
768m

Augrabies

Marchand

Bysteek se Berg
962m

Witklip se Berg
913m

DIE SWARTRANTE

Alheid

Kakamas

Bloukop
979m

N14

Garingberg
959m

Orange River Wineries

Letterkop
745m

Ysterberg
1075m

Picnic Site

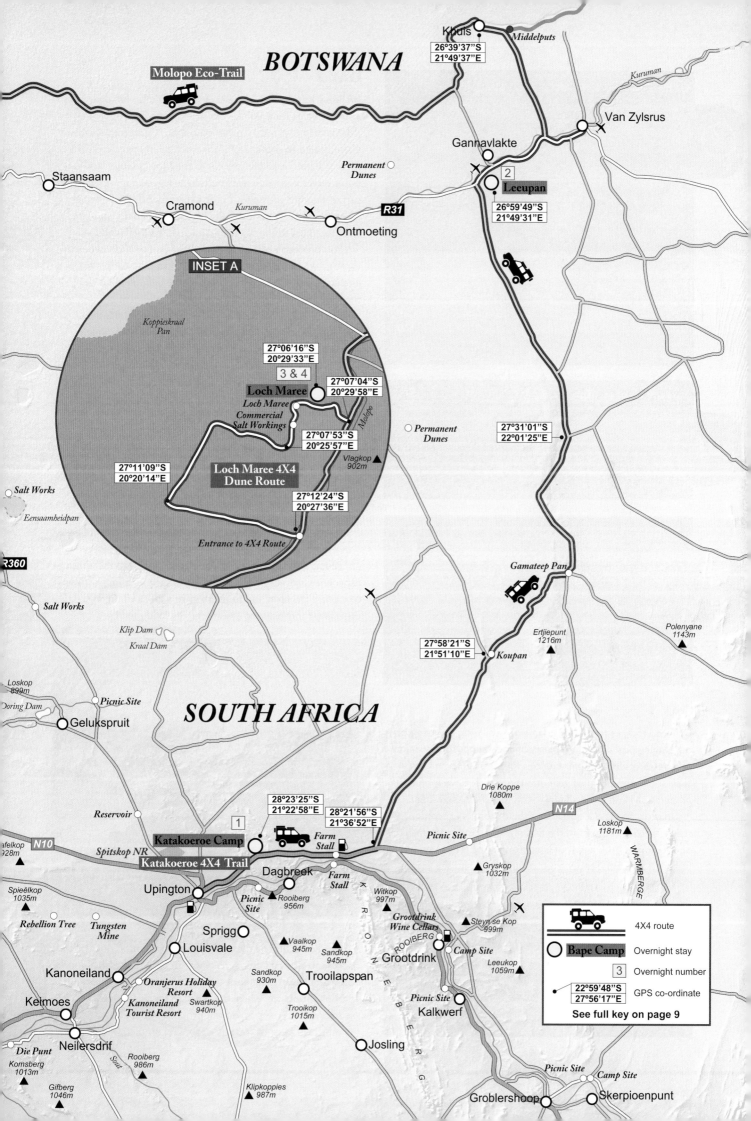

BOTSWANA

Molopo Eco-Trail

Kpuis
Middelputs
26°39'37"S
21°49'37"E

Kuruman

Van Zylsrus

Gannavlakte

2 Leeupan
26°59'49"S
21°49'31"E

Staansaam

Cramond
Kuruman
Ontmoeting
R31

Permanent
Dunes

INSET A

Koppieskraal
Pan

27°06'16"S
20°29'33"E

3 & 4

Loch Maree
Loch Maree
Commercial
Salt Workings

27°07'04"S
20°29'58"E

27°07'53"S
20°25'57"E

Molopo

Permanent
Dunes

27°31'01"S
22°01'25"E

Salt Works

27°11'09"S
20°20'14"E

Loch Maree 4X4
Dune Route

Vlagkop
902m

Eensaamheidpan

27°12'24"S
20°27'36"E

Entrance to 4X4 Route

R360

Salt Works

Gamateep Pan

Klip Dam
Kraal Dam

Polenyane
1143m

27°58'21"S
21°51'10"E

Ertjiepunt
1216m

Koupan

Loskop
899m
Doring Dam
Picnic Site

Gelukspruit

SOUTH AFRICA

Drie Koppe
1080m

N14

Picnic Site

Loskop
1181m

Reservoir

28°23'25"S
21°22'58"E

28°21'56"S
21°36'52"E

WARMBERGE

1 Katakoeroe Camp

Farm
Stall

Picnic Site

Spitskop NR
Katakoeroe 4X4 Trail

ofelkop
028m
N10

Dagbreek

Gryskop
1032m

Upington

Picnic
Site
Rooiberg
956m

Farm
Stall

Witkop
997m

Grootdrink
Wine Cellars

Steyn se Kop
999m

Spieëlkop
1035m

Rebellion Tree
Tungsten
Mine

Sprigg

Vaalkop
945m

Sandkop
945m

ROOIBERG

Grootdrink

Camp Site

Louisvale

Sandkop
930m

Trooilapspan

Leeukop
1059m

Kanoneiland

Oranjerus Holiday
Resort

Swartkop
940m

Picnic Site

Kanoneiland
Tourist Resort

Trooikop
1015m

Kalkwerf

Keimoes

Die Punt

Komsberg
1013m

Rooiberg
986m

Sout

Klipkoppies
987m

Josling

Gifberg
1046m

Neilersdrif

Picnic Site

Camp Site

Groblershoop

Skerpioenpunt

4X4 route

Bape Camp   Overnight stay

3   Overnight number

22°59'48"S
27°56'17"E   GPS co-ordinate

See full key on page 9

DAILY DRIVING DISTANCE AND TIME

Day 1	Travel from home and meet group in Upington		
Day 2	Upington to Van Zylsrus	245km	6hr
Day 3	Van Zylsrus to Loch Maree	240km	7hr
Day 4	Drive Loch Maree 4X4 Trail	100km	5hr
Day 5	Loch Maree to Kakamas to Riemvasmaak	310km	8hr
Day 6	Drive Riemvasmaak's Molopo 4X4 Trail	100km	5hr
Day 7	Riemvasmaak to Augrabies to Daberas	160km	6hr
Day 8	Drive Daberas 4X4 Trail	75km	6hr
Day 9	Depart Daberas for home		

VEHICLE REQUIREMENTS

▸ Four-wheel-drive with low-range transfer case
▸ Recovery points front and back
▸ Good ground clearance
▸ Proper off-road tyres
▸ Rear diff-lock or traction control would be an advantage

TRAILER-FRIENDLY RATING

5/5

This trip is definitely suited to those who like to tow their creature comforts with them.
▸ Towing is from camp site to camp site on Grade 2–3 dirt roads and tracks
▸ There are some short but steep inclines and declines so braked axles are an advantage
▸ We stay at two camps for one night each, and for two nights at three camp sites

DAY 1

Off-road tourists to this area come from all over, so Upington is our staging post. There are plenty of good shops for last-minute purchases as well as repair facilities for most vehicle makes, 4X4 accessories and camping gear. It is the perfect town for final preparations and to fill all tanks with fuel and fresh water.

In order to get our guests into the rhythm of expedition-style travel, we camp from the first night and utilise the facilities of Katakoeroe, 16km east of Upington on the N14. A quaint feature is that tame emus graze around the camp site among the horses.

ORANGE RIVER

Known to the San as Nu-Gariep ('Great River'), it was renamed in 1779 after Prince William V of Orange by the Dutch explorer, Captain Robert Gordon.

The area north of the Orange River up to the Kgalagadi Transfrontier Park was known as Gordonia, after this same Captain Gordon.

DAY 2

We leave Katakoeroe in the early morning after breaking camp and head east for 23km before turning northwards for Van Zylsrus on gravel roads, passing Koupan, Gamateep Pan and Gannavlakte en route. This 245km stretch through typical green Kalahari is just to get you to the Molopo River itself, but it serves as a good acclimatisation leg, during which you can reacquaint yourself with the necessary off-road driving techniques, shrug off and leave big city life behind you, and start to adjust to the space and pace of the Kgalagadi.

You proceed northwards towards Koupan and Gamateep through grasslands, where the odd acacia tree really sticks out and sociable weaver nests dominate the telephone poles by the roadside.

On arrival in Van Zylsrus you will be greeted by a sign reading, 'Relax, this is Van Zylsrus', which kind of sums up this sleepy town. There is a hotel, shop, petrol station, police station and post office, otherwise there aren't many more facilities. This small town is the hub of numerous prosperous cattle farms and game ranches, many of which offer accommodation or camping facilities.

Our choice is to camp at Leeupan, a privately owned hunting and cattle farm which has its own bush camp set among red dunes. Leeupan boasts a couple of grass thatch-type fenced-off braai lapas and an outdoor shower with adjacent long-drop. The shower water is heated by a simple wood-burning donkey geyser, the norm at such places.

If you leave Upington early enough, you should arrive at Van Zylsrus around midday, so by the time you get settled in at Leeupan, the timing is perfect to enjoy a quick sand-driving experience around their eco-trail. This is the ideal opportunity to explore the farm and to get to grips with sand driving, especially for those who are new to off-road driving.

A tricky sandy bit, day 2

The eco-trail is neither difficult nor long, but it does provide good sand-driving practice for those in need. It is also a good opportunity to teach people about off-road driving procedures and bush etiquette, where they can see for themselves the wisdom in such rules as 'do not proceed into an obstacle until the vehicle in front of you has cleared it completely' and 'you are responsible for the vehicle behind you – make sure they don't miss any turns' and 'don't overdo it at an obstacle, rather do it over'. The trail sets the scene for what is to come at Loch Maree and Riemvasmaak.

A worthwhile side trip, time permitting, is to visit the Meerkat Manor of TV fame, which is next door. They are closed on Sundays and you have to book in advance, so don't just arrive.

Van Zylsrus lies on the Kuruman River at the start of the Raptor Route, so the birding enthusiasts will be pleased to be able to tick off bateleur and martial eagles while hoping for a sighting of African white-backed vultures (there are 100 breeding pairs near Askham) and lappet-faced vultures which are common in the area.

The first night of camping under pitch-black skies on such a trip is always the best as one marvels at the stars and how busy the bush can be at night. Nightjars, bats, jackal and the continual buzzing of insect life will keep your attention as the camp fire burns down and everyone turns in for an early night.

DAY 3

Morning dawns early in the Kalahari, with birdsong treating the ears as the aroma of percolating coffee drifts across the camp site. Today you pack up camp at Leeupan, leave Van Zylsrus to the south and head via sand tracks for the Botswana border post of Middelputs some 40km off.

Just short of the border post lies the turn-off to the start of the Molopo Eco-Trail, the section of 4X4 track in the river bed. This is where you meet the Molopo for the first time. Initially the track is made up of compacted rock, which is very uneven and delivers a very bumpy half-hour ride until you get to the edge of the southern bank of the Molopo River. At this stage of its course, the river is a permanently dry flood plain ranging from 100m to around 400m wide in places. Continuing down the winding track into the river bed, you arrive at a shady section of acacia thorn trees, a picnic spot according to Tracks 4 Africa on the GPS.

From here you drive westwards downstream along the meandering river bed, where you can see large herds of springbok, some 60 to 70 in number. These are hunting farms and the animals are skittish, galloping off when they catch sight of vehicles. On your right-hand side, Botswana has tarred its road along the border fence, but fortunately it is not so on the South African side, which makes for a more genuine experience.

You will encounter many farm gates between Middelputs and Bokspits, all of which will have to be closed behind you.

The track widens and becomes smoother the further westwards you go, indicating a return to some form of civilisation, however gradual this may be. Along the way you can see ostrich, secretary bird, kori bustard and many soaring raptors.

Presently you will arrive at the turn-off to the Bokspits border post on your right, which lies just to the south of Twee Rivieren in the Kgalagadi Transfrontier Park. This is where the Nossob River joins with the Molopo from the north. Just down the road is that well-known watering hole and camp site, the Molopo Lodge. It is crucial to refuel here or you won't reach Kakamas in two days' time. Having just driven 240km, you should observe the golden rule of overlanding and 'fill up whenever you can'.

Molopo Lodge is an icon in the area, with its classic Kalahari chic décor and its themed bar in particular. The accommodation offerings are varied, from basic to luxury suites with air conditioning. Game drives are offered in their vehicles, plus you can fly in by light aircraft. They cater for conferences and weddings too.

The nearby co-op stocks basic supplies, so if you are running low you can top up with fresh items.

Some travellers may prefer to break their journey at this point and divert up to the Kgalagadi Transfrontier Park for a few days to view lion, cheetah, leopard and giraffe as well as plenty of plains game such as springbok, wildebeest and gemsbok.

Proceeding south from Molopo Lodge you come to a crossroads with the R360 which travels in a west-east direction. Should you turn left here and drive east for 5.6km, you will come to a place called Witdraai, perched on the southern side of the dry Kuruman River.

Molopo Eco-Trail

Continuing southwards, we reach another cattle and game farm, Loch Maree, where we stop for two nights.

Loch Maree is mainly a sheep and cattle farm, but in the game camps there are also giraffe, springbok, eland, zebra, gemsbok, white blesbok, hartebeest, blue wildebeest, ostrich, duiker and steenbok. It is named after a huge salt pan which lies 5km off the main gravel road. The pan is 24km in circumference and covered in a 1m-thick layer of salt, the equivalent of 9 million tons. Its shimmering white surface is surrounded by red dunes, and the vivid blue sky provides opportunities for dramatic photography, especially late-afternoon sunsets.

Quite how it was named Loch Maree we have never been able to establish, but knowing that outlaw Scotty Smith at one time had a base not far north of here, known as Scotty's Fort, he may well have stumbled across the pan and named it.

Camping at Loch Maree

Camping is once again in a bush camp among the red dunes. On arrival at the bush camp, you may be treated to the delightful sight of giraffe browsing off the tops of camel thorn and acacia trees. The toilet is a long-drop type, and the showers are once again heated by donkey. The camp is situated between parallel 'dune streets' and as such offers limited protection against the wind and no protection whatsoever against the cold, as the cold air cannot escape. In winter temperatures can drop to -8°C, so come prepared. Also, don't expect to get any water out of the pipes until the sun has thawed everything out.

THE KALAHARI CAMELS

In 1902 four circus camels and their handler, Saali Salomon, arrived in South Africa from Egypt. They were sold to a farmer who ran the mail service between Swartmodder near Upington and Rietfontein in the Kalahari. He then resold them to the Cape Mounted Police to use for patrolling the borders with what are now Namibia and Botswana.

The camels were bred, initially at Rietfontein in the Mier district, but the programme was relocated to Witdraai in 1920, from where the successful patrols continued. At the height of the programme there were over 300 camels at Witdraai.

The arrival of the Ford pick-up in the late 1940s made the camels redundant, so they were sold off by public auction in 1951. Many of their descendants are still found all over South Africa, Namibia and Botswana.

DAY 4

Retha, wife of third-generation farm-owner Johan Stadler, briefs us on what to expect during our 4X4 tour of their farm. 'Soft sand (deflate to 1 bar) and Kalahari views to die for!'

The 4X4 trail begins 10km south of the farmhouse down the main gravel road running alongside the dry Molopo, opposite a trading store where you can stop if you need fresh bread and milk. The start is through a gate next to a cattle-loading pen. The twin track is fairly firm as you set off in a west-northwesterly direction through numerous gates and livestock enclosures. The veld is typical Kalahari, with tallish grass, red sand and camel thorn trees dominating the landscape. Grey camel thorn and shepherd's tree are also numerous in the area, as well as black-thorn, three-thorn (*driedoring*) bushes and the tsamma, or Kalahari desert melon.

After 13km you reach a sign marked '50km Roete' where you turn right in a north-northeasterly direction. Now it gets interesting, as you have to drive across the dunes, rising to their crests and gently rolling down their faces before repeating this pattern again and again. Initially they are small with easy gradients, but now and again the slopes are longer, the sand softer and the gradients steeper. Novices learn plenty from this experience, as Loch Maree tests your driving skills and nurtures your off-roading abilities. The practice session back at Leeupan stands you in good stead.

The route is an inspection track along the cattle fence. As the trail gets difficult to follow when you momentarily lose it (either where the grass has become overgrown or the wind has erased the tracks of previous vehicles), you simply veer towards the fence and you're sure to find it and regain your path once again. After 4km the trail rises up onto a plateau and from the edge the amazing sight of the Eenbeker ('One Cup') Salt Pan opens up before you – a white expanse of open flatness, unexpected among the rolling red of the grassed dunes.

From this vantage point we once observed three gemsbok trekking across the pan, their tiny silhouettes recognisable only for their distinctive horn shape – a true Kalahari image.

You drive a further 3km to a large dune, the ideal stop for a well-earned lunch break, once everyone in your group has made it to the top, that is. The approach is in very soft sand and the S-shape of the track saps energy from the vehicles so that momentum is easily lost and you can get bogged down, especially if you floor the accelerator and wheel-spin yourself into a nice deep hole! With a bit of pushing and shoving and backtracking it shouldn't be too much of a performance to get all the vehicles in your group up to the summit of this dune, the most

Loch Maree 4X4 Trail

challenging part of the trail. Novices shouldn't feel daunted by making repeated attempts in a variety of gear selections in order to find what works best for their particular vehicle. 'Rather do it over than overdo it', as overdoing it can see you fly over the top of the dune, becoming airborne and doing substantial damage to your suspension system when the whole lot comes crashing back to earth.

The track down this dune isn't simple either, as a serious side slope draws the unsuspecting down and into a nearby thorn bush. Those with rooftop tents or overloaded roof racks will get particularly nervous as the roll-over angle seems too close for comfort. Once successfully past this character-building section, the track proceeds more sedately through a further 7km of rollicking dunes, before turning 90° to the right in an east-southeasterly direction towards the really massive Loch Maree Pan. The track descends down to the southern shore of the pan, where you are requested to drive along the outer edges and follow the shoreline around the pan.

If you turn left, you will come to the base of a really high dune, labelled 'Impossible Dune' on the maps provided. Here you can play nicely and test your vehicle's dune-climbing abilities in preparation for that Namibian trip on your bucket list. Few make it to the top, we're told.

This pan is commercially worked, so proceed with care as there is large earth-moving equipment around. Stop and investigate the workings – it is interesting. The trail at this point veers away from the pan and a short climb leads you around a small kopje, before finally veering eastwards away from the pan and climbing up to a superb lookout site with panoramic views. This spot has a covered shelter with concrete tables and benches and a place to braai. It is a lovely setting for a picnic stop en route and, since it is only a few kilometres from the bush camp at the end of the trail, many campers even drive back here to enjoy sundowners and photograph the sunset over the pure whiteness of the pan to the west. To the east the view takes in the parallel dunes as they disappear to the horizon. Oh, and there's cellphone reception here too, so you can contact family and friends and make them jealous with a few MMSs should you so please.

From here you descend down the eastern face of the dune and wend your way on a firmer twin track, through much shorter grass than at the start of the trail, back to camp to relax and ruminate on another great day under Kalahari skies.

In general, the sandy tracks are firm and the *middelmannetjie* is not too high to create problems. Things get interesting, though, when you need to crest the dunes. This is where tyre pressure and momentum play such an important role.

The scale of the place is immense. It is so easy to lose yourself in the vastness of the solitude and the quiet. Yet there is a lot to take in, as it teems with life on these dunes – the spoor of field mice, small buck, ground squirrel and birds are all over. You must get out of your vehicle to investigate these things.

Back at camp you light a huge fire, braai massive amounts of meat and maybe someone will haul out a guitar and treat the creatures of the night to an off-key rendition of *Ver in die Ou Kalahari*. It just seems appropriate! Either way, you are guaranteed a good night's rest after this eventful day.

DAY 5

At sunrise, throw some twigs onto last night's coals and a few puffs later the camp fire is burning once more, re-boiling the *moerkoffie* for the fourth time. What a way to wash down a few Ouma rusks and a bowl of steaming porridge. This is the life!

Leaving Loch Maree you head south on the longest leg of the journey – a 310km stage to Kakamas for fuel and provisions, and then on to Riemvasmaak for the next two nights where you'll camp in a canyon close to a hot spring.

Initially the gravel road leads to Abiekwaput se Pan in the area where the border with Namibia is the dead straight north-south boundary that stands up like a spear point on a map. You then pass through Noenieput, named after a noenie tree that grew there at an old drinking well dug by the San.

And so you continue towards Lutzputs ('Lutz's Well') in the south. Along the way the road follows the Molopo. In this more southerly section of its course, it is evident that water flow isn't too far below the surface, as there is plenty of greenery about, and also patches of marshy ground, while reeds abound in some sections of the river bed. The terrain changes the further south you travel, the red dunes making way for flat expanses of rock-strewn grassy landscape, with kopjes that look as though a giant hand has scraped all the loose stones in the surrounding area up into neat symmetrical piles. The road is rocky too, and on this stretch you could expect punctures. Should this happen on your trip, relax with a nice cup of tea while you set about plugging holes and reinflating or changing tyres as required.

Your arrival in Kakamas feels like a semi-return to civilisation. There are bottle stores, shops, ATMs and smooth

tar! Kakamas is also a compulsory refuel stop and the last opportunity for the next four days to make purchases.

Leaving town, you re-cross the Orange River and head northwest on gravel, making for Riemvasmaak, your home for the next two nights. This is an area of some 14,000ha nestling between the Augrabies Falls National Park and the southern Kalahari. It is a unique, isolated and spectacular mountain desert-like destination, with Namibia to the west and the Orange River its southern border. The scenery is dramatic, with craggy mountains, a hot spring and a colourful local population only too willing to share their history with you.

Once through the entrance gates, you drive through the small village and follow signs to the hot spring via a very steep descent down to the canyon camp site. The Molopo River lies at the bottom of this ravine, just about 10km as the crow flies to where it joins the Orange River. Tall cliffs surround you and the echoes of bird calls at dawn are deafeningly beautiful.

Having settled in, you should lounge in the hot spring to soothe away the aches and dust of the road. Thereafter light your camp fire and settle in feeling fresh and relaxed.

DAY 6

Tourism Officer Clarissa Damara will brief you on the history of Riemvasmaak and tell how the original Damara, Nama and Xhosa inhabitants had been forcefully removed in the mid-1970s, as the property was deemed to be of strategic military importance to the defense of the nearby border with the former South West Africa (Namibia). A military base was established and weapons testing took place for the next 20 years, until the property was handed back to the original owners in 1995 after one of the country's first land restitution claims.

Clarissa will discuss their four 4X4 trails with you, but naturally you should opt for the Molopo Trail so as to visit its junction with the Orange River. It is the most difficult of the trails, and you will have fun picking your way down the two mountain passes over wash-aways, heavily eroded sections and axle-twisters.

Keep your eyes peeled for small buck species and also the remnants of mortars and small rifle grenades stacked next to the roadway in a grim reminder of our hostile past. Some of the early returning residents tragically suffered loss of limb due to the area not having been thoroughly cleared of ordnance.

The track soon meets up with the course of the Molopo and the ravine gives way to a wide and extensive ancient flood plain. The sand here is very fine

The Molopo Trail within Riemvasmaak, day 6

dried silt, which billows up in huge clouds behind the vehicles as you pass on your way to the Orange River.

Many amazing features are visible en route, such as the dried waterfall, with its smooth rock ledge over which flood waters flowed in days gone by. The entire area is rich in geological formations and minerals. Rose-quartz rocks the size of soccer balls litter the landscape. There is a powerful mystical feel about the place.

The Orange River itself hides behind a curtain of acacia trees, but once you find a gap, you can make your way down to the cool green waters and enjoy a leisurely lunch on her banks.

Driving the return loop away from the Orange River takes you back to the village of Riemvasmaak, where you can collect the fresh oven-baked bread or *roosterbrood* you ordered in the morning and buy some firewood before you head back to camp for an early end to the day.

A short drive north of the village takes you to the remains of the military base. There isn't much to see these days but for the concrete slab floors of some of the buildings and the surrounding earth mound embankment around the boundary.

And so your mission is now complete. You have successfully traced the lower course of the ancient Molopo – this great enigmatic African river which thousands of years ago provided many villages and vast herds of wild animals with sweet life-giving water. This same river, at one time the ancestral home of the Barolong tribe, has given you and your companions such joy as you have journeyed down her now dry bed.

It is our wish that we all live long enough to see the effects of global warming reversed so that the world's great rivers, such as the Molopo, are able to flow once more.

DAY 7

To complete the balance of this nine-day trip, you need to spend a day (day seven) in transit, travelling to Daberas Adventures, to the west of the Augrabies Falls National Park. You should leave Riemvasmaak at midmorning and travel over the Blouputs Bridge to view the Augrabies Falls and maybe enjoy a light lunch at their restaurant. You are assured of dramatic photos and a pleasant amble along the wooden walkways. Time permitting, try to fit in a game drive in your own vehicle. The camping and chalet facilities are well maintained and you are certain to enjoy some respite from the rigours of dirt-road travel if you choose to stay over for a night or two.

Neighbouring Daberas Adventures is a 4X4 trail and camp site where you enjoy your last

RIEMVASMAAK

The name Riemvasmaak relates to the tale of how the local Damara farmers once caught a cattle-rustling San, tied him to a rock and left him overnight to the elements and his fate. When they returned the next morning they found that the leather thongs (*rieme*) with which he had been tied up (*vasmaak*) had been miraculously loosened and the man had escaped, seemingly without any assistance.

Along the Orange River near Daberas, day 8

SOME OVERLANDING TIPS AND ETHICS
- It is wise to refuel whenever you have the opportunity, as you never know whether or not the next town will have fuel
- Always leave farm gates as you found them
- It is generally acceptable to stop by the roadside for a cup of tea or to enjoy a quick bite to eat before continuing unhurriedly on your journey

two nights of the trip. Their bush camp is well appointed, complete with flushing toilets and gas showers. The water is not drinkable, however, due to high mineral contents.

The Daberas owners take responsible tourism, conservation and good off-road driving practices seriously, so expect a detailed briefing on the do's and don'ts.

DAY 8

Day eight will be spent driving their 4X4 trails, yet another highlight in a trip full of highlights. The serious section of the trail, and one which only vehicles with rear diff-lock should attempt, is the long, steep incline up to Aubrey's Viewpoint. The steep track is full of loose, round rocks the size of bowling woods, which make for very limited traction. Then there are cross-axles and erosion furrows, which tend to pull the wheels into their grips.

After this section, the going is much easier, although very rocky and bumpy, and you are certain to enjoy a most memorable day's driving. There are climbs, there is loose rock, there are steep sand dunes, and the great views over to the southern Namibian plateau away to the north have to be seen to be believed. At midday, you can enjoy a lunch break on the banks of the Orange River where it flows languidly over the rocky rapids that give the farm its name of Daberas – an alliterative Damara word mimicking the sound that water makes as it flows over rocks at a fording point.

DAY 9

Leaving Daberas, you travel south on gravel farm roads until you reach the N14 tar road between Springbok and Upington. Gautengers will turn left, Capetonians will turn right towards Pofadder ...

But that is another chapter!

19 The Old Ox-wagon Route – a pioneering experience in the Southern Cape

by Philip Sackville-Scott

TOP 10 ATTRACTIONS OF THIS TRIP

❶ Mountain-trail driving conditions – rocky and side slopes ❷ A guided tour of the Knysna Forest with lunch at a community-owned restaurant ❸ Beautiful surroundings, from indigenous forests to abundant fynbos ❹ Dramatic Cape Fold Mountains at every turn ❺ Photographic opportunities ❻ Relics and ruins from days gone by ❼ Three separate 4X4 trails ❽ Interesting snippets of the local history ❾ Local characters who are truly passionate about conservation ❿ Visit a local 'charcoal from invading plants' initiative

TRIP OUTLINE

The Old Ox-wagon Route runs inland between Knysna and Heidelberg, almost parallel to the N2, but in the glorious mountains of the Southern Cape. The route is the initiative of three local 4X4 trail owners – Nico Hesterman at Bonniedale, Nico Bester at Louvain and Katot Meyer at the Burchell's Trail – who devised a way to link their three trails together into an 'off-road tour with an exciting story behind it'. The result is a journey of discovery that every off-road enthusiast should experience at least once, no matter their level of experience.

The adventure starts just east of Knysna on the N2, proceeds inland up to Die Vlug, before returning southwards for a bit and then heading west via Millwood Forest, Homtini and Karatara and on into the Attaquaskloof to Bonniedale. Continuing west you then cross the Gouritz River, climb the Witblits Pass and enter a hidden valley known by early travellers as the 'Land van Egypten' (who knows why), before eventually descending Ertjiesvlei-se-Berg and ending at the small town of Heidelberg on the N2.

SEE DETAILED MAP ON PAGE 200 ▶▶

APPEAL RATING

5/5

The indigenous forests of the Knysna area are universally appreciated for their uniqueness and tranquillity. This trip takes in three separate 4X4 trails linked together by forestry roads, public roads and gravel tracks, as you trace the transport routes of the early settlers and transport teams between the Cape and Knysna.

▶ Learn about the history of the transport riders and Knysna woodcutters
▶ Experience contrasting flora, from indigenous forests to fynbos
▶ Get away from it all within two hours' drive of the Garden Route
▶ Scenic tracks and challenging 4X4 trails provide great driving

THE BEST TIME TO TRAVEL HERE

▶ The winters are surprisingly mild during the day, but can be cold in the evenings and at altitude
▶ From the spring months through summer and into autumn the whole extent of the trip can show different facets of the region's beauty depending when you visit (various protea species flower at different times)
▶ August to October is best, as this is when the veld starts to awaken

FAMILY-FRIENDLY RATING

5/5

▶ There is plenty to entertain all ages on this route
▶ Children in the 4–10 age bracket could get bored during extended periods in the car
▶ Regular stops at places of interest keep the attention of everyone of all ages
▶ Although ours is a camping trip, alternative accommodation is available at all the places where we stay

SELF-SUFFICIENCY RATING

3/5

At all times you will be within two hours' drive of help, so this is a safe route and you don't need to be 'hard core' to thoroughly enjoy it.

▶ Fuel is available along the route, so no long-range capacity is necessary
▶ A comprehensive selection of food is available in Knysna, and general stores along the route stock the basics
▶ Water is available and safely drinkable at all camps
▶ All camps have hot showers and flushing toilets
▶ All camps have formal accommodation nearby if tents don't do it for you

Koup

Bloukop
948m ▲

Heuningneskop
549m ▲

Gamka

33º51'30"S
21º53'05"E

Quteniqua
NR

33º52'26"S
21º51'36"E

John Tom
4 & 5

Viewpoint

Sunbird Camp

Swartberg
NR

Bonniedale Lodge

Kruisrivier

33º52'37"S
21º52'44"E

Viewpoint

33º53'32"S
21º50'55"E

Rietfontein
Ostrich Palace

Ladismith

Koerug
518m ▲

Gamka

Badshoogte

Touwsberg
1491m ▲

Swartrug
517m ▲

Touws

Olifants

Plathuis

Witteberg
514m ▲

Die Hoek

Gamkaberg
NR

Rooiberg
1480m ▲

Groot

Van Wyksdorp

33º52'26"S
21º51'36"E

Bont Huis
Hotel Ruins

Radioactive
Spring

Brand

ATTAQUASKLOO

4 & 5

Sunbird *Attaquas*
Camp

33º53'28"S
21º03'36"E

Bonniedale Lodge

Robinson
Quteniqua
NR

Brandrivier

Langberg

R327

Woeska

SEE INSET A

Boosmansbos
Wilderness
Area

Vreysberg
1110m ▲

Grootberg
634m ▲

Rooielsberg
1299m ▲

Duiwelsbosberg
1294m ▲

Weyers

Moederskop
440m ▲

Herbertsdale

34º05'35"S
20º57'54"E

Kruis

Gourits

Heidelberg

N2

Zeekoegat 1795

Riversdale

Platkop
294m ▲

Klipberg
224m ▲

Vals

Stink

Pienaars

Swartheuwel
161m ▲

Dekriet

Aloe Factory

Albertinia

N2

Gouritz

Kleinberg
280m ▲

Danabaa

Rietheuwel
153m ▲

Goukou

Aasvoëlberg
490m ▲

Johnson's Post

Vermaaklikheid

Trompskop
289m ▲

Riethuiskraal

Droëvlakte

Olifantsberg
357m ▲

Vleesbaai

Kapstylhuise
1887

Puntjie

Blomboskop
164m ▲

Still Bay

Baken se Kop
325m ▲

Gouritzmond

N
NW NE
W   E
SW SE
S

I N D I A N

0   20 km
0   10 miles

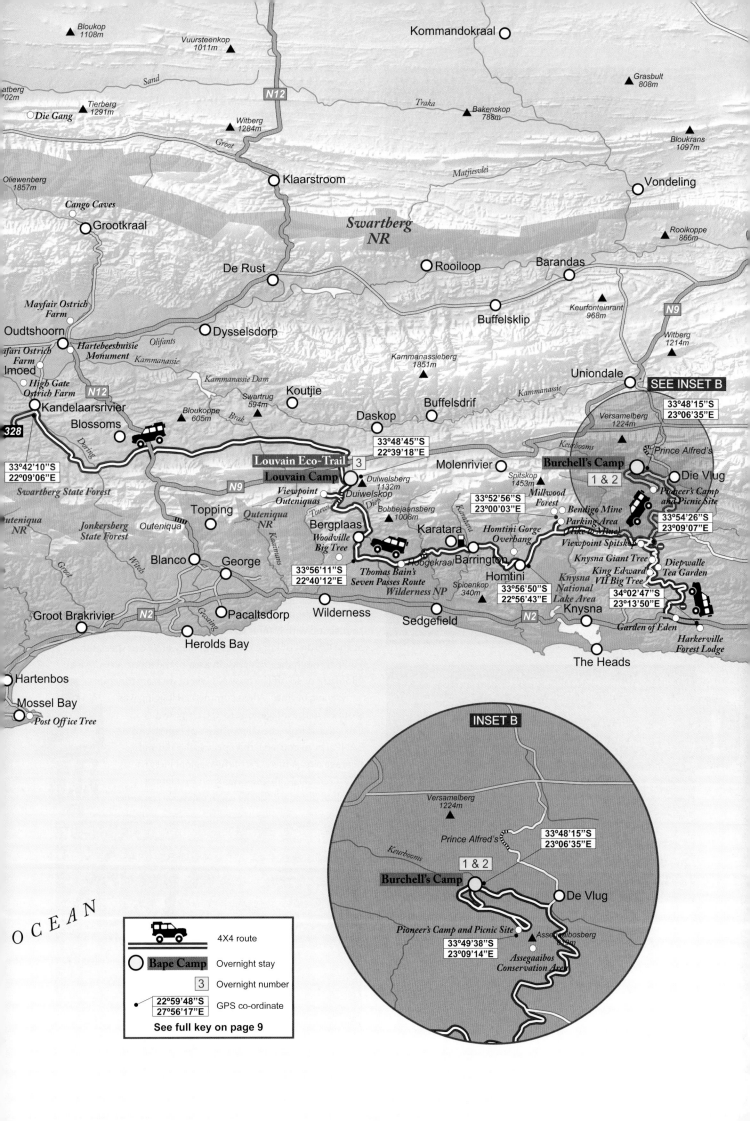

Bloukop
1108m

Vuursteenkop
1011m

Kommandokraal

Grasbult
808m

Sand

atberg
'02m

N12

Traka

Tierberg
1291m

Die Gang

Witberg
1284m

Bakenskop
788m

Bloukrans
1097m

Groot

Oliewenberg
1857m

Cango Caves

Klaarstroom

Matjiesvlei

Vondeling

Swartberg
NR

Rooikoppe
866m

Grootkraal

De Rust

Rooiloop

Barandas

Keurfonteinrant
968m

N9

Mayfair Ostrich
Farm

Dysselsdorp

Buffelsklip

Olifants

Oudtshoorn

Hartebeeshuisie
Monument

Kammanassie

Witberg
1214m

afari Ostrich
Farm
Imoed

Kammanassie Dam

Kammanassieberg
1851m

Uniondale

SEE INSET B

High Gate
Ostrich Farm

N12

Koutjie

Kammanassie

33°48'15"S
23°06'35"E

Versamelberg
1224m

Kandelaarsrivier

Swartrug
594m

Buffelsdrif

Prince Alfred's

328

Blossoms

Bloukoppe
605m

Daskop

33°48'45"S
22°39'18"E

Molenrivier

Burchell's Camp

Die Vlug

33°42'10"S
22°09'06"E

Brak

Louvain Eco-Trail

3

1 & 2

Pioneer's Camp
and Picnic Site

Doring

Swartberg State Forest

Louvain Camp

Duiwelsberg
1132m

Spitskop
1453m

Millwood
Forest

33°54'26"S
23°09'07"E

N9

Viewpoint
Outeniquas

Duiwelskop

33°52'56"S
23°00'03"E

Bendigo Mine
Parking Area
(Hike to Mine)

Outeniqua
NR

Topping

Outeniqua
NR

Bergplaas

Diep

Bobbejaansberg
1008m

Karatara

Homtini Gorge
Overhang

Viewpoint Spitskop

Jonkersberg
State Forest

Outeniqua

Woodville
Big Tree

Tourws

Karatara

Knysna Giant Tree

Diepwalle
Tea Garden

Blanco

George

33°56'11"S
22°40'12"E

Thomas Bain's
Seven Passes Route
Wilderness NP

Hoogekraal

Barrington

Homtini

Spioenkop
340m

33°56'50"S
22°56'43"E

Knysna
National
Lake Area

King Edward
VII Big Tree

34°02'47"S
23°13'50"E

Kaaimans

Groot

Gwaing

N2

Pacaltsdorp

Wilderness

Sedgefield

N2

Knysna

Garden of Eden

Groot Brakrivier

Herolds Bay

The Heads

Harkerville
Forest Lodge

Hartenbos

Mossel Bay

Post Office Tree

INSET B

O C E A N

Versamelberg
1224m

Prince Alfred's

33°48'15"S
23°06'35"E

Keurbooms

1 & 2

4X4 route

Burchell's Camp

De Vlug

Bape Camp   Overnight stay

3   Overnight number

Pioneer's Camp and Picnic Site

Assegaaibosberg

22°59'48"S
27°56'17"E   GPS co-ordinate

33°49'38"S
23°09'14"E

Assegaaibos
Conservation Area

See full key on page 9

VEHICLE REQUIREMENTS

- Four-wheel-drive with low-range transfer case
- Recovery points front and back
- Good ground clearance
- Proper off-road tyres
- Trailers and caravans should have proper off-road chassis, suspensions and tyres
- Rear diff-lock or traction control an advantage

TRAILER-FRIENDLY RATING

5/5

This trip is definitely suited to those who like to tow their creature comforts with them.

- Towing is from camp site to camp site on Grade 2–3 dirt roads and tracks
- There are some short but steep inclines and declines, so braked axles are an advantage and make the trip safer
- We spend two nights at two of the camp sites and one night at each of the others, so there's not too much packing and unpacking

GENERAL WARNINGS FOR THIS ROUTE

There are no major safety concerns on this trip; however, you do need to be bush-wise and take basic common-sense precautionary measures.

- Use sun-protection creams, hats and long-sleeved shirts
- Wet-weather clothing as mountains can be cold and wet all year round
- Protect eyes against glare
- Hydrate regularly
- Malaria-free throughout
- No large predators on this route
- Local population is sparse, so criminal activity is low and unwanted attention is rare

Most of the early ox-wagon trails were not constructed as such, but travellers merely followed existing game and elephant tracks or the footpaths made by the Khoi people. The first ox-wagon trail to cross the Langeberg/Outeniqua range was the Attaquaskloof Pass north of Mossel Bay. This became the main road to the north for 180 years from 1689 to 1869. Only with the arrival of John Montagu, Colonial Secretary at the Cape from 1843 to 1852, and the expertise of Andrew Geddes Bain and his son Thomas, did proper road construction begin in the Cape.

The first properly constructed passes over the Cape Fold Mountains between the coast and the Little Karoo were the Montagu Pass (1848), between George and Oudtshoorn, and the Robinson Pass (1869), between Mossel Bay and Oudtshoorn. Nowhere else in South Africa is there such a concentration of mountain passes in one area, nor such a variety of scenery and vegetation, as in the Southern Cape.

These passes are an important part of the Little Karoo story: without them there would have been no access, nor settlement of farms and no way for the farmer to communicate with, and bring his products to, the outside world. This trip explores some lesser-known passes and ox-wagon trails.

The group gathers the previous afternoon at Harkerville Forest Lodge where we all meet and enjoy a sociable evening becoming acquainted in the private lapa. Those not wishing to camp may book a chalet here instead.

Harkerville is situated just 20km east of Knysna, and you can plan to arrive a day or two earlier to explore Knysna and stock up on provisions for the trip ahead. Being a large town, Knysna offers vehicle maintenance, camping stores and the full range of retail shops for those last-minute repairs and purchases.

DAY 1

After an unhurried breakfast we leave camp at 08:30 in order to meet up with Dennis Carlisle of Bhejane 4X4 Adventures at the Garden of Eden on the N2. He will be our specialist guide through their concession area of the forest. We drive a kilometre or so off the busy N2 where we start the tour.

Dennis begins: 'When commercial logging was stopped in the indigenous forest, responsibility was passed from the Department of Forestry to SANParks to conserve this spectacular natural heritage site. A mere 2% of the original indigenous forest remains – an indictment on mankind's absolute disregard for the earth's natural resources.

The tour starts off through lush indigenous forests

The forest used to extend from Mossel Bay all the way to Humansdorp! One of the greatest contributing factors was the demand for hardwood sleepers to construct Cecil John Rhodes's dream railway line from the Cape to Cairo.'

Our tour takes us into the Diepwalle Forest along restricted tracks (Bhejane are the sole concession holders) and Dennis's commentary over the 29MHz radios is hugely informative as he describes the inter-dependency between the lichen, fungus, moss, ferns and trees. One realises that the forest is like one huge living organism and that if any of the constituent parts is removed from the system, the whole will suffer and perish.

We learn about the logging operations of old, we hear stories of mishaps, air crashes and missing persons, and we make regular stops to take photos or to listen to stories of the more interesting aspects of the forest. Dennis describes the life of a *houtkapper* (woodcutter) 100 years ago, tells tales of elephant sightings and explains about the narrow-gauge railway that was constructed when all the horses were recalled for duty in the Anglo-Boer War. There are many other interesting tidbits, but you'll have to do the tour yourself to get the full run-down.

The quiet is deafening and the green lushness is a total onslaught on the eyes. One's hearing is also assailed as the bird calls are noticeably lower in frequency, which is nature's way of capitalising on the fact that low-frequency sound travels further through dense undergrowth. The temperature in the forest is fairly constant all year round, peaking at around 22°C. This means that you will find fewer insects in the forest than you would expect, but amphibians thrive in the many streams. The constant dampness allows the dead tree branches to decompose relatively rapidly. A welcome side-effect of the cool and damp conditions is that it is virtually impossible for this forest to be destroyed by fire.

At around midmorning we stop for coffee in one of the large 'fynbos islands' we periodically encounter. Apparently these areas were previously cleared for habitation purposes and the

forest hasn't reclaimed them, allowing the fynbos to establish itself instead. (Or that's one theory anyway.) Bhejane provides the coffee and rusks – a most welcome midmorning snack.

We continue past huge 1000-year-old yellowwoods, known as *Gelandes* to the foresters of old, as well as massive stinkwoods, eucalyptus and ironwood trees. Radio chatter dies down to zero as everyone absorbs the enormity of these forests and their importance to the local ecology.

We end off this wonderful morning's activities with a quick visit to the King Edward VII Big Tree before proceeding to the Diepwalle Tea Garden, an initiative of the local community which is well worth supporting, for a traditional lunch of savoury *vetkoek*, coffee and scones.

Proceeding up Prince Alfred's Pass after lunch, we detour to the top of the Spitskop lookout, from where we can appreciate panoramic views of the whole area right to the sea.

As we approach the tiny village of Die Vlug, we are met by one of the 4X4 community's most eccentric and colourful characters, and owner of the Burchell's Trail, Katot Meyer, who first escorts us to the Assegaaibos Conservation Area to view various conservation projects. Invasive alien trees and vegetation are a major problem in the area and the Working for Water teams have their hands full trying to make inroads into eradicating these unwelcome water guzzlers. (As the convoy curls its way over very steep and twisting tracks through the bushy mountainous terrain, evidence is all around you of their hard labours in cutting out black wattle trees and saplings in

BOTANIST – WILLIAM JOHN BURCHELL

In 1998 a fire started at Die Vlug and spread westwards, destroying vegetation, but exposing a track which was described by Burchell in 1814 in the publication *Catalogus Geographicus*. He had collected many specimens in this area, including one, *Oxylaena acicularis*, which has not been found again.

Burchell arrived at the Cape in 1810, learnt to speak Dutch and prepared for the explorations to come. He had a wagon custom-built to cope with the narrow bridle paths over the mountainous areas, its width being only 700mm. It was well equipped with presses, sketch paper, magnifying glasses and over 50 reference books. Leaving Cape Town in 1811, he trekked through regions 'never before trodden by European foot'.

He travelled over 7200km, exploring as far as Botswana, collected over 63,000 specimens and objects, more than any man before or since. He made over 500 drawings of landscapes, portraits and zoological and botanical sketches. He returned to England in 1815 and spent the rest of his life identifying his collection.

particular.) We pass an initiative to convert all this unwanted alien wood into charcoal, but the price seems high as the process produces much unwanted smoke.

Another interesting sideshow is a visit to an electrically self-sufficient farm. Two banks of solar panels (each the size of roadside advertising hoardings), wind turbines and a battery storage room, complete with an array of inverters, provide an interesting and impressive display. Apparently this small farm had been purchased by a group of paranoid families from Johannesburg during the last days of Nationalist rule. Bunkers were dug and stocked with about a decade's supply of paraffin, candles and tinned food. It seems crazy now, looking back!

Katot Meyer at Burchell's Camp

From here we divert into Die Vlug to visit the information centre where various displays portray the history of the area and also map out the conservation schemes, both government and private, which are currently active.

Arriving at the Burchell's camp in the mid-afternoon, we set up camp, relax and chat about the day's experiences. This is an ideal setting for the guitar to come out. We are visited by our host, Katot Meyer, who recounts the history of his Burchell's Route, named after the famed botanist William Burchell who toured the area collecting samples and documenting thousands of new species. Out comes the 'laptop' (a jerry can cut in half with a hinged lid!) and the hand-drawn maps and charts showing the route and his passion – the way in which one could 'travel on gravel' all the way to Bellville if you wanted to!

Before leaving us to ourselves, Katot promises to meet us at '16 minutes past eight' the next morning for a quick briefing for those wanting to drive his trail. Then he is gone.

This is truly a bush camp, with the levelled sites hidden away among the undergrowth providing some privacy, unlike the fresh-air bush toilets. (The toilets are the proper flushing type that you find at home, but with just a rope which you can span between two poles to indicate 'occupied' status!)

A feature of this camp is the many and varied little hand-painted signs that Katot has erected around the place indicating directions to everything you could wish to know. Another is a display of rocks in the shape of Africa, labelled with their places of origin. It is quiet here, but for the birdsong and twittering emanating from the surrounding trees and dam.

For the non-campers, various chalet accommodation options are available at Die Vlug, 5km away.

DAY 2

True to his word, Katot arrives at '16 minutes past eight' to introduce the drivers to the wonders of his trail. First, he unpacks a contraption made out of battered corrugated roof sheeting, which he has adapted and painted to represent the geographical relief of the surrounding area. (It even has folding legs like a table to make the presentation easier!)

The group then departs on what must be the most picturesque 4X4 trail in the country. It is tucked into a secluded valley and the route winds its way over streams and through protea forests, and traverses three different fynbos zones as the altitude varies. Essentially the route is one full day's travel as undertaken by WJ Burchell. The track was only recently rediscovered when a veld fire swept through the area and exposed the old tracks. After doing much research, old maps indicated that these were the tracks made originally by William Burchell on his specimen-collecting travels.

Initially you climb a fairly steep hill as the rocky 4X4 trail crosses over the hill to the south of the camp to gain access to the picturesque valley beyond. The descent down the other side is steep and the traction is rather poor as you make your way over the uneven ground. This is first-gear low-range work for your transmission, but it isn't long before the whole group has been guided over the obstacles and the track follows a stream in the pretty valley floor towards the southeast.

At the end of this section is a copse of alien trees where each driver is requested to do their bit for conservation and to ring-bark a tree each. There is a nice mud hole here to test your tyres' traction, followed by a steep loose rocky climb before you descend down to Pioneer's Camp, a rustic site in a clearing among a thicket of trees. (Both these obstacles are optional and have bypasses.)

Mud hole

Having enjoyed a light lunch here, we retrace our tracks in a northwesterly direction, taking a left fork in the track to end the Burchell's experience with a descent down the steep pass.

This track isn't so much about the driving challenges, but rather the amazing beauty that you will find during the day. If you are fortunate, Katot will be on hand to lead you through; if not, join an organised tour which almost guarantees his presence.

We return to camp, get the unique showers fired up, start the camp fire and then the storytelling commences as we compare notes and reminisce on the day.

DAY 3

Today is what in rally terms would be called a liaison stage. Packing up after breakfast, we drive east back towards Die Vlug and then zigzag southwards down the Prince Alfred's Pass. Shortly after the turn-off to Plettenberg Bay, we take a forestry road westwards into the Ysterhoek, Gouna and Goldfields forests, stopping near a stream for morning coffee. Here you

have the opportunity to visit the Bendigo Mine and other interesting aspects of the Millwood Forest.

From here it's south to Homtini village, and then west again via Barrington and Karatara, where you can refuel and stock up on basic provisions if necessary.

We continue west for around 25km along Thomas Bain's Seven Passes Route before turning north towards the Bergplaas Forest Station and the start of the Louvain Eco-Trail. This is a combination of forestry tracks and private trails over the Duiwelskop. You drive through mountain fynbos, indigenous forest and pine plantations, experiencing all the area has to offer. Our route regularly crosses that of the Outeniqua Hiking

Down we go!

Trail as we ascend the Duiwelskop Pass. We try to imagine the ox-wagons of old wearily trudging their way along these precipitous tracks, where the margin for error would have been negligible. Letting your imagination run wild, you can almost hear the complaining lowing of the oxen and the rifle cracks of the long whips as the wagon train creaks its way forwards.

Nearing the end of the day's drive, a turning to the left leads to the most magnificent climb up a very steep track. Trailers need to be unhitched and parked by the roadside as the gradient is too steep and there is not enough space on top to turn a rig around. The track is lined with overgrown hakea, so be prepared to get your car buffed up when you get home! The views from up here are well worth it, however, as you really feel 'on top of the world'.

DUIWELSKOP PASS

This, the most difficult pass to cross in the 18th century, was realigned by Thomas Bain in 1864 and the present 4X4 track follows this new alignment along the western slope of the mountain, rather than over the summit. The pass was regularly used to transport timber to Graaff-Reinet from 1776 to 1869, until the Montagu Pass (1847) and Prince Alfred's Pass (1868) were opened.

Governor Van Plettenberg made the first wagon crossing in 1778, travelling south from the Langkloof. For today's 4X4 travellers, the Duiwelskop Pass features magnificent views of the Garden Route and the Indian Ocean, the original tracks of the ox-wagons and the unparalleled and characteristic smell of mountain fynbos.

This 30km trip is between Bergplaas Forest and Louvain, where permits must be obtained.

Continuing back to the Duiwelskop Pass, we soon start descending down to the farm of Louvain and their camp, where we will be spending the night. Nico Bester is on hand to welcome us and show us around. There is a beautiful stone church designed by the wife of Bishop Grey, which serves as a great wedding venue.

DAY 4

Leaving Louvain northwards, you soon meet the N9. Turn right and almost immediately left again for a short while through the Eseljagtpoort until the gravel road turns to the west, crossing the Brak River to the N12 and Outeniqua Pass (Oudtshoorn to George), which you cross and then head for Zebra station and the R328 – Robinson Pass (Oudtshoorn to Mossel Bay). From here it's on to Kandelaarsrivier, Volmoed and a quick detour down Saffraansrivier to view the Bont Huis Hotel ruins. Volmoed was known to the explorer Patterson in 1779 as 'Poverty'; the name was changed to Armoed in the 1800s, then back to Volmoed again in the 1900s ('Full of Hope' changed to 'Poverty' and then back to 'Full of Hope' once more).

The ruin of the Bont Huis Hotel is surprisingly intact, having been abandoned over 150 years ago when the new Robinson Pass was completed and the ox-wagon trains no longer passed by. Stopping at the ruins, we have time to try to make out how the various buildings must have looked and what functions they were built to perform in their heyday. Clearly visible still is a channel leading to a water mill which must have been used to

THE ATTAQUASKLOOF OX-WAGON TRAIL

This was the 'N1 for ox-wagons' for 200 years until 1869, when the Robinson Pass was completed. The first expedition on this route was sent out by Simon van der Stel under the leadership of Isaac Schrijver in January 1689. Gouriqua Khoi pointed out the elephant route to them and it took seven days to cross the Attaquas Mountains. Many famous explorers and celebrities used this pass, which became known as 'the gateway to the Karoo and East Cape'.

The new Robinson Pass in 1869 ended the 180-year reign of one of the most beautiful and attractive passes over the Langeberg and Outeniqua mountains, yet during the Anglo-Boer War, the Mossel Bay Town Guard built a series of small blockhouses along the Outeniqua Mountains – one well-preserved example is situated near the top of this pass, overlooking the part of the Attaquas Pass leading to Oudtshoorn.

Off-road travellers can enjoy spectacular scenery, fynbos, natural rock pools and relics of blockhouses, tollhouses and the remains of ox-wagons alongside the road.

CapeNature has an overnight hut for hikers for the third day of the Attaquas Hiking Trail.

grind flour, bearing in mind that a 'country hotel' in those days would have had to have been pretty independent. The double-storey main structure hints at its former design, which must have presented a most welcoming sight to weary travellers of the day.

We drive on, westwards on the Attaquas Ox-wagon Pass (a national monument) and past an Anglo-Boer War blockhouse placed (for strategic reasons, no doubt) at the head of the most stunningly beautiful fynbos-filled narrow green valley. The journey leads along the path of the original ox-wagons. It follows more or less the route taken by the early explorers, the likes of Schrijver (1689), Thunberg (1772), Sparrman (1775), Swellengrebel (1776), Van Plettenberg (1778), Patterson (1779), Miller and Holtzhauzen (1782), Gordon (1786) and Van Reenen (1790).

Your arrival at Bonniedale is naturally at their eastern boundary, near which are the ruins of the old Attaquas Tollhouse, where the circular outspan area can still be made out among the low-lying vegetation. Nico Hesterman, the route owner and our on-site guide, joins us around the fire and regales the group with entertaining snippets on the history of

Getting comfy at Bonniedale's camp site

the area, from the Khoi skirmishes with the early settlers to the San and their rock art, the Anglo-Boer War, the early ox-wagon trains, and a few ghost stories.

Chalets are available, as well as accommodation in permanent tents.

DAY 5

We rise early, partly due to the full day's activities ahead and partly due to the anticipation of a breakfast of bacon and eggs. The first ones to wake up stoke last night's embers, and a kettle soon produces steaming hot water for coffee. By 09:00 everyone is ready to commence with the first half of Nico's trail. After the driver's briefing and a radio check we engage four-wheel-drive and roll out of camp onto the trail.

The going is rough and bumpy, as one would expect from a rocky 4X4 mountain trail, but the views and the diversity of the flora are what holds our attention. We stop regularly for photo opportunities or for a chat about a specific bush, a protea or an anthill, and Nico's running commentary is informative and light-hearted. Of particular interest is his explanation of the biological onslaught being waged against the invasive hakea. A specific bug and a specific orange dusty fungus can only survive on hakea, and they work together to kill the trees, after which they die off as they don't attack the surrounding indigenous floral types. 'It's far preferable to poisons and a lot easier than chopping them out. We tried that, but it was too much work,' laments Nico in typical fashion.

Numerous cross-axle sections and much loose stone and rock are negotiated in first gear low range, especially where the inclines are steep. In parts the dense foliage scrapes the vehicle's sides, but no one complains as the environment is so exquisite.

Around midday, just before completing the first half of the trail, Nico leads us about 100m off the track on foot to visit one of the rock art sites on his farm. His detailed explanation of the meaning of the paintings and the techniques employed by those ancient peoples is fascinating to say the least.

In the afternoon we tackle the second half of the trail. It delivers tougher driving challenges, especially the loose ascent up to Sunbird Camp which requires diff-lock or traction control to be engaged, but the more cautious drivers can opt for escape routes if they feel unsure of their (or their vehicles') abilities. The 43° descent down John Tom Pass has to be experienced to be believed. Fortunately we all survive without mishap, but there have been roll-overs here before!

Back at camp in the evening, we all enjoy hot showers to rid us of the day's dust and most retire after supper for a relatively early night after a most enjoyable day.

DAY 6

Leaving Bonniedale farm, the gravel road leads westwards to the old village of Woeska, an old wagon post, and along the Attaquaskloof, crossing the Gouritz River via the long concrete causeway and up the Witblits Pass to the farm Welgevonden in the Langberg. We continue through rural farming area before ultimately descending from the mountains to arrive at Heidelberg, our journey's end.

Here we refuel and say our goodbyes to our new friends before dispersing to our respective homes.

Although amusing, this warning sign at Bonniedale should be heeded.

Rock paintings

BONNIEDALE – ITS HISTORY, MYTHS AND LEGENDS

The Attaquaskloof was inhabited by the San until the 1700s, as can be seen by their rock art on the farm, which includes paintings of armed horse riders. They lived in the valley with the Attaqua Khoi.

The first European to set foot on Bonniedale was the adventurer-explorer Isaac Schrijver on the expedition commissioned by Simon van der Stel to barter for sheep and cattle with the Inqua Khoi near Aberdeen. On his return, the party was attacked by the Attaqua Khoi who stole their sheep and drove them into Grootkloof on Bonniedale. Schrijver followed them the next day and killed 41 Khoi.

A Scotsman (name unknown) was the first European to settle on Bonniedale (hence the name) in 1860, supplying produce, mules and oxen to the passing travellers up the Attaquaskloof. He also had the toll concession to maintain that section of the pass, but once the Robinson Pass was complete this was no longer viable. He returned to Scotland in 1880 and never came back.

The ghosts of the slain Khoi are still said to spook horses in the Grootkloof, where an archaeological dig uncovered the remains of an entire Khoi village.

THE LEGEND OF BLUEBEARD SWANEPOEL

This was the last person to be publicly hanged in South Africa, when he met his fate in the town square of George, having been convicted on many counts of murder. His modus operandi included killing those who came to buy cattle from him. After the sale, he would ride over the Attaquas Mountains and ambush them, killing everyone and taking back the cattle. He did this four times successfully, but was caught on the fifth attempt at this grizzly scam, when he missed one lucky person, who had skipped off into the bush to relieve himself.

Another of his practices was to kill the labourers who took out honey for him on the cliff faces of the upper Gouritz River. After retrieving the honey from them, he'd push them over the edge of the cliff into the whirlpool of the river below. As their bodies could never be recovered, he was never convicted of these charges.

His grave lies behind the hut used on day three of the Attaquaskloof Hiking Trail.

20 Lesotho – Kwahlamba, the barrier of spears

by Johann du Toit

TOP 10 ATTRACTIONS OF THIS TRIP

❶ 4X4 driving on some of Africa's highest mountain passes ❷ Mecca of high mountains, deep secluded valleys and crystal-clear mountain-river crossings ❸ Magical drive up 'The Dragon' – Sani Pass, South Africa's highest mountain pass ❹ Unspoilt nature in the Lost Valley of Khubelu ❺ Camping next to the Khubelu River deep inside the Maluti Mountains ❻ High mountain 4X4 tracks crossing from the Khubelu River to Katse Dam ❼ Camping at our Crusader Camp ❽ A full tour of that engineering wonder, the Katse Dam ❾ Driving 11 of Southern Africa's highest mountain passes, all over 2500m in height ❿ Visit the highest diamond mine in the world at 3100m

TRIP OUTLINE

Lesotho is roughly 30,000km^2 in size – about the same size as the Kgalagadi Transfrontier Park or Belgium. The entire country is above 1000m in altitude, with only 10% of the land suitable for agricultural use.

This is in every respect a mountain country, formed by volcanic eruptions some 160 million years ago. Generally, the large valleys were formed by the erosive action of the major river systems like the Senqu, Khubelu and Malibamatso. Lesotho is indeed a country born by fire and flood.

These mountain ramparts are the breeding ground of storms in summer and snow in winter. Known as 'Mountains of the Dragon', they were called by early Bantu peoples *Kwahlamba* – 'Barrier of Spears'.

During our expedition we will ascend Sani Pass and cross the escarpment and the Sani Flats on our way to Black Mountain (3241m), called Kotisephola by the locals. Stopping at the ridge, we look to the north where some 12km away lies Thabana Ntlenyana (3482m), meaning 'beautiful little mountain'. The next highest point to the north is the mighty Kilimanjaro.

From the escarpment we will explore the northeastern region of Lesotho, also know as the Roof of Africa – yes, before the world-famous off-road race was moved to the Maseru area, it used to take place here, even at one time including an ascent up Sani Pass.

This area is widely affected by the Khubelu, Senqu (known as the Orange in South Africa) and Malibamatso rivers, and these unspoilt valleys created by the mighty rivers will be explored in our 4X4s over the next couple of days.

SEE DETAILED MAP ON PAGE 210 ▶▶

APPEAL RATING

5/5

This African kingdom in the sky offers similar alpine conditions as the mountain ranges of Europe, the only difference (for South Africans) being that Lesotho is much closer to home. With an altitude in excess of 1000m for the entire country, travellers have to be well prepared for this remote and rugged mountain kingdom.

▶ The Kwahlamba Expedition offers the opportunity to drive 11 of Southern Africa's highest mountain passes, all over 2500m
▶ Drive Sani Pass – South Africa's highest mountain pass at 2874m
▶ The staggering natural splendour of the Lost Valley of Khubelu
▶ 300 days of brilliant sunshine per year
▶ Countryside formed by fire and ice dating back some 160 million years
▶ Crystal-clear mountain streams
▶ Katse Dam and the Lesotho Highlands Water Project, modern-day engineering wonders
▶ Heights, depths, sizes, distances and temperatures are all extreme in Lesotho
▶ The Basotho people are friendly

THE BEST TIME TO TRAVEL HERE

The weather in Lesotho varies considerably between seasons and can also change very rapidly on any given day.

▶ You need to be well prepared for the rains between October and March
▶ Likewise for the very cold winters from May to August
▶ Bear in mind that at an altitude of 2000m the temperature can drop below freezing at any time of the year, so travellers must be equipped for cold and snow conditions all year round
▶ Routes accessible during winter can be dangerous in summer as a result of flash flooding and high river levels
▶ Camping is not advisable in the winter unless you are really well equipped with -5°C rated sleeping gear
▶ It is essential to plan routes with the particular season in mind
▶ Without good snowfalls, Lesotho is pale and grey in winter compared to being lush and green during the summer – almost a different country

Don't ever underestimate the weather in Lesotho – travellers have lost their lives as a result of this.

GENERAL WARNINGS FOR THIS ROUTE

▶ All the rivers in Lesotho are fast flowing – do not attempt to cross a fast-flowing river (in most cases the level will drop within a couple of hours after heavy rain; the general rule is 'if you can walk it, you can drive it' up to manufacturer's specifications for wading depth)
▶ Be well equipped for the cold and fast-changing weather conditions
▶ Don't camp alone in isolated areas – travel in groups or with an organised tour operator
▶ We always recommend the use of a reputable local guide
▶ Without a qualified 4WD guide, the roads and tracks can become very demanding – you will not only require considerable local knowledge but also a fair amount of 4X4 driving experience if travelling on your own

MAP 20 LESOTHO – Kwahlamba, the barrier of spears

Caledonspoort

Qalo

Khukhune

28°41'43"S
28°14'00"E

Moshoeshoe's Fortress

Butha-Buthe

Qhobela

Liphofung
Cave

28°45'20"S
28°36'03"E

Tsehlanyane

Tlholohatsi

Khatibe

Moteng

28°46'16"S
28°37'29"E

Levi's Nek

Pitsi's Nek

Khabo

28°45'16"S
28°29'39"E

7

'Camp Running Water'

Oxbow Lodge

Afri-Ski Resort

Khoro-ea-Mahlasela

Pass of Gu

Moshoeshoe's Birthplace

Tsehlanyane National Park

Matlameng

Matseng

Lekhalong-la-Rampai

Kao

Kao Mine

Pitseng

LESOTHO

Lejone

Malibamatso

29°20'06"S
28°29'30"E

Seshote

*Lesotho Highlands
Water Project*

Makhoaba

*Makhoaba
Waterfall*

Lehlabatheng
2905m

Katse Dam

Katse Dam Viewpoint

Katse

Orion Katse Lodge

6

29°22'36"S
28°39'35"E

29°20'31"S
28°30'37"E

5

Crusader Camp

29°23'43"S
28°40'06"E

Marakabei

Cheche's

Mantsonyane

Mokhoabong

Thaba-Tseka

Thaba-Putsoa
3065m

Taung

Sehonghong

Legend

	4X4 route
Bape Camp	Overnight stay
3	Overnight number
22°59'48"S 27°56'17"E	GPS co-ordinate

See full key on page 9

DAILY DRIVING DISTANCE AND TIME

Day 1	Travel from home to meet at Himeville		
Day 2	Travel via Sani Pass to Mokhotlong	93km	10hr
Day 3	Lost Valley of Khubelu to camp site	84km	10hr
Day 4	Rest day at camp site		
Day 5	James Pass to 'Crusader Camp'	118km	8hr
Day 6	To Katse Dam	56km	4hr
Day 7	Lejone to 'Camp Running Water'	165km	10hr
Day 8	Moteng Pass to Caledonspoort	82km	2hr

FAMILY-FRIENDLY RATING

2/5

▶ Since this is an expedition-style trip you should be wary of travelling with small children
▶ Small children aren't equipped for the long hours of travelling over some very challenging and rocky terrain – their little bodies get shaken around to a point of irritation, both for themselves and for their parents
▶ We would not recommend taking children younger than seven (unless they are seasoned off-road drivers) on this trip as we will be camping and conditions can become very demanding
▶ Altitude sickness can affect children and the elderly
▶ During winter trips children cope better, being able to play and have fun in the snow ('white gold')
▶ Formal accommodation is recommended and a well-prepared 4X4 essential to cope with the freezing cold and snow-covered road conditions
▶ The possibility of being 'snowed in' for a few days is real; however, if you are well prepared with food and drink, in the end this becomes an adventure to be remembered for a very long time
▶ Many other accommodation and route alternatives are available in Lesotho to the family with very small children

UNDERBERG

Underberg is a busy little town, despite being in predominantly farming country. The town is pretty functional and now includes a number of commercial ventures.

The annual Splashy Fen Music Festival sees hundreds of people make their way through Underberg and this part of the southern Drakensberg to spend the Easter weekend enjoying the local music, arts and crafts, food and drink.

DAY 1

With Himeville being fairly remote for travellers from both the Cape and Gauteng, people tend to arrive in the late afternoon or early evening, so we recommend that you book into the Sani Pass Hotel and Leisure Resort rather than set up camp. The resort lies in the foothills of the southern Drakensberg, a declared World Heritage Site.

On the way in, the traveller will drive via Underberg and Himeville, where the last supplies and fuel can be obtained for the epic adventure that lies ahead.

Please note that you may not transport liquor into Lesotho. We don't understand why, but have witnessed many unnecessary arguments with customs officials at the border post that only lead to bad service and very unfriendly officials. Remember that this is the law as laid down by their government and not the border officials, so don't blame them.

Book into the hotel and enjoy their hospitality and good food to get ready for the adventure lying ahead. The hotel is up to date with weather conditions in Lesotho, and in the case of a breakdown or medical emergency they know whom to contact.

DAY 2

Today we will enter Lesotho. In preparation for the border crossing, be sure you have a valid passport for every traveller (since 2010 Lesotho has not accepted temporary passports), a pen for completing the entry document, and money for the road tax. Make sure your vehicle's licence disc is still valid, and always have your ID and driver's licence at hand. Be friendly – it is amazing what a smile can achieve!

The drive up Sani Pass, irrespective of how many times you have done this, remains a very pleasant experience. In 4X4 circles, driving the Sani Pass is often regarded as the icon of 4X4 driving. But this is one of the more beautiful passes in South Africa, and anybody doing the ascent purely for the sake of a 4X4 challenge is definitely missing the point.

During the last couple of years we have seen an increase in the number of non-registered quad bikes racing up the pass, showering vehicles and pedestrians with dust and rocks. Not only is this an irritation, it's illegal as this is a public road. Nowadays we are very happy to notice a clampdown on this practice, as police on the South African side are putting a stop to it.

HIMEVILLE

Named after Sir Alfred Hime, a road engineer and Prime Minister of Natal, Himeville and the surrounding region present more fly-fishing opportunities than anywhere else in the country. The district further boasts three golf courses and numerous rivers for swimming, rafting, canoeing and tubing. Horse trails and polo fields add a further dimension to the available fun and excitement.

The building housing Himeville's museum was constructed in 1900 as the last of Natal's forts, before it became a prison until 1972. Its displays include military, African traditional and even trout-fishing memorabilia. The museum is home to a collection of San artefacts providing insight into their life and times.

Sani Pass

SANI PASS

The name Sani was originally taken to be a derivation of the name San (for Bushmen), but this is incorrect. In 1890 Chief Letsie, the son of Moshoeshoe, sent his son Rafoltsane to the area currently known as Mokhotlong to establish a centre of local government, and to act as District Chief. The name Sani is thus thought to be an abbreviation of the name Rafoltsane.

Once the Sani Pass (at 2874m Southern Africa's highest pass) was a rough mule trail descending the eastern highlands of old Basutoland into Natal. Tough drovers brought wool and mohair down the pass on donkeys and mules to trade for blankets, clothing and maize meal – the essentials for life in a remote, impoverished country. One young man had a dream of operating a motor vehicle service up this fantastic pass, using the four-wheel-drive vehicles he had seen on service in World War II. His name was David Alexander, and the company he founded in 1955 has operated on the Sani Pass ever since. (It is illegal to drive up Sani in a 2X4.)

Many have played a big role in transforming this former bridle path into a driveable 4X4 road, and many lives were lost in the process. For a more comprehensive history of this pass and the road to Mokhotlong, we strongly recommend that you read *Sani Pass – Riding the Dragon* by David Alexander and *The Sage of the Sani Pass and Mokhotlong* by Michael Clark.

Many outdoor activities can be enjoyed from the Sani Top Chalets, such as hiking, mountain biking, horse trails and cultural tours to a traditional Basotho home.

The first 15km to the South African border post is a relatively easy and enjoyable drive up the valley, and here you'll pass the first of the signposts where it is stated that by law you require a 4X4 vehicle to drive up the pass.

Formalities at the South African border post will be swift and well organised. You can also make use of their very clean and well-maintained ablution facilities, which are likely to be the best that you will encounter for a long time.

As a rule of thumb we always engage low range from here onwards. It's amazing that in 4X4 conversations you will frequently hear somebody boasting, 'I drove up Sani in my two-wheel drive' or 'I never used low range all the way to the top'. This is a sure sign of a driver not only abusing nature but having no respect for the lives of his passengers.

The last 8km is very scenic and you need time to take it all in and really appreciate your surroundings. This is the reason why we do not recommend that you race up Sani and onwards to Katse Dam or Fouriesburg. Rather give yourselves enough time to explore this magical pass.

Always remember that ascending vehicles have right of way. There is no way that a heavily laden truck can stop and then pull away again on these inclines.

Once you reach the top you can take your hat off to Godfrey Edmunds, an ex RAF Spitfire pilot, who drove the first vehicle up Sani Pass, which at that stage was nothing more than a bridle path. This epic journey took place on 26 October 1948 in a Jeep and took just on six hours to complete with the aid of a team of ponies and a chain block pulley.

Once you've finished all the border post formalities on the Lesotho side, you can pay a quick visit to Sani Top Chalets and take some refreshments at the 'highest pub in Africa' (actually the highest *licensed* pub in *Southern* Africa). Don't stay too long, as from here it's still a good hour's drive to tonight's recommended overnight stay.

From Sani we climb higher via the Kotisephola Pass (3241m), the second highest road in Lesotho. Some 13km from Sani, stop at the top here, look in a northeasterly direction and you will just be able to spot the highest peak in Lesotho, Thabana Ntlenyana (3482m).

The last 46km section on the way to the recommended accommodation is via the very scenic Sehonghong River Valley to the Mokhotlong district.

We recommend St James Guest House (camping and self-catering options), Mokhotlong Farmer Training Centre (rooms but with no hot water), or Senqu Hotel (rooms with safe parking, and they make an excellent hamburger). Keep in mind that accommodation in the rural areas of Lesotho will have very basic facilities; however, they are well maintained and clean.

This will be a long day; all travellers still need to acclimatise to the high altitude and 'thin air', and this is also the main reason why we recommend formal accommodation for this night and not camping – a good night's rest will prepare everybody for the challenges in the days to come.

A local donkey

SELF-SUFFICIENCY RATING

3/5

Every day of this adventure sees us passing through one village or another. No matter how small in size, the basic commodities are obtainable. However, the following is critical:

▶ Carry emergency food for days in the vehicle, should unforeseen extreme weather patterns or mechanical breakdowns strike

▶ Stream water high up in the mountains is probably some of the sweetest water you can drink; however, in the villages the streams will be contaminated and you are advised to use bottled water only – this will also be obtainable at most of the smaller stores

▶ Having a mechanical breakdown will be problematic as it will be very difficult to obtain the services of a 4X4 tow truck to reach the very remote spots – do not rely on roadside assistance and rather take care of recoveries yourself

▶ Never travel alone

▶ Because of the relatively short distances involved for this trip, normal fuel ranges will be more than adequate for most vehicles; you are able to refuel at many of the smaller towns encountered along the route

VEHICLE REQUIREMENTS

This trail, although demanding in places, was not developed to be a 4X4 tester, but rather an off-road expedition for the whole family.

▶ 4X4 with low range (this is critical for the steep descents and ascents)

▶ High road clearance as per standard D caps 4X4, but remove the running boards

▶ Recovery points front and rear

▶ Good-quality tyres with at least 60% tread

▶ Mud-terrain tyres will be an added benefit

▶ Secure points to strap down all luggage items – when packing, plan to have all the heavy equipment and water as low as possible in the vehicle, as this will have a positive effect on the centre of gravity, especially when driving some of the steep passes

▶ Make sure that the cooling system is well maintained, with enough antifreeze (as per manufacturer's specifications) in the radiator

▶ Rear diff-lock will be an added bonus

▶ Make sure licence disc is valid and visible

▶ Confirm with your insurance company that your vehicle will be covered in Lesotho for driving 'off a given road'

TRAILER-FRIENDLY RATING

0/5

None of these trails are suitable for the towing of any sort of trailer. Track and trail conditions are just not safe for a 4X4 towing a trailer or caravan of any description, no matter how small or rugged.

DAY 3

After only a short drive from Mokhotlong, in the relative luxury of driving on tar, we cross the Senqu River, known in South Africa as the Orange River. Just before the bridge you turn to the right, going off the tar and onto a twin-track trail that will take you down to the banks of the river. This is a truly beautiful spot for an early breakfast.

The tar road winds through the mountains and we pass Fraser's Trading Store – a good place for some cold refreshments and fuel. Just 3km further on the tar road we have to turn right onto an unmarked gravel road that will open up the Lost Valley of Khubelu.

It is very important to take a short detour at this stage and drive further along the tar road until it crosses the Khubelu River. The reason for this is to inspect the condition of the Khubelu (which also means 'red river') for possible flooding. Further up the track, on the way to Khubelu, you will need to cross this very scenic river no fewer than 11 times without the luxury of a bridge! If there is flooding it might be a good idea to put plan B in place.

Up to this point on the Kwahlamba Expedition we have travelled in areas that are frequently visited by tourists. The Lost Valley of Khubelu is just the opposite, with large areas that are rarely, if ever, visited by any tourists. Therefore it is true that we are just as interesting to the locals as they are to us – show respect and don't give the children any

ASPECTS OF BASOTHO CULTURE

Moshoeshoe I is the father of the Basotho people as he was responsible for drawing together the scattered Sotho peoples who had been driven apart by Zulu and Ndebele raids, and for creating Lesotho, the Basotho Kingdom.

The Basotho people have developed a unique culture. Due to being one of the few African peoples living in a mountainous environment, they have made many adaptations to their conditions. The beautifully patterned woollen Basotho blanket is one example.

Most villages are located high in the mountains and are formally structured. They are made up of a number of kraals, i.e. a collection of buildings belonging to one family. Some are for sleeping, some for storage and one for cooking. Each kraal will also have an enclosure for livestock. The Basotho are agriculturalists and the chief allocates the fields around the villages to villagers. Many crops are cultivated, including maize, wheat, sorghum, beans and peas as well as vegetables such as onions and cabbage. Many local herbs are also gathered as green vegetables, which the Basotho call *moroho*.

The Basotho pony is the best form of transport in the mountains, while donkeys are often used as pack animals. Most families own cattle, and oxen are used to plough. Wool from merino sheep is a major source of income, as is mohair from Angora goats. The shepherds are often young boys who stay in simple huts, called *motebo*, perched on ridges at well over 3000m and very well hidden.

When passing a village you will frequently see a flag flying from a tall pole. This indicates a place where something is being sold. A white flag means *joala*, a locally brewed sorghum beer. Yellow means maize beer, red means meat and green means vegetables.

River crossing

sweets, as this will only encourage future begging.

The first couple of kilometres will be via a very good gravel road, but this will soon change as the road winds its way among various villages until it changes to a mere track and we reach the first river crossing.

It is very important to get your feet wet at this stage and walk the crossing in both directions – make sure there are no hidden holes or large rocks before crossing. The area will be more and more sparsely populated from this point. In the most isolated places and on the steepest of gradients, the local people not only survive, but actually live very happily in their traditional villages. Getting lost here is very difficult as there is only one track to follow and any wrong turns will only lead to a dead stop in a village or against a mountain. About four river crossings further on, the track will ascend the mountain via a very beautiful pass that we have named Moluoane Pass, after the willow trees in the river.

The last big village we enter is Maloraneng, and we strongly recommend a quick stop at David's Shop for some very traditional refreshments before tackling the last 8km (two hours) to our camp site. Arriving at camp will be a relief after the day's travels. We have the luxury of long-drop toilets and cold-water showers and are surrounded by the devastating beauty of the mountains. We consider this site the most scenic and most remote in Lesotho.

THE ROOF OF AFRICA RALLY

The Roof of Africa Rally was first run in 1965, and is commonly thought to have put off-road racing on the map in Southern Africa. The event started in Johannesburg and then travelled down to Butha-Buthe, where participants entered Lesotho and proceeded over the Moteng Pass to Oxbow, the diamond diggings at Letseng-la-Terae and on to Tlokoeng. The route then wound down the Sani Pass and finished in Durban.

Jan Hettema won the first event in a standard Volvo. In 1969 Eddie Keizan won in a Land Rover, and it was only 25 years later that a Land Rover won again when Cliff Barker and Mike Reddin won in a Defender 110.

The 'Roof' is now a motorcycle and quad race, cars having last competed in 2000.

DAY 4

We strongly recommend a full day of rest in camp. Fear not, there is plenty to do, with the crystal-clear mountain pools waiting for you to try and catch those elusive wild trout. Otherwise negotiate with the locals from Lichecheng village for the use of their horses for a pony trail. Or, for the more adventurous, take a three- to four-hour hike with our guide to a local hot spring, totally natural and uncommercialised.

This will also be a day to reflect on the unspoilt beauty of the Maluti Mountains and to prepare man and machine for the next phase of the expedition.

There is no firewood available at the camp site and we have to be totally self-sufficient during our stay here. Be warned – although water is available in abundance, it isn't safe for drinking purposes.

DAY 5

This next day of our Lesotho adventure will take us up and beyond 3000m in elevation, via the very challenging James Pass to the highest diamond mine in the world at Letseng-la-Terae (meaning 'swamp in the corner'). But be warned: the Basotho love their 'diamonds' and they will display a wide variety of items for sale, from broken glass to quartz and even, in some cases, real diamonds – don't support this highly illegal industry.

LETSENG DIAMOND MINE

The Drakensberg and Lesotho highlands, being of volcanic origin, have pipes, fissures and pockets of diamonds hidden in the rock. Over the years many men have spent long periods and large amounts of capital to release this wealth from Lesotho – as far back as 1950 Colonel Jack Scott had teams of geologists roaming the mountains and locating the bigger deposits.

Currently the Letseng Diamond Mine, owned by Gem Diamonds Limited, is noted for its high percentage of large diamonds in the 10+ carat range, although the mine is expensive to operate, with a yield of around 2 carats per 100 tons. However, with its large amount of sizable roughs, the Letseng mine has the highest dollar per carat ratio of any diamond mine in the world. One of the most notable diamonds to come from the mine was the 603 carat 'Lesotho Promise' found in 2006.

Joining the Roof of Africa tar road again at the Letseng gate, we proceed southwards down to Mapholaneng, one of the bigger villages in the area. It is amazing to note that the nearest clinic for all the villages we passed in the Lost Valley of Khubelu is at Mapholaneng, some 6–8 days away on horseback!

Mapholaneng has a big shop full of Western commodities, and you can also get fuel here. The adventurous can sample and buy the locally brewed traditional beer (you need a strong stomach). Outside Mapholaneng we turn right at what must be one of the most misleading signposts in Lesotho. This signpost, in the very friendly brown tourist colour, advertises Katse Dam, Pony trekking and Kayaking. The real story here is, yes, the road will take you to Katse Dam – eventually, with the aid of GPS and a 4X4 and some 12 hours of extreme 4X4 driving. This has caught out many a tourist travelling on the Roof of Africa tar road to Butha-Buthe and Fouriesburg, driving in small rented sedan cars.

SPECIFIC KIT REQUIRED FOR THIS TRIP

Camping in Lesotho, even in summer, can become very demanding and will require some foul-weather equipment.

▶ Full camping gear, with good weather-resistant tents and -5°C rated sleeping bags
▶ Cold-weather clothing (good jacket, beanie, gloves and boots)
▶ Colouring-in books and educational toys for the local children, which should be distributed only via legitimate sources or schools – no sweets
▶ Passports for all occupants and a valid South African driver's licence
▶ With 300 days of brilliant sunshine, don't forget the sun block
▶ Fishing gear, as most of the streams are well stocked with wild trout

ESSENTIAL REQUIREMENTS FOR THIS TRIP

▶ Full recovery kit to include a minimum of two 10m recovery straps with bow shackles
▶ Spade
▶ High-lift jack (if compatible with 4X4) or air jack, wooden block as base for bottle jack (practise jacking your vehicle up at home prior to embarking on the trip)
▶ Spare keys and extra immobiliser batteries
▶ Full puncture-repair kit, with tyre-pressure gauge and compressor (test this at home prior to the trip)
▶ Tool kit, with extra fuses, radiator leak-blocking gum and metal fixative
▶ Full first-aid kit, including emergency medication for allergies, especially bee stings; make sure that the kit is stocked with some extra medication for nausea and headaches as these are some of the first symptoms of altitude sickness
▶ Headlamps for all passengers
▶ Gumboots are handy
▶ Strong plastic bags for rubbish (don't dispose of rubbish inside Lesotho, not even in the villages – it will all be opened by the local people and animals and will end up strewn all over the countryside)
▶ There is no firewood inside Lesotho, so pack some for all the camping evenings

SEE FULL PACKING LIST ON PAGE 218 ▶▶

Needless to say, we are prepared and follow the gravel road with a spectacular view of the Senqu River on the left-hand side. Unfortunately this very scenic spot may not look the same in future, when a proposed new dam (at a cost of R7 billion), which will dam the Khubelu and Orange rivers, is erected near this site. What the effect of this dam will be on this unspoilt area remains to be seen.

The road now changes to twin tracks and leads us to the St Martin's Mission Station. On the way there we will pass the very scenic Makhoaba Waterfall in the Makhoaba River. It is highly recommended to stop at the mission and enjoy

the singing of the children. This is also one of the places in Lesotho where we support the local communities by delivering educational toys.

With one eye firmly on the clock, soon we have to depart to 'Crusader Camp' for the evening. As a result of the very high mountain slopes, the sun sets rather early in Lesotho, so we have to be at camp no later than 16:00. The last section is via the 'Crawler' and 'Long Drop' passes.

Our camp was chosen not so much because of its scenic properties, but rather because this is a rare spot where it is possible to pitch the tents on level ground. Camping will be under the stars with no ablution facilities or running water – true Lesotho-style.

Camping, Lesotho-style

DAY 6

Descending Bernard's Baboon Pass, we enter the low-lying areas on our way to the third of the big rivers – the Malibamatso. This area can become very slippery during wet conditions and one has to drive with great caution. Nowadays the traveller is blessed with a new bridge over the Malibamatso River that will link the trail to the main gravel road from Thaba-Tseka to Katse Dam.

Many years ago, before there were bridges over the Malibamatso River, we came across a truck firmly stuck in the river and no fewer than 24 oxen trying their best to clear the truck out of the river crossing. Needless to say we had our old reliable tool, the high-lift jack, with us and were able to lift this eight-ton truck so that rocks could be placed under the wheels.

KATSE DAM AND LESOTHO HIGHLANDS WATER PROJECT

The Katse Dam on the Malibamatso River is the second largest in Africa and was identified during the 1990s to supplement South Africa's water supply. The World Bank arranged for a treaty between South Africa and Lesotho, allowing for the execution of the project to proceed.

The project was completed by a consortium of construction and engineering companies and was subject to widespread corruption, which is not uncommon with large dam projects. The Lesotho courts have taken the unusual step of prosecuting the large companies involved in the scandal in addition to the Lesotho bureaucrat who took the bribes. Thus far, there have been a number of convictions and at least one company debarred by the World Bank for its role in the scandal.

Eventually, to the joy of the driver (and probably the oxen as well), we managed to get the truck out. Since that day we have called this crossing 'Jack'!

The main gravel road will take us to the luxury of Orion Katse Lodge, where we have a variety of accommodation options available to us, ranging from two- and three-bedroom houses, hotels or the more cost-effective dormitory-style (sharing ablutions) accommodation. With three camping nights behind us, we strongly recommend the comfort of a hot shower and a bed with some clean white linen. The chef at the lodge is famous for preparing the local trout, which makes for an excellent supper.

Very near to the lodge we take a secluded track up Simon's Hill. This scenic view over the Katse Dam is named after a very dear friend, a guide at Katse Lodge who lost his life at a very young age in a tragic swimming accident in the Malibamatso River.

Close to Simon's Hill, at the shop at Katse village, you can stock up with all the commodities as well as some traditional Basotho blankets. Time permitting, we definitely recommend an additional night's stay here at Katse Dam in order to visit the botanical garden and also enjoy a boat cruise on the dam.

DAY 7

We start our day with a tour of an engineering wonder, the Katse Dam and the Lesotho Highlands Water Project (LHWP). This highly educational tour is conducted from the head office (the biggest building at the dam) at 09:00 daily for a small fee. Their specialist guides will give a comprehensive briefing regarding the project, followed by a tour of the dam wall, an experience not to be missed.

The LHWP has changed the way of life in Lesotho. The new roads across the breathtaking mountain passes have unlocked the many secrets of this harsh mountainous hinterland to tourists. At the same time the benefit to the local population of routes accessible to motorised transport, upgraded health services and more shops have all contributed to a better way of life for those living in these high and previously inaccessible places.

After completing our educational tour we travel on what must be one of the best mountain passes in the world. While driving, bear in mind that all the materials used for building Katse Dam had to be transported via these mountain passes, requiring a solid road of world-class standards. The road follows the edges of Katse Dam and then crosses the dam via what is known as the main bridge to the massive intake towers before reaching the town of Lejone. Here we say farewell to tarmac and switch back to 4X4.

Our next 60km, travelling via Kao Mine, will offer not only some of the best views in Lesotho but will also be a test for man and machine, taking the best part of 4–5 hours to complete. This is one of the most isolated tracks in Lesotho, with no villages between Kao Mine and the Roof Of Africa tar road. After this section, the sighting of the tar road at Tlaeeng Pass (the highest drivable pass in Africa at 3270m) will be most welcome.

The last section to 'Camp Running Water' next to the Malibamatso River will take us via the Pass of Guns, Khoro-ea-Mahlasela Pass and Afri-Ski Resort to our turn-off just after Oxbow Lodge. Camping for the last night will be without any facilities except the Malibamatso River for water.

Snow-covered track

DAY 8

Following the Roof of Africa tar road back to Butha-Buthe and Caledonspoort, we cross one of our last mountain passes as we descend down the escarpment via the famous Moteng Pass (2815m), passing the Liphofung Cave along the way. (With the prospective tarring of Sani Pass on the cards, we imagine that Sani will look very similar to Moteng once the contract is completed.) When descending Moteng Pass, be very careful of trucks and taxis – the local drivers seem to harbour no fear of these mountain passes. As you will note from the bent railings and wrecks in the valleys below, they are inclined to put far too much trust in their brakes.

Caledonspoort is a very efficient border post with Fouriesburg just on the other side. Once through the border control posts, the tour is over and you can look back on a magnificent week's discovery of just a corner of the great mountain kingdom that is Lesotho.

THE LIPHOFUNG CAVE

This cave has been in use since prehistoric times, as evidenced by the San rock art on the walls and the rich archaeological deposits of Stone Age implements on the floor. Later, the first Basotho monarch, King Moshoeshoe the Great, inhabited the cave when visiting that part of his kingdom.

The small visitor centre includes a display of San rock art and Basotho culture and also has a curio shop, as well as ablution facilities. This heritage site was developed almost entirely with the help of local labour and artisans, which means that most of the costs of the development have been ploughed back into the community. Visitors can purchase keepsakes from the small craft outlet, which carries an assortment of handiwork made by members of surrounding communities.

There is self-catering overnight accommodation in two huts, and camp sites are available. There is also accommodation offered in the nearby village.

Packing list

Specific items from these lists should be selected according to the nature and duration of the trip and your proximity to medical and mechanical assistance.

Camping equipment

- free-standing tent
- groundsheet
- guy ropes
- tent poles
- ladder and stays for rooftop tent
- tent pegs
- canvas repair kit
- mallet
- axe or bow saw
- spade
- table
- chairs
- beach umbrella, gazebo or awning
- picnic mat
- mattresses
- sleeping bags
- extra blankets
- space blankets
- pillow
- mosquito net
- solar shower
- funnel for water tank
- fold-up wash basin
- fold-up toilet seat
- spare washbasin plug
- torch
- spotlight
- headlamps
- double-bulb light
- cigarette lighter socket charger
- cigarette lighter socket adapter
- lighter
- matches
- spare batteries
- battery charger
- fire extinguisher
- high/low thermometer
- magnet
- magnifying glass

Basic and recovery equipment

(These are essential items that should always accompany you, even if just on a day outing.)

- leather work gloves
- tyre-pressure gauge
- tyre-valve spanner and spare valves
- winch remote control cable
- winch block
- tree protector strap
- bow-shackles
- spade
- high-lift jack
- kinetic strap
- tow strap
- puncture-repair kit
- special anti-theft wheel nut socket
- air compressor

Tool box

- bottle jack
- wheel spanners
- jump leads
- block and tackle
- tyre levers
- pump pliers
- screwdriver set
- small adjustable spanner
- small hacksaw
- brake fluid
- clutch fluid
- engine oil
- gear oil
- auto transmission oil
- 3-in-1 oil
- Q20 lubricant or moisture repelling spray
- sealant
- reusable putty adhesive
- double-sided sticky tape
- insulating tape
- duct tape
- silicon spray
- instant glue
- exhaust pipe/silencer repair paste
- quick-set putty
- quick-set steel
- tie-downs
- cable ties (various lengths)
- fan belts
- fuel pump filter
- gasket material
- gasket sealant
- fuel hose
- windscreen cleaner
- hand pump
- hose and pipe repair kit
- radiator hose bottom
- hand drill
- saw set
- bow saw
- spare bow saw blades
- hacksaw
- spare hacksaw blades
- Allen keys
- assortment of files
- ball hammer
- claw hammer
- file with handle
- rivet gun
- rivets
- crowbar
- monkey wrench
- drill bits
- portable vice
- large adjustable spanner
- large fencing pliers
- large pliers
- long-nose pliers
- socket arm
- 25mm socket
- socket set
- socket universal joint
- spanner set
- vice grips
- wire cutters
- tin snips
- fuses (in fuse box)
- gas jets
- gas washers
- circuit tester
- copper wire
- fishing line and box
- knife-sharpening kit
- baling wire (thick and thin)
- large pencil
- large tenting needle
- leather punch
- sandpaper (assorted)
- selection of hose clips
- selection of washers, nuts, bolts and screws
- selection of wire
- set square
- super lock
- tape measure
- wood clamps
- wooden rule
- light bulbs
- electrical lead
- siphon hose
- spare bulbs
- spare tubes
- plumber's twine
- wire coat hangers
- wire stay shackles
- wire stays
- water tank dipstick

Kitchen equipment and food

- gas cylinder
- cooker attachments
- skottel-braai
- potjiekos cast-iron pot and lid
- Cobb
- wok
- gas ring
- kettle
- bowls
- wash-up basin
- drying rack

two-plate burner and hose
braai grid
bread baking tin
charcoal
cool box, large
cool box, small
wood
pots
frying pan
absorbent cloth
black refuse bags
candles
clingwrap
washing powder
dishwashing liquid
firelighters
paper plates
paper towels
clothes pegs
toothpicks
aluminium foil
grater
funnel
kitchen cloths
household cleaner
soft drinks
beer, wine, spirits, liqueurs
long-life milk
fruit juice
yoghurt
coffee, tea, coffee creamer
condensed milk
biscuits (sweet and savoury)
rusks
breakfast cereals
bread
butter
cheese
jam
honey
eggs
fresh vegetables
baking powder
flour
rice
sugar
salt, pepper, herbs, spices,
    seasoning
oil
stock cubes
vinegar

meat marinade
mayonnaise
salad dressing
tinned foods
snacks (e.g. peanuts, chips,
    olives)
energy bars
sweets
meat

Clothing and personal items
trousers
shorts
shirts
T-shirts
underwear
thermal underwear
pyjamas
hat
cap
sunglasses
beanie
scarf
bed socks
gloves
jacket
jersey
sweatshirt
hooded sweatshirt
raincoat
swimming costume and
    towel
wet shoes
hiking footwear
spare shoelaces
shoes
sandals
sunblock
shampoo
conditioner
toothbrush
toothpaste
dental floss
mouthwash
face cloth
bath towel
liquid soap
hand cream
moisturiser
lip salve
scrubbing brush

soap
shower cap
tissues
toilet rolls
cotton wool
emery board
nail clippers
hairbrush and comb
hairdryer
mirror
sewing kit
Swiss army knife or multi-
    tool
small backpack
water bottles
waist pack
binoculars
camera and charger
memory sticks
cellphone and charger
ID document and passport

Medical supplies
medicine for:
    colds
    hay fever
    upset stomach
    insect bites and stings
    headaches
    inflammation of eyes
    sunburn
    toothache
    backache
    stress injuries
    cuts and scratches
    burns
    mouth ulcers
    chafing and grazes
    constipation
    diarrhoea
    cramps
    snake bite
    sprains
other medical supplies:
    antibiotic cream
    antibacterial cream
    antiseptic ointment
    insect repellent
    eye bath and patch
    eye drops
    anti-inflammatory gel

gauze dressings
bandages and grips
swabs
antihistamine tablets
antihistamine cream
thermometer
hot and cold compresses
inhaler (if required)
malaria prophylactics
calamine lotion
throat lozenges
water purification tablets
disinfectant
assorted plasters
vitamin tablets
needles and cotton
charcoal tablets
safety pins
rehydration powders
peroxide
clove oil
rubber gloves
scissors
tweezers
splints
sponge
sterile pads
dropper
ear buds

Reference books and leisure items
books on:
    birds
    mammals
    insects
    trees
    grasses
    snakes
    spiders
    stars
    geology
    animal tracks
field note book
road maps
board games
playing cards
song book

Responsible behaviour and off-road etiquette

The topics of driving techniques, safety aspects of off-road driving and how you should prepare yourself and your vehicle have all been comprehensively covered in many training manuals, on training courses and in other off-road media and publications, so we won't even mention things like 'always stay in the tracks'. It is mainly our behaviour when we go off-road and into wilderness areas that will determine whether this wonderful lifestyle will remain open to us in future.

Irrespective of how we choose to experience off-road destinations, we have certain responsibilities and there are basic principles to be upheld – firstly to the local inhabitants of rural areas, secondly to the wildlife that we encounter, and lastly to our fellow travellers, all of whom deserve our respect. Regarding the first two, always remember that we are the visitors to their domain. Our social norms are irrelevant in the bush and our actions should at all times be non-confrontational and subservient to the customs and living patterns of the permanent inhabitants.

Just because you're in the wild, don't go wild!

Here are a few tips on off-road etiquette to make you a welcome visitor and not an unwelcome intruder.

Etiquette towards local villagers and rural inhabitants

- Never drive into a village billowing clouds of dust and sending goats, chickens and children scattering for cover. Stop on the outskirts and approach slowly on foot. Rural villages and settlements usually comprise a grouping of huts that serve different uses, such as sleeping quarters, social rooms and food-preparation areas. (Consider the huts as you would consider the rooms of your house.) Driving into their midst is like having uninvited individuals parking their 4X4s in your entrance hall or lounge.
- Ask permission to camp alongside or near kraals and villages, and always offer to pay. The spot you sought out for yourself under a nice shady tree may well be a meeting place, dance area or sacred spot. Imagine arriving home from work to find a group of campers merrily setting up tents on your front lawn and digging up the garden to make a camp fire.
- Ask permission to photograph people and their possessions, and always offer some sort of remuneration. Some rural people still harbour deep superstitions. No-one likes a camera lens thrust into their face – just ask Colin Farrell or Russell Crowe.
- Drive slowly when passing kraals, villages and farmhouses so as not to cover everyone and their washing in layers of dust – in areas where water is scarce, having to rewash clothes will cause ill feelings. This also applies to crops planted close to the road – the pores of leaves clog up, stunting their growth.
- When donating medicines, food, clothing or educational gifts, don't just give them to the first person you see. There is a social hierarchy to be respected, so seek out the chief or headman and allow him to distribute according to the priorities and needs of the villagers. Don't give out sweets to children.

- Be selective and frugal when gathering firewood in the bush (rather bring wood from home, or use charcoal or gas). Logs should be allowed to decay naturally as they sustain many insects at the bottom of the food chain; removing such logs impacts negatively on creatures that in turn feed on the insects. Also, the soil needs the nutrients they provide to ensure healthier vegetation. In addition to these considerations, remember that the local people depend on firewood and, when it is scarce, they often have to walk miles to gather it. They regard large bonfires as wanton wastage. This fuel is essential for their cooking, and thus their survival.
- Always leave gates as you found them.

Etiquette towards the wildlife

- When camping in the wild, be aware of locating your camp site correctly. Avoid settling in close proximity to water holes, game paths and hippo runs.
- Always approach wild animals slowly and quietly – avoid jerky or sudden movements and don't rev your engine. This tactic may work in the traffic at Sandton City, but although 4X4s may look tough, they don't actually offer much resistance to an elephant, rhino or hippo!
- Allow herds to cross your path at their leisure, without trying to barge through among the animals. The young and sick are often protected in the centre of a herd and this provocation will be regarded as an attack.
- Never, under any circumstances, feed any wild animal. Some fools like to throw food out of the vehicle to attract animals and get a good photograph. This makes them lose their natural fear of humans and they then expect to be fed in future, often 'insisting' on food in an aggressive manner. This could be detrimental to your long-standing relationship with your leg! Often these animals have to be destroyed as they pose a threat.
- Remember that you are in their domain, they are not in yours. Shine a torch regularly around the outskirts of your camp at night to see if you have any fireside 'visitors'.
- Don't wear white clothing in the bush. Not only does this pose a laundering nightmare, but white also attracts unwanted insects. Avoid bright colours and rather wear greens, tans or khaki to blend in. Camouflage clothing may be hip, but in many African countries you will be arrested for wearing so much as a camo cap!

Feeding of wild animals can cause them to lose their healthy fear of humans

Helping a fellow adventurer out of soft sand

Etiquette towards your fellow travellers

▶ Observe the personal space of others when pitching your tent; spread out rather than camp on each other's doorsteps.

▶ Don't shine torches into people's eyes as it is irritating and the pupils take a while to recover.

▶ Dim your headlights when driving into a camp site after dark or you may see more than you'd bargained for!

▶ Having a light on inside a thin nylon tent casts a remarkably clear silhouette of human forms, so be aware that everything you do inside could be screened to the entire camp site.

▶ Teach children what is acceptable and what is unacceptable behaviour; your version of cute may not correspond with other people's.

▶ Respect the right to privacy of others. Call out as you approach another's tent. Also, walk around their site, not through it.

▶ Always ask the guide or group leader if you can braai at your own site and not at the communal fire. We understand that a little family bonding is required now and again, but check first whether it is safe to do so.

▶ Avoid continually opening and closing car doors, any audible music from your car, and excessively loud talking and laughter. Allow a sense of quiet serenity to prevail so that everyone can tune into 'bush radio' and appreciate the sounds of nature.

▶ Not everyone is an early riser. Try to be quiet and allow the late sleepers to enjoy their last minutes of shut-eye. Rather let birdsong be their alarm clock.

▶ Ensure that you have the right equipment with you – people start to lose patience if you continually want to borrow this and that.

▶ Kinetic straps and ropes have a limited number of times they can be used. If you have to be recovered with somebody else's kinetic strap, the right thing to do is to offer to buy it from them. (Or you could pay a pro rata amount of the replacement value. Typically they cost R1000 and have 10 'pulls' in them, so offer to pay R100 for each 'pull'.)

▶ Naturally, foul or abusive language and blasphemy is unacceptable.

▶ And guys, it isn't funny to pee on the fire to kill the coals!

Just apply common sense and good manners to all you encounter and everyone will be able to co-exist happily and in harmony.

Don't forget to pack your sense of humour and use it frequently.

Camp fire

Author information

PHILIP SACKVILLE-SCOTT

Owner-manager of **Sackville Safaris**, Philip is a registered Four Wheel Drive Guide and currently the chairman of the 4 Wheel Drive Guides Association (4WDGA). He regularly contributes articles to various off road publications and is keen on many outdoor activities.

Philip was born and grew up in Lusaka, Zambia, where he was fortunate enough to be introduced to the African bush by the legendary Norman Carr, at Luangwa Game Reserve. He matriculated from Rondebosch Boys' High School. Coming from a marketing background, he has spent many years in the advertising and sports marketing arenas and currently also owns a sign-making business.

Sackville Safaris is a Cape Town-based off-road tour business, offering self-drive camping tours to the back of beyond. They regularly visit the West Coast, Northern Cape and Richtersveld, Kalahari, Karoo, Garden Route and Tankwa areas, as well as embarking on extended trips into the Eastern Cape to visit the Baviaanskloof, Addo and Transkei coastline. They don't only do the extended tours, but also visit many local 4X4 trails for weekend trips.

All Sackville Safaris tours are family-orientated outings – they believe that the peace and tranquillity of Africa's natural splendour is the ultimate setting for spending quality time together as a family. Whether your specific interest is photography, game-viewing, geology, botany, birding, rock art, astronomy or just plain chilling in wide open spaces under clear blue African skies, any trip with them will be an unforgettable experience of the off-roading lifestyle.

So, join Sackville Safaris in your 4X4 for the adventure of a lifetime as you go off-road and explore the hidden gems of the South African landscape. If you don't have a 4X4, they can arrange a fully kitted rental unit at competitive prices.

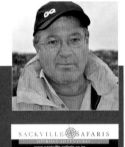

Contact details
Tel: +27 21 558 3930
Cell: +27 82 446 1981
Website: www.sackville-safaris.co.za
Email: philip@sackville-safaris.co.za

JURGENS SCHOEMAN

Jurgens grew up on an African farm, in the Prince Albert district of the Western Cape province, South Africa. He studied at the University of Stellenbosch and qualified as Agricultural Economist. He worked at KWV in Paarl, South Africa's largest winery. He then worked for a rural development organisation prior to being appointed Development Manager with the Western Cape Tourism Board, and later CEO of Breedekloof Tourism.

In 1998 Jurgens started his own travel company, **Live the Journey Tours**, founded on his desire to share exceptional travel experiences with others. He is a 'people's person' and enjoys being in touch with nature, which he strongly believes has a distinct healing and uplifting effect so essential to counteract today's hectic lifestyles. He has a passion for people, for nature, for travel, and for discovering new horizons. He has a dynamic personality and has a special gift that nurtures enjoyable group dynamics.

The essence of the Live the Journey brand is 'life-enriching travel'. They differentiate themselves by arranging itineraries based on our world's unique, often off-the-beaten-track natural and cultural assets; trips are highly experiential, enjoyable and interactive; you see places, people and phenomena that the average traveller would not be able to experience.

Trips are operated strictly in accordance with sustainable tourism principles, and they are informed and facilitated by specialists who are very knowledgeable about the natural and cultural environments in which they travel. Live the Journey Tours provides the highest level of personalised service and value for money, with clients being treated with utmost care, the prime objective being their enjoyment and fulfilment. Tours are flexible so as to accommodate a variety of age groups and cost levels.

Destinations include South Africa, Lesotho, Namibia, Botswana, Zimbabwe, Mozambique, Angola, Zambia, Tanzania, Kenya, Rwanda, Uganda, Ethiopia, Zanzibar, Madagascar and Jordan. Live the Journey Tours in conjunction with the concession holders operates the 'Faces of the Namib' tour.

Contact details
Tel (Bellville): +27 21 912 4090
Tel (Worcester): +27 23 347 7427
Cell: +27 82 341 6733
Fax (Bellville): +27 21 912 4099
Fax (Worcester): +27 23 347 6972
Email: info@livethejourney.co.za
Website: www.livethejourney.co.za or
www.facesofthenamib.com

ANDREW BROWN

Andy climbed his first mountain at the age of seven. It was a relatively minor peak in the Snowdonia region of North Wales, and he was carried on his father's back as much as he walked, but from these humble beginnings was born a passion for mountains that eventually led him to fulfil a lifelong dream to climb among the high-altitude peaks of the Himalayas.

In more recent years the call of the great outdoors has nurtured an intense love affair with the African bush and a keen interest in conservation. Accompanied by his wife Veronica, Andy has been very privileged to be able to enjoy travelling through Africa on journeys that have taken him to Tanzania, Kenya, Botswana, Namibia, Zimbabwe, Zambia and Mozambique. He was the expedition leader on many of these trips, and he experienced at first hand the diversity of the region, not only in its topography, flora and fauna, but more importantly in the cultures, traditions and ways of life of the modern-day citizens of these exciting countries.

South Africa is, first and foremost, his homeland but Andy enjoys a feeling of wonderful homecoming on every trip he makes to the countries north of our borders.

Andy guides for the **4X4 Offroad Adventure Club** in his spare time. He is a co-founder, with Greg van der Reis, of the **Adventurer's Club of Southern Africa**, which attracts people who explore by foot, plane, bicycle, kayak, yacht, 4X4, diving, paragliding, hunting, climbing, trekking and just about everything else. Full membership is only open 'to those who have already lived their adventure'. Between adventures, Andy lives in the scenic Cape village of Villiersdorp.

Contact details
Cell: +27 82 654 7400
Email: Andrew.brown@nexusrs.co.za

SIMON STEADMAN

Simon Steadman is a registered Professional 4X4 Trails and Overland Tourist Guide and sits on the committee of the 4 Wheel Drive Guides Association. He has been guiding off-road trails and tours since 2006 and has several years of off-road experience in some of Africa's wildest destinations. One of his greatest assets as a tour guide is his ability to remain calm in the most trying of situations and to think clearly and logically while under pressure. Other good traits that go down well with his clients are his fine cooking skills, his warm and gentle nature, and the great hospitality he extends to all of his clients.

Simon is the owner of **Mafunyane Adventures**, a 4X4 adventure company that specialises in guided self-drive 4X4 tours to some of Southern Africa's most remote and awe-inspiring destinations. All trips are fully catered and family-orientated, as Simon feels it is important for families to enjoy the bush together in a safe and well-controlled environment. Mafunyane Adventures supports the responsible use of 4X4 vehicles in the wild and they ensure that all their tour groups are well informed about the impact their 4X4 vehicles can have on the environment when used incorrectly and irresponsibly. They strive to cause as little impact on the environment as possible in all the areas visited.

Contact details
Cell: +27 84 447 4666
Fax: +27 11 252 9240
Website: www.mafunyaneadventures.com
Email: info@mafunyaneadventures.com

HUGO POTGIETER

Hugo is an experienced member of the 4X4 community and is a national committee member of the 4 Wheel Drive Guides Association. He is a registered and qualified 4X4 Adventure Guide and has been taking groups to Mozambique since 1994. He has a wealth of 4X4 and diving experience in Mozambique and along the KwaZulu-Natal North Coast, and he loves to share his knowledge. He is also experienced in deep-sea fishing, scuba diving, underwater photography, powerboating and sailing.

Hugo runs **Mozambique 4X4 Safaris**, which specialises in family-orientated self-drive and guided 4X4 vacations to out-of-the-way destinations in Mozambique. Economy packages and customised safaris are available, tailored to your specific vacation and adventure needs. Mozambique 4X4 Safaris go off the beaten track, taking you deep into tropical jungle, coastal forest areas and breathtaking secluded bays, while taking utmost care of your needs and of eco-sensitive areas. They also offer ocean safaris, enabling you to snorkel with whale sharks and dolphins.

Contact details
Cell: +27 82 453 8318
Email: hpotgieter@oldmutual.com

ANDRÉ VAN VUUREN

In 1997 André bought a small safari company in Botswana. In the meantime he was working as a Regional Manager in the corporate banking environment. With a BSc and an MBA to his name, the young André was ready to take on the corporate world. Or was he?

'After operating the safari business on the sideline for two years, I reached a crossroads where I had to make a decision: do I swap the corporate world for nature, tours and tourists, or do I climb the corporate ladder? I chose the first option, changed the company's name to **Explore Africa Adventures**, and set off into the wild world of self-drive 4X4 safaris with an emphasis on wildlife photography.'

Explore Africa Adventures is a privately owned safari company and has specialised in self-drive 4X4 safaris since 1997. Most of the safaris are self-catered but Explore Africa also offers tailor-made safaris for small groups and fully catered options on request.

André is one of the leading safari guides in Southern Africa. He is registered with the Field Guides Association of Southern Africa (FGASA) and is a specialist on Zambia, Malawi and Tanzania. He is also a keen conservationist, a businessman and a man with a soft spot for Africa's biggest mammal – the elephant.

Contact details
Tel: +27 12 663 5319
Cell: +27 82 935 7405
Fax: +27 86 518 9649
Website: www.explore-africa.co.za
Email: info@explore-africa.co.za or andre@explore-africa.co.za

JOHAN SNYMAN

Johan grew up in Durbanville in the Western Cape and lived and worked in Stellenbosch for 21 years as a Project Manager on Municipal Infrastructure projects. After qualifying as a 4X4 and Overland Tour Guide in 2006, he joined **Kumnandi Getaways** as a part-time 4X4 guide.

He did his military service in Namibia during 1981 and 1982, and thought that he would never set foot on Namibian soil again. But then he met Adri, who grew up there, and his love affair with Namibia started in 1994. Between June 1994 and October 2010 they toured through Namibia 58 times, and have visited almost every town and place of interest and have travelled on just about every road in the country. They know the country better than many Namibians do.

During their travels they kept detailed notes and accumulated a vast number of photographs, and this culminated in Johan's writing a comprehensive guide to Kaokoland (yet to be published, and to be followed by similar guides to the rest of Namibia).

Johan and Adri emigrated to Namibia in November 2010 and now reside in Windhoek.

Contact details
Email: johans@iway.na

JOHANN DU TOIT

Johann's passion for adventure travel started early – he was always outdoors, whether on motorbikes (he won provincial colours in 1986 for off-road racing) or in 4X4s.

He started by exploring Lesotho with a borrowed 4X4, and graduated to being in charge of catering and logistics for the then Camel Trophy SA. He obtained a vast amount of experience that naturally progressed to 4X4 driver's training. With his logistical knowledge and the support of his 'bush-wise' wife, Karen, he started taking the first fully logistical tours into Botswana, Lesotho, Namibia and Swaziland, being in charge of the then Beeld 4X4 Adventures and Leisure Wheels Adventures.

Johann and Karen run **African Expeditions**, offering catered camping self-drive tours to interesting off-road destinations in Southern Africa. They have recently started offering tours for dual-purpose motorcyclists. Most of their current routes (in Namibia, Botswana, Lesotho and other parts of Southern Africa) are tourist-friendly and, with very capable people like the late Jan Joubert, they also developed the routes into Kaokoland and the famous Dorsland Trek into Khaudum.

In addition to enjoying the African bush, especially Lesotho, they have also, under the guidance of Volker Jahnke, developed the very successful Forbidden Land route in Namibia, sharing Jahnke's love of the Skeleton Coast and the art of big-dune driving.

Johann and Karen have two sons, with whom they hope to do many years of 4X4 adventure travel.

Contact details
Tel: +27 44 272 4576 or +27 44 272 4816
Cell: +27 82 884 3444
Website: www.2wheelsafaris.co.za
Email: africanex@mweb.co.za

DAVE VAN GRAAN

Masazane Expeditions is a reputable, established expedition company specialising in African overland expeditions, where visiting remote places is the norm rather than the exception.

In 2000 Masazane achieved SATOUR accreditation as a training institution to present their Professional 4X4 Trails and Overland (Adventure) Tourist Guides course. The company has received exposure in various South African publications, including magazines, such as *Drive Out*, *SA 4X4*, *Leisure Wheels*, *Getaway*, and several newspapers.

Husband-and-wife team Dave and Jacqui van Graan founded Masazane Expeditions in 1995 and have operated it ever since, specialising in long-distance self-drive expeditions high into Africa and beyond. They are both registered as 4X4 Trails and Overland Tourist Guides. They are committed to the management of natural resources, which is reflected in their motto: 'We support the responsible use of 4X4 vehicles in sensitive areas.' Dave also founded the 4WDGA (4 Wheel Drive Guides Association).

Extended trans-Africa expeditions is the Masazane speciality, but the company also offers expeditions to the southern and central parts of East Africa, as well as short tours in the Soutpansberg (Limpopo, South Africa). Although the focus is on self-drive adventurers, they also take clients on an African experience in the Masazane vehicle. Masazane provides logistical support to the film industry by way of bush catering, tented camps, drivers and location advice. Dave has successfully completed eight trans-Africa expeditions with clients.

He is a registered paramedic with much experience in medical emergencies, and his most important asset is his calmness in adverse situations. In order to complete these expeditions, Dave relies on the organising and administrative skills of Jacqui.

Contact details
Cell: +27 82 829 5421 (Jacqui)
Cell: +27 82 772 6682 (Dave)
Website: www.masazane.co.za
Email: info@masazane.co.za

GREG VAN DER REIS

Greg is an adventurer. True to his surname (meaning 'of the journey'), he has travelled almost 2 million kilometres in Africa over the past 25 years.

Qualified as a quantity surveyor, he holds a pilot's licence, 4X4 driving instructor's certificate, yacht skipper qualification, skiboat skipper's ticket, scuba diving ticket, radio amateur license, has had his own 4X4 radio programmes in both English and Afrikaans, completed a 4X4 TV documentary for Super Sport in 2010 with Andrew St Pierre White, and has had over 50 articles published on various aspects of off-road and adventure travel.

In 1998 he founded the **4X4 Offroad Adventure Club**, one of South Africa's largest clubs for family-orientated off-roading enthusiasts. He also founded the Land Rover Society of Explorers and various business enterprises, and was a member of the National Sea Rescue Institute (NSRI). He is currently a member of the National Geographic Society, Stellenbosch Flying Club and Royal Cape Yacht Club, among others.

He has led eight expeditions. One of the most exciting was to search for the Lost City of the Kalahari, and another was finding an as yet undocumented meteorite crater. He has been documenting the petroglyphs in the Northern Cape since 2007, and has led a diving expedition of shipwrecks in the West Indies. He fell in love with the Richtersveld in 1998 and, having returned to explore the region on over 130 separate trips, he can justifiably be called an expert on the area.

Contact details
Tel: +27 21 913 1262
Fax: +27 21 913 2709
Cell: +27 82 566 1821
Website: www.4x4offroad.co.za
Email: offroad@iafrica.com

4x4
Offroad Adventure
Club
"The Best Thing Since 4wd"